THE DISTRICT OFFICER IN INDIA
1930–1947

THE DISTRICT OFFICER IN INDIA
1930–1947

Roland Hunt and John Harrison

LONDON
SCOLAR PRESS
1980

First published 1980 by Scolar Press
90/91 Great Russell Street, London WC1B 3PY

Scolar Press is an imprint of Bemrose UK Limited

BRITISH LIBRARY CATALOGUING IN PUBLICATION DATA
Hunt, Roland
The district officer in India, 1930–1947
1. India – Politics and government – 1919–1947
I. Title. II. Harrison, John
325′.341′0954   DS448

ISBN 0–85967–560–2

Printed in Great Britain by
Western Printing Services Ltd
Bristol

CONTENTS

MAPS

The publishers would like to acknowledge advice and help on the maps, so generously given by Andrew Cook of the India Office Library and Records.

PREFACE

This book has its origin in an approach made in 1974 by three former members of the ICS, John Christie, Dick Slater and Roland Hunt, to Miss Joan Lancaster who was then Director of the India Office Library and Records. It was their feeling that though some individuals had published interesting reminiscences of their life in the ICS, the full variety of the experience had yet to be explored. There seemed, therefore, to be scope for a compendious approach, with Indian and Pakistani participation and with attention to areas which had been neglected in earlier accounts. They suggested that the India Office Library might be interested in acquiring accounts by former members of the ICS and Burma Civil Service of their service in India and Burma between 1930 and 1947 for deposit in the India Office Library and possibly as the basis of a published book. The period chosen was perhaps arbitrary. But given its distance from the present and the average age of the, contributors it would scarcely have been realistic to have gone back earlier in time, tempting though that would have been.

Miss Lancaster welcomed the idea and kindly agreed to circularize a number of retired members of the ICS and the Burma Civil Service. The response was generally favourable, and a considerable number of those approached agreed to write an account. To jog their memories after so many years and to ensure a degree of structure and form in their accounts they were sent guidelines indicating areas and topics they might care to cover in compiling their contributions. During the course of some three years over seventy people sent in contributions and in some cases photographs and drawings too. The quality of the material was almost uniformly high, its authors having taken great trouble in assembling it, often by research into old letters and other contemporary documents. The editors have been able only to reproduce a small proportion in this book. Fortunately the complete accounts are available in the India Office Library so that scholars and students will be able to make full use of this enormously interesting material, which gives a straight-forward, first-hand account of the work of the district officer during the final years of the Raj as seen from a wide variety of differing standpoints.

In preparing a book based on the contributions, with a few additions from already published material, the editors have been assisted greatly in their task by a small advisory committee set up under the chairmanship of Miss Lancaster. Its membership has included senior staff of the India Office Library and the retired members of the ICS already mentioned. It has also included Vernon Donnison, a former member of the Burma Civil Service, who is largely responsible for the chapter on Burma and has given unstinted help in many other ways. The editors are specially grateful to Victor Martin, a former member of the Diplomatic Service with a special interest in India, who did invaluable work over a long period in organizing the collection of the material and encouraging the contributors. Arthur Platt, a former member of the ICS in Madras has also given most useful advice and information.

This book is essentially about the last generation of men who joined the ICS and the Burma Civil Service. It attempts to show, using their own words, the sort of men they were, their background and training, the work they had to do and the way in which they set about it. In a sense it is a successor to, and complement of, Philip Mason's two-volume study of the ICS, *The Men Who Ruled India*. It does not offer a general history of the India and Burma services, nor does it directly concern itself with the phenomenon of empire, nor with the vanished social world of the Raj so vividly captured by Charles Allen in *Plain Tales from the Raj*. It is not concerned with individuals as individuals, even though the personalities of the contributors may make themselves felt. The book does not deal with policy as formulated in London or Delhi, except to the extent that the actions or feelings of the men on the ground reveal the presence, or absence, of policies laid down from above. Rather it concentrates attention upon one vital area of government – that of the district, the basic unit of Indian administration since Mughal times, the most important point of interaction between governors and governed. It focuses upon only one stage of the career of these officials, but the formative, most testing and most vividly recalled of all.

What we have done is to attempt a balanced abridgement of the large body of material at our disposal in the way we think best illustrates the work of the ICS district officer in our period in all its wide variety of content and settings. We are, so to speak, setting out the evidence with the minimum of editorial explanation or comment. Our contributors cover a great range of experience and work in every province. But they are self-selected and cannot be regarded as wholly representative. For instance the number of Indian and Pakistani contributors is smaller than we would have wished and there is none from Bangladesh or Burma. Nevertheless we present what we believe to be a fair cross-section.

We have used a variety of approaches in this study. There is necessarily a biographical element in the setting-out of the social and intellectual background of the contributors and a personal one in the reporting of individual reactions to the pleasures and pains of an ICS career. The tasks of the district officer on the other hand have been handled analytically, separating out their major constituents: revenue, magisterial and executive. The nature of his relationship with other services in the district and with such groups as missionaries, planters or businessmen, and the investigation of the instruments, official and non-official, which he used in the management of his district have been subjected to the same treatment. There is an obviously artificial element in such distinctions, but, we hope, a gain in clarity. And having established the common structure underlying the day-to-day work of the district officer, the recorded experience of the contributors has been used to demonstrate at each point the extraordinary variety of circumstance, geographical, social and political, in which that work was carried out in the twelve provinces of India and Burma with their multitude of regular, tribal and frontier districts.

Moreover the work of the district officer was quite as varied over time as over space. 1930 to 1947 were years of drastic economic change, of constitution building, of war and of tense bargaining and communal conflict as independence approached. New tasks were imposed on the district officer such as civil defence, food procurement, large-scale rationing and, in Burma, post-war reconstruction. Politics and violence pressed ever more hardly on the forces of law and order in the district. The district officer from being an agent of an alien bureaucratic rule became the instrument of elected Indian governments, required to accommodate himself to the wishes and requests of politicians. The concluding chapters of the book are therefore cast in a more narrative form designed to demonstrate some of the fundamental shifts in the work and position of the district officer, a foreshadowing of the new, though still vital role he had to play in the two successor states of India and Pakistan which emerged from the old India after 1947.

Roland Hunt, formerly ICS Madras   John Harrison
Charlton   Department of History
Charlton Lodge   School of Oriental and African Studies
Nr. Banbury, Oxfordshire   University of London

CONTRIBUTORS BY PROVINCES

Assam Hayley, Lydall, Maitra, Murray.

Bengal Bell, Christie, Gupta, McInerny, Martyn, Rahmatullah, Saumarez Smith, Woodford.

Bihar and Orissa Flack, Kemp, Lines, Macdonald, Martin, Orr, Ray, Solomon, Swann.

Bombay and Sind Barty, Faruqui, Lambrick, Raza, Symington.

Central Provinces Hyde, Matthews, Paterson, Ramsden, Watson, Mrs Brown.

Madras Carleston, Downing, Dunlop, Georgeson, Hope, Lamarque, Maher, Masterman, Narasimham, Platt, Thompson.

Punjab Arthur, Belcher, Cowley, Curtis, Emerson, Fearn, Hubbard, Husain, Le Bailly, Slater, Williams.

United Provinces Banks, Bonarjee, Bowman, Cook, Haig, Lane, Lloyd-Jones, Midgley, Mudie, Radice, Shukla, Symons, Venkatachar.

Burma Cockburn, Donnison, Fowler, McGuire, Richards, Wallace.

A. J. V. Arthur, MBE, DL (Punjab 1938–47)
b. 16 September 1915.
ed. Rugby and Cambridge.
SDO Murree and Kasur. DC Attock and Multan. Sudan Political Service 1949–54, finishing as Deputy Governor.
Chairman of Woodhouse, Drake and Carey, Ltd, London. Chairman, Chelmsford District Council and Mayor of Chelmsford. Vice Lord Lieutenant for the County of Essex, 1978.

J. D. Banks (United Provinces 1939–47)
b. 3 January 1917.
ed. Nottingham High School and Cambridge.
Joint Magistrate, Roorkee. Town Rationing Officer, Agra. Deputy Secretary to Government, Lucknow.
Hospital administrator: House Governor, King's College Hospital; Assistant Secretary, DHSS.

D. C. Barty, CBE (Sind 1937–47)
b. 27 February 1914.
ed. Fettes College and St Andrews.
Secretary to the Governor of Sind, 1942–6. Collector and District Magistrate, Hyderabad, Sind, 1946–7.
Served in Colonial Administrative Service, Hong Kong, 1948–68.

R. H. Belcher, CMG (Punjab 1939–48)
b. 5 January 1916.
ed. Christ's Hospital and Cambridge.
SDO Kasur. Assistant Director, Civil Supplies and Colonization Officer. Acting Commissioner, Multan Division.
Commonwealth Relations Office, 1948–65, finishing as Deputy High Commissioner in India. Under-Secretary, Ministry of Overseas Development, 1965–76.

F. O. Bell, OBE (Bengal 1930–47)
b. 2 February 1907.
ed. Christ's Hospital and Cambridge.
SDO Siliguri and Tangail. Settlement Officer. District Magistrate and Collector, Bakarganj, Midnapore, Dacca and 24 Parganas.
Solicitor. Served in Legal Department of LCC and GLC. Chairman of Chesham District Council and member of Buckinghamshire County Council.

N. B. Bonarjee (United Provinces 1925–50)
b. 10 March 1901.
ed. Dulwich College and Oxford.
Joint Magistrate in various districts. Collector and Magistrate, Meerut. Secretary to Government. Commissioner, Benares division. Chief Secretary to Government.
Served after 1947 as Commissioner and Chief Commissioner.

A. I. Bowman (United Provinces and Assam 1937–47)
b. 11 May 1915.
ed. Glasgow High School and Glasgow University.
DC Khasi and Jaintia Hills, and Political Officer, Khasi States, Assam. District Magistrate and Collector, Mirzapur, UP. Served in Indian Army with rank of Captain. Acting Registrar and Lecturer in Classics, University of Ibadan. Head of Department of General Studies, Falkirk College of Technology. Justice of the Peace.

H. H. Carleston, CIE, OBE (Madras 1927–47)
b. 25 July 1904.
ed. St Olave's, Southwark and Cambridge.
Additional District Magistrate, Malabar. Collector of Ramnad, Guntur, Chittoor and Vizagapatam districts.
University administrator: Secretary, St Cuthbert's Society, University of Durham; Administrative Secretary, Cambridge University School of Veterinary Medicine.

W. H. Christie, CSI, CIE, OBE (Bengal 1928–47)
b. 17 December 1905.
ed. Eton and Cambridge.
Under-Secretary, Government of Bengal. DC Chittagong Hill Tracts. Appointments in Delhi, finishing as Joint Private Secretary to the Viceroy.
Adviser in India to the Central Commercial Committee. Managing Director and Vice-Chairman, British India Corporation, Ltd, Kanpur. Controller of Operations, Commonwealth Development Finance Company Ltd, and consultant to the IBRD.

G. W. Cockburn (Burma 1937–48)
b. 27 May 1913.
ed. Fettes College and St Andrews.
Senior Civil Affairs Officer in Bassein and Thaton districts. DC Hanthawaddy district. BBC 1948–73, finishing as Controller, Staff Training and Appointments.

B. C. A. Cook, CMG, OBE (United Provinces 1929–47)
b. 20 July 1906.
ed. Radley College and Oxford.
Magistrate and Collector, Jhansi and Budaun. Under-Secretary and Joint Secretary, Government of India Finance Department.
Joined British Foreign Service, last appointment being HM Consul-General, Barcelona.

W. Cowley (Punjab 1939–47)
b. 17 November 1915.
ed. Middlesborough High School and Cambridge.
Assistant Commissioner, Firuzpur, Hissar and Jullundur districts. Assistant Director, National War Front, Punjab, and Provincial Youth Organizer.
Farmed in North Yorkshire. Writer and broadcaster on farming and local history.

G. C. S. Curtis (Punjab and later Indian Political Service 1929–47)
b. 4 September 1904.
ed. Westminster School and Oxford.
SDO Pindi Gheb. Colonization Officer, Nasirabad, Baluchistan. DC Hazara and Mardan. Political Agent, South Waziristan. Secretary to Government of NWFP. Became a farmer. County Councillor in Essex and Chairman of County Planning Committee.

F. S. V. Donnison, CBE (Burma 1922–46)
b. 3 July 1898.
ed. Marlborough and Oxford.
Assistant Superintendent, Shan States. DC Mergui and Thaton districts. Commissioner, Pegu division. Chief Secretary to Government of Burma.
subsequently worked as an historian in the Historical Section of the Cabinet Office. Has written a number of books on Burma.

H. J. Downing (Madras 1941–7)
b. 22 March 1919.
ed. High School for Boys, Trowbridge, and Oxford.
Sub-Collector Dindigul, Madanapalle, Coonoor and Chicacole. Special Assistant Agent, Bhadrachalam.
Later joined British Foreign Service, finishing as Consul-General, Cape Town.

S. W. C. Dunlop (Madras 1937–47)
b. 9 May 1914.
ed. Epsom College and Cambridge.
Sub-Collector Chingleput and Bezwada. Under-Secretary and Deputy Secretary, Government of Madras.
HM Colonial Service, Cyprus, 1947–50. Malayan Civil Service 1951–62. Subsequently a schoolmaster.

G. H. Emerson, OBE (Punjab and Indian Political Service 1930–47)
b. 3 December 1907.
ed. Rugby and Cambridge.
SDO Murree and Rupar. DC Kangra. Political Agent in NWFP and Baluchistan. Secretary to Governor, NWFP, 1941–3.
National Council of Social Service 1947–72.

M. A. Faruqui, OBE, SPk (Pakistan), **HQA** (Pakistan) (Bombay and Sind 1931–47)
b. 15 December 1906.
ed. Government College, Lahore.
SDO Surat and Nasik. Under-Secretary, Government of Bombay and Government of India. Collector, Thana, Bombay and Karachi. Secretary to Governor of Sind.
Continued in the service of the Government of Pakistan, holding appointments of Chief Secretary, Sind and West Pakistan, Cabinet Secretary and Principal Private Secretary to the President.

J. M. Fearn, CB (Punjab 1940–7)
b. 24 June 1916.
ed. High School of Dundee and St Andrews.
SDO Kasur. DC Lahore.
Joined Home Civil Service in 1947, and served in Scottish Office, finishing as Secretary of Scottish Education Department.

A. W. Flack (Bihar 1937–47)
b. 1 November 1913.
ed. City of London School and Cambridge.
SDO Kishanganj and Dhalbhum. Superintendent, Hazaribagh Central Jail. District Magistrate, Monghyr.
Lecturer in Physics and Astronomy, University of Canterbury, Christchurch, New Zealand.

R. W. D. (Sir Robert) Fowler, KCMG (Burma 1937–48)
b. 6 March 1914.
ed. Queen Elizabeth's Grammar School, Mansfield, and Cambridge.
SDO Moulmein and Maymyo. Under-Secretary, Defence Department. Senior Civil Affairs Officer, Amherst District. Additional Governor's Secretary.
Joined Commonwealth Relations Office. Deputy High Commissioner in Pakistan, Canada and Nigeria. High Commissioner in Tanzania and British Ambassador to the Sudan.

W. W. Georgeson (Madras 1930–50)
b. 13 October 1909.
ed. Aberdeen Grammar School, Aberdeen University and Oxford.
Sub-Collector and District and Sessions Judge.
Later business executive.

H. C. Gupta (Bengal 1935–47)
b. 15 July 1910.
ed. Ewing Christian College, Allahabad, and Allahabad University.
Joint Magistrate, Bankura. SDM Cox's Bazar. Ramporehat. Additional District Magistrate and Collector, Alipore and Dacca. District Magistrate and Collector, Khulna. After independence served in the UP and the Government of India, retiring as Chairman, Board of Revenue, UP 1970.

G. A. Haig, OBE (United Provinces 1931–47)
b. 19 May 1909.
ed. Winchester and Oxford.
Settlement Officer, Shahjahanpur. Collector, Moradabad, Regional Food Controller, Lucknow and Secretary to UP Government, Food and Civil Supplies.
Joined Home Civil Service and served in Ministry of Food and Ministry of Supply as Assistant Secretary.

T. S. S. Hayley, PhD (Assam 1938–50)
b. 4 October 1913.
ed. Clifton College and Cambridge.
Served as Under-Secretary to the Government of Assam, Director of Publicity and Deputy Commissioner.
After independence was Secretary to the Government of Assam. Later Chairman of the British Psycho-Analytical Society and the Institute of Psycho-Analysis. Editor of journals dealing with psycho-analysis.

R. C. Hope (Madras 1938–47)
b. 25 September 1915.
ed. St Edward's School, Oxford, and Oxford.
Sub-Collector Chingleput, Vizianagram, Pollachi, Coonoor, and Tuticorin. Assistant Commissioner, Civil Supplies, Madras.
Later practised as a solicitor in London.

P. M. Hubbard (Punjab 1934–47)
b. 9 November 1910.
ed. Elizabeth College, Guernsey, and Oxford.
SDO Pindigheb. DC Bahawalpur and Mianwali. Assistant Colonization Officer. District and Sessions Judge.
Later Director of Central Secretariat, British Council and Director, National Union of Manufacturers.

M. A. Husain (Punjab 1937–70)
b. 5 October 1913.
ed. Government College, Lahore, and Cambridge.
Assistant Commissioner and Under-Secretary in Punjab. Under-Secretary and Deputy Secretary, Government of India.
Later joined Indian Diplomatic Service and served as Ambassador and Secretary, Ministry of External Affairs. Commonwealth Deputy Secretary-General 1970–8.

E. S. Hyde (Central Provinces and Assam 1928–47)
b. 6 March 1906.
ed. Sedbergh and Cambridge.
SDO Ellichpur and Seoni. Dewan and Administrator, Bastar State. Additional Superintendent, Lushai Hills, Assam. DC Mandla and Jabalpur.
Worked for ICI. Subsequently director and secretary of a London art gallery.

A. H. Kemp, CIE (Bihar and Orissa 1928–47)
b. 28 February 1905.
ed. Portsmouth Grammar School and Cambridge.
DO in five districts. Secretary to Government of Orissa and officiating Chief Secretary.
Served as a UK Trade Commissioner in Pakistan and later practised as a solicitor.

W. G. Lamarque, MBE (Madras 1937–47)
b. 12 February 1913.
ed. Marlborough and Oxford.
Sub-Collector, Sivakasi and Pollachi. Under-Secretary and Deputy Secretary, Government of India.
Served as UK Trade Commissioner and Deputy High Commissioner in Enugu, Nigeria. Later worked with Ministry of Overseas Development. Was UK Representative to FAO.

H. T. Lambrick, CIE, D.Litt, FSA (Sind and Bombay 1927–47)
b. 20 April 1904.
ed. Rossall and Oxford.
Served as Assistant Commissioner in Sind, DC Upper Sind Frontier, Secretary to the Governor of Sind. Civil Adviser to the GOC Upper Sind Force and Chief Martial Law Administrator, 1942. Special Commissioner for Sind, 1942–6.
Fellow and Treasurer of Oriel College, Oxford, and lecturer in modern history.

H. T. Lane, MBE (United Provinces 1937–47)
b. 26 April 1914.
ed. Rossall and Cambridge.
SDO in Lucknow district followed by settlement work in Jhansi. Regional Food Controller, Meerut. Collector and District Magistrate, Ballia.
Home Civil Service. Subsequently Bursar of Rossall School for 25 years.

W. F. G. Le Bailly (Punjab 1927–47)
b. 17 October 1904.
ed. Wellington and Oxford.
DC Montgomery, Attock and Delhi.
Malayan Civil Service and Commonwealth Relations Office.

R. N. Lines, MBE (Bihar 1937–47)
b. 11 September 1914.
ed. Royal Latin School, Buckingham, and Oxford.
After service in various districts as SDO was Collector of Darbhanga, Bhagalpur and Patna. Deputy Controller of Civil Supplies and DC Singbhum.
Colonial Administrative Service in Northern Rhodesia. Worked with the Commonwealth Development Corporation. Member of Buckinghamshire County Council since 1977.

C. M. Lloyd-Jones (United Provinces 1938–47)
b. 11 January 1914.
ed. Oundle and Cambridge.
City Magistrate, Lucknow. SDO Roorkee. Collector Ballia and Muzaffarnagar.
With Calico Printers' Association, later Tootal Ltd, 1948–77.

E. F. Lydall (Assam 1932–5, then served principally in Baluchistan and North West Frontier Province as member of the Indian Political Service)
b. 4 August 1907.
ed. Marlborough and Cambridge.
Assistant Commissioner Lakhimpur and Gauhati. SDO North Lakhimpur. Assistant Commissioner at Loralai and Kalat. Assistant Political Agent, North Waziristan, President Manipur State Durbar, Imphal, and Secretary to the Resident at Baroda. With Legal Department of Shell from 1952–66. Then Director of a charitable foundation in Switzerland.

I. H. Macdonald (Bihar and Orissa 1938–47)
b. 19 July 1915.
ed. Daniel Stewart's College, Edinburgh, and Edinburgh University.
After service in Ganjam, Koraput, was Collector of Balasore and Ganjam districts in

Orissa and Gaya in Bihar. Deputy Secretary with Bihar Government in Patna. Studied law and was admitted a Writer to HM Signet. Partner in Edinburgh law firm from 1953–73.

R. E. McGuire, CMG, OBE (Burma 1925–48)
b. 22 August 1901.
ed. High School, Dublin, and Trinity College, Dublin.
DC Yamethin, Bhamo and Myitkyina. Warden, Burma Oilfields. Deputy Director of Civil Affairs. Commissioner, Sagaing and Magwe Divisions. Governor's Secretary. In business after retirement.

E. F. McInerny, MBE (Bengal 1935–47)
b. 8 May 1910.
ed. Swansea Grammar School and Oxford.
Assistant Magistrate, Barisal and Alipore. Additional District Magistrate, Chittagong and District Magistrate 1941–6. District Magistrate, Noakhali.
Stayed on doing missionary and educational work in Chittagong and Barisal until 1970.

J. E. Maher (Madras 1928–47)
b. 5 September 1904.
ed. Cheltenham and Oxford.
Assistant and Sub-Collector in Madras. District Judge in Madras and Orissa. Legal Remembrancer, Orissa and Chief Secretary.
Ministry of Agriculture, London 1947–58. Then with Country Landowners' Association.

S. N. Maitra (Assam 1935–47)
b. 7 June 1912.
ed. Mitra Institution, Bhowanipore, Presidency College and Scottish Churches College, Calcutta, and King's College, London.
SDO Mangaldai and North Lakhimpur. DC Cachar and Darrang. After independence served in West Bengal. Collector, 24 Parganas and Chief Commissioner, Andaman Islands.
Indian Deputy High Commissioner in East Pakistan, acting High Commissioner in Karachi and finally Indian Ambassador to Manila 1959–62.

H. B. Martin, MBE (Bihar 1939–47)
b. 6 October 1915.
ed. Harrow and Oxford.
SDO Hajipur and Sasaram. Under-Secretary and Deputy Secretary, Supply and Price Control, Government of Bihar. Regional Grain Supply Officer, Gaya.
1947–72 with ICI Plastics Division. Then master in a preparatory school.

P. D. Martyn, CIE, CBE (Bengal 1927–47)
b. 7 April 1904.
ed. Stockport Grammar School and Manchester University.
SDO Kushtia and Kalimpong, followed by settlement work. District Magistrate in Faridpur, Midnapore, Noakhali and Jessore. Home Department, Bengal Government finishing as Additional Secretary. Civil Representative, Eastern Command.
Principal, and later Assistant Secretary, Ministry of Defence, 1947–64.

C. H. (Sir Christopher) Masterman, CSI, CIE (Madras 1914–47)
b. 7 October 1889.
ed. Winchester and Oxford.
Collector and District Magistrate in various districts. Later Secretary to Government of Madras and Member of the Board of Revenue. Chief Secretary and Adviser to the Governor.
UK Deputy High Commissioner in Southern India 1947–9.

V. G. Matthews, CMG, OBE (Central Provinces 1931–47)
b. 3 March 1907.
ed. Latymer School and London University.
Deputy Commissioner, Under-Secretary and Private Secretary to the Governor, CP. Under- and Deputy Secretary, Government of India. Accountant-General, Bihar. Collector of Customs, Madras, Karachi and Bombay.
Director of Imports and Supplies, Government of Kenya; later Minister of Finance. Commissioner for East Africa in London.

E. A. Midgley, CMG, MBE (United Provinces 1937–47)
b. 25 March 1913.
ed. Christ's Hospital and Oxford.
Joint Magistrate, Saharanpur, Lansdowne and Agra. Deputy Secretary to UP Government. Manager, Balrampur Estate.
HM Principal Trade Commissioner in Delhi. Minister (Economic and Commercial), Delhi and Minister (Commercial), Washington. Ambassador in Berne.

R. F. (Sir Francis) Mudie, KCSI, KCIE, OBE (United Provinces 1915–47)
b. 24 August 1890.
ed. Fettes College and Cambridge.
Magistrate and Collector in the UP. Settlement Officer Agra. Revenue Secretary and Chief Secretary, Government of UP. Acting Governor of Bihar, Home Member, Viceroy's Executive Council and Governor of Sind.
Stayed on to be Governor of West Punjab, Government of Pakistan. Chairman and member of various British Government missions of enquiry.

D. C. Murray (Assam 1939–46, North West Frontier Province 1946–7)
b. 26 April 1916.
ed. Hymer's College and Oxford.
SDO Naga Hills and Golaghat. Additional DC Darrang. DC Cachar. Assistant Political Officer, Miranshah, North Waziristan.
Later farmed in Scotland.

C. V. Narasimham, MBE (Madras 1937–63)
b. 21 May 1915.
ed. Madras PS High School and Tiruchi National High School, and Madras and Oxford Universities.
Assistant Collector and Sub-collector, Vizagapatam. Sub-Collector, Dindigul. Under-Secretary and Deputy Secretary, Government of Madras.
Later served as Joint Secretary, Ministries of Food and Agriculture, and Finance, Government of India. Executive Secretary, Economic Commission for Asia and the Far East in Bangkok. Under-Secretary-General, United Nations, New York.

J. W. Orr (Bihar and Orissa 1939–55)
b. 1 January 1916.
ed. Fettes College and St Andrew's.
Assistant Magistrate, Bhagalpur, Bihar. ARP Officer, Patna. SDO, Angul, Berhampur and Orissa. District Magistrate and Collector, Cuttack. Secretary to Governor of Orissa.
After independence served as Deputy Secretary, Ministry of Finance, New Delhi. Collector of Customs, Bombay and Director of Inspection, Customs and Excise (All India) in Delhi. After retirement served with Consolidated Gold Fields Ltd, London.

N. K. Paterson, CIE, OBE (Central Provinces 1929–47)
b. 25 December 1905.
ed. George Heriot's, Edinburgh, and Edinburgh University.
Under-Secretary and DC in the CP. Deputy Commissioner and Chief Commissioner, Andaman Islands.

A. J. Platt, CBE (Madras 1932–47)
b. 13 August 1908.
ed. Liverpool Collegiate School and Cambridge.
DC with Revenue Secretariat, Government of Madras. Private Secretary to the Governor.
Later with HM Treasury, Establishments and Finance.

P. W. Radice (United Provinces 1931–48)
b. 18 June 1908.
ed. Blundells and Oxford.
Additional DC Naini Tal. DC Andaman and Nicobar Islands. Collector of Etah and Deoria. Secretary to the UP Government.
1949–73 Clerk to the States and Court of Alderney, Channel Islands. From 1974 Member of the States of Alderney.

S. Rahmatullah (Bengal 1937–47)
b. 9 June 1913.
ed. Arrah Zillah High School, Arrah (Bihar), and Patna University.
Assistant Magistrate and Collector, Bankura. SDO Metrokona, Sirajganj and Narayanganj. District Magistrate and Collector, Howrah, Murshidabad and Midnapore.
Joined Civil Service of Pakistan, Secretary to Government of East Bengal and Commissioner in Rajshahi and Dacca. Secretary, Central Planning Commission, Government of Pakistan.

G. C. F. (Sir Geoffrey) Ramsden, CIE (Central Provinces 1920–47)
b. 21 April 1893.
ed. Haileybury and Cambridge.
Served as DC, Commissioner and Adviser to the Governor of the CP.

G. M. Ray, MBE (Bihar and Orissa 1937–47)
b. 2 August 1912.
ed. Caterham and Oxford.
SDO at Bhabua and Dinapore, Superintendent, Central Jail, Bhagalpur. District Magistrate and Collector, Gaya.

S. H. Raza, SQA (Pakistan), **SP** (Pakistan) (Bombay and Sind 1934–47)
b. 16 February 1910.
ed. Government High School, Hardoi, UP and Lucknow University.
Assistant Collector in Ahmadnagar and Nasik districts, Bombay. Deputy Secretary to the Government of Sind and Collector and District Magistrate of Larkana and Tharparkar. Secretary to the Governor of Sind. Collector of Karachi.
Entered service in the Government of Pakistan. Appointments have included Chief Secretary in Sind and East Pakistan, Secretary of Pakistan Government departments.

C. J. Richards (Burma 1921–47)
b. 8 March 1894.
ed. Haileybury and Cambridge.
After service as SDO and Settlement Officer was DC in Meiktila, Katha, Henzada, Tharrawaddy and Myingyan districts. Commissioner of Settlements and Land Records. DC Pegu.
Later worked for the Burmese Service of the BBC and as a schoolmaster.

W. H. Saumarez Smith, OBE (Bengal 1934–47)
b. 31 December 1911.
ed. Winchester and Cambridge.
Under-Secretary, Government of Bengal and Government of India. District Magistrate, Malda.
Later held administrative posts in the Church of England, including Appointments Secretary to the Archbishops of Canterbury and York.

J. D. Shukla, D.Phil (United Provinces 1939–73)
b. 1 January 1915.
ed. GIC Allahabad, and Allahabad University.
Served in Aligarh and Saharanpur districts, then as Collector of Sultanpur and Budaun.
Vice-Principal, Indian Administrative Service Training School, Director-General, Indian Stores Department, Indian High Commission in London. Commissioner and Member of the Board of Revenue in the UP. Author of books on Indian administration matters.

R. M. K. Slater, CMG (Punjab 1939–47)
b. 27 May 1915.
ed. Eton and Cambridge.
Under-Secretary to Government. SDO Pindigheb and DC Dera Ghazi Khan.
Joined British Foreign Service and served as Ambassador to Cuba and High Commissioner, Uganda, Assistant Under-Secretary, Foreign and Commonwealth Office.

S. Solomon (Bihar and Orissa 1927–47)
b. 20 September 1904.
ed. Clifton College and Cambridge.
SDO Giridih, Gumla and Bettiah. DC Singhbhum. Collector of Balasore (Orissa) and Director of Development, Orissa. Secretary of Provincial War Committee, Bihar. DC Hazaribagh.
Liberal candidate in local and parliamentary elections. Author and translator.

R. S. Swann, MBE (Bihar and Orissa 1939–47)
b. 17 November 1915.
ed. George Watson's Boys' College, Edinburgh, and Edinburgh University.
SDO Khurda and Berhampur. Secretary to Governor of Orissa. DC Sambalpur.
British Diplomatic Service 1947–74, finishing as Counsellor in British Embassy, Bonn.

D. Symington, CSI, CIE (Bombay and Sind 1926–47)
b. 4 July 1904.
ed. Cheltenham and Oxford.
DO Karachi, Mirpurkhas, Dharwar, Ratnagiri, Nasik and Sholapur districts. Backward Classes Officer, Bombay Province. Municipal Commissioner and ARP Controller, Bombay City. Secretary, Home Department and Governor's Secretary. Director, Northern Rhodesia Chamber of Mines.

R. S. Symons, CMG, CIE (United Provinces 1926–47)
b. 24 July 1904.
ed. Christ's Hospital and Cambridge.
Revenue and Finance Minister, Rampur State. Joint Secretary, Government of India Finance Department.
With HM Treasury. Minister to UK Delegation, OECD, Paris.

H. (Sir Herbert) Thompson, CIE (Madras and Indian Political Service, 1922–48)
b. 9 March 1898.
ed. Manchester Grammar School and Oxford.
District work in Madras and NWFP. Revenue Commissioner, NWFP. Resident Kolhapur and Deccan States. Resident Punjab States.
Later Rowing Correspondent of the *Sunday Times* and Governor of St Thomas' Hospital.

C. S. Venkatachar, CIE, OBE (United Provinces and Indian Political Service 1922–60)
b. 11 July 1899.
ed. Maharaja's High School, Bangalore, Madras and London Universities.
DO in the UP. Agent to the Governor-General in British Malaya (now Malaysia).

Later Rural Development Commissioner and President of the Court of Wards in the UP.

Appointments since independence include Diwan of Jodhpur and Jaipur, Secretary to the Government of India, Ministry of States, and Secretary to the President of India. Indian High Commissioner in Canada.

W. I. J. Wallace, CMG, OBE (Burma 1928–47)
b. 18 December 1905.
ed. Bedford Modern and Cambridge.
DC Pakokku, Amherst and four other districts. Deputy Director of Civil Affairs with rank of Colonel. Commissioner, Tenasserim and last British Chief Secretary.
Served in Colonial Office, London 1947–66, retiring as Assistant Under-Secretary.

G. L. Watson (Central Provinces 1932–46)
b. 13 December 1909.
ed. Whitby Secondary School and Cambridge.
DC Betul, Balaghat, Raipur, Amraoti and Nagpur districts.
Lecturer at Acton Technical College. Lecturer, Reader and Professor of Mathematics, University College, London. Now Emeritus Professor and Honorary Research Associate.

A. A. Williams, OBE (Punjab 1932–47)
b. 16 May 1910.
ed. Merchant Taylors' School, Crosby, and Cambridge.
DC Rawalpindi, Jullundur, Attock and Lahore districts. Secretary to Punjab Government.
Colonial Administrative Service 1948–57, serving in Nigeria and Singapore (as Deputy Chief Secretary). Bursar and Fellow, The Queen's College, Oxford, 1958–77.

G. P. Woodford (Bengal 1940–8)
b. 21 December 1915.
ed. Kingswood School, Bath, and Oxford.
SDO Diamond Harbour and Asansol. Deputy Controller of Rationing.
Later Senior Planning Officer, Ministry of Housing and Local Government, Department of the Environment.

*   *   *

Mrs Janet Brown, widow of Leslie N. Brown, has also contributed. L. N. Brown served in the ICS between 1910 and 1936 in Bombay and Sind. He was Collector of a number of districts, including Ahmedabad in Bombay and Sukkur in Sind.

INTRODUCTION

Englishmen first went east, in 1601, in search of spices from the Indonesian islands – pepper, cloves, nutmeg and mace. They turned to India only when they realized the importance of Indian hand-spun, woven and printed cottons in the spice trade and indeed in the whole network of Asian trade from East Africa to China. The English East India Company set up its main trading settlements where it could tap Indian textile production: in Gujarat, along the Madras coast and in Bengal.

When in the 1750s the Company was drawn into the power struggle set off by the decline of the Mughal empire in India, it was from these trading settlements, the port cities of Bombay, Madras and Calcutta, that its conquests spread out. Within the next seventy years territory under British control had expanded to form the western Presidency of Bombay, the Presidency of Madras on the east coast, and the Bengal Presidency spreading far up the Ganges valley towards Delhi, all three subordinated to a Governor-General and Council at Calcutta.

By the early nineteenth century the industrial revolution in Britain and the growth of machine manufacture of cottons had destroyed the importance of the overseas trade in Indian handloom cottons. But throughout the nineteenth century India continued to play a major role in the British trading system. She became a growing market for British manufactures: mill cottons, track and rolling stock for the Indian railways, machinery for her jute and cotton mills. By 1913 India was Britain's largest single customer. In return India supplied British markets with jute and cotton, hides, oils and tea. Just as important, India's export surplus of commodities helped to balance Britain's trading books in Europe, America and in China where, for example, sales of Indian opium and raw cotton helped pay for British purchases of Chinese tea. India was also a minor but safe field for British investment. As Britain's industrial lead declined in the later nineteenth century and European and American tariffs made the export of British manufactures more difficult, India's value as a market and as a balancing item in Britain's trade network became if anything more pronounced.

If the trade of India was important to Britain, so was the Indian Army which she created. This standing force of nearly 200,000 Indian sepoys, British-armed, officered and led, and stiffened with British troops sent on lengthy tours of duty in India, was the army with which the conquest of Burma, the acquisition of Ceylon and Malaya, and the annexation of East Africa was effected. Indian troops were employed in campaigns in Egypt, Ethiopia, Persia, Afghanistan and South China, and as garrisons along the main imperial lines of communication. It was an enormous advantage that in the creation and maintenance of the British empire in Asia it was often Indian rather than British lives which were at risk or lost. That the whole cost of the Indian Army, and of the British troops in India, was borne by the Indian taxpayer was pure gain.

The value of India to Britain thus depended on her continued 'fit' into the world-wide pattern of British trade and the openness of her markets to British merchants, industrialists and investors, and on the availability for imperial purposes of an effective Indian Army largely paid for by India. But in the twentieth century, and particularly after the First World War, the 'fit' became less good, partly because India's export surpluses were cut back by Japanese and Chinese competition and by difficulties with exchange rates, partly because Britain's manufactures were moving from the old staple industries to the newer technologies of the car, aeroplane, wireless, chemicals and synthetics for which India was less important as a market. At the same time, though the strategic significance of the Indian Army was increased by the opening of the Persian and Near Eastern oilfields, by Malayan rubber planting, and by the exploitation of Burma's rice and oil potential, it became much less easy to use the Indian Army as a purely imperial instrument.

The difficulty was an economic one. India was a relatively poor and underdeveloped country with a large subsistence agriculture sector and a comparatively small industrial base. Per capita income was low, the surplus which government could take in revenue and taxes was small. As alien rulers the British wished to tax as lightly as possible. But 30 to 40 per cent of the total yield was swallowed up by the Army, and another considerable slice went to pay the imperial services. As late as 1919 over 90 per cent of the bureaucrats in the Indian Civil Service – the men who filled the key positions in the Governor-General's Council and the central Secretariat, who staffed the provincial governments with their secretariats, who provided the commissioners of divisions, and the collector-magistrates in the 250 districts – were Europeans. So were over 90 per cent of the members of the all-India Police Service and two-thirds of the other Imperial Services: Customs, Education, Forests and so on. Only in the judiciary had Indians really come into their own. With so much ear-marked for the civil and military instruments of British rule, there was little room for manoeuvre in the Indian budget. War or famine, any growth in the functions of government or in the quality of its services, any technical advance in the equipping of the army, quickly threatened a growth of debt or raised the unwelcome spectre of tax increases.

Two ways of avoiding tax increases had long been tried. One was to replace expensive European officials by Indians wherever it was possible and thought politically safe to do so. By the early twentieth century the Subordinate and the Provincial Services, recruited in India, were largely Indianized. In the judiciary Indians were beginning to occupy even the most senior posts on the High Court benches, and a very few had entered the ICS. The second way was to rely on unpaid, non-official agencies, rather as justices of the peace were used in England, offering titles, honours and favour to those who would serve in municipalities or on university senates, hospital boards and the like, or help government in maintaining law and order in the towns and countryside.

If, however, new tax demands proved unavoidable then the need was to make them more acceptable. One useful method was to associate Indians with the raising, and more important, with the allocation and spending of the increased revenues. Before 1900 this had been done at the local level by the surrender into non-official, elected hands of the taxing and spending powers of the municipalities and district boards. (Usually such powers were small, but the metropolitan city governments such as Bombay or Calcutta handled very considerable revenues.) More tentatively, after the Mutiny of 1857 and the transfer of power from the East India Company to the Crown, the Government of India had also begun to nominate to its central and provincial legislative councils selected Indians whom it could consult on the likely reception of its measures, taxation included. In 1892 the number of such non-officials was increased and nomination was given a less autocratic flavour by a process of consultation with such representative bodies as municipalities, universities, landholder associations and chambers of commerce about suitable persons. In 1909 a second Indian Councils Act (often referred to as the Morley-Minto Reforms after the Secretary of State and Viceroy who worked them out) went much further, providing for non-official majorities in the councils and at provincial level for the direct election by secret ballot of more than half of the non-official members. A constitutional, electoral entry into representative bodies at every level had thus been opened to Indians, though the franchise still restricted the political class very narrowly indeed.

By 1909, however, the improvement of communications in India, the spread of education, through English at the higher levels, the growth of the press, and the slowly accelerating process of urbanization and industrialization had permitted Indians to come together in wider and wider groupings, some religious or sectarian, some cultural, some economic, but others, thanks to the increased pressures of government upon Indian life and society, political. The widest ranging attempt to produce an all-India political community, begun in 1885, was that of the Indian National Congress. In structure Congress was rather a loose assemblage of English-educated, often professional men which met annually to voice Indian grievances and demands. Although it was a limited body, being drawn from the small westernized class, and its appeal was often limited by its wish to secure government approval and by its desire to avoid offending any group within Indian society, Congress did do much to create a sense of nationhood. Moreover, as the Swadeshi and Boycott movements mounted in protest against the Viceroy Curzon's high handed methods demonstrated, Indian nationalism was capable of mobilizing much wider, if mainly middle-class, support when the interests of the sort of men active in Congress seemed seriously threatened. By 1909 the pressures generated outside the constitutional arena were strong enough to require changes within that arena.

The grant of effective power in municipalities and district boards, and of influence and status in the provincial and central legislative councils required men to organize to secure power or exercise influence. The question was on what lines would they do so?

India was the size of Western Europe, and as divided linguistically, historically and culturally as the nations of Europe. Indians identified themselves primarily with the region whose language they spoke, whose saints and heroes they followed and admired, whose distinctive dress and diet they adopted. (In the countryside, indeed, their universe might be much smaller, of merely district size.) Indians were also divided on religious grounds: they were Hindus, Muslims (a quarter of the total population), Sikhs, Christians or Parsis. And if they were Hindus they were hierarchically compartmentalized on caste lines, as Brahmins, Kayasthas, Jats, Kammas, Kalwars and so on – each of those major headings being subdivided yet again for marriage and ritual purposes.

At the same time Indians were men with varied economic interests, as landholders, peasant farmers or landless labourers, money lenders or borrowers, millhands, foremen or millowners, cotton manufacturers who looked to either export or internal markets, government clerks, teachers, lawyers – on the bench, prosperous barristers, struggling vakils – merchants and shopkeepers or their customers, owners of urban property or their tenants. Organization for the new electoral politics which the British had introduced might thus have been on either class and interest or upon group and community lines. In the event, though politics were often about group interests – in the towns for example whether the main tax base should be property or trade or in the countryside about landlord and tenant rights – the mobilization of votes was more often on caste or communal lines. The fact that many castes and sub-castes were occupational as well as social and ritual bodies meant of course that mobilization by caste might also mean mobilization by economic interest.

The British had introduced a parliamentary, electoral style of politics which in Britain was organized round interests and classes. But the British presence in India, the cultural challenge of the West and of Christian missionaries, had served to sharpen Hindu, Muslim, Sikh or Parsi self-consciousness, producing religious reform movements or orthodox restatements which repelled the western challenge, but also served to highlight differences between Indian religious communities. The growth of a sense of nationhood posed the question 'What nation?'. Hindu extremists might deny a place to Muslims in the Indian nation – and Muslims increasingly saw themselves as perhaps a nation within a nation. Moreover the counting of votes made minorities aware of their weakness in a winner-take-all electoral system. From early in the twentieth century seats in the Punjab municipalities had been allocated on tacitly communal (i.e. religious) lines. The Indian Councils Act of 1909 saw the creation of separate electorates for Muslims in response to appeals by the Muslim League, founded in 1906. In 1916 separate electorates were formally introduced in the United Provinces even for local elections. In a society as pluralist and as local or regional as India the creation of a party system to work the constitutional apparatus set up by government was obviously extremely difficult. To build up a nationalist agitational movement powerful and united enough to secure concessions from government might seem even more so.

It was the First World War which forced these issues. Between 1914 and 1918 India was required to shoulder great burdens in the imperial cause: the recruiting of over a million men, a massive debt increase, the dislocation and running down of trade, industry and the transport system, many shortages and accelerating inflation. Such a massive contribution had to be paid for, in both material and political coin – and the general recognition of the importance of India's contribution raised great expectations. More extreme nationalists pressed for early payment. Something was paid on account in August 1917 when the Secretary of State announced that the ultimate goal was responsible government for British India within the Empire and that meanwhile self-governing institutions would be developed and Indians increasingly associated with every branch of the administration. And then, rather late, a final payment was tendered in the form of the Government of India Act of 1919, the Montagu-Chelmsford Reforms.

The Act committed government to an extension of parliamentary government and to a radical devolution of legislative and financial power from the centre to the provinces. At the centre the consultative pattern remained, for although three Indians were appointed to the seven-member Executive Council of the Governor-General and although the elected, non-official majority in the Legislative Council was substantial, the one was not made responsible to the other. The Executive was still responsible to the Secretary of State in London not to the elected Council members in Delhi. Moreover certain key imperial subjects, such as defence, foreign affairs and communications, were listed as reserved to the Government of India.

All other subjects, however, were assigned as provincial subjects to the eight Governor's provinces, which now had very substantial elected majorities in their legislatures and executive councils half of whose members were Indian. More important still, while some of the provincial list subjects, broadly the law and order and revenue subjects, were reserved – to be handled by the executive councillors responsible to the Governor – the others, such as education, public health, agriculture and local government, were put in charge of Indian ministers drawn from the legislative councils and responsible to them under the system of dyarchy. To match the division of subjects between the centre and the provinces a division was made of the heads of revenue – customs and income tax, for example being allotted to the Government of India, land revenue to the provincial governments. Elections to the councils were from territorial constituencies, as in Britain, although, reluctantly, the principle of separate communal electorates was continued for Muslims, and even extended to Sikhs in the Punjab, and Indian Christians, Anglo-Indians and Europeans. The franchise, however, was greatly extended, so that about five million voted for the provincial councils and one million for the central legislative council. Burma, as one of the provinces of British India, shared in these reforms and changes.

The grant to Indian ministers of authority over certain provincial subjects, and of the patronage which went with it, was designed to secure the support of moderate Indian political leaders. The price for their collaboration was a reduction in the bureaucratic control of the administration. Devolution of finance to the provinces restricted central control, while as Montagu, the Secretary of State, put it the Act both required 'the subordination of the Services to the Government in India rather than to the Secretary of State' and 'the general alteration of the Services from a governing caste to an executive agency'. The district officer would henceforth be required to work for elected ministers and to adjust to a situation in which the art of political management would be as important as executive ability. A number of ICS officers took an early retirement rather than adjust to the change.

It was one thing, however, to elaborate a constitution, another to secure for it an Indian welcome. Behind the British proposals lay a search for a means of prolonging, with Indian consent, a colonial relationship serving British purposes. It was accepted that India would be given self-government. But some could scarcely yet discern the end to Indian tutelage and others who welcomed a swifter Indian advance to partnership still expected Britain to be the senior partner. Behind Indian responses lay a deep-seated rejection of that unequal relationship. The question was, therefore, whether Indian politicians would see the reforms as a means or a barrier to the self-government they ultimately sought.

Initially it seemed that the new constitution would work. The older, moderate wing of Congress, outvoted since 1916 inside Congress, chose to break away and form the National Liberal Federation to work the reforms. Even the main, more extreme body of Congress, which had for some years used agitation outside the formal political system as an instrument of change, grudgingly prepared to use them as a stepping-stone to 'full Responsible Government'. In South India the Justice Party, formed in 1916 in opposition to a Brahmin-dominated Congress, was also ready to enter the elections. So were the Muslim League and other Muslim groups.

Unhappily the Government now chose to drive through two bills, the Rowlatt bills designed to continue in peace time the emergency powers of summary trial taken during the war to deal with terrorism. The bills had been attacked by all sections of Indian opinion and unanimously opposed in Council; nevertheless they were rushed through.

At this point Gandhi, a Gujarati lawyer who had won a national reputation by his championing of Indian rights in South Africa and his saintly character, decided to apply the methods he had worked out in South Africa for applying moral pressure on government. He offered satyagraha ('reliance on truth'), refusing to obey the unjust new laws, courting punishment by doing so, and urging others to follow his example. Although he operated outside Congress, Gandhi's ability to voice his demands in the popular idiom of Vaishnavite Hinduism and to tap a wide range of post-war discontents won him a wide backing. Satyagraha was offered by individuals, and a national hartal or stoppage of work was declared, to be non-violently observed on 6 April 1919. The response was stronger in towns than villages and stronger in the Punjab, the United Provinces, Gujarat and Bombay than elsewhere, for organization had been hurried, but it was sufficient to alarm the Government. In the Punjab, where anti-European violence had occurred, it led to the shooting down by General Dyer of some hundreds of demonstrators in the Jallianwala Bagh at Amritsar.

This incident, of itself, did not lead Congress to change its mind about working the new constitution. But the hero's welcome given to General Dyer by the right wing in Britain and the betrayal by Lloyd George of wartime pledges that the Ottoman empire, in whose ruler the leadership or khilafat of the Muslim world rested, would not be dismembered raised doubts about British honesty of purpose. They provided Gandhi with an opportunity in 1920 for a larger, more universal moral assault upon the authority of government, one which would embrace Muslims as well as Hindus, and involve the countryside as well as the towns. Only the government could provide issues universal enough to arouse nationwide emotion – Gandhi recognized that it had now done so.

Not everyone was happy with Gandhi's proposals: older leaders, with strong regional bases, resented his claim to plan and lead the whole movement, more communalist Hindus resented the alliance with the Muslims, and conservatives feared the involvement of the masses. But local and regional leaders also saw that they needed a national movement and national leaders to put real pressure upon government, and when Gandhi asked that the Congress command structure be strengthened they accepted his demand. A new constitution was created for Congress, establishing a structure which paralleled that of the government. To an All-India Congress Committee some three hundred strong, meeting several times a year to discuss policy, was added a compact, standing Working Committee, a Congress cabinet or executive council. From this centre lines of communication, or of command, radiated out to twenty-one Congress provinces, based on language areas, each with its Provincial Congress Committee or PCC. Below these were District Congress Committees and in theory at least, town and village circle committees too. Each unit elected from its own membership representatives for the next higher level. In principle a well-articulated machine had been created for mobilizing political support upon a national scale.

The campaign was one of non-violent non-co-operation with the administration: a symbolic resignation of titles and honours was to be followed by resignation from the civil services and police, by the boycott of government schools, colleges and law courts and so to the boycott of the new councils. In December the goal was set of 'the attainment of Swaraj (self-rule) by all peaceful and legitimate means'. Gandhi intended, it would seem, to create a parallel government.

The movement, first taken up by Muslim Khilafat committees and then endorsed by Congress, drew in far wider numbers, men and women, peasant

as well as urban, than ever before. By 1921 it had reached formidable proportions, seriously straining government administration. The Muslim
leaders, the Ali brothers, were arrested for appealing to sepoys to renounce
their allegiance – but Gandhi and the Congress leaders echoed the appeal.
Fear for military and police loyalty, fear lest the industrial work force, hit
by inflation and post-war readjustments, be radicalized, fear of a growth of
the Kisan Sabhas or peasant associations, fear, as Craddock, Governor of
Burma, put it, that the feeling might spread that the British Government was
a setting sun, led to insistent calls for a crack-down on the non-co-operation
leaders.

What was significant, however, was that two successive Viceroys,
Chelmsford and Reading, and their Home Member Sir William Vincent
refused to do so. They recognized that any considerable interference with
the freedom of speech and liberty of the Press would threaten the working of
the new constitution. More important they recognized the overriding need
to keep moderate Indian opinion on their side, to win a moral victory. In the
face of Gandhi's satyagraha – truth-force – described as the weapon of the
weak against the strong, Government acted with great restraint. Repressive
measures were taken as violence spread among the non-co-operators late in
1921, but Gandhi was met with his own weapon of moral authority. Government allowed moderate Indians to be alienated by Gandhi's arrogance as
campaign commander, by the costs to their children's education, their
businesses or legal practices of non-co-operation, and by the rising tide of
violence. Early in 1922 the violence got out of hand in a savage mobbing at
Chauri Chaura and on 8 January Gandhi called off the whole campaign.
Government by its comparative restraint had won that co-operation of the
Indian people, which had been the basis of British rule in the past and was
essential to its continued success.

British government in India, though ultimately backed up by armed force
– about a third of the Army was ear-marked for internal security and
stationed close to the major towns and cities for that purpose – and by a
police force numbering about 200,000 men, rested in reality upon consent.
Dyarchy had been designed to win that consent, as was the grant of fiscal
autonomy to India, and the moves begun in 1924 to increase the pace of
Indianization of the civil and military services. The widening of the electorate in 1919 to include the more substantial agriculturalists was a necessary
part of any advance towards self-government. But it, too, was designed to
secure consent by enlarging what was thought to be a loyal, conservative
element in the Indian political class. It would be a major task of provincial
governments and their agents in the districts, the collectors, to retain the
loyalty of these men and to sustain the moral authority of the administration.

In 1922 the nationalist opposition was in disarray. Some Congressmen
had been alarmed by the threat to the established social order involved in
Gandhi's appeal for mass support: non-payment of revenue might go on to
non-payment of rent, working-class support for hartals might lead on to

strikes. More radical Congressmen felt betrayed by the calling off of non-co-operation at its peak of agitational effectiveness. For at the end of the day the new constitution had not been aborted: Liberals, Muslims, the Justice Party, the Unionist Party in the Punjab – an alliance of agriculturalists under Muslim leadership but with a significant Hindu element – were in office, exercising power, in possession of patronage. Moreover the opportunist alliance of the non-co-operation and Khilafat movements always viewed with suspicion by some communalists, had ended in mutual recrimination. The Khilafat movement, largely organized by the orthodox ulema, had used the language of Islam, just as Gandhi tended to use a Hindu idiom: by 1922 communal self-consciousness had been increased, not diminished, and from 1924 to 1926 communal violence flared sharply all over India.

The non-co-operation movement of 1920–2, even at the height of its agitational strength, was never a closely organized all-India movement despite the unitary command structure given to the Congress constitution and the large powers entrusted to Gandhi. The breakdown of the alliance with the Muslims was the most serious failure, but there were many others which demonstrated that non-co-operation was often being used not for national but for local and sectional purposes. The Kisan Sabhas in the UP and western Bihar were incorporated into non-co-operation, but when their leaders demonstrated their independence in active campaigns against land-lords they were promptly disowned. After Gandhi had called off non-co-operation, ending his current usefulness, he too in his turn was disowned by many of those who had earlier accepted his leadership. For some years he retired to his ashram, busy with his campaign for the uplift of the un-touchable Hindus and with his economic programme for the poor, the spread of domestic cotton spinning and weaving.

If all-India cohesion was difficult to sustain, so was party unity. In 1922 Congress as a movement was uncertain how to proceed. Gandhian No-Changers proposed to continue the boycott of the new councils. Pro-Changers wished to enter the councils, but only to disrupt them from within, and in January 1923 they formed themselves into the Swaraj Party to do so. Yet the No-Changers and the Pro-Changer members of the Swaraj Party were able to remain within the Congress. Such accommodation of powerful regional forces or individuals was essential, if undignified. The new party in the second elections under the new constitution showed the extent of the support Congress could muster, winning many seats, a majority in Bengal and the Central Provinces. But they were unable effectively to disrupt the working of the councils. In 1925, frustrated by the sight of others enjoying the fruits of office, more and more Congressmen prepared to break loose and seek office. Once ministers could be seen to be enjoying real power to push through their programmes and to reward their followers, the temptation to subordinate long-term national ends to short-term regional gains was very great. (The Liberals, for one, argued that the effective working of the consti-tution was the best way forward to self-government.) National leadership for the movement had only a very limited role – this was as true of the Muslim

League as it was of Congress – for it was time to abandon agitational politics in favour of politics within the system.

A new strategy was certainly needed, for while Congress sought a way forward, the Muslims were digesting the possibilities and implications of the 1919 constitution and moving steadily away from the Congress vision of the future. In 1923 Muslim attendance at the annual Congress session dropped to less than 4 per cent, and in 1924 for the first time in several years the Muslim League met apart from the Congress for its annual session. The Act of 1919 had devolved power to the provinces in order to protect British authority at the centre. But the shift of power to the provinces provoked in Muslims a reflection, occasionally voiced earlier, that though a minority in India as a whole, in several provinces they were, or might be, a majority. At the 1924 and 1925 League sessions the point was made that protection for Muslim interests might best be achieved in a federal structure with a minimal centre and virtual provincial autonomy. In 1927, indeed, Jinnah, speaking for the League, offered to give up separate Muslim electorates in return for the separation of Muslim-majority Sind from the Bombay Presidency and its elevation, with Baluchistan and with the North Western Frontier Province into full Governor's provinces. The offer was turned down, however, by the Hindu members of the central legislature, and attacked by the Hindu Mahasabha. Congress, uneasily outside constitutional politics, saw its claim to be a nationalist movement speaking for all India being discredited.

At this point a British blunder again altered the picture. The 1919 Act had provided for a review in 1929 of its effectiveness and of the possibilities of further advance. In 1927 the Conservative Government brought the date forward – to avoid the danger of its being out of office and unable to choose the review body at the later date – and announced the setting up of the Simon Commission to go out to India. The blunder was to make the Commission an all-white body, seemingly intended to judge Indians' performance and deal out or withhold favours accordingly. The Congress – joined by the Liberals – was able to rouse Indian pride and anger and to boycott the Simon Commission wherever it moved in India on its fact-finding tour. The 1928 Congress session went on to declare for complete independence or purna swaraj. What purna swaraj might mean was worked out in the Nehru Report prepared by an All-Parties Conference Committee, attended by Liberals, Muslims and Congressmen representing the older more conservative wing as well as the younger radicals and socialists. The Report envisaged a fully responsible government, with an executive responsible to an elected legislature, at the centre and in the provinces, and with the status of a Dominion as newly defined by the Statute of Westminster. It was to be a government with a strong centre and weaker provinces, while all electorates should be general, without any special electoral provision for minorities as befitted a united nation. The change in status of Sind, the NWFP and Baluchistan to full governor's provinces was to wait until self-government had been achieved.

As soon as it was published the terms of the Report were declared unacceptable both by the Muslim League presided over by Jinnah and by an All-Parties Muslim Conference presided over by the Aga Khan. It was also attacked by the younger, radical generation of Congress leaders such as Jawaharlal Nehru and Subhas Chandra Bose who argued for immediate independence. Motilal Nehru, author of the Report, made it clear that he would resign office if their demand was met, and it was certain that a demand for independence would alienate many other more conservative Congressmen, and the Liberals outside Congress. The compromise suggested by Gandhi was that government be allowed until 31 December 1930 to grant the Dominion Status which the Viceroy, on 1 November, had defined as the eventual goal for India. Failure to win Dominion Status by that date would be met by a renewal of non-violent non-co-operation. The challenge both to Britain and to the Muslims was complete, and the prospect that a way out of the divisions and frustrations of constitutional politics would be sought by Gandhi through renewed agitation loomed.

In 1930 anyone joining the Indian Civil Service could expect a very difficult start to his career. The old certainties of a bureaucratically-run India had largely disappeared. It was abundantly clear that the new ICS recruit would have to operate in a most uncertain, fluid political environment, that he would need to display a new and more sensitive approach, and be ready to face disruption to his work, even perhaps an early termination to his career. He might well have to preside over the quite novel process of the demission of empire.

FURTHER READING

On the ICS as an institution and as a body of men four older books can be strongly recommended as general introductions, both sound and highly readable: L. S. S. O'Malley, *The Indian Civil Service, 1601–1930* (London 1931); E. A. H. Blunt, *The ICS* (London 1937); Philip Woodruff (Philip Mason), *The Men Who Ruled India* (2 vols, London 1953–4); and N. C. Ray, *The Civil Service in India* (Calcutta 1958). Their various qualities have been neatly summed up by Professor Bernard Cohn:

> Blunt emphasises the actual functioning of the civil service during the twentieth century and gives a vivid description of the types of work that officials did. O'Malley's work is more of a history of the development of the services, and Woodruff's was consciously written as a monument and salute to a service and tradition which, although it is continuing in post-Independence India, is rapidly changing. N. C. Roy's [sic] *The Civil Service in India*, while it ably discusses the British period of civil service, emphasises the changes which have taken place in the service since Independence, particularly in relation to recruitment, training, and internal structure.

More recent studies are: G. P. Srivastava, *The Indian Civil Service* (Delhi 1965); K. L. Panjabi (ed), *The Civil Servant in India* (Bombay 1965), which like Woodruff is an assemblage of personal experiences; S. S. Khera, *District Administration in India* (New Delhi 1960); and B. B. Misra, *Bureaucracy in India: an historical analysis of development up to 1947* (Delhi 1977). Two works which look at district work from a post-Independence view point, but which are of value for an understanding of the subject of this book are J. D. Shukla, *State and District Administration in India* (New Delhi 1976) which surveys the whole range from district officer to village servant, with helpful distinctions between the practice of the various provinces, and

E. N. Mangat Rai, *Patterns of Administrative Development in Independent India* (London 1976).

Two semi-fictional works describing the district officer in action, at once lively and instructive, are Penderel Moon, *Strangers in India* (London 1944) and Philip Woodruff, *Call the next Witness* (London 1945). On the social setting in India of the district officers Charles Allen (ed), *Plain Tales from the Raj* (Andre Deutsch 1975, Futura Publications 1977) is admirably readable. For a convenient, compact and very perceptive overview of the whole period of British rule and administration in India, the best value is offered by Percival Spear, *A History of India* (London 1965), vol II, and for a more close-range study Sir Reginald Coupland, *The Constitutional Problem in India* (Oxford 1944) is still valuable.

A number of contributors to this volume have written from their ICS experiences: N. B. Bonarjee, *Under Two Masters* (Oxford 1970); F. S. V. Donnison, *Burma* (London 1979) and *British Military Administration in the Far East 1943–46* (London 1956); James Halliday (B. Symington), *A Special India* (London 1968) and J. D. Shukla, already listed. So have R. P. Noronha, *A Tale Told by an Idiot* (New Delhi 1976) and Humphrey Trevelyan, *The India We Left* (London 1972).

CHAPTER 1

RECRUITMENT AND PROBATIONARY YEAR

When in the mid-eighteenth century the English East India Company moved from trade to conquest in India and was faced with the task of administering its acquisitions, it turned to the practice of its Mughal predecessors, whose empire had been divided into provinces, and further subdivided into sarkars or districts, the key units. It was upon this pattern that the vast new areas brought by conquest and treaty into British India came to be administered. Over the same years the Company set out to change its servants in India from clerks and merchants into administrators and rulers.

The Court of Directors of the Company, exercising a personal patronage, had selected the merchants and factors, bound by covenants to loyal service, to drive their trade in India. They were sent out young to learn commercial skills in the corporate life of the factories. But for a Company turned ruler new methods were needed to train their agents in administration. A formal period of instruction was added to learning on the job. Lord Wellesley, Governor-General 1798–1805, noting the 'obstacles imposed by an unfavourable climate, by foreign language, by the peculiar usages and laws of India and by the manners of the inhabitants', established Fort William College at Calcutta where new entrants underwent a three-year course in Indian languages (whose study he did much to foster), in Indian history and law, and in the Regulations of the Company, together with English literature, modern history, international law, ethics and jurisprudence. Fort William College lasted for only seven years, but the training of the Company's recruits was then transferred to Haileybury College, north of London, where the same novel experiment of educating civil servants continued. As in India, vocational training was joined to a broad, liberal education, given by teachers such as Malthus and William Empson to a body of young men grounded together 'in one uniform system of right principles'.

The novelty of training the Company's servants was followed in 1855 by the startling decision to select them, not by patronage, but by open competition from among the products of British universities and public schools. After the examination the successful probationers were given a specialist training in Indian languages, law and procedures.

The adoption of open competition widened the field for the middle-class products of British public schools, universities and crammers, particularly the sons of professional men and the clergy. But it also opened the door in principle to Indian entrants willing to prepare for the examination. In 1857 three universities, at Calcutta, Madras and Bombay, were added to the growing system of westernized schools and colleges in India and the appointment of Indians to government posts, even quite senior on the legal side, was extended. After the Indian Councils Act of 1861, more-over, Indians were associated, as non-official members of legislative councils, with policy making at the highest level. In 1862 accordingly Satyendra Nath Tagore, brother of the Bengali poet, sailed for England to sit the ICS examination, leaving his eight-year-old wife in the care of his grandmother. He was successful and served for thirty-three years in Bombay, mostly as a district judge. Three more Bengalis were successful in 1868 and there was a steady trickle of Indian candidates thereafter. The educational investment was high, however, as indeed it was for British families, and for caste Hindus with their fears of ritual pollution there were social as well as economic costs in travelling to Britain. Indian entry by way of an examination con-ducted in a foreign language in the subjects of an alien culture and sat in London was necessarily slow; even by 1909 there were only sixty Indians in the total cadre of 1,142 members of the ICS. This was so despite the opening of a proportion of the government posts formally reserved since 1861 to the Covenanted Civil Service recruited by the Secretary of State in London to the Indian members of the Uncovenanted Provincial Civil Services recruited in India, on the grounds of proven merit.

The First World War, however, materially altered the position of the ICS. British war losses thinned the ranks of those from whom recruits had traditionally been drawn while a growth of government activity made the Home Civil Service, also now recruited by competitive examination, more attractive. It is likely, too, that the Colonial Service, to which entry was by selection not examination, had also become a significant competitor for recruits as conditions of service and the scope of administration within the colonies improved. At the same time constitutional changes in India made the outlook for British entrants seem less secure and appealing. A first breach in the ICS monopoly of top executive and policy-making positions had been made in 1909 in response to nationalist demands and the need to make increased government activity and taxation more palatable. Indians were thereafter appointed even to the Governor-General's and Secretary of State's councils, while elected Indian members of the legislative councils secured the right to initiate policy discussions, not merely to be consulted. Then in 1919 the same two pressures, grown much more formidable thanks to British economic weakness and the significance of India's contribution to the Allied cause, led to far greater inroads upon the position of the ICS. Under the Government of India Act of that year the ICS, like the Indian Police, was still to be recruited by the Secretary of State, but the holding of the ICS examination concurrently in London, Delhi and Rangoon made it much easier for Indians and Burmese to sit it, while British recruitment faltered. In the provinces, moreover, where the great bulk of the ICS served, the executive councils were equally shared between British and Indian members in every case but that of Bihar. Under dyarchy ministers were given charge of those departmental subjects designated as transferred and so ICS district officers, though they were still ultimately responsible to the Secretary of State, often found themselves, for practical, day-to-day purposes working under Indian ministers. To some at least this was a most unwelcome development. As Bonarjee, who was at school in England at the time, puts it: 'In Britain itself old-timers and old-stylers were by no means enthusiastic, particularly at the prospect of their sons and nephews serving with, and quite possibly even under, Indians.' The early 1920s were thus years of disquiet, at least for the British members of the ICS. That disquiet was increased by the prospect of further constitutional reform which might affect the security of a career in India and by the immediate situation after the introduction of the Act of 1919, which was marked by outbursts of anti-British feeling and communal bitterness and violence, a constant pre-occupation and source of anxiety to all officials in India.

So serious did the problem of attracting British entrants to the ICS become that in August 1922 Sir Samuel Hoare introduced a motion in the House of Commons asking the Government to institute an enquiry into the situation. One immediate response was to restate the moral value of an Indian career, although what this involved was seen rather differently by the two front benches. The Prime Minister, Lloyd George, in what now seems oddly florid words, stressed that there was a continuing and crucial role for the British ICS:

Their every word is a command, every sentence a decree, accepted by the people, accepted willingly with trust in their judgement and fairness which might be the pride of our race. I can see no period when the Indians can dispense with the guidance and assistance of the small nucleus of the British Civil Service of British officials in India – this twelve hundred in a population of three hundred and fifteen million. They are the steel frame of the whole structure. I do not care what you build on to it – if you take that steel frame out, the fabric will collapse. There is an institution which we will not cripple; there is an institution which we will not deprive of its freedom and privileges – and that is the institution which built up the British Raj in India – the British Civil Service in India.

Colonel Wedgwood, speaking for the Labour Party, also stressed the contribution which British ICS men had still to make, but in very different terms. He observed that 'the best of the British officers in India realise that they are doing their finest service to the Mother Country when they assist forward the process of their own extinction'.

The longer term reaction was to set up the Lee Commission in 1923 to review service conditions. Inflation in India had made the pay and pension rights of the service, which had once seemed so generous, increasingly unattractive, while the decline of the rupee against sterling had made the cost of remittances from India to Britain to support homes and families there much more burdensome.

For grievances over pay and conditions of service the Lee Commission provided satisfactory remedies. The new pay scale for British members of the ICS started at about £560 a year, rising to £900 after five years and to £1800 after fifteen years, with a top figure for a district officer of some £2400 a year and still higher salaries for commissioners, chief secretaries, provincial governors or High Court judges. By the standards of that time this was generous enough, but there were no comfortable answers to the other reasons for disquiet. Indianization of the ICS continued, and the Lee Commission proposed that half the places annually filled should go to Indian candidates so as to achieve racial parity among serving officers within fifteen years. One of the contributors, Symons, recalls a letter he wrote in 1925 when assessing the possibility of a career in the ICS: 'I want to hold before me always the Toc H ideal of service... I want my life to be an unselfish one and if the ICS is going to offer me such a life ... the ICS will do; but if the ICS offers a life which is allowed me, under protest, by Indians, with every prospect of it being taken away from me at a moment's notice, then I don't think it will do; it would be ghastly to be thrown out of India at 40 with nothing to do and no qualifications for doing it.'

Not all ICS candidates were perhaps as idealistic and dedicated as Symons, though most probably many shared his sentiments to some degree. His doubts about the long term prospects of a career in India were, however, quite widespread. They could only have been intensified by the appointment of the Simon Commission in 1927 to review the working of the Act of 1919, for that made it clear that a further advance towards self-government was on the way.

The long and painful gestation of a new Government of India Act, which was accompanied by another bout of civil disobedience, was a further discouragement to British recruitment to the ICS. A consequence was that in the first five years of the 1930s only ninety-one British were appointed to the ICS as against one hundred and thirty Indians. In 1935 only seventy-one British candidates sat the examination to compete with two hundred and twenty-one Indian candidates appearing in London alone. The parity at entry envisaged by the Lee Commission had broken down.

The remedy was to 'top up' the British examination entrants with a number of entrants by selection from among university graduates. (In India selection already operated since 20 per cent of ICS posts were open to Indians promoted on merit from the provincial services or by nomination from the minority communities.' The provision of this double channel of entry, coupled with a publicity drive in British schools and universities, restored the situation. With the outbreak of the Second World War in 1939 the London examinations came to an end, but some candidates were selected in 1940 and 1941 and a few were even appointed after 1945.

Despite these fluctuations in the popularity and prospects of an ICS career, recruits, both British and Indian, regularly offered themselves. Why and with what hopes and motives they did so, they themselves reveal. Haig is a good example of a candidate with a positive web of Indian connections. His father was Governor of the UP; an uncle was in the Indian Army; an aunt was married to an Anglican Bishop in India; and a grandfather had been a Judicial Commissioner in the UP. With his parents away in India and visiting him only on rare occasions, Haig had not enjoyed his school holidays staying in country vicarages, and he was determined not to subject his own family to such experiences. But a chance encounter with an Indian

ICS officer at his father's table was nevertheless enough to persuade him to follow in his father's footsteps.

Another follower of family tradition, Symington had decided at the age of ten that he must go into the ICS. In his case there was a family connection going back over a century to brightly-uniformed ancestors serving in the Bombay Light Cavalry and the Bombay Artillery of the Honourable Company's Army.

With some of the Indian candidates, parental authority was evidently expressed in a very decisive way. N. Baksi, who served in Bihar, was pressed hard by a family friend to apply for the ICS, although he wanted to become a surgeon. He is quoted in K. L. Panjabi, *A Civil Servant in India* (Bombay 1965) as follows:

My mother finally clinched matters by saying to me, 'Our country will be free and our leaders will need the assistance of administrators with honesty, character and integrity. If you have drunk my milk, no one will be able to purchase your character. Take my blessing, go and compete at the ICS and you will succeed.' That was the end of my dream to become a surgeon.

In another instance, too, maternal influence was the decisive factor, as R. P. Noronha, who served in the CP, relates on the first page of his *Tale told by an Idiot* (New Delhi 1976):

I got into the I.C.S. in a pleasantly casual fashion. When I went to England, my mother had impressed on me the need to appear for the competitive examination, which I had no intention of doing (my heart was set on a career as a photo-journalist). After I had refrained from taking my first shot at the examination, my mother lost patience – but also some of her abounding faith in an only child – and sent me all the forms and certificates duly filled up for the I.C.S. She also indicated delicately that if I did not appear, my allowance would die a sudden death. I appeared; and, much to my surprise, I got in. Even more to my surprise, I topped the list of Indian candidates, and ever since then I have had no faith in competitive exams.

Mudie was a Cambridge Mathematics Wrangler in 1911 and went on to become an assistant master at Clifton and later for four terms at Eton. He writes,

I then came to the conclusion that I had no interest in school-mastering and decided to get into the I.C.S. My father had always wanted me to do this, but my mother was against it and that is why I first tried school-mastering. After about six months at home, I went to a crammer's in London – the well-known Wren's – an establishment almost entirely devoted to cramming candidates for the I.C.S. examination, which they did efficiently and with great success. The I.C.S. examination started on 2 August 1914, two days before the war broke out. Having been a Sergeant in the Cambridge Officers' Training Corps, I applied at once for a commission and was gazetted on 26 August to a London Territorial Battalion. My welcome to the battalion was hardly heartening. I arrived after mess was over, so sat down alone with everyone watching me, except the Colonel who came across to me and said, 'I would like to know how you got into this battalion, Sir, for we have many fellows on our waiting-list whom we want.'

Mudie did not, however, stay long with this battalion because the War Office decided that successful candidates for the ICS who had joined the Army should be sent to India as soldiers though with the proviso that they should

not be sent to the Front and with the promise that they would be taken back
into the ICS at the end of the war, provided that, within a year, they then
passed in riding, health and the vernacular. Mudie was transferred to a
battalion which was going to India and eventually ended up on the staff of a
musketry school in India before entering service in the UP after the war.

But to many, and possibly most, of the candidates it was a combination of
circumstances which dictated the choice: the attraction of the job, having
the scholastic proficiency to pass the exam, and the example of others, which
was sometimes purely accidental, as in Belcher's case:

My family had no connection with India, and before the end of my university career,
I myself had no special interest in that country. At nine, I won a scholarship to
Christ's Hospital; at eighteen, a scholarship in Classics at Jesus College, Cambridge;
in 1937, with a moderately good honours degree, I hesitated what career to follow.
For those of my generation, there was a natural tendency, if one had jumped the
established scholastic hurdles with reasonable success, to attempt another somewhat
similar hurdle, the Civil Service competition. One might say it was the path of least
resistance; at any rate it was somewhat in that spirit – after half-hearted looks at two
alternatives – that I decided to compete. But, first, on the advice of my tutor, I stayed
a further year at Cambridge, reading for the Diploma in Classical Archaeology. So it
was in the summer of 1938 that I filled in the forms for the Civil Service competition,
and in the course of doing so was confronted with the question which services I
wanted to be considered for – Northern Ireland Civil Service? Clerkship in the House
of Commons? Inland Revenue Inspectorate? Indian Civil Service or only the Home
Civil Service? The last was what I thought I really wanted, the first three I knew I did
not. The I.C.S. was not then such a prestigious service as it had been before the 1919
and 1935 reforms, but still well-thought of, and it appeared to me to be remarkably
well-paid. I decided to put my tick against the Home and Indian; and, in the event
not coming quite high enough in the list for an immediate job in the Home, accepted
the offer of one in the Indian.

Bell, from an L.C.C. school in South London, went on to Christ's Hospital
and Cambridge, where he took a second in History. Like Belcher, Bell
hankered after a career in the Home Civil Service:

The question was, should one take a chance on the Home Civil only, and in the event
of failure, try again the following year, or also enter for the Indian Civil Service and
the Colonial Service Eastern Cadetships (for Ceylon, Malaya and Hong Kong) which
were recruited on the same examination? Another possibility was to be less ambitious
and enter for Inspector of Taxes or Third Class Officer, Ministry of Labour which
recruited by a similar, but easier, examination. In my last year at Cambridge, when a
career was much in my thoughts, I had sought advice from the University Appointments Board. The Board rather directed men's ideas towards India and at the same
time, the India Office was bringing its influence to bear.

Bell was given the final push towards a career in India by the advice of a
family friend to the effect that 'there was still something worth-while to do
in India'.

Midgley, the son of an Ilford customs officer, had a similar background to
Bell and he writes:

My father's plans for me were explicit, I was to be what was then called a 'First
Division Man'. Occasionally, my father, in flights of fancy, saw me as Secretary of
the Board of Customs and Excise. But first he had to get me to the right school. I
had no great difficulty in being top of my class at the local elementary school. At that

age I passed for a bright boy and there was not much competition. Moreover, my home was full of books, including the informative and improving works of Arthur Mee, *The Children's Encylopaedia*, bound volumes of *My Magazine*, *To The Boy who is going to be Prime Minister*, *To The Boy who is going to be Lord Chancellor* – and so on. *Elitism* was unabashed in those days, and I was sometimes called out to stand before the rest of the class to be publicly commended. Fortunately for my character, I was soon to discover that the world outside Ilford was full of even brighter boys, for my father hit on Christ's Hospital as the place for me. He drafted a careful letter to the Lord Mayor of London, through whose good offices I was nominated to sit for a competitive examination for limited entry to that great school. At the age of eleven, I assumed the blue gown and yellow stockings. Even before leaving school, my thoughts had turned to India. For schoolboys of my era, India was full of romance. When I was very young, the Mutiny was still alive in English folk lore. My grandfather used to play on the piano a dramatic piece called 'The Relief of Lucknow'. This was a series of themes introduced by captions. 'General Havelock's forces are sighted – tara, tara'. 'The Mutineers flee – hurry music'. Then there were Henty and Manville Fenn – stories of young sons of the vicarage, who, joining the Indian cavalry, were looked down on for their piety and lack of private means, but who, having spent their youth careering on horseback over Dartmoor on half-broken ponies, soon abashed the regiment by mastering some previously unmanageable steed. And of course Kipling. A friend of my father's would bring his family to tea on Sundays and, afterwards, read the *Jungle Book* aloud to the assembled families. I made a conscious decision to try for the I.C.S. at the age of seventeen. My father gave me a book 'Careers in the Civil Service'. The first chapter was on the I.C.S., and discovering that probationers were required to pass an examination in riding, I read no further. I would not be a 'First Division Man' or even (my father's fall-back position) an Inspector of Taxes. I would go to India and ride about the countryside administering justice and being the father of my people.

A very different route to the ICS is described by Venkatachar:

My ancestors lived for several generations in an *agrahara*, a village or area of land given to Brahmins, about twenty-five miles from Bangalore (in the Indian Princely State of Mysore). My father and his elder brother, both born in the 1860s, were the first members of the village community to take to English education in Bangalore. My school education was entirely through the medium of English. Mysore State had two prestigious government colleges – the Maharaja's College in Mysore taught humanities, the Central College in Bangalore taught various branches of science. I studied in the Central College from 1916 to 1918; in 1918, I joined the Presidency College at Madras from where I graduated in Chemistry in 1920. Till I went to Madras, I knew nothing of British India and of the events happening there. I did not know how the British ruled India. I had not even visited a British-administered district. We read no newspapers in our home. The Indian State of Mysore was completely isolated from British India.

Contact in Madras with the 'intellectually alert Tamilian students' who talked endlessly about jobs in the ICS and other imperial Services changed what Venkatachar calls 'his somewhat parochial outlook'. After graduating in Chemistry, he decided to go to England to sit the ICS exam. He describes it in detail:

The examination for 1921 was based on an entirely new syllabus which was an innovatory departure from the old, time-honoured one. It was in three parts: a number of compulsory papers such as essay, précis-writing, general knowledge, everyday science and a modern European language; secondly, groups of optional subjects; and thirdly, a *viva voce* conducted nearly a month before the written tests. The last was a radical innovation. It carried three hundred marks out of a total of nineteen hundred. The Civil Service Commission explained that the marks for oral examination were purposely kept high so as to test the capacity of the students to give decisive answers in an intelligible way, for one of the necessary accomplishments of an I.C.S. officer must be the power to talk, argue and reason, above all be quick in decision.

The new system favoured the chances of Indian students. The old syllabus which lasted from Victorian times to 1920 rested on a system of written examination which was a wide-ranging test of detailed knowledge based on the English school curriculum. I should say the new system assisted the process of Indianisation of the Service as it enabled a larger number of Indians to compete successfully in the London examination. I attribute my own success to the new system.

Venkatachar recalls that about one hundred and fifty candidates took the examination. Of the sixteen candidates who were declared successful, thirteen were Indian and three were British. 'No entrant to the Service in 1922', he writes, 'had any idea that the Service would become extinct in his time. On the other hand, he was buoyant and hopeful of a successful career, of rising to dizzy heights of power and responsibility.'

In contrast with Venkatachar, a Brahmin from the South, who entered the ICS by means of the London examination, Faruqui was a Muslim from the North who was successful in the examination held in New Delhi in 1929.

I belonged to a middle-class family of the Western Punjab, which now falls in Pakistan. My father was a medical officer in Government Service. He was transferred from district to district and took his family with him wherever he went. My schooling, therefore, suffered a lot, particularly as my father was usually transferred in the middle of the school year. What is surprising is that in those days the text books taught in each school were usually different for the same class. It set me back every time I went to a new school. And my father had to engage a special tutor to coach me after school hours. This state of constant flux came to an end when I joined college in Lahore. My ambition was to become a professor. And all my preparations were for that career. The ideal of a professorship was before my mind all the time. One night, however, I dreamt that I was holding a card with my name written thereon like this:

Nasir Ahmad Faruqui
_____
Indian Civil Service (Junior)

When I did eventually join the I.C.S., I learnt that those who sat for it in New Delhi were junior to those who joined from London, and a year's difference in the probationary training set us still lower down. Fate, however, intervened in my plans. When the B.A. examination result came out, I was surprised to find that I stood first among the Muslims of the whole province. Friends who came to congratulate my father, strongly urged him to enter me for the I.C.S. competition. When my father asked me, I agreed. But in all my life before that, I had never considered myself good enough for the I.C.S. which was then the premier service in India and to which went the most able students, which I was not. If I was successful in entering the I.C.S. in 1929, it was a special act of grace by God. I was the least deserving candidate.

Narasimham, who was, like Faruqui, the son of an official, was born in Srirangam in Madras. With the aid of an Indian scholarship and help from his father, Narasimham got to Oxford and obtained a second in modern History after only two years. At the age of twenty-one, he passed into the ICS, fourth of the combined list in the 1936 examination and first among the Indians. On the reasons which prompted him to apply, Narasimham writes:

I may say that first of all it was one of the conditions of the scholarship given to me by the Tata Fund that I should take the Indian Civil Service examination. In those days, for an Indian, the Indian Civil Service presented the finest possible career prospects, even though a few positions in private industry, especially the oil companies, were quite attractive. Conditions in India have changed very much since then, but in those days, anybody's first preference was the Indian Civil Service. I recall very vividly those days in Burlington House, where the Civil Service exams were held, and I must say that the atmosphere was very congenial to a person giving of his best, particularly in the viva which carried three hundred marks. In my own case I thought I had done fairly well until the very end of my oral examination. At that point I was asked a number of questions such as whether I rode or swam, or whether I shot. I gave a straight-forward 'No' to all such questions, and I was afraid that these negative answers would pull me down in the viva. I was very surprised and pleased when the results came out, and I found that I had received three hundred marks out of three hundred.

A considerably less enthusiastic picture of Burlington House and of the advantages of candour is given by Matthews:

At the suggestion of an Indian university friend of mine, I examined the prospects of a career in India and I was greatly attracted to it – especially, to be frank, by the high rate of emoluments and security offered by the Indian Civil Service. This was 1929. With the economy of the world collapsing in ruins, security and high pay were considerations of the highest appeal. The written exam was preceded by the *viva voce* at the HQ of the Civil Service Commissioners in Burlington Gardens. On the appointed morning, I found myself facing across a wide table a crescent-shaped line of seated people, indistinctly discernible because the line fronted an enormous window through which the light of the summer morning shone full in the face of the candidate. The examination was stern, but fair. Unfortunately, I made a grave strategic error. In due course I was asked the stock question, 'And why do you want to go to India?'. The most welcome reply was, of course, 'My great grandfather, my grandfather, and my father all served in India and I want to follow the family tradition' or at least, 'I have a feeling for India and have an ambition to serve in that part of the British Empire'. Unfortunately, I was unable to answer in either of these senses. I told the truth, and this was my undoing. I said, in effect, that with the economic uncertainties then existing, I thought it desirable to seek security in the Indian Civil Service – especially as it was the highest-paid civil service in the world. This reply was greeted with a long silence from my examiners and the rapid termination of my interview. The result was that, in spite of my highly successful university career, supplemented by my university colours for athletics, I was marked down to one hundred out of three hundred. However, in the written examination the gods smiled upon me, and I stood first, with enough leeway completely to offset the low viva mark and I came fifth overall in my year.

The candidates who had been successful in the examinations or the selection procedures in Britain, India or Burma then went forward to a period of specialist training in Britain. This was one year for British candidates but two years for candidates selected in India or Burma, until 1937, and one year from then onwards. During their training period the probationers received three hundred pounds a year if British, three hundred and fifty if Indian or Burmese. For many people who had scraped through a degree course at the university on one hundred and fifty pounds a year or less, such a sum seemed riches.

Their training took place at one of three universities in Britain, namely

Oxford, Cambridge and London with, up to 1937, Trinity College, Dublin, a fourth but little-used alternative. These four universities were recognized by the Secretary of State for India as centres which could assemble the necessary teaching expertise. The probationary course included Indian law, Indian history and a vernacular language appropriate to the province to which the probationer was going. The allocation of candidates to their respective provinces, ten in India plus Burma by 1938, was made as soon as they had been selected. The cadets, as they were called, were allowed to state their preferences, but the authorities were able to satisfy only a minority since it was the custom for most of the British candidates to put the Punjab or the UP as their first choice. The range of choice was a little wider after 1937 with the creation of the new provinces of Orissa and Sind which had formerly been parts of Bihar and Bombay respectively. The separation of Burma from India in 1935 brought a change of nomenclature to the ICS cadre in Burma who were now called The Burma Civil Service (Class I), but Burma remained one of the choices open to ICS candidates. The Burma cadets underwent the same general instruction as the Indian cadets, but they received special tuition in Burmese language and history and Buddhist law.

At the end of the course all cadets sat a final examination in law, history and their vernacular, which was prescribed and set by the Civil Service Commission, but they also had to pass a riding test. Many cadets found this the most unexpected and unfamiliar part of their course. The individual was expected to arrange and pay for a course of instruction at some approved stables. He was issued with official instructions entitled *Hints on Riding* which contained some pretty pithy advice on the care of horses in India such as 'If the syce does not keep your horse in proper condition and fit to travel, change the syce.' However, though for many cadets who came from urban homes in Britain and India a riding course might be both beneficial and enjoyable, the horse was in fact becoming increasingly irrelevant as a means of transport in many parts of India and Burma.

The probationary year meant very different things to different people. To the Indians selected in India who had not been abroad before, the probationary period was their introduction to the British environment and culture which they had read about, but not so far experienced. For British entrants, probation provided an opportunity for change, a graduate from a Scottish university going perhaps to Oxford or an Oxford man to London. Once they had arrived at their respective universities reactions among the probationers naturally varied. Venkatachar, who went to Cambridge in 1920, felt both isolated and detached:

In Cambridge, I was more an observer than a participant in the University life. As a probationer, I had nothing to do with academic life. I made no friendship with any Englishman. We Indian students kept the company of our fellow Indians. We regularly attended the Indian *Majlis*, occasionally debates in the Cambridge Union or a talk by some eminent person. I still remember the address by Edwin Montague after his dismissal by Lloyd George. We considered him to be a benefactor of India. On the whole, our understanding of English life was on the surface, quite superficial.

The syllabus for the probationers was anything but inspiring. The lectures on

Indan Codes and laws were dull. No one told us what sort of work awaited us in India. No meaningful and intelligent ideas enlightened the probationers on the nature of Indian administration nor was he burdened with any mystique of imperialism. After the strenuous competitive examination, the probationary period was somewhat of an anticlimax from an intellectual point. The year of leisure could have been utilised for more profitable purpose.

I carried no ideas from Cambridge about Britain's empire in India or how to rule it. My entry into the Civil Service was mainly a means of furnishing myself with a career with handsome emoluments and a pension at the end of it – both of which were generous, at any rate, to the end of the Second World War. In my Cambridge days, I had acquired the habit of discursive reading which has continued up to this day. The one idea I carried in my head on leaving England was the saying (the source of which I do not remember) of Walter Raleigh – man of letters, a great don of Oxford – the I.C.S. was a university in which you never graduated; you went on learning by experience till the end of your career; also, that first degree achievements and the Day of Judgement were two separate examinations and not one.

Gupta spent two years at Oxford from 1933 to 1934 and unlike Venkatachar he certainly made the most of it, not least the opportunities for travel in Europe at a very interesting time.

Having passed the Medical Board, I sailed by the S. S. Narkunda – a strange, new experience. Leaving the boat at Suez, we paid a quick visit to the Egyptian pyramids and rejoined it at Port Said. I would not wax eloquent over the stone masses that are the pyramids – a colossal squandering of slave labour. While our sea-sickness was soon over, home sickness persisted. From Marseilles, we travelled overland and an Indian friend received me in London. The same night, I had my first sight of Piccadilly Circus, its ceaseless flow of motor traffic and the flashing neon signs – a strange world. After buying the minimum essential clothing, I reached Oxford, New College (only six hundred years old).

I soon joined the I.C.S. Society, the Union Society, the League of Nations Union, the Lotus Club, the Indian Majlis and the Labour Club. Most evenings were thus occupied.

If one were to ask me which single factor I would call the most potent influence over me there, I should reply the Oxford Union Society debates. The phenomenal standard of speech, the delicate wit and humour, the eminently fair hearing accorded to the contestants, the rapier thrusts of argument and the matchless repartees combined to make for a feast of reason and flow of soul. I looked forward keenly to the weekly debate every Thursday. Here one saw facets of the British democratic way of life from which the foreigner could draw an inspiration. It is modelled on Westminster and no wonder it has been the cradle of parliamentarians. A brilliant Indian, Doosoo Karaka (later editor of the 'Current') was President one term. Others included Michael Foot and John Cripps. Among visitors who spoke to us were Sir Winston Churchill, Sir Samuel Hoare, Father D'Arcy and Gillie Potter. A German undergraduate asked Sir Winston if he considered the German people, as opposed to the German Government, responsible for the First World War. With his neck stuck out the bulldoggish way, he snapped back 'Yes'. The German stalked out of the hall in protest accompanied by sarcastic cheers.

We had three longish vacations – Christmas, Easter and Summer. Travelling is said to be a part of liberal education. In those days, circular, concessional return tickets over continental railways were easily available; there was little rush of traffic and there were plenty of moderate hotels. In fact, staying put in England would have cost about as much as going round there. Baedekear's guide books provided all the requisite help.

In the Easter vac I visited Switzerland, Italy and the Rivieras. Swiss towns were spotlessly clean and the people friendly. In Italy I saw the priceless paintings of the old Italian masters, the Uffizi, the Pitti, the picturesque bridge over the Arno, the Bridge of Sighs, the gondolas of Venice and the fountains of Rome. Mussolini was lording it over there. How shortly was the power and glory of that dictator to be crushed and buried for ever – a warning to all budding dictators. In Pompeii, I climbed the Vesuvius on foot and nearly perished in the wilderness until guided by woodcutters. I walked across the crater with steam sizzling out of innumerable holes and peered down into the cavernous, smoking mouth of the volcano! It is a marvel none of the spluttering spouts gave way under my ignorant steps, and I was alone there. I was horrified to see the skeletons in the Pompeii Museum on return. Verily, 'in the midst of life we are in death!'

The summer term at Oxford passed with incredible swiftness. It was more or less a perpetual festival on the river in preparation for the great event, the summer 'eights'. In lovely weather, we played tennis or did punting on the river (I was left hanging on the pole once), attended end of term parties in our clubs and read for the exams. It was a scene of youth and gaiety. Thereafter, having taken the exam in London, I betook myself to the Continent – this time the Netherlands. Thence to Hitler's Deutschland, the ominous Swastika fluttering thickly all over the land. 'Heil Hitler' was the order of the day. It was clear that the smug complacency of the British was only day-dreaming. There was a bellicose air all round. Hitler was deified as happens in all countries practising hero worship. Like dumb, driven cattle, men and women, boys and girls were marching the streets, throwing up their arms in the ludicrous Hitler salute.

In one town I noticed Hitler's motorcade, the roadsides thick with the populace screaming themselves hoarse. I felt convinced that the British democratic system was peerless. Such mental ferment is perhaps not the least gain of foreign experience. It is a pity that our successor Service has been denied this opportunity. Crossing over, I saw Prague, then over to Budapest. On the way back to England, I passed through Munich, seeing the gigantic Deutschemuseum and the wonderful Planetarium. I then enjoyed the famous steamer trip up the Rhine from Coblenz to Cologne. By this time, the purse had dwindled down so much that I had to be content with semi-starvation meals in Belgium before rushing pell-mell to Oxford and throwing myself on the goodies in the Dining Hall! And so began my second year there in autumn '34. I paid a weekend visit to Cambridge, 'founded by those who had been sent down from Oxford', and was reminded that 'while the Cambridge man walked as though all the world belonged to him, the Oxford man walked as though he didn't care a hang to whom the world belonged!'

After a further account of a second year Christmas vac spent in Spain and France it is almost a surprise to have a brief aside:

During probation we also had to take down notes of criminal cases during actual hearings in a criminal court. I attended the Bow Street Police Court in London for a fortnight. It was most interesting and business-like.

Slater was one of those who decided to go elsewhere for his probationary year and therefore deserted Cambridge for London. He writes:

I chose to do my probationary year at the School of Oriental Studies [SOS] in London. I had enjoyed Cambridge, but there seemed little point in going back, and personal ties were in the south. It was a congenial group, with a high proportion of Indian entrants. Our Common Room and Dining Room were in slightly dingy premises off Victoria Street, strategically placed for the various SOS classrooms in which we absorbed the elements of Indian history, law, revenue and language. I had no criticism of the course. Apart from the early history of India, an academic discipline which it would nevertheless have been short-sighted to neglect, the practical relevance of our studies to the work we were to do became clear the moment I arrived in India. I owe a special debt of gratitude to the phonetics expert who, with fantastic perseverance, got me to move lips, tongue and teeth in a way which produced sounds positively recognisable as Urdu. I acquired in London a feel for the language which later yielded a First Class Interpretership.

Lamarque exchanged Oxford for London where he was impressed by the quality – and the idiosyncrasies – of some of the academic staff:

I had worked exceedingly hard during my last year at Oxford, culminating in Finals, followed by the Civil Service exam, and the comparatively relaxed atmosphere at the School of Oriental Studies provided a welcome change. To my Indian colleagues, the probationary period may well have been a waste of time and they might have done better to have gone straight back to India after the entrance exam. But for me it proved a gentle introduction into a completely new world. I knew nothing of India and her affairs, and to go from the Greek to the Tamil language was to experience an extraordinary transition. It was helpful to be broken into these unfamiliar things in a familiar environment. It was an obvious anachronism that in 1937 the authorities should require us probationers to pass a riding test, and this was an irritation to the Indians among us, most of whom did not care for horses anyway. But, having done some riding already, I quite enjoyed this and found it an interesting experience to take a test first on the beautifully schooled horses of the Metropolitan Police at Imber Court and finally on the equally well-trained horses of the Gunners at Woolwich (even though some of us thought that at that stage of our history the Army was wasting its time with horses as much as we were).

The supervisor of I.C.S. probationers at the School of Oriental Studies was Dr S. Vesey-Fitzgerald, a genial and scholarly man who had retired prematurely from the I.C.S. and devoted himself to the study of Hindu and Muhammedan law. He first introduced me to those astonishing and surely under-rated works, the Indian Penal Code, for which Lord Macaulay was mainly responsible, and the Indian Evidence Act of Fitzjames Stephen. It has always seemed to me since that English criminal law would be more simply and more efficiently administered if those two Acts had been applied here also.

Vesey-Fitzgerald had served in the Central Provinces and would regale us with stories of life in Amraoti, of which he clearly had happy memories, but which we in turn would gently mock behind his back. Three other of the teachers at the School stand out in my memory; a gentle and rather sad little Madrassi, who had anglicized his name to Pathy and who had the hard task of trying to teach me Tamil; in complete contrast, the ebullient Sir Denison Ross, the Principal of the School who seemed to know every one of the world's languages, had a fund of good stories, and for one reason or another, gave me a rather alcoholic lunch one day in White's Club; and Professor Lloyd-James, master of phonetics who tutored the BBC's announcers in what, in those days, was regarded as correct English pronunciation, and introduced us probationers into such mysteries as the glottal stop and how to control the tongue and lips so as to make (in my case) Tamil sound more realistic. Looking back on it, we were lucky to encounter such men.

All of us London-based probationers got to know each other quite well, and this itself was a useful experience. At least half of us were Indian. I had scarcely ever met an Indian before and I discovered for the first time that where people have similar educational backgrounds and professional interests, differences of race, colour or class are of no consequence. (Some of the Indians, as I discovered later, came from the humblest homes.) My parents had a tennis court and we could sometimes have tennis parties for the probationers which provided a useful means of getting to know them. Some of the Indians, Narasimham, Tarlok Singh and others have risen to the top in Government service since independence. It was, however, of the nature of Government service in India that, particularly at the junior levels, one saw very little of one's contemporaries, certainly outside one's own province, and I have never seen many of my fellow probationers since we left London.

Watson stayed on at Cambridge to do his probationary year there in 1931–2. He found the curriculum somewhat academic and not sufficiently geared to the practical needs of the trainee.

I learnt Indian history from someone who got it from a book; I could have got it direct from the book. There was too much about Asoka and little or nothing about modern developments. I did, however, learn that the Holy Roman Empire was neither holy, nor Roman, nor an empire. Someone told me later that, as an I.C.S. officer, I was neither Indian, nor civil, nor a servant.

I learnt Hindi from a retired Indian Army officer who would have preferred to teach me Urdu, but as he pointed out, the two languages are not so very different. Urdu is written in the Arabic script which only the writer can read, and Hindi in the much less illegible Devanagari script. There was also a course in phonetics which I found interesting and useful. Later I found myself as well prepared in Hindi as could have been expected.

The course in Criminal Law, including the Law of Evidence, was given by a retired High Court Judge from Lahore. I consider it satisfactory on the whole, except that it was not possible, in my time, to be as firm as he advised in controlling a criminal trial. There were things that the Bar did not like and were too strong to let one get away with.

The great omission in the probationary year was the administrative system of British India; I arrived in India knowing nothing of what I was to do, except for the magisterial work.

Paterson is also somewhat critical and comments, as many do – though Venkatachar is an exception – on the lack of any briefing during the probationary year on the complexities of the political and constitutional situation in India at the time.

Cambridge was great fun and I enjoyed every minute of it, but I also did a certain amount of work, particularly on language and on the law since it seemed to me quite basic that one should be able to speak the language easily, and also basic that one should be really conversant with the law that one would have to administer. Looking back later on, I really had only one criticism, or perhaps two, of the training year at Cambridge. The language I had to learn was Hindi, and when I did get to the Central Provinces, I found that we had been taught far too high-flown a version of Hindi and what I had learnt was almost useless. The second criticism, I think, is that we could well have stood a lecture or two by a person with sufficient authority and knowledge to tell us more precisely what the constitutional and political position was, since there seemed to be almost a blank in my year at Cambridge on this subject, and it was only when one got to India that one began to pick up the threads of the political and constitutional set-up.

Belcher, who came from Cambridge to Oxford for the probationary year 1938–9, takes the point about political briefing further.

The, as it were, academic element in my choice of a Civil Service career persisted into the probationary year, for which I was allowed to attach myself to Brasenose College. Indian history, Indian language (in my case, for the Punjab, Urdu), and Indian economics were studied as for a university course – all naturally useful, but not for the most part with any sharp focus on the India of the present day in which we were to work or the particular job we were to do there. Apart from learning the basic essentials of British Indian law, and how to ride a horse, the only preparation that was sharply focussed in this sense was given by a very praiseworthy course of phonetics (so that some of the probationers were ultimately able to talk 'their' language as the natives of their province did instead of in the painful accents of

'Sahibs'), and a brief series of talks on what was called 'social service' which at least described, if often rather paternalistically, some of the truths and the major day-to-day problems of Indian life concerned with agriculture, health, and general social conditions. To these I would add the preparation that came from conversations with the Indian probationers, most of whom had passed the examination in India and came to join us in the United Kingdom for the probationary year. But even with these more realistic elements, it remains true that we were taught very little about the current political situation in India, though it necessarily affected the work we were to do there and the policies we were to implement. All this had to come on the job later, and at no stage, even in India, did we have any authoritative instruction in these matters. (Far less was there anything said about the possibility of our not serving out our full twenty-five year contract.) Perhaps it was wise, or at least inevitable, that this should be so: such instruction would have risked discord between the British and the Indian probationers and perhaps wider controversy than that. And its absence naturally mattered less to those among us who came from families with an Indian service background and so grew up into a natural interest in, and knowledge of, things Indian. But the lack of realistic information and discussion meant that to many of us, with our ignorance of life – even in our country – the various realities of India often came as something of a shock – could well have had undesirable repercussions on our conduct of our duties or on the spirit in which we performed them.

In the case, however, of Carleston, who did his probationary year at Cambridge in 1926–7, a taste of India broke into formal instruction in a most curious, indeed surprising, way:

This was a year of affluence – three hundred pounds! There were useful lectures on the Indian Penal Code, the Code of Criminal Procedure, the Indian Evidence Act and on Hindu and Mohammedan Law from a retired District and Sessions Judge (we were advised to insist on a body before convicting anyone of murder and warned that sometimes very aged Indians consented to be murdered so that a case might be foisted on enemies of the family!); on Indian history and Tamil. Examinations came in the summer and that in Tamil provided a mild surprise – and shock. It was conducted by a retired Indian 'professor' (apparently a stopgap). During the oral examination, we were each invited to tea at his house in an obscure part of London – Indians and Europeans in two separate groups. We had our suspicions, but duly went. The 'professor', who had our papers on his desk, told us that we had all done very badly; and then went on to say that he and his family badly wanted to get back to India, but had not the wherewithal – so could we help him? There was a stony silence as we nearly sank through the floor. He left us alone for a spell, then returned and said no more on the subject; nor did we broach the subject, having agreed that it would be improper to make contributions in such circumstances. He was more successful with the Indian group whose hearts were melted at his tale of woe. In the event, we all passed our Tamil with good marks! We felt that this was a foretaste of what we might expect east of Suez – a practical end to a useful probationary year.

Many contributors have referred to the riding, and to the riding examination which came as a memorable, and for some traumatic, finale to the year. Matthews gives a description which highlights the comic aspects:

I found that I would be required to learn to ride so, in common with other successful candidates at Cambridge, I repaired one day to the establishment of a British ex-cavalry man, Captain Cooper. In the riding school, we spent much time falling on to the floor attempting to go over jumps with 'arms folded and stirrups crossed'. Among the standard jumps was a five-bar gate which the horsey Captain set great store on our being able to clear – why, I cannot imagine because I never saw a five-bar gate during sixteen years in India. In any case, the horses at the riding school all jibbed at this gate, putting on all four brakes at the last minute and either throwing the rider over the gate or, when sufficiently urged by the crack of the attendant captain's whip, taking a standing jump at the gate – often with dire consequences. This, we were informed by our superior and sarcastic mentor, was known as the 'I.C.S. jump'.

At the end of this pleasant year of relaxed learning, we sat our 'final' examination at which no one had ever been known to fail in spite of dark hints of what could happen if the post-appointment year was taken too lightly. The examination included a riding test at the Royal Artillery School, Woolwich. This annual event must have been looked forward to greatly by the junior officers of that establishment because they gathered in large numbers to watch the pale, bespectacled, pigeon-chested examinees bump along like sacks of potatoes on their nags in the wake of the handsome young Irish Sergeant who, on a magnificent palomino, its tail streaming and mane flying, led the hotch-potch group over the formidable jumps in the arena.

With this hurdle passed and a pleasant year drawing to its close, the probationers had then to go to the India Office to sign their covenants. Shukla recalls that at the end of his year, 1939, the probationers were asked to meet Lord Zetland, the Secretary of State for India, at Whitehall:

Lord Zetland received us all; there were some other officials of the India Office. We were served tea and Lord Zetland addressed us and we signed the covenant and became members of the Civil Service of India. Lord Linlithgow, the Viceroy of India, was, exceptionally, present on the occasion and I remember Lord Zetland gently asked him if he would like to say a few words to us, but he declined.

With their covenants signed, it was the custom for the probationers to travel to Bombay with a first-class ticket on the P & O, the shipping line which regarded itself, and was generally thought of, as the official mode of transport for British officials serving in India. Matthews writes of his voyage out to India in 1931:

One cold, drizzly, grey November day, I left Liverpool Street Station *en route* for a Channel crossing and Paris. There followed a change from the Gare du Nord to the Gare de Lyons and an all night journey to Marseilles. It rained all across France and it was still raining when I boarded the P & O *Viceroy of India* lying alongside the quay. It was still grey and raining when I went to bed. I awoke to the motion of a ship at sea. I went on deck and was greeted by the brilliant sun and the blue, so blue, of the Mediterranean. Life had begun!

The voyage was the usual thrilling fairy tale-like existence to somebody who had never been on a ship bigger than the cross-Channel boat to Boulogne, but it came to an end as suddenly as it had begun when we were all ushered, with expert efficiency, off the boat at Bombay to find ourselves, unaided once more, face to face with the hard facts of life. Official instructions established my posting to be Nagpur and a few days later saw me in a four berth compartment to myself on the Calcutta Mail, destination Nagpur. The train left in the late afternoon and was due at Nagpur on the morning of the next day. I got little sleep – the racket of the train inhibited this. I spent the night gazing into the darkness – what darkness it was too – hoping to see some of India's wildlife, even a tiger. Needless to say, I was disappointed. Next morning the train steamed into Nagpur station. I hastily threw out my bedding roll and grabbed my two suitcases for a rapid disembarkation before the train began to move out. I need not have worried. The Calcutta Mail was still there two hours later. I was met by a tall bearded person resplendent in a high white pugree with a fan flash and a white robe embellished with a crimson sash to which, near the waist, a brass plate was attached. I was puzzled as to how he knew I was the right person until I noted that I was the only European disembarking. He made me a profound salaam which was just as well as I was about to do something similar to him – he looked so magnificently important! He shook his head when I tried my Cambridge-learnt Hindi on him, but invited me, by gesture, to read the brass plate. I read the words 'Deputy Commissioner, Nagpur'. Although confused by a feeling that I was in a place where anything could happen, I dismissed the very transient thought that this could be the great man himself and seeing him summon two almost naked persons (which I soon learnt were better known as coolies), I gathered that this splendid person had been sent by the D.C. to meet me. And so it proved, for we were soon leaving the station and driving through the *busti* or town streets and bazaars of Nagpur in the D.C.'s car, driven by his driver (not called chauffeur in India). The township left behind, the landscape became more open and we passed here and there big, isolated and highly dignified buildings with the Union Jack floating over them. These I learnt later were Government offices like the Secretariat, etc. These gave way to an area of tree-lined roads with verandah bungalows in spacious compounds and approached by considerable drives through pillared gates. Through one of these gates we now turned and I noticed on one of the pillars a black nameboard with white lettering announcing W. V. Grigson I.C.S. The car drove up the drive, stopping under a portico from which steps led up to a wide verandah and thence to the wide open door of the drawing room. I was greeted most kindly by a tall, bespectacled and prematurely balding man and his smiling wife who soon set an apprehensive griffin completely at ease. My luggage was bundled out of the car and proceded me to the house where my kindly hostess showed me to an immense bedroom of which one of the many doors led to a stone bathroom with a zinc portable bath and other appropriate apparatus. I noted with a little thrill that the bed was enclosed in a frame covered by a mosquito net. Now, I thought, I am really in pioneering country!

Later in his service Matthews may have smiled at this early vision of Nagpur and its bungalows as pioneering country, but for Maitra when he made the long haul from Bombay to the far corner of the Assam valley there were still reminders in regulations of genuine old frontiersman days:

The voyage by the P & O ship 'Strathnaver' was memorable as I used to sit at meals at the same table as the famous Mr M. A. Jinnah and his somewhat forbidding sister, Miss Fatima Jinnah. Mr Jinnah was then at a loose end, having given up his London practice at the Privy Council and not yet taken up the Muslim League. He was always immaculately dressed, often communicative, and quite willing to talk on any subject with his young and brash fellow diner.

It was a long haul, 2277 miles by rail from Bombay to Dibrugarh in Upper Assam. The Assam railway train creeps like a snail; you have to spend two nights and two days on the route from Calcutta. Still, one should not grumble, the old steamers took weeks.

The regulations issued in 1851 expressly authorised passengers to take pianos in their cabins free of freight, provided they were required for use during the voyage and were not in packing cases.

Macdonald had a chilly, pretty off-hand reception on arrival at Bombay:

I sailed for India on the *Viceroy of India* in October 1936 and arrived in Bombay after a ten-day voyage from Marseilles. The Viceroy himself, Lord Linlithgow, returning from leave, was on board and we were therefore treated to a very impressive ceremony at the time of his arrival, with salutes from various naval vessels in Bombay harbour and a grand military display on the quay-side. The Deputy Secretary in charge at the Bombay Secretariat, to whom I reported, handed me a telegram and said, 'Gaya for you.' 'Where is Gaya?', I said. How the hell do I know?' he said. Such was my introduction to the Indian sub-continent, but I went to the railway station and found an obliging official who told me exactly how to get to Gaya.

For Slater, on the other hand, India was a familiar, welcoming place. He had been born in India, and was therefore, in a sense, returning:

The 'déjà vu' theme of the newcomer to India is fairly hackneyed, but I make no apology for playing it. From the moment of docking in Bombay, there was the odd sensation of coming home. Memory could have played no part; I was an infant when I left India. I must have absorbed, during my twenty years of conscious life, far more than I realised of the India-related literature, photographs, pictures and miscellaneous mementos which were still part of the cultural heritage of so many of my generation, whether or not their links with India were direct. The Gateway of India was as familiar as the bustling crowds, the poverty and wealth, the squalor and the splendour of Bombay, even the smells. The green-upholstered twilight of the Frontier Mail compartment in which I headed for the Punjab, so unlike anything in the experience of a traveller at home, was nevertheless not unexpected, any more than the white incandescence of midday over the endless plain as we rattled north, the wallowing buffaloes, the toy villages barely distinguishable from the mud from which they were made, the Persian wheels, the temples and the mosques – at once a preview of the environment in which we were to live and a glimpse into, as it seemed, a remembered past.

Midgley went out married:

My wife and I boarded the RMS *Strathmore* at the beginning of October 1937. There were a dozen of us probationers aboard, about half Indian and half European. We took over the large centre table in the dining saloon and did our best to liven up the ship. Ian Bowman, kilted and playing his bagpipes, led a Conga of children in fancy dress through the public rooms. We danced every evening and I was rebuked by the wife of a High Court Judge for allowing my wife to dance with our Indian colleagues. 'You will find', she said, 'that, in India, Indians will not allow their wives to dance with you'. The argument from reciprocity seemed pointless and she was already out of date. The outstation clubs were already what is now called 'integrated'. It all depended on the degree of orthodoxy of one's Indian colleagues and friends. I can recall no social embarrassment arising from the racial difference and my wife, even when travelling alone in railway carriages entirely occupied by Indian men, never experienced the slightest discourtesy. In this respect, Delhi has always been a great deal safer than Rome. Indian sexual manners are old fashioned. There is more prudery than licence.

When the ship docked at Bombay, Mohammed Shafi, a grave gentleman from Saharanpur, was there to meet us. I had engaged him in advance as our bearer. First go off, we made a poor impression on Mohammed Shafi. He presented a list of stores to be purchased in Bombay. The first item, looking a little odd in the Urdu script, was 'wine'. This turned out to mean mainly whiskey, but even at eleven rupees a bottle, we could not afford it.

At the Bombay Secretariat, I learned that I was posted to Muzaffarnagar, one station beyond Meerut, for which place we set out on the Frontier Mail, sharing a compartment with Ian Alexander. Ian was posted to Meerut and the next evening was taken off the train there by the Collector's daughters. After the noise and bustle of the crowded stations we had passed through, it was extraordinary to see two young English girls, gowned for a cocktail party, coming towards us through the throng. I had already begun to wonder how a handful of Europeans could presume to manage, much less govern, such a mass as we had seen of Indian humanity. The nonchalance of these charming girls reassured me.

It was midnight on 24 October when the train drew into Muzaffarnagar.

As I stood in the carriage door, a dark company moved towards us, faces barely distinguishable in the dim light of the station's oil lamps. The leader, speaking only Hindustani, introduced himself.

'Sahib, I am the nazir.'

'And who are these people?'

'Sahib, these people own bungalows in Muzaffarnagar. I brought them so that you could arrange some bungalow that might suit you.'

I was baffled. But then an English face appeared.

'I'm Hartley. Canal Officer. I've only just heard you were coming. I'm the only European in the district at present so I thought I'd come to meet you. Come out to my camp.'

'How kind of you. May I introduce you to my wife.'

'Good God man. You haven't brought a wife?'

'How do you do, madam, you'll have to rough it.'

With which he made off, calling back, 'You'd better go to the Inspection Bungalow; no place for a lady in my camp.'

'What did the Sahib say?' said the nazir.

'To go to the Inspection Bungalow.'

The nazir did not have the appearance of a high-ranking officer, but at least he knew what an Inspection Bungalow was, which was more than I did. So off we went in a T-model Ford, commandeered no doubt from a local zamindar.

The Inspection Bungalow was bare and clean and smelt of disinfectant. There was no bedding. Touring officers carried their own, but we, of course, had none. An enamel pot in a beautifully joinered and polished wooden stand might, we thought, be a device for boiling stew, but turned out to be a commode. A man arrived with a bottle of whisky, thoughtfully sent by Hartley. This, and our greatcoats, kept us passably warm through the night, but jackals surrounded the bungalow and howled till dawn like lost souls.

With the express approval of the Secretary of State, probationers were permitted to travel overland to their destinations. Fowler (later Sir Robert Fowler) was one who did so:

Seven of my colleagues and I decided to go out to India overland. There were two parties and of the four in my car, two were for Bengal, one for Bihar and I had to go on the last leg by sea, so Calcutta was our destination. We were given great help and encouragement by the India Office and when we left on 1 October, we were given an official send-off from Clive's steps.

After numerous adventures, by mid-November we were in Iran and beginning to feel the excitement of journey's end. The nearer we got to India, the more friendliness and help we met. The Embassy in Tehran came under the sphere of influence of the India Office and the Government of India and we received a special welcome there. This was even more marked when we arrived in Meshed and were bidden to dinner by the Consul General who was a senior member of the Indian Political Service. After a hard drive south, we entered India through Zahedan and the first representative of the Raj we met was a charming junior official doing the passport and immigration control. He was in a small office opening off the central courtyard of the fort-like frontier building and as it was still rather hot and there was little business to occupy him, he was sitting reading with his feet in an enamel bowl of cold water. He stood up, still in the bowl of water, and shook hands with great ceremony as we introduced ourselves to him. I have always treasured the picture of my first meeting with Indian officialdom. Soon afterwards, we had a breakdown and were camping in our tents for two nights while we made rather a laborious repair to a broken front spring. This time it was Baluchi road menders who gave us freshly-baked chappattis. Eventually we reached Quetta, cold and very tired and at a loss to find our way to the Rest House in the dark. We knocked at the first door which showed signs of life and were ushered into the Sergeants' Mess of a British Regiment and our welcome to India was complete! We were given black beer and short eats and eventually sent on our way to the Circuit House glowing from the heat of their blazing fire and the warmth of their hospitality.

Paterson too saw something of the Middle East on his way out, but he was given an insight into the seamier side of life:

I had a brother in Baghdad and I went via Marseilles and the Messageries Maritimes to Beirut and from Beirut to Damascus by car where, incidentally, the French were having really quite an affair down in the old town, with a first class riot on their hands, and I was not allowed to go and look at the old Damascus. From Damascus, I crossed the desert by hired car in convoy with the Nairn transport – an exciting and exhausting journey which lasted some thirty hours, broken only by dinner (of a kind) at a P. C. Wren kind of fort in the middle of the desert at Rutbah Wells. I spent three weeks with my brother and got my first glimpse of the East, or Middle East – its poverty, its squalor, its population crowded together in a city like Baghdad – and also some idea of the rougher life that lay outside the capital city. My brother and I took his car and we did a tour across the desert to Kirkuk, Sulaimanya, Erbit and up into the Rowanduz gorge where a New Zealand engineer was building a road through this fantastic gorge up towards Persia. We stayed a night or two with him and then went on, on muleback, to Diana where a section of the Iraq Frontier Force, officered by British troops, was stationed. This was a wonderful experience for me, and one that I immensely enjoyed, but it also gave me a slight insight into the rougher bits, or wilder bits, of countries in perhaps that part of the world.

Then I caught a boat from Basra bound for Karachi and Bombay, calling at Muscat, Mohammarah and other ports in the Persian Gulf, and here another experience hit me. At Mohammarah, I think it was, we took on board a colourful, extremely wild-looking bunch of passengers who, the First Mate told me, were Persian gypsies who travelled on the boat down to Karachi and then begged, borrowed and stole their way back through the Punjab and the North West and round again into Persia. I was sitting up on deck one night and down in the well deck, where these Persian gypsies were living, a fight started, possibly over a woman, I do not know; but before a few minutes had passed, one man had pulled a knife and had killed his opponent. This was the first time I had seen raw, explosive violence – my only experience of violence up to that time had been perhaps some mild skul-duggery in the rugger scrum – and this sudden explosion, and death, hit me very forcibly. I think I realised that violence lay not very far below the surface and this was something that was to be well worth remembering.

The probationers appointed to the ICS at the end of 1939 got through most of their training during the 'phoney war' period. But, as Fearn reports,

The sea voyage to India brought direct contact with the war when the 'City of Simla' was torpedoed in convoy in the early hours of 21 September 1940 a day and a half after sailing from Gourock. Eleven of the year's intake to the I.C.S. were on board. All survived to start again, about a month later, the tedious voyage round the Cape to Bombay.

Woodford was in the other batch of probationers, in the *City of Hong Kong*, which 'took them on a wavering course past burning ships off the north coast of Ireland and in convoy way out into the Atlantic. News came through of the sinking of the *Empress of Britain* with children on their way to Canada.' It was a seven-weeks' voyage to Bombay at that hazardous time.

The final intake for the ICS were trained, as some earlier entrants would have liked, in India. Downing describes the probationary year at Dehra Dun in the UP where the syllabus was similar to that followed in the UK, but in rather different surroundings:

At Dehra Dun, where we met the remaining sixteen Indian entrants of our year, we found ourselves accommodated in a pleasant tented camp in the grounds of the Imperial Forest Institute looking up to the foothills of the Himalayas and the lights of Mussoorie.

Dehra Dun was very much the traditional India of the British Raj in its most military form, a military centre the site of the Indian Military Academy and the headquarters of the Gurkhas. It was also a time of war when the Indian Army was engaged in the Western Desert and Abyssinia in Wavell's campaigns against the Italians. There were several thousand Italian prisoners of war at Dehra Dun and, of an evening, we often saw General 'Electric Whiskers' Berganzoli and other senior Italian officers taking their escorted constitutionals. It was a pleasant life for us, with tennis, swimming and long country rides to fill our leisure, but we remained rather spectators of the life going around our camp and were not to any great extent drawn into the social life of the station which was perhaps as well for our studies.

Reflecting on the curriculum of our probationary year, I have sometimes wondered if more could not have been done to take advantage of the fact that, for the first time, probationers were spending their probationary year in India to give us more experience of administration rather than following the same academic course of studies that we would have pursued at Oxford or Cambridge, but I am not sure that this would be a fair criticism.

However, one could not spend several months in India without something of the feeling of the country and its government rubbing off on one. We also had the advantage to a greater degree than we could in England of meeting senior members of the Government of India and the various public services who came to talk to us – members of the Viceroy's Council, the Chief Justice, senior members of the Indian Medical Service and others. In this respect, I think the British members of my year were fortunate in spending our probationary period in India though some of our Indian colleagues who had not been abroad may have missed the experience of a year at a British university.

As for the content of our studies, in retrospect, they may appear to reflect a rather old fashioned concept of government intended for a static agrarian society and based on the omnicompetent and paternalistic district administrator. The emphasis was on the impartial maintenance of law and order, the collection of the land revenue, a little on rural development, but not much attention to such subjects as public finance or economic management. But India in 1941, although in rapid transition, was still so far as the majority of its population were concerned, a traditional agrarian society; the land revenue, the traditional support of Indian governments since the dawn of history, was still the largest single item of government revenue. All this was going to change and before the war was over, many members of our service would be doing jobs very different from those for which they had been trained. The economic impact of the war effort was itself a potent factor in the modernisation of the Indian economy. However, these changes could only be dimly foreseen in 1941. In the meantime, the administration had to be kept running and could only be kept running on traditional lines. Most of us were bound to be district officers in the early years of our career and the future was uncertain.

Another advantage of the probationary year was the opportunity it afforded of getting to know well so many of our Indian contemporaries in the Service. On the whole, we were a very happy party, though occasionally the arguments could become sharp. All the Indian probationers were keen nationalists, some with family connections in the Congress Party. At first, I think, the British element found this rather surprising. Not that we were unsympathetic. Most of us, I think, at that time, had the mildly left wing views which were prevalent in the British universities in the thirties. We accepted that India would become self-governing in some form or other after the war, but, at first sight, it seemed odd that men whose object was the end of foreign rule yet saw nothing strange in entering government service while that rule was still in being. In practice, I think they made a subconscious distinction between the Government as the instrument of foreign power and in its purely administrative capacity, as the established Government of the country, which, in all non-political matters, they expected to operate impartially in the public interest and hence had no inhibitions about taking part in it. That this distinction could be made says something, I think, to the credit of the British administration, and also accounts for the ease with which, at the transfer of power, the administration of the country continued virtually undisturbed – except in those areas disrupted by partition.

So far only a small fraction of the contributors have been introduced. The others will present themselves in action as the book progresses. The contributors can best be described as a self-selected cross-section of the Service, but they constitute a better than 5 per cent sample of its total size (roughly 1,200) during their day and may be thought reasonably representative. All of them came from middle-class households, upper-middle-class professional families, lower-middle-class teachers, clerks or minor civil servants, in a pattern already set by the 1880s and 1890s. About a third of the British contributors' families had some link with India, though not often with the ICS itself. They were very much the sort of young men the examiners had aimed at – two-thirds of them from English and Scottish public schools, three-quarters from Oxford and Cambridge, and with at least twenty-five firsts between them. Yet what is striking is for how few of the British entrants the ICS was an obvious, compelling choice. No doubt some were attracted by the glamour and romance that India still possessed, and some had a genuine missionary zeal to serve its people. But many who sat the combined examination in the hope of securing a place in the Home Civil Service took India when they found that their marks were just below the level required for a Home appointment.

Whatever the ups and downs in British recruitment there was never any shortage of aspirants from India, however. For an Indian the ICS was of course a Home appointment, and a job unmatched in lustre and prestige. Parents certainly encouraged their children to try for the ICS and even those active in nationalist politics do not seem to have objected to their compatriots entering the ICS, presumably because they recognized that Indianization of the services was a useful step on the road to independence. Meanwhile for both British and Indians the ICS offered a well-paid career right from probation onwards, with a high degree of job security and a generous pension at the end of the day. (A note about the career structure with a chart is appended at the end of this chapter.)

The process of training a raw graduate in England before he went to India was a somewhat arbitrary affair, even when one considers that all training techniques were still rather primitive in those days. The probationary course itself had been grafted a little artificially onto the university structure, and there had been some who felt that cadets – about ninety at any given time – should be trained together at some separate establishment created for the purpose. For the cadets themselves the year was relaxing rather than demanding, and though the Law course was useful, many thought the formal training in a written language of uncertain value when first faced with the country dialects of the court or the village in India. Undoubtedly the year helped to create a body of common experiences and expectations in British and Indian cadets, the one making their first acquaintance with Indians and matters Indian, the other with Britain and British people of their own class. But the cultural exchange was a casual, individual affair and given the scatter of Oxford and Cambridge colleges and the amorphousness of London contact could be quite slight. And what was entirely missing – and was missed by both British and Indian cadets alike – was any full account of the whole structure of government and administration in India, and any deliberate attempt to explain British policies and purposes in India.

FURTHER READING

The pioneering nature of the East India Company's decision to make a competitive examination the means of entry to their service has of late attracted the attention of historians. R. J. Moore has traced the genesis of the measure in 'The abolition of patronage in the ICS and the closure of Haileybury College', *Historical Journal*, VII (1964), 246–57, and in his *Sir Charles Wood's Indian Policy, 1853–66* (Manchester 1966). His discussion of the type of recruit the competition was intended to produce is carried forward in a review of the actual recruits and how far they answered the hopes of the reformers, for the earlier years by J. M. Compton, 'Open competition and the ICS, 1854–76', *English Historical Review*, 326 (1968) and for later years by B. Spandenberg, 'The problem of recruitment for the Indian Civil Service in the late nineteenth century', *Journal of Asian Studies*, XXX (1971), 341–60. Something of the same ground is covered by C. J. Dewey, 'The education of a ruling caste: the Indian Civil Service in the era of competitive examination', *English Historical Review*, 408 (1973), 262–85, but with an interesting look at the content of the reading lists and examination papers set. The most recent study, covering the last years of the ICS is by T. H. Beaglehole, 'Rulers and servants. The ICS and the British demission of power in India', *Modern Asian Studies* XI (1977), a reply to the question raised in D. C. Potter, 'Manpower Shortage and the End of Colonialism: the Case of the Indian Civil Service', in *Modern Asian Studies*, VII (1973), 47–73.

For those interested in the earlier Company experiment of providing a college education for its civil service recruits there is a wide ranging cultural study of Wellesley's experiment at Fort William College in D. Kopf, *British Orientalism and the Bengal Renaissance* (Berkeley 1969), and on Haileybury an excellent chapter by B. Cohn, 'Recruitment and training of British civil servants in India, 1800–1860', in Ralph Braibanti (ed), *Asian Bureaucratic Systems Emergent from the British Imperial Tradition* (Durham 1966).

Career Structure – Indian Civil Service

On appointment to the ICS, a new entrant was posted to a district of his province, where he would serve for one or two years as an Assistant Collector or Assistant Commissioner under training. When he had passed his law and language examinations he would receive his first independent posting as a sub-divisional officer in charge of the magisterial and revenue work in a subdivision of a district. In between his seventh and his tenth year he might expect to be given charge of a district or a posting as an under- or deputy secretary in a provincial secretariat. Alternatively he might at this point choose a judicial career starting, after a legal training, as an additional district and sessions judge. Further alternatives at this stage were to apply for selection for the Indian Political Service, one-third of whose members were recruited from the ICS, or for certain specialist services – customs, audit or posts and telegraph for example. There was a common time-scale of pay for the ICS, starting at about £400 a year and finishing at slightly over £2000, whatever the choice they made or the pattern of their early career. Retirement was compulsory after thirty-five years' service, though full pension of £1000 a year could be claimed after twenty-five years' service. District officers seconded for service in the provincial or central secretariats, which were staffed entirely in this way, received small supplements to their pay. Additional allowances were also paid, up to a limit of £3600 a year, to those who were appointed, usually after twenty-five years' service, by selection to such senior posts as commissioner, member of a Board of Revenue, chief secretary or secretary to a governor or judge of a provincial High Court.

CAREER STRUCTURE

YEARS OF SERVICE	Executive Branch	Judicial Branch	Other Careers
1–2	Assistant Collector/Assistant Commissioner under training.		
2–10	Sub-Divisional Officer/Sub-Collector/Joint Magistrate. Under- or Deputy Secretary in a provincial secretariat.		
7–10 onwards	Collector/Deputy Commissioner and District Magistrate. Secretary or Joint Secretary in a provincial headquarters. A few other senior jobs at headquarters	Judicial training followed by appointment as Additional District and Sessions Judge and District and Sessions Judge.	Indian Political Service, Indian Posts and Telegraph Service, Imperial Customs Service, Indian Audit and Accounts Service.
	Selection Posts		
25 onwards	Chief Secretary, Commissioner, Member of Board of Revenue, Secretary to Governor.	Judge of Provincial High Court.	

CHAPTER 2

DISTRICT TRAINING

On arrival in his province, the new junior civilian often spent a short time in the capital calling on the senior officials. Up to the time of the Second World War, when the practice mercifully ceased, he had to perambulate round the bungalows of the High Court judges, secretaries of the provincial government and other officials dropping visiting cards. The junior civilian was at this stage gazetted as assistant collector/commissioner in the destined district, the appointment being published in the Government Gazette.

On his arrival in the district, it was the accepted practice for the collector or some other senior officer to accommodate the newcomer for a time; indeed, this was often necessary because the assistant collector or assistant commissioner was a supernumerary in the district, and there was no accommodation reserved for him. There are many tributes to the kindnesses the trainees received and the warmth and generosity of the hospitality shown to them, whether it was being included in the governor's Christmas shooting camp, or, as in the case of the Midgleys, being welcomed in the household of an Indian Provincial Service deputy commissioner, thereafter a close friend, or being accepted for six months as a paying guest by his DC as was Murray in Assam. This open-handedness in hospitality, coupled with the instant freemasonry of the Service, a special feature of life throughout India and Burma and particularly in the smaller stations, did much to mitigate the pangs of homesickness.

It did not take the junior civilian very long to realize that his training would be a fully-documented affair. In Madras, for instance, the junior civilian was given on the occasion of his first call on the Secretariat no less than six books of rules of one sort or another. Of these, the most important for his immediate purposes was the Indian Civil Service Manual which set out the training procedures in considerable detail. Generally speaking, the training schedule was broadly similar for junior civilians throughout India. On the one side, there was the language training with the emphasis on the spoken word and the 'deciphering', as the Manual put it, of vernacular writing. This, together with revenue laws and regulations, accounts procedures and other administrative practices was tested in two departmental examinations held at the provincial capitals at six-monthly intervals. Since the grant of increments depended on success in these tests at the lower and the higher standard, there was a strong incentive to satisfy the examiners.

The second part of the training was the practical side, under the eye of the collector. Of the seriousness and value of this part of the training the ICS Manual in Madras left collectors in no doubt:

Collectors will not fail to observe the great importance of paying attention to the training of the young men who are entrusted to their guidance, and whose success in life and influence for good depend so greatly on the assistance which they receive at the outset of their career. The object to be kept in view in training an assistant is to fit him for useful service hereafter rather than to obtain immediate assistance from him.

Its usefulness in practice, it may be said, depended on the aptitude and industry of the junior civilian, the degree of attention and interest the collector or deputy commissioner could bring to bear and, perhaps most important of all, the ability of the subordinate officials and clerks to impart instruction to the man in training. This part of the training began with a study of village administration. During this the trainee, assisted by the village headman and the village accountant and by the revenue inspector or qanungo who was in charge of the revenue administration in a circle of up to fifty villages, became responsible, nominally at least, for the management of a village and the keeping of accounts for a period of three months. Sometimes the trainee had to submit an economic survey of his village which would not only cover 'the economic condition of the village, including prosperity or otherwise (with causes)', but also more sociological issues such as the customs governing land tenure and rentals.

The village training was followed by a period understudying the qanungo in checking the work of the village officers in his circle. There was also a boring, but no doubt necessary period studying the operation of a government treasury at the headquarters of a taluk or tahsil. (At that time the government operated largely on a cash basis as banks were not to be found in smaller towns, but despite this, defalcations and robberies were rare.) The other side of the assistant's training was concerned with magisterial work which will be described in a later chapter.

The training period which lasted for a year to eighteen months was a remarkable experience in many ways. It could also be rather lonely, for the assistant was a somewhat isolated figure. Except when he went to the provincial capital for examinations or for some official gathering, he seldom met those who had been his contemporaries as probationers and who were now under training in other districts. Even the Indian newcomer would often find himself in quite unfamiliar surroundings, serving away from his home province and under the eye of a British mentor. For the British assistant, there was the total unfamiliarity and strangeness of the whole environment. In most cases his first collector or deputy commissioner would be British like himself, in some cases he would be Indian.

The isolation, but also the immense amount of detailed experience, of work and of Indian society, which was involved in the field training period is well brought out by Georgeson. He arrived in India in November 1930 and was posted as Assistant Collector, popularly and more aptly called a 'learning boy', to Ganjam district, then in Madras Presidency but subsequently in Orissa:

Ganjam was near the border between the Telugu and Oriya countries and for my departmental examination I had to learn Telugu. In one way I was lucky; there was an Assistant Collector's bungalow; I think the only one in the Presidency.

Socially, the district was unusual. The largest town was Berhampur and certain district officials were stationed there, but the District Collector and the District Police and Forest Officers were stationed at Chatrapur, a small town thirteen miles away. There was a club at Berhampur, and we normally went there on Saturday evenings and rather monotonously played tennis as long as daylight and monsoon permitted, and then a game on the billiard table which we called 'Fleece' (otherwise I think called Russian pool) – always the same game.

The work consisted partly of study and mainly of the acquisition of practical experience. First, I served, in theory, as a village karnam or accountant. I say in theory because I never actually took over as karnam. That would scarcely have been possible. Apart from the fact that I did not really know the language well enough, a karnam could not do his work properly until he knew his village. In the Presidency of Madras, except for some areas held by great landlords or zemindars, every field and every subdivision of a field in separate occupation was registered and mapped separately for the entire village, which was more like a parish in British terms. Because it was the practice, when land was being divided among the heirs of the holder, to divide every plot, these subdivisions could be very small. The smallest I came across was a hundredth of an acre. This practice, combined with the practice by which if a peasant had some money available to buy land he would buy any plot that happened to be on the market, led to a degree of fragmentation of holdings by which each cultivator owned a great number of small plots scattered throughout the village. The karnam had to inspect every plot as necessary and record particulars of the cultivation. He was supplied with a key-map of the village printed on cloth showing every field, but to identify each field from that would be an impossibly long task.

I was therefore attached to a certain village karnam whose qualification was that he could speak English. I camped in a tent, not at the village, but about two miles from it in the outskirts of a small town called Icchapur, where it was possible for my cook to get simple daily supplies. My servants had a smaller tent. My clerk, who was more a mentor than a clerk, must have found some quarters in Icchapur. My karnam came to me by bicycle each day, except when I went myself to the village by motor-bicycle. He kept all his registers and accounts and I made copies of them and of the entries he made from time to time. When I went to the village, he showed me round the fields.

My karnam was, like most karnams, a Brahmin. When he arrived one morning on a day which was a fast-day for orthodox Hindus, he said that he hoped that I was fasting. While I was searching for words to explain that such observances did not apply to my community, the clerk, who was of low caste, broke in with a tirade against Brahmin superstitions. Yet my karnam was justifiably proud of his command of English and also of his *savoir-faire*.

There was no time in my service at which I was so much among the people: though always, indeed, somewhat apart. Frequently in the evenings, I went to a little local club, composed mainly of clerks and other men (only men) of similar status. They knew English and, in my company at least, generally spoke it, or, at least, that mixture of English and Telugu in which the significant words were English and the connecting words Telugu. I remember hearing a well-educated Indian say to another, 'Wadu (he) most unpopular ayinadu (became).'

On the other side of the peninsula, Faruqui, who hailed from the Punjab, found that, though he was no stranger to India, he was an utter stranger to the Bombay Presidency. He thought that he was fortunate to be posted to Surat district – where, if the language was unfamiliar, at least there were cultural links with fellow Muslims:

Surat was the port from which Muslim pilgrims used to sail for Mecca and Madina during the Muslim rule of the sub-continent. And Surat was the first place where the

British opened their so-called 'factories', which were really commercial warehouses.

The people in Surat are Gujratis, their language being soft and sweet-sounding and they were then much more cultured than people of other areas in the Bombay Presidency because of their long history and association with international cultures. Even in the villages, I found people with clean clothes and clean huts and utensils. There were three Nawabs (Muslim aristocrats) and the Muslims were generally better off than Muslims in other parts of the Presidency. The Hindus and Parsis were equally cultured people. All the three communities ate well-cooked food and lived in average, but clean houses.

My first Collector was a Parsi belonging to the Provincial Civil Service. But he and his wife were highly westernized and modern. The other officers were a mixture of British and Indian origin. An advantage in serving in the Bombay Presidency was that there was less distance between the British and the Indians, and they mixed freely. There were instances, before my time, of one or two Indian members of the ICS being black balled for membership of the club in predominantly British military stations. In one case, the British Commissioner of the division, who was President of the club, resigned in protest. In another case, the British Governor, on his visit to the district, gave a dressing down to the members. The situation was rectified in both cases. And that had a salutary effect on the rest of the Presidency. I must also say that the British Government's policy of posting men from the British aristocracy to the three Presidencies as Governors was an extremely wise step. They brought with them nobility and social charm. And they did not have the pre-formed notions and even prejudices of the ICS Governors in other provinces.

Soon after my arrival in Surat district, I was sent out on tour with a subdivisional officer. I did not like touring then. But soon I got used to it. And I soon found out the policy of my superiors was a wise one. Firstly, it helped me financially (in the form of travelling and daily allowances) when I was hard up. Secondly, and this was the real advantage, it got the rural areas into my blood, into my system. India is a predominantly rural country, and District Officers who spend most of their time at headquarters of towns with rest-houses to stay in, can never get under the skin of the villager. I had to live mostly in tents. In my monthly diary, I had to specify how long I had stayed in bungalows. And if it was more than one-third of the period of the tour, the commissioner of the division criticised the touring officer and asked him to stay longer in out-of-the-way places where there was no roof except a canvas one.

In Farrukhabad in the UP, Venkatachar was trained, to a large extent, by two deputy collectors, touring with them in their subdivisions and watching them at work. But the British Collector, A. P. Collett kept an eye on his progress, and Venkatachar remembers some general advice he received:

Collett's administrative wisdom and philosophy of service were informally conveyed in a chat, never as a set task or a lesson. One piece of advice was most valuable. The Indian officer should be natural. He should not imitate the Englishman. He should have the courage to hold on to values which he feels are good for him. Indianisation of the service does not mean the Anglicanisation of the individual.

This was very much the advice which Azim Husain, in the neighbouring province of the Punjab, received from his DC, S. Partab: 'You shall never become a "Sahib". This simply would not do in 1938.'

Venkatachar's training was completed by attendance for three months at the Provincial Training School which the UP Government organized at Moradabad. ICS officers and Provincial Service officers were trained together at this establishment and, as a result, got to know each other at an early stage in their careers. The system of group training, which was peculiar to the UP, was abandoned in the 1930s. Symons who, like Venkatachar and

Cook trained at Moradabad, very much deplored the closure, as an economy measure, of a course which he found to be of lasting value.

Arthur, from the letter written to his parents, seems to be in a very different milieu as he gives glimpses of his training in the Punjab:

I really cannot drum up much enthusiasm for the so-called Society (European) of Amritsar. The people are all right in their own way, but their way does not happen to be my way. The outlook of nearly everyone here seems to be so narrow and petty, and the only things in which they seem at all interested are gossip and drinking whisky, neither of which is in my line. Much the nicest people whom I have met so far are the cultured and educated Indians, some of whom are extraordinarily nice. They, of course, are excluded from the Club, which is a pity. One does not meet the Indian members of the ICS much, except at official dinner parties and ceremonies.

Arthur was able to write with much more enthusiasm of his Deputy Commissioner, Ivan Jones:

Jonah is an Irishman from Trinity College, Dublin, where he was a classical scholar and got a first. He looks rather like a don. He is a good chap and I am extremely lucky to be with him. He is rather a contrast to M————. The latter is a superb example of the official of the old type, frightfully arrogant and sceptical of all Indians, and yet certainly efficient at the same time. Whereas Jonah is probably just as efficient, but in a much quieter and more pleasant way. The comic thing is that the Indians like being treated roughly – they are a queer people and need a good deal of understanding.

Jonah and I have now been on tour for ten days, and it has been enormous fun. We tour for three hours or so in the morning and inspect three villages usually, in company with the *tahsildar, zaildar, lambardars*, police sub-inspector and various other functionaries. After inspecting the village and examining the well, the drains, paving, various houses, school (if any), Jonah and I sit in state and listen to various orations of welcome and complaints. Jonah listens patiently and then addresses the assembled villagers in a paternal manner and encourages them with a lecture on rural uplift – *dehat sudhar*. Of course I don't understand much of what is actually said, except by implication, as proceedings are conducted in Punjabi.

Five or six weeks later it was time for Arthur to take the plunge:

I have just been out on tour alone, which has been the greatest fun. I only saw one or two villages each morning and undertook a thorough inspection of each one, asking all manner of questions about crops, revenue, irrigation, etc. I learnt an immense amount about each village, and as I had to talk in Urdu the whole time, I made some progress in that wretched language. I used to spend about two hours in each village – first, I inspected the village for three-quarters of an hour or so, after which we all sat down and I asked my questions. Finally, I gave a short lecture in halting Urdu on the benefits of Rural Uplift.

I had some comic moments, particularly when I mixed up the words *bikri* and *bakri*, and the villagers thought that I was talking about goats, whereas really I was trying to ask them about fragmentation of holdings. At first, I felt rather a laughing-stock, but during the last few days, I really felt that I had got contact with the villagers and the British prestige had been enhanced somewhat. In one village, all the villagers crowded round me and shook my hand warmly, and there were general cries of 'shabash' (well done) as I mounted my horse and rode away.

Not all Arthur's early days were routine, however, and the regular round of revenue survey and village inspection could be agreeably, even bizarrely interrupted, as by 'Pohli week':

This is for the destruction of *pohli*, a weed rather like a thistle. I was in charge in the Amritsar tahsil and had a grand time dashing round by car, inspecting the work and setting light to the bonfires. I went out three times and covered one hundred and fifty miles in all. When I was going along the canal bank, I saw a boy strung up to a tree with his feet tied to a branch and his head hanging down. He was surrounded by about five or six men who were pummelling his body and chanting. I ran over to the tree, but only caught one of the men while the others escaped. I arrested the man and found that the boy was deaf and dumb and could not explain what had been happening. I took them both off to the police station and returned two or three hours later to make a report. I was then told that it was all in accordance with religious custom and they had no alternative but to release the man. But it seems a dreadful practice to me – almost on a par with Suttee. Apparently, the boy is the *chela* [disciple] of a *fakir* and when people sing, he goes into a trance, is immediately strung up to a tree and not taken down until he becomes absolutely stiff. I mean to investigate this, but have had little time this week. It certainly ought to be prohibited, but Government are always terrified to interfere with the religious customs of the people. These men were Mohammedans.

For his treasury training, Arthur was sent to Dalhousie, a small hill-station in Gurdaspur district. He writes,

My duties are not onerous. I have to be at the Treasury from 10 a.m. to 4.30 p.m., but I have very little work to do except on Fridays, and I spend most of my time learning Punjabi, which is rather fun. I can now write the script, but I find it very difficult to read. The great advantage about conversation is that once you know the elementary rules of grammar, if you are stuck for a word, you can always shove in an Urdu word which, in most cases, will be correct.

Most of the people have an anti-Indian prejudice which is unfortunately so common among the British in India and particularly among the military. The sub-divisional officer, and my immediate superior, is an Indian. I lunch with him at the Treasury each day, and find him an extremely pleasant fellow and very easy to get on with. His one weakness is a slightly over-hearty manner. He is a clever fellow and competent at his job, and works much harder than is really necessary here. The fact that he is an Indian puts off most of the English here, and I have met few who can say a good word for him. This is really a disgraceful state of affairs. On several occasions, I have not been able to contain myself and have had to defend him. This absurd superiority complex and chosen race complex of the British is one of our worst characteristics.

The early experiences of Bell who travelled to Calcutta in November 1930 on his way to a posting in eastern Bengal, provide a sharp contrast with those of Arthur. Whereas the Punjab was a new province, Bengal was an old, regulation-bound Presidency which had direct links with the days of Clive and Hastings. Bell writes,

The touts and hangers-on at shops and streets of Calcutta gave an unfavourable impression of the land in which we had come to serve. We were met on arrival at Howrah Station by G. B. Synge, the Under-Secretary of the Home Department, lodged in the United Services Club and were supplied with bearers [personal servants] by Synge, and formally reported our arrival at Writers' Building, the headquarters of the Bengal Government. There we were taken to meet many of the senior officials and were also taken for an interview with the Governor, Sir Stanley Jackson, the former England cricket captain and Conservative MP.

My career started in a very orthodox way, along the lines which had been followed by Assistant Magistrates for generations. I was posted to Jessore, a small town which was the headquarters station of the district of that name. Jessore had been a Collectorate from the time of the Permanent Settlement (1793), the town lying some seventy-five miles north-east of Calcutta, some two hours on the broad-gauge line which ran to Khulna. A fine 'marching road', tree-lined, connected Jessore with Calcutta and continued on a route which must have led to Dacca, but I do not think that anyone would have tried to travel to Calcutta by motor-car in 1930 – still less to the East.

I lived with the Collector (A. S. Larkin) and his wife in the big two-storeyed 'Colonial'- or 'Planter'-style house which was his residence. The only other British official in the district was E. H. Le Brocq, the Superintendent of Police, a bachelor some four years older than myself and having his first independent charge of a district. The Judge was a senior member of the ICS, (P. C. De), and there was an additional Judge (Guha Roy) who was also a member of the ICS. There were three lady members of the Baptist Mission at Jessore, but no other Britishers. The district had, in by-gone days, been one in which indigo-planting had flourished, and it had achieved notice during the indigo troubles of 1860, but the only trace of the once-powerful and flourishing planters was a very broken-down old man at a place some way North. In a sense, Jessore was a very suitable place to start one's service, for the only 'Club' life was at the tennis club, and our evening amusements were confined to bridge at the house. Contact with the local population was easy. My first task was to prepare myself for the departmental exams, held in Calcutta in May and November. As was customary, I had the help of a young man to take me through the Bengali set-books and to help me with the basic grammar, but practice in speaking Bengali was not very effective. I had to take the initiative in indicating what I wanted to do. I learnt a good deal in the practical application of Indian Criminal Law by sitting with the experienced Bengali magistrates, hearing the headquarters SDO recording complaints and issuing processes, and sometimes sitting through a case-hearing. Everyone was very patient with me, explaining the reason for the action taken, and the provisions of law involved. I gradually learnt more Bengali and got into the 'atmosphere' of the country, and learnt what was expected and what was not 'done'. I gradually came to learn – perhaps even to understand – the normal assumptions of Bengali life. Women were rarely to be seen around the Courts, and when they were, they came with the end of their clothes tucked round their faces, and as complainants or witnesses mumbled replies which were often too much for the Bengali Magistrates and Police Officers to understand. One learnt that there was an accepted difference between the 'educated' gentleman [bhadralokh] (usually of higher Hindu caste) and the general run of the peasantry or the town labourer. Caste loyalty of a witness in a case was expected; 'This witness is, of course, a caste man of the complainant, but there is nothing else against his credit.'

The net result was that I gained respect for the Bengali Deputy Magistrate who, with occasional exceptions, was a man who knew his job, and did a good job for his country. Conversations with these men were rewarding. I learnt the value which they put on schooling or formal educational qualifications, and I learnt too, of the importance attached to family matters, such as the intricate arrangements made to secure the right marriage for son or daughter. Very young marriage was normal (or had been when these men were young). Astrology, too, played an important part in the lives of some of them. At this time, none of the senior officers in the Collectorate were Moslems, although the district had a majority of Moslem inhabitants, and the Moslems had acquired much local government power including the Chairmanship of the District Board.

My training in the Revenue Law which was also a prescribed subject for the departmental exams, was in some measure 'self-taught'. I was attached to various divisions of the office, read through case-papers, and read and noted the various statutes starting with the Permanent Settlement Regulation of 1793 which had to be mastered. The question of the transferability of raiyati holdings and the conditions upon which the landlord must be required to recognise and accept the purchaser of a raiyati tenancy was the burning issue of the Bengal District Administration of the day, and a large staff was employed by the Collectorate in receiving fees paid on registration of the purchase deed and forwarding them to the landlord.

But life was not wholly detailed office administration. There were sometimes journeys out with the Collector to visit local personages. Here one met some extraordinary people, such as the elderly Khan Bahadur who entertained us with gramophone music from 'Our Miss Gibbs' and with a record 'Johnny get your trousers on'. There was a visit to an important 'bhadralokh' village, after a local land-owner had been murdered by Moslem tenants, and where the Congress-minded inhabitants were begging for the protection of the Government.

The district had had its share of political trouble in the summer of 1930, but by the winter of my arrival was quiet. Larkin, who was a man for pouring oil on troubled waters, encouraged hockey matches between the police and the local schools, in which I took part, and also Le Brocq, who was an excellent hockey player. At the beginning of the football season I played with the Collectorate team, and learnt something of the enthusiasm which young Bengalis had for soccer. We also made a point of attending various school functions. Gradually, I acquired a fair acquaintance with the Government Officers and clerks employed in the Collectorate and with some members of the Bar who appeared in the Criminal or Revenue Courts. Once or twice, I visited the Jessore Institute, which was the 'Town Club', patronised by the same sort of men – Government Officers and some members of the Bar. My main impression of the Institute was the decrepit and untidy furnishings and surroundings of the building. A billiard-table repaired with sticky paper, exposed cushions and a red ball spot like a pit.

This, in fact, was only one aspect of what seemed to Bell to be the dominant feature of Indian life – its untidiness. The town and villages or bazaars, through which he went on journeys out, were full of waste paper and coconut shells. It was nobody's business to tidy them up.

Before going to Hooghly, I had two experiences of very varied content. The first was a practical demonstration of what could happen when religion and politics got mixed – an event in miniature of what was to happen all over India in the next sixteen years. A fanatical Moslem was insisting on sacrificing a cow in the middle of the village of Panjia on the occasion of Bakr-Id. This was the 'bhadralokh' village where I had been with Larkin a few months earlier when there was a panic following the murder of a landlord. Investigation had shown that there was no custom of holding cow sacrifice in the village, and this made it impossible for the authorities to sanction one this year. In view of the danger in the situation, the Subdivisional Officer (a Brahmin) went out to the village with a party of armed police, and I went too. At first, the Moslem party seemed quite intractable, but eventually some Hindu landlord offered a site for the sacrifice. There was much argument as to whether the spot was visible from any house, and after further bargaining we worked the difference down to a radius of about ten yards. Someone then gave way a little, and I marked the position by planting my walking-stick in the ground, amid loud shouts of 'Allah, Allah' from the Moslems. This after about two hours' patient work. The Moslem leader had been carried away by his emotions and at one time had caught hold of my leg and asked me to kill him if he did not kill a cow in the village, or in his date-palm grove. This I declined to do on the grounds that he was a good man. The Moslems then became very happy, the actual place of sacrifice having been agreed, and I was provided with a chair to sit and watch the ceremony. I did not look closely, but ate my sandwiches and read H. G. Wells' 'The King who was King' while the mess was cleared up. I came away from the village with a great respect for the SDO – reputedly an orthodox Brahmin – who, in spite of all his convictions and instincts against cow sacrifice, had taken great trouble to secure an agreement upon a place for the sacrifice.

In the adjoining province of Bihar, Ray sounds a more critical note in his description of his early days there. He writes,

One of my first impressions, and to be confirmed later, was the extreme parsimony of the Government. In fact the Raj, in Bihar at any rate, seemed to be run on a shoe-string. For example, the magnificent new capital at Patna was without water-borne sanitation, and, compared with the comfortable modern houses of business and commercial representatives, some of the subdivisional bungalows were little better than barns. Nor did many district headquarters even have official bungalows for Assistant Magistrates, which meant boarding with one's Collector. The struggle with the Public Works Department to get a bungalow cheaply white-washed after a previous occupant would take a chapter in itself. French and Dutch colonial officials of comparable status whom I met early on expressed astonishment and attributed such Spartan living to British phlegm, the stiff upper lip and the belief that anyone reasonably lodged couldn't possibly do the job properly.

The salaries for all cadres of the services, both Imperial and provincial, were extremely modest considering the responsibilities involved, and when I rashly asked a very senior colleague on arrival about office hours, I was curtly told that district officials were on duty for twenty-four hours. Without being extravagant, it was often difficult in the early days to make ends meet (I could only do so with subventions from home), what with the wages of servants, and Mess and club bills, and I often wondered how young members of the Indian Police managed.

Much of the administration seemed entirely out of date and out of touch. For example, we were elaborately trained in survey and settlement work, but seldom afterwards put it to any practical use, and our set-book for the Hindi examination was almost pure Sanskrit and bore little relation to modern idiom (compare teaching English to Indians out of Beowulf and Chaucer). The cultural and historical background of the people among whom we were to work and serve was almost entirely neglected, and, looking back, I realise how valuable and helpful courses would have been in local art, literature and architecture, the basic elements of the Hindu and Moslem religious beliefs and everyday customs and usages. All this we were supposed to pick up as we went along; it was not much encouraged. We were urged to buy horses with which to tour our districts, as was leisurely done in the old days, but even by 1937, the work and the population had so increased as to make this virtually impossible. Most of us acquired second-hand cars soon after arrival, a move which was not well-received in the highest quarters. Finally, each of us was presented with a confidential 'Memorandum on the Subject of Social and Official Intercourse between European Officers and Indian Gentlemen'. This pompous publication was dated Ranchi, 1913, with an Appendix of 1821. Nothing seemed to have moved very much since then.

Ray's comments on the failure to provide courses on the Indian arts, religious beliefs and customs is a valid one, and is echoed by others. But as Shukla records, writing of his early days at Bareilly (UP), there were still British officials ready to share an interest in Indian religion and philosophy or a literary enthusiasm. On the very first evening of his Bareilly posting the Collector with whom he was staying thus engaged him in a long conversation:

War had broken out, and Mr Acton was keen to know all about England, London and Oxford. There were other subjects discussed. Two of them I remember; one was Indian independence and the other Buddhism. On Indian independence, I had strong views. He agreed that India should be independent, but it was for the Indian parties and the main elements in its political life to agree on a political settlement. We sat up late after dinner and, on retiring, he said to me that next morning at 6 a.m., he was going to inspect the jail and asked if I would care to accompany him. I agreed. I did not realise that my training had begun.

Mr Acton was an early riser. I reached his room at five past six and he had left. By the time I reached the jail, he had already started on his round and publicly reprimanded me for being late. I said that I was only five minutes late and had reached his room at five past six. In that case, I was ten minutes late, he said. I got the point, which I have ever since remembered, that the junior has to be five minutes earlier than the time fixed by the senior. Later on the round, I put my hands in the pocket of my pants and Mr Acton asked me to take them out, for he said, 'You do not look smart that way'.

Like other officers under training, Shukla was asked by his Collector to go out and pitch his tent in the villages. Shukla writes on the ideas underlying this stress upon touring:

The welfare of the man behind the plough was our paramount duty. We must not forget the interests of the non-vocal sections of the people, it is the poor and illiterate who need our attention. I am of the view that the British rulers ignored the middle classes which they themselves had raised and called them 'a microscopic minority'. The view of most officers was that the middle classes could look after themselves, and municipalities had been handed down to them, but villagers needed looking after, they needed a paternal government. Otherwise the strong would oppress the weak. While there was substance in this view, lack of contact with middle classes was a grave mistake, it kept the rulers not fully aware of the newly-emerging India. They had no doubt the widest possible contacts with the villagers and also individual contacts. As regards the middle classes, they had good relations with industrialists and some others, but not with lawyers and some other English-educated professionals whom they regarded as rivals and who constantly criticised British rule.

Before the winter was out, Mr Acton arranged for my going on tour. This was called winter touring. I thoroughly enjoyed this outing learning a lot of things amidst the atmosphere of a picnic. We would go out to villages in the morning, riding from our camp and would do what was called 'partal', that is going from field to field and verifying the correctness of the entries in the patwari's papers. Very great importance was attached to this work, and the testing and verification of entries was done publicly before all the village folk assembled. These papers define the right of Government to land revenue, and at the same time they define the rights of various people to land.

I learnt a lot about village life and the problems and interests of villagers during this tour, and this education continued throughout my service.

Shukla studied judicial matters with the District and Sessions Judge of Bareilly, but also enjoyed much more general discussions with him too:

Mr Plowden was a very senior officer having joined the ICS in 1913. His acquitting judgments sometimes upset the district administration. He was a great intellectual and full of ideas which he liked to communicate. But he was lonely. He lived with the Commissioner who had gone on leave. I sat with him on several days taking notes of cases. But even when this training ended, he insisted that twice or thrice a week I met him when he rose from his court in the evening. Then we had a long walk, lasting for over an hour, in the compound of the Commissioner's house which had an extensive area and was full of trees and foliage (now a whole colony of officers' bungalows exists there). After we had finished our walk, we would have our baths; for this purpose, one bathroom in the Commissioner's house was opened for me. Meantime, my servant would bring my dinner-jacket from my house and I would get ready. Mr Plowden would come out dressed for dinner. We would then sit down over drinks and Mr Plowden would then start his discourses on comparative religion, philosophy, early history of man and the life of Englishmen of letters, some of whom he knew personally. For example, when I mentioned Lytton Strachey, he told me that he was his cousin and he gave me an account of the life and the style of living of the Stracheys. I was young and full of my own ideas and not very reverential and would project my views, but I learnt a lot from him and many ideas became clear. I still remember those evenings and conversations with delight.

For Murray, making the long journey to Assam, it was the beauty of the countryside which made the first sharp impression, the easy generosity of the people, the hospitality of officialdom:

To reach Assam in the north-east, you had to cross by rail to Calcutta which we found agog with the excitements of the Lal Puja celebrations. Then I went on by train to North Bengal where the track turns east and finally reached Amingaon early one wet morning on the north bank of the Bhramaputra opposite Pandu and Gauhati. The great river, which is locally called the Lohit, is here a mile wide though still five hundred miles from the sea.

A Bengal Police Officer, also travelling to Shillong, the provincial capital, invited me to share his taxi, and to my delight, we were almost at once climbing up into the cooler climate of the Khasi Hills by a narrow winding road through bamboo jungle which gave way to more open country and then to heath country. It was beautiful and totally different from the flat and fertile plains of the delta of the Ganges or the parched and rocky terrain of Madras, but not unlike the Nilgiri Hills of the far south.

Mr Harold Dennehy, the Chief Secretary, who had been a boxing blue at Cambridge and was sometimes referred to as the 'extinguished-looking gentleman' because of the large topee he used to wear when out riding, put me up for a day or two, and I was bidden to dine at Government House.

The easy hospitality which one met everywhere in India was remarkable. Hillmen offered bamboo 'chungas' of rice-beer, plains villagers gave bananas and pineapples and merchants and pleaders and planters all were equally generous. These unsought and unrequited kindnesses from strangers to a passing young official remain permanent memories to me. Good manners and graciousness were part of the unhurried simple life of rural India in those days.

I was posted to Sylhet district in the Surma Valley south of the Khasi Hills. Its population of about three million was more than half Mussalman. It was a wide and fertile plain traversed by frequent waterways and dotted by lakes called 'haors' and striped by higher ridges of infertile gravel called 'tilas'. In the rains, the western half went largely under water. As Cherrapunji, on the escarpment to the north, has an annual rainfall of four hundred and fifty inches, this anuual flooding is not surprising. It has one good, it restricts communal rioting. In 1939, the Deputy Commissioner was Gerald Packenham Stewart, a Cork-bred Irishman of Ulster descent and he and his wife, Liz, put me up for my first six months, charging me ninety-nine rupees a month (just over seven pounds) and one rupee for bananas of which I ate large quantities. Their rambling and thatched bungalow stood in an ample compound between the river and a tank (pond), with the little station club conveniently near the front gate. He was only thirty-three, and the amount of work he got through was enormous, a never-ceasing stream of chaprassis carried endless baskets of files between his office at the house and the Kacheri and they stood in stacks across the floor.

The rather carefree, cheerful atmosphere which Murray found in Assam was perhaps more typical of the hills than of the plains. Certainly Swann, down in the Orissan delta, a rather lonely posting, was oppressed by the mass poverty of the cultivators there:

On arriving in Orissa, I soon realised that I was in a quiet backwater, an almost purely Hindu rice-bowl without strong communal or political passions and with the bare minimum of staff from the Imperial services. It was also a province recently cobbled together on a linguistic basis from chunks of Bihar, Madras and the Central Provinces, all with different administrative procedures and land tenure systems, and the process of integrating these had not even started. As a result, my period of training in Cuttack was, except for magisterial work, of little relevance to my future work in other districts. However, the crude, but effective discipline employed in obliging young officers to learn the local language (increments stopped until you passed the lower and higher standards) was certainly of great value, as I became one of the very few ICS officers with any command of Oriya, the others having fulfilled the language requirement by passing the Hindi examination before being exiled from Bihar. In relations with colleagues, I felt decidedly isolated; in nearly every case, there was a sizeable age gap, and my own lack of interest in sports, and, one might as well admit it, a degree of intellectual snobbery on my part did not help matters. However, this perhaps stood me in good stead later in the lonely life of the districts. As regards relations with subordinates, these were easy and agreeable, even if one was irked by what seemed excessive subservience. Looking back, my impression is that cultural difference between British and Indians made little personal impact. One's social and working contacts were with the more or less Europeanised, and though, for practical purposes, it was essential to get some knowledge of Hinduism in its social aspect, there was simply no time for any study of its philosophy. First experiences of revenue and magisterial work – obviously extremely amateurish – left me with mixed feelings; fascination with the job or the case immediately in hand, coupled with growing realisation – not diminished by later experience in the districts – of how little could be achieved even with the maximum effort and goodwill. Of course some matters could be put to rights and what one hoped was justice could be done in individual cases, but this was merely scratching the surface. The great mass of people would still remain on the border-line of starvation and oppression, at the mercy of the money-lender and other leeches. Looking back, it now seems remarkable that this realization did not produce disillusioned inactivity: quite the contrary, one slaved away regardless, perhaps with the sub-conscious wish to escape from a sense of futility.

Symington had the unusual experience of having some of his training afloat when touring in Sind with the Commissioner (the chief official in that area before it was detached from Bombay). Each year, so Symington recalls, the Commissioner went up the Indus in a flat-bottomed paddle-steamer to show the flag and to meet the people.

Whenever the SS Jhelum tied up, a crowd of visitors was waiting along with a guard of honour from the local police-force and a fresh pile of fuel. Hudson would spend the day interviewing the officers of the district and land-owners, the latter – some of them men of vast estates – magnificent in huge turbans, snow-white shirts and embroidered coats, and enormous billowing trousers. While each man waited his turn, he chatted to the Assistant Commissioner; and some of the extra punctilious ones, hearing that a new sahib was on board, even paid courtesy calls on me. Since they spoke nothing but Sindhi, and since my Marathi would have been about as useful as Spanish in talking to a Finn, these rather embarrassing meetings could only consist of smiles, bows, gestured invitations to be seated, and silent leave-takings.

Although he arrived in Burma after its separation from India, the early experiences of Cockburn seem to have resembled closely those of his Indian colleagues.

I spent three days in Rangoon meeting various senior members of my Service and acquiring a considerable variety of equipment – from a bed-roll to cooking pots, from tough boots to wide airy shorts. But my most important acquisition was Maung

Mya (Mr Emerald), my lugale. He would be my personal servant organising the rest of my staff, running my house, looking after my needs and so on. A good lugale was essential to a District Officer; most were good, loyal and competent, and Maung Mya was no exception.

For all the beauty of the approach to Rangoon, the place itself was just another city, surprising me only in the large number of Indians in this the capital of Burma. Anyway, I was glad when we caught the night-mail train to Mandalay and then on further north the following morning.

I was to spend the next ten months under training in the district of Shwebo (sixty miles north of Mandalay) and then, after two months, in Mandalay district. Both these districts are in the Dry Zone of Burma. This zone lies in the rain shadow of mountain ranges lying to the west, and the half-dozen or so districts within it get about thirty inches of rain a year as compared with nearly two hundred inches a year in the rest of Burma. As a result, the land is less fertile and green, the crops different – cotton, sesamum, groundnuts, etc. – and less abundant, the villages smaller and further apart. My first impression was, therefore, of a brown, hot, dry and empty landscape. Later I came to know and love it and would not have changed my Dry Zone life for anywhere in Lower Burma.

For the first few months, training meant largely looking over someone else's shoulder. I chased dacoits (robbers) with the District Superintendent of Police, I toured the villages with the Subdivisional Officer, I inspected crops and fields and maps with the Superintendent of Land Records, I sat in court while criminal cases were tried, I sat in offices and studied the papers and cases that various Burmese officials were dealing with, I acted briefly as Treasury Officer. But above all, I studied the Burmese language – not an easy one with its three different tones: I had a junior clerk attached to me and he went everywhere interpreting, teaching and encouraging.

After three or four months, I took local exams in Burmese, Criminal Law, Treasury and Revenue procedure and passed by the Lower Standard. As a result, I was gazetted a Third Class Magistrate and appointed 9th Additional Magistrate, Mandalay.

One of the delights of Mandalay was that one of its subdivisional headquarters, forty miles away and four thousand feet up, was Maymyo, the hot weather seat of the Governor, though no longer of the Government. I visited it frequently for cool air, golf, squash and so on. One Sunday, I was sitting in the cinema when a slide was shown saying 'Communal Rioting in Mandalay'. It took a moment or two to realise that this meant me; then I dashed to my car, drove down the hill to Mandalay, changed into my kilt – worn in the cold weather and on all occasions of serious trouble – put my automatic in my sporran and reported for duty. For the next five nights, I was on duty at riot headquarters, going out as necessary with patrols of troops or military police. This was because the agreement of a magistrate was necessary before a patrol opened fire.

Normally, training took place on an individual basis in the district to which the junior civilian had been assigned. But there were exceptions to this: The UP had had a system of group training, though it was discontinued, and in Bihar, a sudden and surprising jump in the size of the ICS intake for one year – ten against the usual two or three – led the Government of Bihar to arrange for the training of all of them in a single district under a special officer with the powers of a deputy commissioner or collector. Kemp was chosen for this unusual assignment:

I was accordingly appointed to organise a training establishment for six months to give the newly-arrived Assistants training in magisterial work and revenue work, camp life in the villages and to prepare them for the departmental exams. In the Provincial Legislative Council, scoring points were always seized upon with avidity and the creation of special posts invariably came up for scrutiny. One joker tabled a question what were the special qualifications of Mr Kemp to be appointed in charge of a training establishment for young officers, to which the Government reply was, not quite to the point, that Mr Kemp had plenty of recent subdivisional and district experience.

To judge by exam results, the experiment was a success. A training camp in the interior of Gaya district proved most useful. Five of the Assistants were Indian and five British. It was noticeable that there was more sheer mental ability among the Indians than the Britishers, doubtless partly explicable by the much greater competition by Indians to enter the ICS than was to be found among British students at that time.

The proper training and acclimatization of the newcomer to a district, with its strange language, customs and culture was a formidable process for the man himself and sometimes for his wife too. It was also a considerable commitment for his subordinates as well as his superiors, for it was largely his subordinates who had to shepherd him through the revenue procedures, the treasury work and all the multifarious routines which he had to learn. In fact they did more than that, acting as guides and instructors on many of the practical problems of life as well as on the social and cultural background to the administrative task. The contributors often pay tribute to the patience and kindness of their mentors in the provincial and subordinate services. Fearn, in the Punjab, adds: 'It says much for the tolerance of members of the Provincial Service that the young ICS entry was cheerfully acknowledged as "the senior officer of the not too distant future".' The contribution of these men was the more valuable because they were a comparatively stable element in the administration. The collector's ability to guide his assistant was limited by his own heavy work-load. But it was also limited by the frequency with which he and other senior district staff were transferred, whether on leave or because of other service factors.

The training programme followed a time-hallowed routine. Set examinations had to be passed, and there were many books of rules and procedures to be mastered. Language imposed its own routine and discipline. Nominally at least, the trainee had to work his way up the revenue hierarchy, accepting charge of first a single village and later of a group. A diary had to be kept and submitted to the collector. In Madras certainly, and probably in most other provinces too, the training routine was also diversified by attaching trainees for specific periods to district officers in other departments – the district superintendent of police or the district forest officer for example. Much, nevertheless, depended on the industry, receptivity and adaptability of the trainee if he was to benefit from the training offered and understand the underlying realities of district life. In a small, fully-stretched service the newcomer was expected to take his place in the line as soon as possible and learn his job there with the minimum of introductory formalities.

But if there was a structure to training little seems to have been done to make instruction methods more up-to-date. Individual collectors or Provincial Service officers were left to teach – or not teach – trainees by any method they chose. Some were evidently ill at ease or diffident in such a relationship, none received any formal training in the art of instruction, and the promising experiment of establishing training schools, which would have made it possible to build up experience and perhaps to select men with a flair for instruction foundered in the economic stringency of the early 1930s.

Even in the training schools and camps instruction seems to have suffered somewhat from the formal, academic approach on which probationers commented in their years in Britain, and the content seems at times rather archaic. The emphasis was placed more on the correctness and efficiency of procedures rather than the basic purposes and aims of the elaborate administrative effort in which all were so strenuously engaged. Moreover, even at its most thorough, as in revenue training, instruction seems to have lacked dynamism – training was for the immediate job in hand, pressing and necessary no doubt, rather than for the changing task of tomorrow. It is also of interest that even after the passing of the India Acts of 1919 and 1935, when district officers would of necessity be operating within a politicized rather than a purely bureaucratic setting, little or nothing was done to give the trainee a wider perspective of policy at the provincial level.

FURTHER READING

Whereas a great deal of attention has been paid to the social background, selection, college training and examination of ICS candidates, little has so far been paid to their inservice training and social formation in the district in India. One skirmish with the theme by David C. Potter, 'The shaping of young recruits in the Indian Civil Service' has appeared in the *Indian Journal of Public Administration*, XXIII:4 (1977), 875–89, and he has also worked on post-independence attitudes to training in the field. Even the full bibliographical survey by H. K. Paranjape and V. A. Pai Panandikar (eds), *A Survey of Research in Public Administration* (New Delhi 1973), has little more to offer.

CHAPTER 3

THE COLLECTOR IN HIS COUNTRYSIDE

The classic picture of the district officer on tour is of him galloping over sunlit fields in the invigorating air of the cold weather in northern India, with a highly supportive retinue, and among a friendly, if not subservient peasantry. Lambrick, in Sind, gives the flavour:

> Up heaves the blood-red sun-rim, now we shall soon be warm;
> Meanwhile a rousing gallop will do our nags no harm –
> The startled shepherd stares, while his flock together throng,
> Then laughs me back a greeting in the rough Balochi tongue.

But in a country the size of India there were many pictures, in some cases no cold weather, and the environment in which the district officer worked had an almost infinite variety. This chapter will therefore provide sketches of these differing worlds and set out the work of the district officer as it related to the land and the people living on it, who formed four-fifths of the country's population. The administrative objectives were everywhere much the same, but the nature of particular places and people affected the tenor and tone of the methods used.

In the south-west corner of the peninsula, in what was then the Malabar district of Madras, lies a particularly distinctive world. In a sub-continent dominated by the male is found an important Hindu caste practising a matriarchal system of law (marumakkathayam), and in the countryside are found not villages but individual houses dotted across the steamy sub-tropical landscape. Carleston describes this landscape as he saw it as Sub-Collector in Malappuram:

It was a complete change from Coimbatore; a land flowing with water; luxuriant vegetation; paddy flats on all sides; coconut and banana plantations. Instead of regular villages – scattered houses on their own estates, large and small, with small rows of shops at intervals by the roadside; rivers (with plenty of water in them), hills and forests. My own bungalow in the upper part of Malappuram looked out over a forest of coconut trees and night and morning one could hear incessant drum-beating and music from the many houses scattered among those trees.

Most of the land was owned by Nambudiris and by Nayar *tarwads* (families), as owners (*jenmis*) who paid the Government tax, and leased to Moplahs, Thiyyas and others (Kanomdars) who paid them part of the produce. The Nambudiris were the highest caste of Brahmin anywhere in India, and though in many cases poorly educated, were held in considerable reverence and had often acquired extensive properties. The Nayars were governed by a matriarchal system of law. Children remained with the mother and her family of brothers and sisters, mother, aunts and uncles, etc. which formed the tarwad. The father had no place in that family, but remained a member of his own tarwad. There was no legal marriage, but a man visited the woman of his (or hers or her family's) choice when and for so long as she was willing to receive him. On account of their status and wealth, Nambudiris were specially welcome in these liaisons as they were expected to bring gifts of lands and other things to increase the wealth of the woman's family. So these Nayar tarwads grew in wealth and influence and owned large areas of fertile land, which they leased out to other Hindu and Moplah tenants. The Nayars were perhaps the most educated community in India and were to be found in different parts of India and the world.

Malappuram was chosen as the Sub Collector's headquarters as being centrally situated in the heart of the [Muslim] Moplah country. The inhabitants were almost entirely Moplah, with a few Nayars, Thiyyas (the tree-climbing toddy tappers) and Cherumas (untouchables). There had been a succession of Moplah rebellions, directed mainly against the Hindu land-owners, whom they tried forcibly to convert to Islam. The Moplahs had themselves centuries before been converted from Hinduism, and were generally poor, ill-educated and fanatical in South Malabar. The last rebellion had taken place in 1921 and had been put down with considerable severity. Many of the Moplahs had been sent to the Andaman Islands for life imprisonment.

Most Moplah women, being poor, generally earned money by agricultural work, and very attractive they looked with their dark blue dresses and white or bluish bodice and headdress. Their companions at work, sometimes knee-deep in water in the paddy fields, were the Cherumas and Cherumis, the depressed and outcaste members of the Hindu community, who dared not come within specified distances of the caste Hindus for fear of polluting them; they went about and worked topless, but laden with cheap 'jewelry' round their necks. Some wealthy Moplahs, mostly traders, had a large number of concubines besides the full complement of wives, and this was expected of them in order to support the female population, which seemed considerably to exceed the male.

In Malappuram the district officer was operating in an ancient, literate but very stratified social structure. Bowman in Jhansi in the UP also found himself in old-established and possibly even more conservative surroundings. There he encountered a splendidly feudal social order, recalling a distant period when the Maratha chiefs sent their horsemen east and northwards across the collapsing Mughal empire, carving out kingdoms for themselves:

Jhansi had its own peculiar fascination, very different from that of Agra, but equally compelling. Where Agra district was flat, khaki and redolent of Moghul greatness, Jhansi was rugged, red, rocky and full of Mahratta individualism. Jhansi lays claim to be the geographical centre of the Indian sub-continent. Just at the edge of the Civil Lines, there is a small hill with a trigonometrical survey mark on it which is said to be the centre of India, geometrically and cartographically speaking. Bundelkhand is a delightfully jungli place, straight out of Kipling's Jungle Book, with all the requisite animals except the wolves. In Jhansi, I obtained my Revenue powers and began my real work as Subdivisional Officer, in charge of Mau and Garautha Tahsils.

The land in my Subdivision was held mainly by Maratha zamindars or Bundela Thakurs, a proud race who believed in keeping up appearances at all costs. When the Raja of Katera came to visit me in Jhansi, he would appear impressively dressed, with a band of followers carrying guns and swords. The Raja would present his sword to me, a splendid, curved weapon with delicate carvings at the hilt. I would touch it and return it to him, and we would converse very politely and conventionally. On one occasion, when I was returning from Mau by train, we stopped at Katera and I saw the Raja on the platform, clad in simple dhoti and shirt. I invited him into my first class carriage, but he made an excuse and went elsewhere. I discovered that he travelled third class to save money, and changed into his grandeur behind a bush in my garden, before calling on me. He and his brother, equally proud, reminded me of the leaders of the Greeks in the Trojan War and I privately named them Menelaus and Agamemnon. The role of Nestor I gave to the Rais of Gurserai, a delightful and talkative old Maratha, much given to quoting wise adages and old jingles of sage advice. He lived in a strong fort out in the jungle, which dated from the times of Maratha supremacy. The fort had a zigzag entrance gate between two towers. When I first visited it, I had some difficulty in manoeuvering my car. As we entered the first zig, there was a tremendous explosion. Somewhat shaken, I tried the zag. There was another explosion. I found out that the Rais was firing a salute for me on the old mutiny-period cannons that still lined his walls. The Raja of Katera used to do the same when I visited him. A two-gun salute was my ration as SDO.

The zamindars ruled their tenants in mediaeval style. There was an air of humble subservience among the kashtkars, who greeted one with the one word 'bandgi' (your slave), instead of the 'Jia Ham' of the Hindus of Agra, or the 'Salaam' of the Muslims. But they were a pleasant, simple race and very responsive to any interest one showed in them.

Some districts, however, contrived to contain both the very ancient and the most modern. Singhbhum in Bihar was a particularly good example of this with age-old jungles and aboriginal tribes set alongside the huge industrial complex founded by Jamshed Tata, a Parsi from Bombay. Lines, who went there as Deputy Commissioner in 1945 describes the contrast:

Jamshedpur was a great contrast to the rest of Bihar, very urban and cosmopolitan. The great Jamshed Tata came to the area early in the century, when it was just jungle, and chose it as the site for his steel works. By 1945 it was a well planned city with a population of a quarter of a million, drawn mainly from northern India but substantially also from America and Europe. The steel works were by then churning out a million tons of steel a year, more in quantity than any other plant at that time in the Empire and Commonwealth, including the U.K. Its satellite factories in Tatanagar and Golmoni, employing up to 6,000 people each, turned out cables and tin plate, and railway rolling stock and, latterly, armoured cars. Its union affairs could become a flash point for the whole of India. Industrial problems loomed large in the district office. Mining and labour problems also came up at the extensive iron mines at Noamundi and Gua in Chaibasa subdivision, and at the copper mines and smelter at Maubhandar in Dhalbhum subdivision. The work was hard and exacting but when things became too pent up, or I wanted to get away for a time from some mistake, I could always escape to the jungles and the Ho aboriginals in the Kolhan part of Singhbhum. Things moved at a gentle pace there with much song and dance at harvest time, and beautiful villages of clean and brightly painted houses quite unlike those in the plains to the north. The jungles and hills could be very beautiful especially during the monsoon. Small errors did not count for too much. The engineer in charge of minor agricultural works was very anxious to show me a site he had chosen for an irrigation dam. As his description did not tally with my reading of the map, I decided to go and see. In the village near the stream he brought out his map again and explained why he had sited the dam so, just up-stream from a sharp bend. We went to see. As I had read from the map, the bend was in fact down-stream from the site, and I pointed out that the stream was flowing north at that point, not south. The engineer stood bewildered for a moment, and then conceded 'Why, so it is, your honour! I shall have to redesign this scheme!'

Others were working in a much rawer, frontier atmosphere, where the district officer was not so much functioning in an existing pattern as creating a system and order where there had been little before. Curtis filled such a role when he was appointed Assistant Political Agent at Nasirabad in Baluchistan, a border province adjoining the NWFP and Sind:

Nasirabad, a subdivision of the Political Agency of Sibi, was a wedge of territory, about eighty miles long and five to fifteen miles wide which separated the Upper Sind Frontier district from Kalat State and from the Mari and Bugti hills. Its eastern extremity was a few miles short of the banks of the Indus. This end of it for thirty miles or so westward was irrigated by the Bengari Canal, a part of the Sind system of inundation canals. These only flowed in the summer when the melting snows of the Himalayas caused the Indus to rise, and much depended on the course the river took. Some years it might leave the canal heads high and dry and the engineers would have to strive frantically to induce a little water to flow their way. As the average rainfall amounted to only four inches annually, everything depended upon their efforts. Irrigation was, however, sufficiently regular each summer to enable this end of Nasirabad to support a settled population of Baluchi tribesmen housed in mud-walled villages. But where thirty miles west of the Indus canals petered out, the desert began. Here it took the form of a level plain, bare as board, called by the Baluchis 'put' (rhyming with but), but which in the high-flown Indian Persian beloved of the babu was termed the Dasht-i-Amwaut – the Plain of Death. Northwards, it stretched for over a hundred miles to the neighbourhood of the Bolan Pass. This terrible land was entirely without water and supported no life other than small rodents and a snake or two. Occasionally, as a result of exceptionally heavy rains in the hills, a surge would cross the plain and vegetation would spring into life, but it soon died away. There was no shade and the heat in summer was lethal.

The Karachi–Jacobabad–Quetta railway crossed Nasirabad territory on the way to the Bolan Pass. The capital of my little kingdom was situated upon it, at the first station north of Jacobabad, on the edge of the 'put'. When the railway came, there was nothing there. But it was a convenient place for a station as there was a limited water supply available. It had to be called something; so it was named Jhatpat, which, being interpreted from the Punjabi, means 'Immediately' and was a frequent objurgation of the engineer who built this stretch of the railway. Here, in a stark settlement, were the subdivisional offices, the houses of the officials, the levy post and a small jail. There was no water to spare for irrigation, no gardens, and few trees. All around the lone and level 'put' stretched far away.

The 'put' had originally extended for fifty miles west of Jhatpat. But when the Lloyd Barrage was built on the Indus, the Khirtar perennial irrigation canal was constructed which crossed into Nasirabad ten miles west at Jhatpat and then followed a semi-circular course back into Sind. It thereby made it possible to irrigate four hundred or so square miles of 'put'. It was to people this empty country that I was appointed Colonization Officer.

It was a very different world in which Bell worked with his settlement staff, the flat, green, watery world of Bengal, and his form of transport was also very different from any used by Curtis:

I spent most of the time cycling from village to village where work was in progress, and spending the nights at the local dak bungalows, which were situated at convenient distances from the various circle offices. After an early breakfast, I would leave about 8.30 and normally return about 5 p.m. having taken sandwiches with me. My bearer acted as cook, and his nephew, who had been taken on to my staff, was 'paniwallah' [waterboy]. A large box of basic groceries would go with us, as well as a filter for drinking-water, for one never trusted the local water supply. Milk and eggs were always available locally, as were chickens, which were almost the only available meat. Bread would be brought out from headquarters by the messenger who would come out every day with office papers. Vegetables were obtained locally, but, at some stage, extra supplies were obtained from the hills – from Darjeeling or Kalimpong. The evening meal would consist of chicken cooked in some form, sometimes varied by fish, followed by a milk pudding. As the weather got hotter at the end of March, the staff, adapting themselves to the ways of their own country, started work earlier, soon after dawn, and my trips out were from about 6.30 to

2.00 p.m. or a little later. Field work was thus stopped before the worst of the day's heat, but might sometimes, if progress was slow, be continued for a little time in the evening.

Bell used the humble bicycle, Saumarez Smith and Christie the splendid elephant, but as there were no motor roads in half of the sub-division of Salin in Burma, something which he found a 'positive advantage for a beginner', Wallace sometimes had to go on foot:

You saw and heard much en route and you slept in the villages, meeting headmen and elders on their own ground. If you saw them later in headquarters, you knew their background. You might set out at dawn or soon after, riding or walking (a headman, or more than one, and others used to ride or walk with one), stop a dozen times on the way to look at the crops, or a village canal, or village fences (useful, if well kept up, in making things more difficult for cattle-thieves), a village school, inspect the headman's books (birth and death registers, etc. – sometimes this could throw up the need for a visit by the vaccinator; sometimes it simply showed that the headman wasn't doing his job). After perhaps ten or fifteen miles and five or six hours later, you would arrive at your stop for the night, or a few nights. With luck, your kit and staff, spare pony, syce, etc. would have arrived, having travelled by bullock cart, perhaps by a more direct route, certainly without the detours and stops that had taken up your time. After a meal and a rest in the heat of the day, came what would now perhaps be called 'walk-about', probably with your gun, in hope of a shot at a jungle-fowl (game was pretty safe from me for I was a poor shot), and the same sort of thing you had been doing in the morning.

In just a few cases the absence of regular land communications required the district officer to move in a much more stately way by ship or river-boat. That was Symington's experience as Collector of Ratnagiri in the Bombay Presidency:

It was a novel experience to go on tour by sea. The coast is bursting at the seams with history. It is studded with ancient forts that used to command the entrances to its creeks and estuaries, and most of its diminutive and unknown towns were important emporia in past centuries and still exhibit the buildings that once were Dutch or Portuguese or English. Perhaps the most exciting harbour is that of Vijaydrug (The Fort of Victory). The mediaeval towers and curtain-walls, which embrace the entire headland, had the look of some great castle in Wales.

Donnison's first district command, at Mergui in the far south of Burma, was a similarly watery one,

This somewhat heady draught of independence and responsibility was made even more exhilarating in Mergui by its geographical location. My commissioner was three hundred miles away; Government even further. The only practicable access was by sea-going steamer, and the vessel came but once a week on the Saturday morning. Between Saturdays, the only communication was by telegraph.

At Yenangyaung, my work had been entirely concerned with oil, in the Shan States with the Sawbwas and their administration. Mergui opened up completely new fields. Apart from the standard activities common to all districts, in Mergui I found myself dealing with tin mines, tin miners, and tin mining concessions; with rubber planters and their leases; with fisheries; with pearl divers; and with the lessees of the right to collect edible birds' nests. All this involved extensive and splendid touring. The town and harbour of Mergui were on an island, some ten miles across. There was one all-weather motor-road that ran northwards out of the district to Tavoy, crossing numerous ferries, and otherwise only short stretches of local road at Tenasserim and Victoria Point. Most touring, and of course all touring to the islands, was by sea-going launch. I had under my control, for the use of government officers, a fleet of five launches.

The great variety of landscape, climate and even accessibility met with from one region to another was matched, as might be expected, by corresponding differences in agriculture and rural society. Land revenue systems tended to match the geography, too. In the dry Deccan uplands of Madras and Bombay were found the scattered villages and hamlets of extensive agriculture. In lush Bengal with its fertile riverine soil, settlement was dense. In the great open plains of the Ganges valley with their moderate rainfall, true cavalry country, the movement of conquering clans led to settlement patterns dictated by the needs of defence. The corresponding revenue systems which the British found and systematized were *ryotwari*, individual revenue agreements with substantial ryots or peasant farmers in Madras and Bombay; *zamindari*, revenue settlements with large landholders and revenue collectors, who would take over, for a commission, the task of dealing with the multitude of smaller cultivators in the difficult rice land of rivers, streams and swamps found in Bengal, Orissa and Bihar; and in the open Ganges valley a form of zamindari settlement which recognized the joint power of the clan brotherhoods and settled with them or their representatives.

To so describe the various revenue systems is, of course, to simplify and also to ignore the history and timing of British acquisitions of territory in India. When the East India Company made their conquests in Bengal and Bihar they found the Mughal zamindari system in being. They kept the system, mainly because they lacked the experience and the manpower to dispense with intermediaries with local knowledge in the collection of revenue. As the Governor-General Lord Cornwallis said, had the zamindars not existed it would have been necessary to invent them. He also hoped, of course, that they would turn out to be progressive landlords if they were secured in their property, on the model of English landlords, and so in 1793 he made with them a Permanent Settlement of government revenue demand. Starting from the premise that 'nothing could be so ruinous to the public interest as that the land should be retained as the property of the Government', he argued that it was 'unnecessary to enter into any discussion of the grounds on which their right appears to be founded. It is the most effectual mode for promoting the general improvement that I look upon as the important object of our present consideration.' Under this settlement, Macdonald noted in Bihar,

the amount of land revenue to be paid to the Government by the zamindars (mistakenly identified at the time as equivalent to land-holders in England and Scotland) was fixed for all time and the zamindars given a free hand to collect what they could from the cultivators within their own areas, accounting to Government for a fixed proportion of their takings.

When the Deccan was conquered a zamindari settlement was again planned. But the great landholders typical of the Bengal ricelands were nowhere to be found on the dry, more sparsely settled, Deccan plateau.

What is more, Company officials were now more numerous and experienced and the surrender of future profits implicit in a Permanent Settlement was already being adversely noted. It was the ryotwari system of direct collection from the individual ryots or peasant farmers, without the interposition of any intermediaries, which was therefore introduced. The system was probably the fairest in its distribution of the revenue burden but it required quite intensive administration.

Variations of the zamindari system were introduced into later acquisitions in northern India. In some places, as in the UP, the power of the clan lineage or village brotherhood was recognized; in the Punjab that of the yeoman farming family; in Sind, which was semi-desert and dependent very often on canal irrigation, the great landholder came into his own again. But there was no further Permanent Settlement, and indeed the government increasingly intervened to protect the interests of the landed tenants against those of the zamindars it had first settled with so as to prevent any accumulation of grievances and tensions in the countryside which might threaten the stability of British rule. Government was therefore led to intervene even in the permanently settled areas. As Rahmatullah saw in Bengal, the 1793 Settlement 'ensured an almost automatic collection of revenue and the creation of a landed aristocracy which could not but be loyal to the British Crown'. But competition for land in Bengal led zamindars to rack-rent, and in the later nineteenth century the government undertook a detailed investigation of landholder-tenant relations in order to maintain a balance between them.

The developed revenue system as encountered by our contributors, whether ryotwari or zamindari, depended, as can be seen, upon a very detailed knowledge of the agriculture and society of each particular district and of relationships between landlords and tenants. This was why such stress was laid upon regular touring of the countryside. The district officer, travelling about on foot, bicycle or elephant, by launch or car, was not just a tourist or amateur anthropologist: good administration depended upon the deepest possible knowledge on his part of his countryside and the people in it. As Bonarjee puts it, 'the work of the District Officer as Collector involved a knowledge of village life, the deeper the better, of the various land tenures and of the general outlook of the rural areas'.

Land revenue was the main form of traditional taxation in India. And although as time went on, other sources of revenue such as sales tax, income tax, excise and stamps assumed greater importance, land revenue almost to the end of our period was the mainstay of the finances of the provinces. (The revenue yield, in terms of today's values, seems ridiculously small – in 1936 the total land revenue collection in India was some twenty-five million pounds – but the average tax burden in Madras, the wealthiest province, was only about twenty-seven pence a head.) The assessment and collection of land revenue was thus one of the main responsibilities of the collector or deputy commissioner. Collection was not, however, an isolated task. In fact it should be regarded as merely the fiscal side of a much wider land administration, which included, among other things, the control and conservation of government land, the acquisition of land for public purposes, the registration of holdings and the regulation in many areas of landlord-tenant relations.

The basis for all these aspects of land administration was the periodic district revenue 'settlement'. Every thirty years or so each district in the province was surveyed, field by field. Titles to land, tenures, and occupation were all checked, soils were classified and government revenue demand was re-assessed, the normal yield being between 25 and 40 per cent of the net output of the land. In permanently settled areas, of course, there was no revision of government demand; settlement was confined to preparing a record of the various rights in land. This immensely laborious, but very thorough, undertaking was directed by settlement officers who were usually ICS officers deputed for the purpose. Settlement work, with its daily inspections in the villages and constant dialogue with the villagers themselves, since the whole process was a very public one, was generally regarded in the Service as a unique opportunity not only of gaining a practical knowledge of agricultural economics, but also of getting to know the people themselves by moving among them continually for long periods. Officers who had done this work were better armed than most to deal with those teasing questions, involving an understanding of the people, their land and farming, which constantly occurred – as in dealing with requests for the remission of land revenue in times of pestilence, flood or drought. Settlement work came to an end in most provinces on the outbreak of war in 1939, or fairly soon after, and was not resumed before independence. One consequence of this was that men who entered the ICS from the middle 1930s onwards were not senior enough to be put on settlement duty before settlement operations ceased and therefore missed an experience regarded by some of the older men as the high point of their career in terms of both interest and enjoyment.

Settlement was a detailed and somewhat technical aspect of the revenue system, but it was a vital element without which the whole system can scarcely be understood. Le Bailly gives a succinct account of the meaning of settlement in the Punjab:

'Settlement' meant fixing – mostly for a period of 30 years – the cash value of the Government's traditional share of the produce based usually upon a 5 year period during the existing settlement when prices in the nearest market, of which a careful record was kept, were at their most stable. The resultant figure represented one of the Government's main financial resources. This rent varied from village to village throughout the district according to the records of crops in past years and contained provision for postponement or even remission in the face of natural disasters. In the Punjab the 'settlement' was made not with the individual owner but with landholders of the village as a community with a careful division of the burden according to the estimated capacity of each holding. The headman (or headmen) usually a coveted hereditary position was responsible for collecting from the individual landowners of the village and drew a commission on his collections.

Lane's description of settlement work as he experienced it in a zamindari area in the UP is related to the general agrarian scene in that province:

I took up my appointment as Assistant to the Settlement Officer in Bijnor. It was my job, under his guidance and general supervision, to carry out the settlement of one of the four tahsils of the district.

For a single district, a Settlement took about three years to complete. The Settlement Officer carried out a field to field inspection of the whole district, classified the soils into various types and grades, worked out the appropriate current rent for each type and grade of soil, fixed statutory rent rates, and then, from these rates and from experience in recent years, deduced what income the *zamindar* might reasonably hope to collect from his holding, taking the good years with the bad. He then notified forty per cent of this sum to the *zamindar* as the annual land revenue he would be expected to pay. He gave him an opportunity of raising objections and, after these had been disposed of, formally notified, with Government approval, the assessment so determined. This was then recorded in the village records and the *zamindar* knew what his liabilities were for the ensuing forty years. We didn't then have to worry about inflation!

If the Settlement Officer had done his work well, the welfare of the village was assured. If he had done it badly, particularly if he had over-assessed, the result could be great hardship and distress for many years to come.

When the assessments had been made, the Settlement Officer prepared a report which gave a detailed account of the history of the area for the previous forty years, or whatever had been the period of the previous settlement. Some of the earlier reports make fascinating reading.

The system as it had evolved seemed to me to have advantages. Legislation had conferred legal rights on the cultivators. Those who had acquired 'occupancy rights' were secured in those rights by that legislation. Their heirs and successors were secured in the same right of occupancy. On all other cultivators was conferred security of tenure for life; their heirs being entitled to continue in possession for five years thereafter, when the *zamindar* was able to regain possession. These occupancy and statutory rights were, of course, dependent upon regular payment of rent which was duly recorded in the officially maintained land records. Default in payment had to be proved in the Courts and possession could only be regained by the *zamindar* through the due process of law. The security of tenure thus conferred on the cultivators gave them the necessary incentive to good husbandry. No tenant is likely to do what is necessary to keep his land in good heart unless he has reasonable security.

But why, it may be asked, interpose a third party, the landlord, between the man who tills the land and the State which receives the revenue from it. To the administrator, unused to philosophising about the merits and demerits of State ownership of land and naturally disinclined to quarrel with the accidents of history, the advantages were obvious. The *zamindars* provided a useful buffer between Government and cultivator. They simplified the task of collecting revenue from millions of cultivators. Those *zamindars* who lived in the villages, especially if they were themselves cultivators, did much to guide and help not only their own tenants but the whole village community. They could generally be counted upon to co-operate with the Collector in coping with the hundreds of problems associated with the running of his district. They were, in short, a stabilising influence. Of course, the system was open to abuse. Frequently, the *zamindar* would get into financial difficulties, often through crop failures or other troubles which were no fault of his. He would then resort to the money lender, usually a town dweller having little or no link with the soil. If his financial troubles proved to be persistent, the *zamindar* might in the end be obliged to sell out to the money lender. Remote from the village, the latter would employ agents to collect his rents for him. These would have little or no understanding of, or concern for, the cultivator's problems. They would not be averse from making a little on the side for themselves. The classical case of the absentee landlord! But, on the whole, the system worked, the cultivators were protected from the worst evils, and the productivity of the land slowly but steadily improved. I for one never doubted that the fourteen-hour days I spent throughout that winter in Bijnor seeking to fix fair and equitable rent rates for all the various types of land in the *tahsil* were producing something of lasting value to those who lived there.

Only recently did I discover that settlement operations had to be closed down after I had left the district because of the catastrophic fall in agricultural prices in the 1930s. It was not until 1939 that the Settlement could be completed. The rent rates we had proposed had to be adjusted to take account of the latest price levels.

At the time, I did not relate this work in any way to the ultimate transfer of power. Although I knew, of course, that the settlement was for forty years, it certainly did not occur to me that, in less than twenty, power would have been transferred and the *zamindars* themselves expropriated.

Bell, whose touring routine has already been mentioned, gives a characteristically detailed account of the survey methods employed, though since he was at training school there was not the usual crowd of villagers, helping and closely following proceedings, which accompanied an actual settlement operation. The first stage of settlement work, the position of the village having been tied into the all-India cadastral survey by a local traverse survey, was to map and measure the individual fields. This was done by running straight lines across the village fields with a standard 22 yard chain of 100 links, and by taking offsets along this line of advance with the aid of an offset square – Anglo-Bengali 'right-angle' – and a straight bamboo pole of 20 links in length. Bell continues,

This pole was always provided by the 'amin' or surveyor himself, and he also found or made up his own survey marker flags. With this simple equipment, we practised making our maps, showing all plot boundaries, by marking the points where the chain line crossed a plot boundary, and the points where the offset established a plot junction or change in the plot boundary. The classes of land, appropriate to the district were determined by the Settlement Officer after careful local enquiry.

Stage two of the work was 'khanapuri', or 'the filling up of columns'. This was the first stage of preparing the record of rights, as distinct from the map. Here the 'amin' wrote up the name of the person or persons in occupation of each plot, showing on the front of the 'khatian' the names of the possessors with their shares in the interest concerned. On the back was the number allotted to each plot of land, and the class of land. Not only were we making a record of rights, but we were getting information about the country and its people, and one met the locals with a long series of questions, directed to find out trade movements, wages and prices, and the infinite variety of trading in the tobacco and jute marketing.

At a later date in Rangpur Bell worked a rather more sophisticated system:

The Rangpur survey and settlement work was based upon Air Survey. A company, specialising in such work, took aerial photos of the land to be surveyed. The photos were then enlarged and adjusted to fit on to corresponding points on the ground which had been set out on the required sixteen inches to the mile scale, by normal traverse survey. The resulting enlargements were pasted on to a zinc sheet of convenient size, which was carried out to the field by the amin or kanungo, and could stand up to hard wear. The amins could thus start upon the 'khanapuri' process straight away and only ran lines to fix plot boundaries when a mass of shadows over homestead or trees and bamboos concealed those boundaries. In ordinary open field cultivation, the plot boundaries were clearly visible on the photographs.

All this detailed field work was very satisfying to Bell because of the contact it gave with rural people in their home setting.

One gained information first hand about houses, methods of cultivation, crops and the interests and assumptions of the country folk that was otherwise unobtainable. Perhaps most reassuring was the apparent peacefulness of the countryside. In the first year of training one saw too much of the Indian in the Law Courts who was in dispute with someone. What was noticeable about the people in the villages was the lack of dispute – the general agreement as to who had cultivated the land at the last harvest, to whom he paid rent, and how much.

As a settlement officer the district officer was personally involved in the detailed tasks of assessment. The actual collection of revenue was usually done by others, often by village headmen under the supervision of the tahsildar and other revenue staff. Thus in Khurda, in Orissa, Swann found that the collection work was done by headmen on a commission basis, as was also the case in the Punjab. Normally the job of the district officer was to watch the progress of collections, but there were occasions, as Maitra relates from Assam, when his direct intervention was necessary:

One day as I was sitting at my desk in the *Kutcherry* (Office) I was handed a letter from the D.C. The letter said that the *Mauzadars* (revenue agents on commission basis) of Tengakhat and Madarkhat had defaulted to the extent of several thousand rupees. I was to proceed to Tengakhat within 24 hours, realise the government dues and credit them into the treasury within 30 days. By way of help I was to take one peon with me, and ask for a copy of the Assam Land and Land Revenue Regulation and six revenue receipt books from the *Sheristadar* (clerical head of the revenue branch at the district office). This was in the middle of the rainy season when village roads turn into quagmires, leeches lurk everywhere and the elephant is the only practical means of travel across jungles and paddy fields. I learnt the gentle art of elephant riding. When the going is heavy you sit astride the beast's thick neck behind the *mahout* (driver). In the course of the allotted time I managed to collect most of the money and deposited it into Dibrugarh treasury. There were a number of re-fractory tenants and some threats had to be used. But on the whole the main reason behind the success of the operation was the enormous prestige the *Sarkar* (government) enjoyed. I also had the first taste of the finality of orders from above which meant without saying so – in this fail not.

In the ryotwari areas of Madras the village accounts were submitted to, and formally approved by, the SDO once a year at an event known as 'Jamabandi'. Because there were no great estates to be dealt with as a single item but a multiplicity of ryot holdings, and because there was no permanent settlement but each field was assessed annually – whether fallow or culti-vated, irrigated or not – the amount of detail was extraordinary. Checking it at Jamabandi, as Dunlop had to do at Chingleput, could be tedious and exhausting work:

I had accompanied the Collector of Coimbatore during training on Jamabandis so knew what to do, in theory. It was exhausting to be solely responsible for it in practice when unfamiliar with the new district. This is what I recorded in my diary (sic) then: I found work very heavy at first. I have been doing Jamabandi of Madurantakam and Conjeeveram Taluqs for two months now ... it became a very tedious procedure, checking accounts and granting 'shavi' (failure of crop) remission; signing my name thousands of times a day. It was in the hottest season of the year – 105–106:
I used to sit under a Pandal (awning) outside the Taluq office at Madurantakam, passing accounts, checking water rates, receiving petitions, around me a sweating,

malodorous crowd pressing in on every side, excluding the air, from 7.30 a.m. till about 3.0 or even 4.0 without rest. After that, Court work and after that judgments had to be written, ordinary revenue work, village officers' enquiries, files, etc. had to be attended to. I snatched a quarter of an hour for tea – rose from Court at about 7.0 p.m. and sometimes even 9.0 p.m. – dined hurriedly and back to the desk again till midnight. It was regularly a sixteen to eighteen hour day.

The assessment and collection of the land revenue was an important part of the district officer's duties, but it was only one aspect of a much wider relationship with the land and its people. Thus in many of the newer provinces, though not Bengal and Madras, district officers were entrusted with semi-judicial responsibilities in pronouncing on land titles and tenancy disputes which touched the interests of the people at a most sensitive point. Watson in the CP describes this aspect of the work:

In parts of the province the agricultural land – the main source of the Government's revenue – was held mainly by village landlords called malguzars [enjoyers of property] who were given proprietary rights in the early days of British rule, but continued liable to make to the Government an annual payment called land revenue. Much of the land was cultivated by tenants who were protected by law against rack-renting; but some of them could themselves sub-let and rack-rent. What we called revenue work – the main task of the DC – was the enforcement of these arrangements and the settlement of disputes (e.g. about illegal eviction) arising from them. All this was done in a quasi-judicial way; the parties could be legally represented and they could appeal at least twice. The Deputy Commissioner did much of this case-work.

The system followed in the Punjab seems to have been broadly similar. Mangat Rai sums it up very neatly in the following extract from an article on the Punjab between 1938 and 1947:

The revenue organisation was by no means merely a collector of government dues, but also the repository of up-to-date knowledge and documentation of all the rights vested in land. Its much bigger function in the Punjab was as arbiter of disputes in regard to these. The law provided that each hierarchy of the revenue agency should determine within defined powers such rights in case of dispute. In this way, levels of appeal and review existed right from the tahsil, through the Collector and his immediate boss, the Divisional Commissioner, to the head of the revenue organisation, the Financial Commissioner, at the provincial capital. A final appeal lay from the Financial Commissioner's Court to the High Court... The system had the advantage that most of the decisions about land rights... were made by a hierarchy of officers who were in constant touch with their administration – and with the people – as executives.

However revenue work was not confined to the protection of existing rights and the apportionment of the output and profits of agriculture between landholder and tenant, and between cultivator and government. Efficient governments had always sought to encourage agricultural development, if only to enlarge the cake of which they took a slice. In many parts of India and Burma the most visible evidence of such an interest in development was in irrigation work, bringing vital water to a thirsty land.

There were ancient irrigation works, canals in the north and anicuts and tanks (reservoirs) in the south, which, in the British period, had been refurbished and sometimes greatly enlarged by additional schemes. New canals had been run from the Ganges and the Jumna in the nineteenth century and followed by further networks from the five rivers of the Punjab and from the Indus in Sind. But the process of bringing irrigation waters to the dry, un-irrigated areas of the Punjab, Sind and Baluchistan was still being extended in our period, and lands which had been almost waterless before now became productive and desirable with the supply of water. The allocation of land and the settling of the people on it was the responsibility of the district officer.

Le Bailly, in the Punjab, was engaged in this task as Assistant Coloniza-tion Officer, Nili Bar. In fact he spent nearly twelve years of his service in this type of work. As he explains, irrigation in his province had a long history:

Irrigation canals to take surplus flood water in the autumn flood season had been a feature of agricultural development in N. India. The obvious defect of these canals, which had no barrage or headworks to store water, was that in times of water scarcity, when of course water was most needed, they were of little use. One of the great problems of the Indian Government in the late nineteenth century was the recurrence of the appalling famines which followed monsoon failures. The Punjab Government's solution was the construction of headworks to provide as much peren-nial irrigation as possible.

It was realised at the same time that there were vast areas of fertile land between the five rivers of the Punjab which were lying untilled for lack of water, being too high for even flood water to reach unless artificially held up at a barrage or head-works. When irrigated, these lands produced food to relieve famine elsewhere as well as overcrowding in parts of the province where holdings were very small and in many ways these lands, when irrigated, added to the general wealth of the province. Nili Bar Colony forms part of the Sutlej Valley Project whereby the last remaining of the five rivers (the Sutlej) was tamed by the construction of four headworks to pro-vide irrigation to parts of the Punjab and to parts of Bahawalpur and Bikanir States. The Nili Bar Colony represented part of the Punjab's share of the irrigable land which was still owned by the state and therefore ripe for colonization.

Once the colonies were established the supply of water had to be con-trolled very strictly, if the very complex structure of canals was to work effectively:

From the headworks over the river, the main canal flows on the highest available contour at roughly an angle of 45° from the river. Again following the contours, the main canal may split into branches from which again 'distributaries' take off. Culti-vators may not take water direct from the main canal or from the branches, but only from distributaries or their sub-distributaries called 'minors'. It is not perhaps correct to speak of cultivators taking water direct at all. What happens is that culverts called 'mogas' are fixed under the high earthern banks to carry water to irrigate at stated intervals the crops on say three hundred acres of land. The periodical irrigation from a single moga is called a 'wari' or turn and is strictly controlled by canal officials and any interference with it makes the perpetrator liable to heavy penalties. The indi-vidual cultivator whose holding is generally twenty-five acres has a fixed turn which is strictly controlled and he is obliged at the end of his turn to block up his irrigation inlet to allow his neighbour lower down the channel to enjoy his allowance of water.

The ingenuity of the engineering, the skilful blending of old with new, and the general recognition among the cultivators that there had to be order and control in the distribution of water were features of the irrigation systems in Burma as in India. This is something Wallace noticed at Salin:

It was canals that gave ancient Salin its importance. They made it one of the granaries for the Dry Zone. The water used is that which comes down from the western mountains on its way to the Irrawaddy. The old main canal dates probably from the great days of the Pagan Kings in the twelfth century. A second canal was being made in the 1920s. Besides these two major works of widely different date, there were many small canals dug and maintained by groups of villagers. Sidoktaya Township had many of these as well as Salin. Some of them show great ingenuity – e.g. in taking the water round the foot of a steep hill-side. These small canals did not come under the Irrigation Department, which had its hands full with the major works going on. They were a real example of democracy in practice. Each had its own canal officials and simple set of rules and only if there was an argument did Government, in the shape of the SDO, come in as arbiter. This was a rather unusual aspect of one's work and a most enjoyable one as a specific object on tour.

This recital of the district officer's duties – and it is very far from being complete – must prompt the question whether, after he had done all his touring, checking, inspecting and verifying, there was any time or energy left over for general welfare and development work.

Traditionally, the general pattern of district administration was not remarkable for any vision of economic and social uplift. The task of running the machine was enough in itself. Shukla argues, indeed, that the British paid too little attention to economic development:

Maintenance work continued to claim priority too long. Positive development work they did not undertake, though they did a lot of basic work like construction of canals, laying of communications, etc. Perhaps they thought that enough was enough ... but surely there was a place for new visions?

Things were, however, beginning to change in the 1930s. The land colonization schemes in the Punjab seem to have engendered a new enthusiasm for village uplift, which was connected in particular with the names of two District Officers, Darling and Brayne. Belcher gives this picture of Brayne with whom he toured in the Simla Hills:

In the course of his ICS career in the Punjab, Brayne became convinced that the most vital task of the British administration in India was not 'good administration', law and order, etc., or even the development of the country's natural resources, but the improvement of the lives of the villagers who are far and away the most numerous of its inhabitants – and by the improvement of their life he meant not just such things as the introduction of improved farming methods, but better sanitation in house and villages, better health and more effective education for rural life, especially bringing education to the women and girls as well as the boys. He believed that if these things could be achieved, all the other traditional objectives of administration would follow. He threw himself passionately into this cause, putting its precepts vigorously into practice in the districts of which he had charge, especially in Gurgaon near Delhi, where he was DC for many years. He spent his leaves in England learning from progressive British farmers what principles and practices of British farming might be applicable also in the Punjab. And he wrote several Plato-style dialogues featuring a 'village Socrates' persuading reluctant villagers of the virtues of the various practices he wanted to inculcate in the fields of education, health and agriculture; these he had translated into Punjabi and published, so that they could be read by, or to, the Punjab villagers, or performed as playlets in village meetings.

Venkatachar found that, in the UP too, rural development was very much in the air in the thirties:

F. L. Brayne's work in the Punjab was much publicized. The Governments of Bombay and Bengal had initiated rural development programs. The work of a missionary near Trivandrum was well known through his book: 'Up from poverty'.

In UP, the co-operative department was organizing 'better living' societies. Consolidation of holdings was making progress. Some enthusiastic Collectors were on their own carrying out activities such as afforestation, contour bunding, prevention of soil erosion, provision of drinking water wells in the villages, and so on.

The immediate impetus to the extension of rural development programme throughout the province was the grant from the Central Government for development work. This necessitated the working out of a scheme covering the province and for the better utilization of financial resources.

The main scheme of rural development was embodied in a handbook which I compiled and had it approved by the Governor. Briefly, the outline of the scheme was to have one or more development circles, each comprising twelve villages. Here the activities of government departments like irrigation, agriculture, public health, education, etc. were to be co-ordinated, schemes of improvement drawn up and implemented with the co-operation of village people. The District Officer was to be the co-ordinating authority with powers to spend the development grant at his discretion.

General ideas about development were admirable, if the villagers could be persuaded to do it themselves. There was also the problem of securing suitable personnel and training them over a period for work in the rural parts. The real question was whether the District Officer was in a position to mobilize public support, and enlist co-operation of the local politicians and workers who were not only suspicious of local authority, but were positively hostile to it.

These problems do not seem to have worried Bowman who was put in charge of rural development in Jhansi in the UP. He enjoyed the work thoroughly: 'It cut across the frustration which so often goes with the bureaucratic system'. But the new emphasis on rural development took many different forms, no doubt with differing degrees of life and success. In Assam, Maitra seems to have seen little impact, when he speaks of 'the musty and airless nature of the administration' which he had joined 'so hopefully'. This was because 'everything that was worth doing had already been done'. But not far away in Bengal, when 'Rural Reconstruction' was the watchword before the war, collectors were busy, so Saumarez Smith recalls, with 'distributing stud-bulls, starting night-schools, sinking tube-wells, re-excavating village canals'. In Bihar, mass literacy was one of the main objectives of rural development. Ray writes, 'I spent many evenings tramping from one village to another supervising night-classes. Our motto of "Each One Teach One" if followed up could easily have halved illiteracy in a decade, but alas, the cynics produced their own slogan "Literacy for Litigation", but even this carrot failed to keep the momentum going.'

Certainly, as Midgley observed in the UP 'all of us in the Service were concerned with the problem of rural poverty and the wretched conditions of life in the villages'. But it was not so easy to get schemes approved and implemented. He found that his attempts to improve drinking-water supplies in his subdivision and to distribute seeds and fodder in a more rational way foundered by reason of failure of the Public Works and Agricultural Departments to co-operate with him. Whatever the nature of the contact between the administrator and the villager, whether it was village uplift or more mundane questions of title or tax, the district officer had to have an understanding of, and sympathy with, the psychology of those with whom he was dealing. The pace of whatever the business was could not be hurried, if it was to be done properly. This is well illustrated by Symington who draws on his Bombay experience to bring before us not only a typical Muslim assistant collector, but the very earthy world of the villagers too – suspicious, uncertain, but conscious that in the register was inscribed their fate.

When Dost Mahomed said he would check the register, Mahars – village servants – were sent running in all directions to summon the interested parties to the pipal tree in front of the village office. A sizeable gathering had already collected there and went on growing through the afternoon.

A series of dialogues ensued, calculated to try the patience of any officer who might fancy himself in a hurry, and to afford entertainment to the audience.

'Vinoba Ramya Koli.' Dost Mahomed read out the name belonging to the first uncertified entry in the register.

A dark-skinned figure in a high-girt dhoti – public opinion permitted only superior folk to wear their dhotis low about their calves – was hustled forward.

'Are you Vinoba Ramya Koli?'

The man addressed smirked sheepishly and looked round at his friends as if in doubt whether he should make such a daring admission. 'Yes, Yes,' cried the audience, 'He is Vinoba.'

'Vinoba, are you the owner of field number 372?'

'Yes.'

'Have you mortgaged it to Tolaram Bhansali?'

'No, sahib. How could I do so? I do not know what a mortgage is.'

'Then what happened about the field?'

'I have given it for three years.'

'And what has Tolaram given you?'

'Given? He has given me nothing. He gave me some cloth.'

'Did he give you money?'

'Yes.'

'How much?'

'One rupee and nine annas.'

Approving murmurs came from the crowd as it settled down to enjoy itself. Obviously Vinoba was not going to disappoint.

'Was that part of the loan?'

'Who knows? It was to buy liquor.'

A cackle of laughter greeted this tit-bit and Vinoba felt encouraged to go on.

'It was to buy liquor. I had no money to drink at his shop, so he gave me money. When I had drunk I signed the paper.'

'And the cloth?' Dost knew he would have to ask that sooner or later, and decided to get it over.

'That was for my nephew's wedding.'

'So the one rupee nine annas and the cloth have nothing to do with your land?'

'Who knows? When he gave them I signed the paper.'

'What was the paper you signed?'

Here the village accountant intervened: 'It was a mortgage. Here is the true copy from the sub-registry.'

Dost Mahomed examined it. He pointed to a cross at the foot of the page.

'Did you make that?'

Vinoba hesitated. He recollected that two witnesses had seen him do it and decided not to disown it.

'Who else?'

'What is written here?'

'Tolaram is renting my field for three years.'

'What is the rent?'

'One hundred and twenty-one rupees.'

'Do you have to pay that back, with interest also?'

'I will pay when my cousin sends me money.'

'What if he does not send and you cannot pay?'

'Tolaram will take my field instead of the money.'

'Then it is not rent. It is a mortgage. This entry seems correct and I must approve it. Have you any objection?'

Vinoba sank back on his haunches. It was someone else's turn now.

'Write what your honour wishes. I am only a poor man.'

'Dhondu Vishram Chavan,' Dost Mahomed announced, and everyone settled down for turn number two.

FURTHER READING

The contributors to this volume have naturally focussed upon the local detail of the day to day administration. There is thus little on overall land revenue policy, covered by W. C. Neale, *Economic Change in Rural India, Land Tenure in Uttar Pradesh, 1800–1955* (New Haven 1962), and only passing reference to rural development, although this did attract district officers such as Malcolm Darling and F. L. Brayne: M. Darling, *The Punjab Peasant*, 4th edn (Bombay 1947); F. L. Brayne, *Socrates in an Indian Village* (London 1931); *Better Villages* (London 1937). The social implications of rural development, including zamindari abolition or land for the landless labourer, receive almost no attention. There is, however, a growing literature on shifts in the balance between landlord-zamindars, peasants and agricultural labourers, noting the problems of revenue and rent collection, which affected both government and landlords and the problem for the Indian political parties of choosing upon which segment of rural society to base their electoral strategy. A sample might include: A. Béteille, *Studies in Agrarian Social Structure* (Delhi 1974); Rajat and Ratna Ray, 'Zamindars and jotedars: a study of rural politics in Bengal', *Modern Asian Studies*, IX:1 (1975), 81–102; B. B. Chaudhuri, 'Agrarian movements in Bengal and Bihar, 1919–37', in B. R. Nanda (ed.), *Socialism in India, 1919–39* (Delhi 1972); W. Hauser, 'The Indian National Congress and land policy in the twentieth century' in *Indian Economic and Social History Review*, I (1963–4), 56–67; N. G. Ranga, *Peasants and Congress* (Madras 1939); D. A. Law (ed.), *Congress and the Raj. Facets of the Indian struggle 1917–47* (Essays by D. Hardiman, G. Pandey, M. Harcourt and G. McDonald).

MAPS

The following maps show the complexity of the administrative structure under a district officer's charge. The first map is of the district of Chingleput, with its seven taluks, of which Saidapet is one. The second map is of Saidapet taluk, showing the villages of which it was composed including Kil Kundiyar. The third map is of Kil Kundiyar village and the surrounding fields.

A fold-out map showing all the districts of India and Burma can be found at the end of the book.

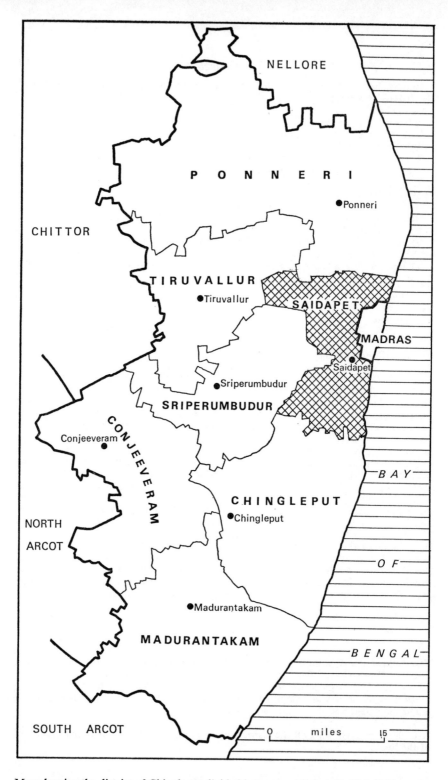

Map showing the district of Chingleput divided into seven taluks, of which Saidapet is one. Chingleput was a district of approximately 1.75 million people with an area of 3,079 square miles. Based on the 'half-inch' Topographical Series maps covering Chingleput district published by the Survey of India.

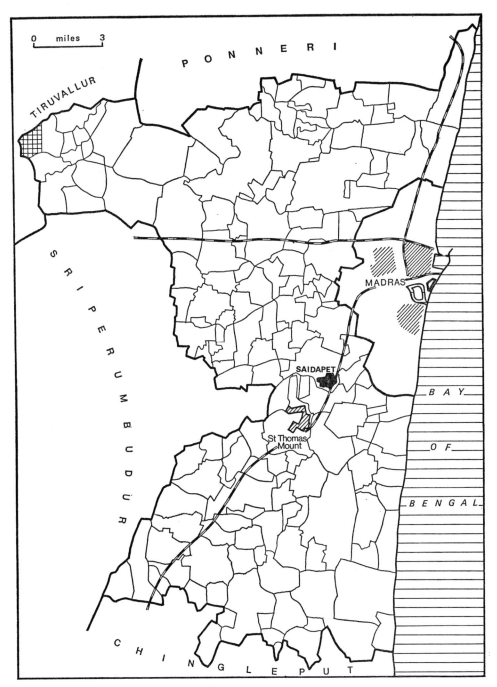

Map showing the taluk of Saidapet and the boundaries of its numerous villages. Kil Kundiyar can be seen in the top left-hand corner. Based on the 'one-inch' map of Saidapet taluk published by the Central Survey Office, Madras 1922.

Map showing the village of Kil Kundiyar and the surrounding fields as they were numbered for revenue purposes. Reduced from a map, on the scale six inches to the mile, kindly supplied by the Tamilnadu State Government.

CHAPTER 4
THE MAGISTRATE

The administration of a single legal system throughout British India (except in special tracts and parts of the frontier areas) required a comprehensive network of courts, both civil and criminal, throughout the country. At the top of the legal pyramid in the provinces were the High Courts under a Chief Justice who was sometimes appointed direct from the British Bar. The puisne judges were mostly promoted district and sessions judges and a few senior members of the local Bar. Each district had a sessions judge, nearly always an ICS officer who had opted for the judicial line. The sessions judge had original jurisdiction in serious criminal cases such as murder and in some civil matters. He heard appeals from first-class magistrates and from subordinate civil judges. He did not tour or go on circuit. The cases came to him.

Nearly all the original criminal work was handled by magistrates sitting individually. Benches of magistrates were relatively uncommon. In the district, there were three levels of magistrate, first, second and third, the last being effectively a training grade. The magistracy was largely staffed by members of the provincial services without specific legal training, the largest number of them being second-class magistrates operating at the taluk/tahsil level. Of the five hundred and eleven criminal offences listed in the Indian Penal Code, most were triable by magistrates of the first or second class.

In his dual role of administrator and magistrate, the ICS district officer fitted into this pattern as a first-class magistrate or joint magistrate in charge of a subdivision, and later as a district magistrate or additional district magistrate. In some of the larger towns, ICS officers held appointments as city magistrates which were full-time assignments.

When he was posted to his first district, the young assistant collector or assistant commissioner was invested with the powers of a magistrate of the third-class; and within a few weeks of his arrival, he would, with the assistance of his clerk, take his first case, often a private complaint of assault. The procedures and doctrines of magisterial work would not be totally unfamiliar to the fledgling magistrate because during his probationary year, as has been seen, he had studied and passed an examination in the Indian Penal Code, the Law of Evidence and the Code of Criminal Procedure, that remarkable trio of legal works, which, edited by two Indian lawyers, Ratanlal and Thakore, and thickly encrusted by them with case-law from a dozen High Courts, guided every one of the thousands of criminal courts up and down the country. The powers of a third-class magistrate were limited. He could imprison for a month or fine up to fifty rupees (£4.50); and the cases which the district magistrate saw fit to pass to him would be trifling ones of assault and theft. In every case, except those tried summarily – and few magistrates were allowed to do this – there had to be a written judgment and the young magistrate's judgment would be submitted to the district magistrate. It would often return with suitable and pithy comment.

Matthews recalls the first case he tried as Assistant Commissioner in Nagpur district (CP):

I started my criminal magisterial work as a third-class magistrate trying small theft cases or 'marpit' (petty assault). I can still remember the unrelaxing sternness with which I confronted my first accused person. This poor wretch had stolen a small bolt of cloth from an open shop in the local bazaar and fled before the hue and cry that was immediately raised by the bystanders – just like Tom, Tom, the piper's son! The case was overwhelming and I had no difficulty in arriving at a decision as to guilt. But what about punishment? I was inclined to award imprisonment up to my maximum powers. Before doing so, however, I decided to consult the City Magistrate, one Mohammed Khan, a man wise in his years and experience. He listened gravely to my reasons for awarding the prison term. He then gently pointed out that the man had no previous convictions and had obviously yielded to a sudden temptation being, as the record showed, out of work and no doubt made desperate by the plight of his deprived family. He suggested that I awarded six strokes of the birch and get the whole thing over. I admired the wisdom of this logic and accordingly the next day when the prisoner was brought before me in the usual chains and escorted by a sub-inspector of police and two constables, I sentenced the man to the said six strokes. There was no great ceremony about the execution of this punishment. A whipping post stood permanently erected in the compound of the Kacheri or court buildings. Thither the prisoner was escorted, his hands bound to the post after his shirt was removed and my own court orderly wielding a four foot rattan cane laid on the six strokes before the motley crowd of petitioners and applicants thronging the compound. The prisoner shrieked his loudest – far beyond the needs of the case, the crowd laughed and all being over, the man was handed his shirt and with a sidelong glance at me (did I detect a half smile) slid away through the crowd doubtless to restore himself to the bosom of his family.

Naturally, the trainee magistrate had to rely heavily on his court clerk or 'reader', particularly over the translation of the evidence since all of this was given in the local language. Belcher in Gurdaspur in the Punjab describes the position in this way:

To help in establishing what witnesses had actually said, in framing questions to put to them myself, and in seeing how to apply to the facts as revealed my recently-acquired knowledge of the Indian Penal Code, the Code of Criminal Procedure, and the Indian Evidence Act, I was given the assistance of an experienced Indian court official called a 'reader', whose functions were similar to those of a Clerk of Court to a Bench of Honorary Magistrates in England, though less authoritative. I felt I ought to be careful not to rely too much on him, a precaution I now believe to have been quite unnecessary in respect of him or of any of the Readers I had during my entire service, all of whom proved to the best of my observation as honest as they were hardworking and professionally reliable. Witnesses naturally spoke Urdu or Punjabi, which I did not as yet understand well enough not to need translation; this could lead to ludicrous delays, since my Reader's translation was closely listened to by the Pleaders on either side, each of whom as like as not challenged it with one of his own, so that if I was not careful I became the helpless observer of an interminable three-cornered and time-wasting dispute. However, increasing familiarity with the language cured this difficulty for me after a few months.

Hayley at Silchar in Assam felt that when he was trying cases as a third-class magistrate,

everybody knew the truth of these cases I had to judge. They all knew, except me. I thought I would try an experiment. I had a very intelligent chaprassi. He is like an office boy, carries one's files to the Court every day and takes messages. I told him to circulate amongst the pleaders who were busy instructing their witnesses as to what tale they should tell, which tale of course might have had little relation to the truth. I would then write my judgement and I would show him that I had written it on my way to Court. I would ask him what was the truth of the case. He would tell me that the truth was so-and-so. Now that might accord with my judgement or it might be quite the opposite, but he knew that I was going to deliver my judgement whatever it was he might have said to me. I found that in spite of all the care and attention that I had given, I might just as well have tossed a coin to discover the truth or otherwise of the case before me.

After passing the first of his departmental examinations, the assistant collector under training would be put on the same level as a taluk or tahsil magistrate and invested with second-class powers. This meant that he could imprison up to six months and fine up to one hundred rupees. He had now rather more important and interesting cases to try.

After the second departmental exam had been passed, the final step in this progression was the grant of first-class powers, with a wider range of cases and authority to inflict up to two years' imprisonment, and fine up to a thousand rupees. He would now receive his first substantive posting as an SDO, equipped to carry out the magisterial responsibilities that fell to a sub-divisional officer as joint magistrate. The volume of the work varied from place to place. For some it was a heavy chore, with the endless procession of witnesses, many false, and the verbose vakils, the tedium being compounded by the need for the magistrate himself to write the official record of the evidence in long-hand, to the grave detriment of his hand-writing. To spend five or six hours a day five days a week doing this and then to write up judgements in the evening might well leave insufficient time for the equally, perhaps more, important general work. Touring provided some escape, but the work seemed to follow the magistrate wherever he was.

Most of the contributors associated their magisterial duty with court work. Many felt that the courts, and indeed the whole process of the criminal law, were sometimes used and manipulated, for the purpose of pursuing private grudges or paying off old scores. They also felt uneasy, when false evidence was so freely offered by the defendants, about the irregular methods, including the manufacture of appropriate evidence, which the police in their turn felt obliged to provide.

Azim Husain, very aware of this dilemma, had, from the outset, strong views about magisterial work as he saw it in the Punjab. He writes,

The magistrate must strike the golden mean. If the story of the police is disbelieved and the public is favoured, there is a grave danger of undermining the authority of the police which, in the long run, may have bad effects. On the other hand, if the police are favoured, they may begin to tyrannize over the public which is equally undesirable. The object is to keep the authority of the police intact and at the same time to treat the police on terms of perfect equality with the litigants whether they are the complainants or the accused. Before a court of justice the accused and the Crown must come begging for justice and not favours.

After his first judgement, Husain noted in his diary that 'witnesses are brought forth not to state the truth within their knowledge, but to show that so-and-so can bring so many men to come and tell lies for him. Most witnesses are fake.' Husain also had a low opinion of the lawyers in the district courts whom he describes as 'of poor ability and intelligence ... beating about the bush ... catching any silly technical objection they can get hold of ... indulging in verbal jugglery as a fine art and thinking it good pleading'. (We have no accounts, of course, of what the lawyers thought about the magistrates.)

Husain's observations are borne out to some extent by the experience of Martin in the Dinapur subdivision of Patna district in Bihar:

At times I was inclined to become cynical about the blessings that the introduction of a British system of justice was often claimed to have bestowed upon the Indian people. Crime was in some areas widespread and the relatively small police force overtaxed in its efforts to contain it. I gained the general impression that while the vast majority of those brought to trial in my court by the police were criminals they had seldom committed the crimes alleged against them in the precise manner presented by the prosecutor.

My sympathies were very largely with the police. One Sub-Inspector with perhaps a dozen constables was responsible for preventing and suppressing crime in an area often as much as one hundred square miles. Robbery and dacoity were in some areas almost endemic and the villagers often too frightened to co-operate with the police. In these circumstances, to bring offenders to court with a reasonable hope of their being convicted under a judicial system which required a high standard of proof, led understandably often to a judicious cooking of the evidence. Identification of the accused was often the key point of the prosecution case. Most of the crimes were committed at night and the defence lawyer's first question was apt to be 'was it a moonlit or dark night? If the latter, what illumination was there?' Many and curious were the explanations why that particular witness had found it necessary to get up and light a lantern at 3 a.m. when by chance he happened to see running away all the accused whom he recognised now in court. It was a game played by very strict rules and if the Sub-Inspector had 'prepared' his case well, the magistrate could do no other than convict and wait to hear in due course whether the Sessions Judge had upset his judgement on appeal.

And so I struggled on, as others had done before me, often engaged for five or six hours a day transcribing long-hand into English the varying evidence vouchsafed in a broad, roughly Hindi dialect by witnesses who were imbued by a number of motives, not least by the, to them, moral necessity of assisting their relatives to the utmost of their powers of imagination and loquacity.

One fact that constantly emerged throughout the cases that came to court was that a large number of the population [of Bihar] really did not know who rightfully owned what piece of land. In a country where the right to cultivate and keep the whole or part of the crops was a vital necessity of life, the vagaries of the Hindu system of succession and the fact that there had been no resettlement of land since the Permanent Settlement over a hundred years before necessitated constant recourse to law. The Civil Courts were the obvious means of redress to any who felt wronged, but although they did indeed grind exceedingly small, they also ground extremely slowly. Quick decisions about ownership of land were time and time again sought through the criminal courts, who had to decide, in a case where two parties had set about each other with lathis [bamboo staffs] causing considerable 'bodily harm', often 'grievous', if the lathi had a sharp piece of iron sticking in the end of it, which party owned the land and were lawfully defending their own and which was the aggressor. To come to a decision on such a point, the magistrate had in fact to listen to all the complicated legal arguments about ownership on each side, often going back twenty years or more and to give a judgement which was really the function of the civil courts. Such judgements could be and very often were appealed against, but in the meantime the successful party would enjoy the comfortable position of knowing that possession was nine parts of law.

Such problems were exemplified in their most extreme form in cases about the possession of 'diara' land. Parts of Dinapur subdivision were situated at the confluence of the Son and the Ganges rivers and every year by the time the monsoon was in full force in August large areas were totally inundated. By October, the floods had receded leaving a vast flat featureless area covered with a rich fertile mud, which could be sown immediately mainly with maize that grew and ripened rapidly to give a valuable crop by next February or March. The onset of the cold weather and the recession of the floods brought each year an almost intolerable increase of criminal cases between often traditionally hostile groups who claimed the right to cultivate and reap the crops.

On one occasion, I made a local inspection in an endeavour to check the mass of conflicting evidence about the ownership of some diara land. It was situated about two miles from the high ground which remained in most years terra firma and contained recognisable landmarks such as trees, temples and 'pukka' houses built of brick. A central feature of this case was the exact situation of a palm tree which was alleged by both sides to constitute one of the boundaries. I had been sceptical about its existence, but on my arrival I found no less than two young palm trees, apparently undamaged by the water of Mother Ganges. As I walked round both of them, my suspicions were aroused and, directing my orderly to wield a spade, I found only too clearly that both of them had been planted the day before, one by each party. I forget what my decision was in this case, but n retrospect I cannot help feeling that it says much for the innate good sense of those tough men from the diara lands that large portions of this kind of land were actually cultivated and crops grown each year.

The accounts of magisterial work give some indication of the violence underlying the tranquil surface of the Indian village scene. Indeed, a great deal – too much perhaps – of the magistrate's work was concerned with murders, riots, gang robberies (dacoities), usually involving violence and assaults. Williams in Sargodha district in the Punjab discovered that disputes over the supply of water for irrigation and illicit amours were the most fertile sources of crimes of violence. On two occasions, he found himself in charge of committal proceedings in murder cases, though in other parts of India more junior magistrates used to do this work. He writes,

My powers as a magistrate extended over the whole district as was usual, but my particular jurisdiction covered the territory of two police stations, one in the canal colony area and the other in the Salt Range. Crimes of physical violence were endemic, springing generally in the one area from canal water being cut off by a greedy neighbour, and in the other from illicit amours. The most sensational Salt Range case of my own time illustrated in full measure the savagery of the local tribesmen and the perpetual handicaps facing the investigating police. A noted local Lothario was in love with a young married girl and planned to elope with her. As she had several male relatives near at hand, he enlisted the help of two accomplices, and one hot weather night, the three invaded the girl's village and carried her off, murdering her husband, father and brother in the process. The uproar created by this slaughter aroused the villagers, and a cousin of the girl tried to prevent the party's escape, but the murderers slew him also. One of the leader's accomplices then sought his help for a similar venture, as he too was enamoured of a girl whose parents would not agree to their marriage, so on the following night, the party entered this second girl's village and although foiled in carrying her off, they did manage to kill the two parents. The police of three districts were then engaged in pursuit of the murderers and the first girl, in and out of the recesses of the Salt Range. and at one stage came so close that the leader of the desperadoes, fearful of the girl not being able to keep up with them and later giving evidence against them if caught, killed her with an axe. Eventually, the three were trapped and arrested, but then came a problem for the police. Four men had been murdered on the first night and some villagers had seen the culprits as they made off, but only one of these three was well known locally. The presence of four dead bodies was too good an opportunity to miss of paying off various private scores, and the villagers named five persons as responsible for the killings, of whom actually only one was a real perpetrator. Fortunately, there was good evidence available for identifying the three genuine murderers with the two killings of the second night, and it was this case which secured their conviction and execution. The preliminary commitment proceedings were conducted in my court, and attracted much interest. At one point, they were suspended for a short time as I was ill; on my recovery, the principal killer assured me that clearly I had been struck down by God and then spared in order that I should then let him and his friends go free.

The tenacity with which vindictive peasants would cling to a false story was further illustrated in the last case I was to hear at Sargodha. A normal case of murder had been investigated, but the police found that the first information report made to them implicated some innocent person as well as genuine culprits, and they prosecuted the latter only. The dead man's father then put in a private complaint against his own original nominees as the murderers. Both cases were in my court, each with different witnesses to the same crime. In the complaint case, witnesses were presented in such a way that no two witnesses on the same point appeared on the same day; when one had been examined, an excuse was made for his corroborator to be held back until a later date – actually, for him to be tutored in what to say under cross-examination, in the light of the first witness's evidence. This had happened on two occasions, and eventually the victim's father had to appear on a fairly minor point. He was to corroborate another witness, and was actually present on the day that evidence was taken, but his lawyer announced that he was not well, since the roof of the tea-shop in the court compound had fallen on him while he was waiting, and so he would have to come on a later day. I called him in and questioned him, but he professed ignorance on all points, including his own name and parentage. It happened that the doctor who had given evidence of the post mortem on the original victim was still present, and I asked him to examine the father. He did so, and pronounced him as perfectly fit to give evidence. After recording this opinion and giving the father another chance to give evidence, which he declined, I remanded him in custody to stand trial for his refusal. He died the following day – of natural causes, as was later ascertained – but the family stated that they wished to prosecute me for his murder, and my forthcoming home leave nearly had to be postponed. I was, of course, covered by the medical view I had recorded, but the story illustrated the lengths to which pertinacity could go. (It ended with the success in the trial Court of the official police version of the original murder.)

Belcher at Kasur in the same province had some rather personal insight into the motivation of crimes of violence over water disputes. His house had a considerable fruit garden:

oranges, grapefruit, pomegranates, guavas, and mangoes – irrigated from the Upper Bari Doab Canal. Being at the very end of the canal, it was natural that we should be affected by any losses of water through accidental breakages in the bank of the canal. But there were those who deliberately broke the canal bank to get water out of their proper turn and as one watched the leaves of one's precious plants and trees shrivel up and the fruit drop off, suspicions of one's neighbours hardened readily into certainties. Hence the urge, with which I came to entertain some sympathy, to pick up metal-tipped staves or even sterner weapons and go off up the canal to take direct action.

Hyde, from the cases which he dealt with as Additional District Magistrate in Ellichpur in the CP, illustrates two other problems which faced the magistrate in India. One was the presence of 'criminal tribes', thieves, cattle-lifters and robbers by custom and heredity. The second, a particularly brutal murder, illustrates the extraordinary difficulties the police sometimes had in getting convictions and having them maintained on appeal when the accused were influential people.

As Additional District Magistrate, I had to try the more important cases where heavy sentences were likely. One such case, a gang robbery, I have never forgotten: the accused were a group belonging to what was classed as a 'criminal tribe', Pardhis I think they were. Most were inter-related and all had 'records', particularly the leader, an elderly man whose son was also one of the accused. As the leader had, in addition to the number of offences of which he was found guilty in the trial, a long list of previous convictions, I had to award a long sentence. When all the gang had been dealt with and were about to be led away, his son asked if he could make a request. I asked what it was. 'My father is an old man', he said, 'and he has been given a long term in jail. Will you not agree to take his years of imprisonment away and add them to my sentence in his place?' I was touched, though of course I could do nothing, but for nearly half a century, I have remembered this offer, by one classed as 'the lowest of the low', as a supreme example of filial piety. I have an abiding respect for this young man.

The most sensational case, however, I did not try myself, but I recorded the key confession and was a witness at the trial in the Court of Session. This was known as 'The Tawlar Case'. The way the case came to light was curious. My police colleague, a very straightforward and keen officer, a Maratha called Ghate, got to hear that surreptitious enquiries were being made by a pleader from Wardha in the CP as to whether the police were investigating the recent death of a young woman in a village called Tawlar, some seventeen miles from Ellichpur. There was in fact no investigation, though the local Sub-Inspector had had a routine report that one Lilawati, a member of a wealthy Kunbi family in the village, had died of fever on 26 July. Ghate ordered the Circle Inspector to go and camp near the village and make confidential enquiries as to whether anything suspicious had happened about that time. The Inspector met with a wall of silence, but after a considerable lapse of time found that a taxi from Ellichpur had come to the nearest point on the main road, about a mile away from the village, some days before the girl had died. This taxi was traced and it was found that the passenger had been a quack doctor from Ellichpur called Balkrishna whom the police started to question.

Early on the morning of the first of September, I was woken by the police who brought in custody a somewhat miserable-looking man and asked me to record his confession. I ordered his handcuffs to be removed, sent the police to the back of my bungalow and asked the man if he wished to make a statement to me. He said he did, so I told him to think it over and left him alone in a small room off my verandah. After some three hours, I again saw him and enquired with the usual warning whether he still wished to make a confession. He clearly said he did and assured me he was not acting under police coercion so I called up my court clerk and recorded in Marathi the extraordinary story he told me.

Balkrishna was an unqualified allopathic practitioner in Ellichpur and was the physician and confidant of a well-to-do Kunbi (a leading Maratha caste) family of Tawlar who had considerable political and local influence. The deceased Lilawati was a member of that family and was considered to have brought disgrace on it by immoral behaviour, having been made pregnant by a Muslim servant. Her two step-brothers, a cousin and an uncle had decided she must be killed and wanted Balkrishna to give her a lethal injection whilst she was asleep: he was to visit the village with the ostensible object of attending the young son of one of the conspirators (Ruprao). Discussions and plottings went on and eventually Balkrishna was driven to Tawlar, complete with lamp, syringe and drugs, in Ruprao's car on Friday, 24 July. Shortly after 11 p.m., he dissolved four grains of strychnine in water and all was ready for the deed, but at the last minute it was foiled by the wakefulness of the wife of Kashirao, another of the conspirators, who was unwell in the part of the house where Lilawati was sleeping. Balkrishna returned to Ellichpur in the morning, but that evening Ruprao and Kashirao came to him and told him that the murder was to take place next day. So he again set out in the car, this time adding chloroform and lint to his leather bag, and at 1.30 a.m., the three of them went into Lilawati's room. Whilst Kashirao ineffectually gagged her with a scarf, Balkrishna injected the strych-nine into her left arm. She cried out, struggled and ran up a stair, collapsing at the top and waking Kashirao's wife to whom she said she was dying. The wife was sent for water and whilst she was away, Lilawati's paroxysms started. Balkrishna was sent for with his chloroform which he administered. The girl was then carried unconscious to her room where she died at 4 a.m. At 8 a.m., her body was taken out to the cremation ground and burnt. Later in the day, the ashes were removed.

Other witnesses were then produced by the police and I recorded their sworn state-ments under a provision of the Criminal Procedure Code. All were villagers, servants, connections or tenants of the conspirators' family. Straight away, strenuous efforts were made to get at them through agents and pleaders employed by the accused and their family – so the police had them temporarily removed to other villages till they appeared before the committing magistrate, my assistant, to whom they repeated the evidence they had given before me. The four conspirators were committed for trial by the Court of Session and Balkrishna was in the circumstances made an 'approver' (King's evidence). However, once the witnesses were allowed back to Tawlar, they were 'got at' by the accuseds' lawyers so that at the Sessions trial, all retracted their previous statements and gave false evidence. The chief counsel for the defence, a very prominent lawyer, had set up his 'camp' at Ellichpur, then moved to Tawlar; a house was hired in Amraoti where the trial was to be held and all the witnesses, prosecution and defence, were taken there and kept under surveillance by the accuseds' family and lawyers. All this was of course known to the administration and indeed came out at the trial, when the defence made allegations of a conspiracy by the police who they accused of tutoring the witnesses.

It was a long and difficult trial, but the judge, C. R. Hemeon, sorted it out well and relying on the confession of the approver and the sworn statements of the prose-cution witnesses before me, together with their evidence in the commital court, found Ruprao and Kashirao guilty and sentenced them to death. The case went to appeal and to everyone's amazement, two judges of the High Court in what was a very flabby judgment acquitted them, saying 'though the case has a ring of probability, it does not take us to the point of reasonable certainty'.

As the magistrates responsible for the maintenance of law and order in the district, I and my immediate supervisor had taken a great interest in the affair in view of the great difficulties the police were having in getting the case through in the face of all the intrigues and obstacles. We had felt that if the prosecution did not succeed in such a manifestly clear and serious case, it would demonstrate that it was almost impossible to secure a conviction against rich, powerful and influential men, such as the accused were. They had used their wealth to secure the services of the most highly paid advocates in India and to bribe witnesses where necessary, though in many cases this was not necessary as their local power was adequate to obtain their ends. We had been defeated and the grave miscarriage of justice was made worse when the false witnesses were prosecuted for perjury and were eventually acquitted on the incredible ground that if they had spoken the truth in their evidence at the Sessions (when they had clearly retracted and lied) a conviction for perjury would dissuade witnesses from changing their false evidence to true.

But if violence, passionate or premeditated, was often present, it could also be feigned in an elaborate and circumstantial way as Hayley discovered in the Sylhet district of Assam. He writes,

Sylhet was a large district with a very packed population. In the days of the East India Company, Thackeray's brother, known as 'Sylhet Thackeray', had been in charge of the district, and it was interesting to read some of his accounts in the Record Room. Most of the district had been under the permanent settlement of Cornwallis, which meant that there were endless lawsuits about land. In fact, they were very litigious people. On my first day in the courts, I was appalled to see about sixty people filing in carrying men on stretchers, most of them covered in blood and with bandages on various parts of their bodies. I turned to my Bench Clerk and told him that I hadn't heard that there had been any riot in the district, and this was very terrible. I listened to a long complaint of how they were peacefully working in their fields, when the other party, armed with sticks, came and beat them up very badly and drove them away. I asked my Clerk what we were to do since the list of the accused numbered between fifty and eighty. 'Sir, you just summon one or two of them' he said. I would not hear of this and said that every single one of them would have to be summoned. My Clerk smiled and said nothing. Then the next case was called on, and a smilar array of bloodstained complainants filed in, carrying their wounded with them. They made exactly the same complaint, but about the other people who had just left the Court. My Bench Clerk said, 'This is very usual, Your Honour'. I ordered some of the bloodstained clothing to be seized and to be sent to the public analyst. It was of course goat's blood, and in fact no sort of fight had taken place at all. It was merely on attempt, through the criminal law, to establish ownership of a piece of land. Had they managed to get me to give judgement on one side or the other, the lucky winners would proceed to the civil courts regarding their claim to the land, which would be greatly bolstered by the fact that the learned magistrate had criminally convicted one of the parties.

Though crimes of violence tended to crowd the magistrate's file, he would sometimes be concerned with family questions, which might have seemed more suitable for a civil than a criminal court. Indeed, it was one of the curiosities of Indian criminal law that first-class magistrates could award maintenance in matrimonial cases. In the Malappuram subdivision of the west coast Malabar district of Madras, Platt had to do a lot of this type of work which raised difficult questions of Muslim marriage law and customs:

The magisterial work was also unusual. Muslims could divorce their wives at will and the Nayar caste could terminate an association merely by the husband leaving the wife who continued to live in her own family home under the matriarchal system. Consequently, there were many claims for maintenance for the children whose fathers had divorced or discarded their wives. In one year, I had two hundred and ninety-seven cases. Paternity was rarely denied and there was a rough and ready scale of maintenance order starting at one rupee per child per month for a coolie earning four annas a day (Rupees seven and a half a month).

In one of these cases, a woman claimed maintenance for two children from two brothers of the stonemason caste and said she had been married to both of them under the caste system of fraternal polyandry. It was clear from the evidence that the younger child could not be the child of the elder brother as she was not living with him at the relevant time. For the elder child, the elder brother denied paternity. One of his witnesses said the caste system of fraternal polyandry had become extinct. He admitted, however, that the elder brother had no other wife at the time and that it was not customary for the younger brother to marry before the elder. I had no doubt that the marrige had been polyandrous at the time and applied the spirit, if not the letter, of the law in ordering maintenance against both brothers for the elder child.

In another matrimonial case, the District Gazetteer [that compendium of information on the geography, ethnology, history, customs and economics, written and periodically revised by district officers] proved useful. A Muslim laid a complaint of bigamy against his wife. He said he had divorced her under duress from her relatives and the divorce was not valid. She had remarried and he argued that this was bigamy. The man belonged to a Muslim sect which, according to the District Gazetteer, followed a particular school of Mohammedan law. Mullah's text book on Mohammedan Law said that this school regarded a forced divorce as valid since the husband could have refused to divorce his wife. I therefore ruled that there was no prima facie case of bigamy unless and until a civil court held the divorce to be invalid, and dismissed the complaint.

Across the Bay from Madras in the Burmese coastal district of Moulmein, Fowler also encountered maintenance cases spicing the familiar magisterial diet of violence and robbery:

Moulmein before the war was a pleasant town, clean and reasonably prosperous. It had timber mills with well-trained elephants bringing teak logs up from the riverside and placing them ready for the saws; there were rice mills to process the big local crop and a good range of craftsmen to make clothing, furniture, boats and so on. The town stood on the south side of the Salween estuary and had a good service of Irrawaddy Flotilla paddle steamers to take passengers to villages along the Salween, Gyaing and Ataran in great comfort, except in the dourian season when the smell of the fruit, usually loaded as deck cargo, was difficult to escape from unless there was a strong breeze blowing from ahead. Railhead was across the estuary at Martaban and cargo ships loaded timber and rice at moorings in midstream. I was kept busy as Subdivisional Magistrate with a steady flow of cases under section 110 of the Criminal Procedure Code [which enabled magistrates to bind over habitual criminals and 'desperate and dangerous' characters]; we won the confidence and co-operation of the village headmen and elders who came forward increasingly readily with evidence against known robbers and dacoits and we gradually managed to get these people into prison with the consequence that there was a great improvement in law and order in the rural areas. From the town, there came the inevitable flow of assault cases and much false evidence was trotted out, mainly in cases in which Bengali lawyers were retained. A Burmese Buddhist marriage could be terminated with great ease and I think I must have acquired a reputation for sympathetic treatment of these cases for numbers of aggrieved Burmese girls used to come before me with maintenance suits and on one occasion I was embarrassed to have my very nice driver brought before me by his wife; on that occasion my judicial decision involved me in some expense when the inevitable request came along for an advance of pay to meet certain unforeseen domestic expenditure. The lawyers who represented most of the parties in the subdivisional court were mostly helpful and competent, but some made the business of arriving at the truth unnecessarily difficult and time consuming. Wherever possible in cases involving rural complainants or accuseds, I used to fix hearings for the appropriate centres on tour. This did not please the lawyers, but it made the hearings much shorter and saved the parties both time and money. In addition, I felt it was desirable to bring the processes of the law to the people in the villages and, especially in cases under the preventive sections where the accused was before the court because he was reputed in the local community to be a robber and a dacoit, I am sure that it was salutary.

In their court cases, magistrates usually were too imprisoned by procedures and rules to be able to innovate, but in the UP, Bowman found an ingenious and happy way of disposing of two ladies who were once brought before him. He writes,

The lock-up in Karwi was a primitive place. The Police Thana was in the old Muslim fort there and the lock-up was one of the dungeons. It was used only for under-trials, who were kept there for short periods. On one occasion, however, the Police picked up a couple of vagrant women who had no fixed abode and who could not explain their presence in Karwi to the satisfaction of the daroga [police superinten-dent]. He had them put in the lock-up and then forgot about them. It was the hot weather and the women were in some distress by the time they were discovered and produced in Court. I felt sorry for the women and was at a loss to know what to do with them. One of the vakils pointed out that they were not unattractive and sug-gested that they might be given into the care of some local citizen, who could be responsible for them. The vakil, with a twinkle in his eye, remarked that it might even be possible to find husbands for them. The idea amused me. I asked if there was any-one in Court prepared to marry either of the women. To my surprise, several men came forward. A small sum of money was set up as a minimum marriage price, to be put aside to the credit of the women, and I called for bids after making sure that the women were agreeable. Both seemed delighted. They went to the highest bidders and were officially married on the spot. Everyone in court was delighted by this break in the monotony of cases, and the married couples were sent on their way with loud applause.

So far the magistrate has been seen dispensing justice in his court-room, or at least doing his best to do so. But his duties were not confined to trying cases in court. Fairs, festivals, commotions and riots all demanded his presence as the man primarily responsible for maintaining law and order. Though the police had the task of physically keeping order, the magistrate would be answerable if things got out of hand. In extreme cases, it would be the magistrate who would order the police to open fire. He also had to keep a close eye on the work of the subordinate magistrates in his area. This took a number of different forms. In some places, the criminal work was so heavy that there was more than one first-class magistrate at subdivisional head-quarters. Arthur and his successor as SDO in the Kasur Subdivision of Lahore District, Fearn, both recall that their magisterial work was shared with six or seven other magistrates, all with first-class powers. The SDO allotted the cases to his team of magistrates. He himself and one other magistrate had enhanced powers which meant that he could award imprison-ment up to seven years. Rahmatullah in Bengal also divided up the magis-terial work among his magisterial colleagues at subdivisional headquarters, keeping some cases on his own file and transferring the rest to the others. All SDOs had to inspect the courts and records of subordinate magistrates to make sure that they were disposing of their cases fast enough. District magistrates had certain appellate powers, and since all judgements of the lower courts were written, district magistrates and SDOs had to read and if necessary comment on these judgements. They also had to inspect the sub-jails, remand prisons which existed at most taluk headquarters, to make sure that there was a valid and current remand order for every prisoner and that the prisoners were being fed properly. Sometimes, magistrates had to

record confessions or carry out the gruesome task of witnessing the hanging
of condemned prisoners.

This was an experience that lingered in the mind and indeed for Shukla,
as a young officer under training in Bareilly district of the UP required to
witness a hanging, it was heart-rending.

> I got up at 4 a.m. and reached the district jail well before sunrise. When I reached
> the jail gates, I saw the wife of the condemned prisoner; soon she was to become a
> widow. She looked at me and suspected that I had come to supervise the execution
> of her husband. When the prisoner was taken out of his cell, there was a commotion
> in the other cells; all were awake. After farewell and goodbye from his fellows, the
> prisoner was taken to the place of execution. When the deed was done, the Civil
> Surgeon certified that the prisoner was dead. It was a most unpleasant sight. When I
> came out, the dead prisoner's wife seeing me, broke her glass bangles, heralding her
> new status of widowhood: I thought what kind of world was it where someone did
> an evil deed, but another suffered. The woman had committed neither dacoity nor
> murder, yet she suffered and so did the children. That morning, I could not enjoy my
> breakfast. But such is the power of repetitive process that after supervising three or
> four executions, I got used to them and thereafter the experience made no difference
> to the enjoyment of my breakfast.

As ninth Additional Magistrate in Mandalay in Burma, Cockburn had
the same macabre duty. He had to see the condemned man and check that
he was the right man. Then he fulfilled his last request by providing him
with a coin to pay for his crossing of 'the Burmese equivalent of the River
Styx'.

The work in the courts was a test of the magistrate's hard-headedness and
acumen as he strove to disentangle the truth from a welter of falsehood.
Attendance at executions was a gruesome, but fairly brief assignment. But
perhaps the most severe test came in the handling of law and order situations,
as they arose, predictably or unexpectedly, in the field, when the magistrate
was standing by, perhaps for long periods, to authorize any police action
which might become necessary. Two contrasting aspects of the magistrate in
action are given below. In the first, Midgley had a baptism of fire as SDO in
Saharanpur district in the UP, when he was on duty at a Hindu festival and
found a frightening situation beginning to develop. He writes,

> A shrine of the goddess Shakumbar Devi is situated in one of the lower folds of the
> wooded Siwalik Hills which mark the northern boundary of the Saharanpur sub-
> division. The shrine is isolated in pleasant jungle country frequented, in those days,
> by the occasional tiger. Once a year, however, in October, at the time of the walnut
> harvest, the goddess demands that silver gifts be brought and deposited in the inner
> sanctuary, a tiny shrine in the middle of a compound, itself about twice the size of a
> tennis court, the whole surrounded by a high wall. This temple compound is set on a
> hill and access to it is by a steep flight of stone steps leading to the high wrought-
> iron gate.
>
> At the propitious period, some twenty thousand pilgrims camp around the temple
> waiting for the hour to strike. From 2 a.m., it is the object of each one of them to get
> into the shrine to deposit his offering.
>
> The crowds seeking entry to the temple compound were controlled by barriers
> manned, traditionally, by members of voluntary Hindu organizations (a sort of
> counterpart of the Boys' Brigade or the Church Army). They were admitted through

the outer compound gate in batches of a hundred or so at a time so that entry into the inner shrine might be orderly. Few police were thought to be needed to control this essentially friendly, non-communal affair. As it happened, at the time of which I speak, only a very few police were available.

I was duly warned that I could count on no police reserves to help me at Shakumbar and I, the Deputy Superintendent of Police and a small squad of constables, of whom half a dozen were armed with smooth bore muskets, were to manage the matter.

Plainly, we must rely heavily on the Boys' Brigade, etc. It had been decreed, however, that these volunteers were not to be allowed inside the shrine itself for, the previous year, they had taken advantage of this post of honour to pilfer some of the silver offerings. Disgruntled at this ruling, the voluntary organizations took out a procession, on the eve of the great day, carrying placards and shouting slogans declaring religion in danger, violation of the people's rights and tyranny of the Joint Sahib (me) who should forthwith be removed.

My wife and I encountered this procession on an evening walk and waved and smiled at them. A feeble gesture. It would have been sensible to arrange a meeting and work out a compromise.

At midnight, I was handed an ultimatum. Either volunteers should be allowed inside the shrine or the voluntary organizations would withdraw. I refused to submit and sent out into the neighbouring villages to collect as many village patwaris and chaukidars as could be found at short notice to replace the volunteers. This was pig-headed. The dispute was still, at this stage, pretty trivial. But the young are pig-headed. The DSP would have managed it all much better on his own, but he fell in loyally with my plan.

As the sun rose and the morning advanced, it became clear that our slender forces were not enough to control the crowd efficiently. Agitators moved among them and a cry was raised that I had defiled the shrine by entering it in my cow leather shoes. I threw my shoes down into the crowd from my post on top of the temple compound wall. There was some laughter and good humour was temporarily restored... The agitators then entered the temple compound among one of the batches of two hundred or so that we admitted at one time. When the gates had closed behind them, the agitators dragooned the crowd into sitting down and began to make impassioned speeches urging the crowd to attack me and the two police orderlies with me. The DSP was out of sight, hemmed in inside the shrine, and I sent one of the orderlies out by a postern to summon the file of armed police.

This show of force excited the opposition to further efforts. I then ordered the police to load and threatened to fire. The agitators bared their breasts and begged to be made martyrs. What does A do now? The situation was obviously beyond me and I did what I should have done in the first place. I sent an orderly to battle through the crowd and extricate the DSP from inside the shrine.

He took in the situation at a glance. 'May I make a suggestion?' he said.

'Certainly. I have made a mess of it. Please tell me what to do.'

'Well', he said, 'I think we should dismiss the armed police and send for two bottles of lemonade.'

The lemonade arrived. The agitators stood awaiting events.

'Now', said the DSP, 'all the bad hats are providentially collected together inside the compound. Outside are twenty thousand pilgrims whose only wish is to get into the shrine to make their offerings before the propitious hours run out. We must abandon our crowd control. Open the main gates and the bad hats will be swept away in the rush of the crowd. To show that all is well, you and I will sit just outside the gates drinking our lemonade.'

In minutes, the situation was transformed. Providentially, no one was crushed in the rush.

The world in which Thompson operated as City Magistrate in Peshawar in the NWFP was a bizarre and turbulent one, an appropriate place for an unusual magisterial adventure worthy of a Henty tale.

Apart from the dangers of inflammable tempers, blood feuds and quarrels over women, boys and land, there was a criminal underworld which, as in Northern Ireland today, bred its own recruits from adolescent youth. That underworld had the additional complication of gang warfare under the direction of bosses of Chicago type. We even had a replica of Al Capone and we nicknamed him accordingly. The basis of his empire was drug smuggling. Peshawar was ideally situated geographically, for with the administrative border of India only nine miles away and a hinterland beyond it of lawless country bordering on areas where poppy was grown, it was easy to carry in the loads of 'charas', the favourite blend. A man need only to have inner linings to the waistcoats which winter and summer were part of his wardrobe and only a policeman would suspect him. Smell did not matter because he had a powerful odour of his own.

In an Arabian Night escapade Twinberrow, the Assistant Superintendent, City, my opposite number in the Police Service, tried to trap 'Al Capone'. He telephoned to me in court one morning with a brief proposition 'Are you willing to come to the city at midnight tonight and disguise yourself as a Pathan?' I knew him well enough to agree without question; for one thing, somebody at the telephone exchange would have been bound to be listening. At midnight, I cycled quietly to the Kabuli Gate of the city (officially known as the 'Edwardes Gate' after the famous nineteenth century hero, Herbert Edwardes) and was let in. Twinberrow was waiting for me in the Thana (police station) just inside. Later it was to play a leading role in the Red Shirt invasion of the city in 1930. Disguise was easy. All that had been provided were baggy Pathan trousers which we pulled on over our shorts and let our shirt tails hang down outside them. Then we put on ready-wound turbans; they were worn over high-peaked caps known as Kullas. As usual amongst young officials in the summer, we were wearing 'chapplis', the tough Pathan sandal. The city inspector started us on our way and then disappeared to make his own way of approach. I had guessed that we were after Al Capone, and so it was. We were to go to the back of his house and wait there for the appearance of a smuggler who was to pick up a consignment of opium to take down country. My presence was necessary for a dissident member of the gang had promised to betray the rendez-vous if the City Magistrate would come in person. The trust in my status was pleasant. Twinberrow and I were taller than we knew, for over six feet in height, our high turbans made us look more menacing than even the tall Pathan at 1 a.m. in the morning. As we wound our way along one of the narrow alleys (I always imagined they must have been like London before the Great Fire), we heard running steps approaching round the corner. I was ready for a dagger in my ribs, but when the runner caught sight of us he stopped dead, turned round and bolted back for all he was worth. So far our disguise seemed perfect. When we arrived outside the house, we squatted in an entrance opposite and waited. In a surprisingly short time, a light came on in an upper window. We presumed that that was the signal for a basket of heroin to be lowered for collection. But nothing happened and after a considerable time, the light went out and we continued to wait. Then footsteps approached. A voice said 'apne' (yours). It was the City Inspector; he whispered that something must have gone wrong. So we walked back to the Thana where the sentry smartly presented arms. So much for our disguise.

At lunch time, Twinberrow came into court. When we had withdrawn to my room, he told me the story. 'We've been had. After an argument over his share of some previous loot, one of Al Capone's crew had threatened to bring you if he did not pay up. When that light went up, all he had to do was to say "there is the City Magistrate"'. But Al Capone had more than the last laugh. The accomplice did not survive long. It was easy to arrange a murder on the frontier if you had money.

Fortunately, lighter moments did sometimes occur to relieve the routine and compensate for the tedium, distastefulness and hazard of certain duties. The supervision of their subordinate magistrates certainly provided some light relief for Raza in Sind and Richards in Burma. As Collector of Mirpurkhas, Raza encountered a curious subordinate magistrate. He writes,

Rughumal had a foul tongue and used to abuse the criminals produced in his court to his heart's content. He then started abusing the witnesses whom he suspected to be giving false evidence and later on extended his abuses to the Advocates who defended confirmed criminals. There was a representation from the Bar against Rughumal. He was pulled up by the District Judge and was cautioned to be more careful in future. After this, Rughumal devised an ingenious way to defend himself. Before commencing the day's proceedings, he showered abuses on himself uttering words like 'Rughu, you must be mad to work with people like those assembled in your Court' or 'Rughu, why don't you take poison and get away from these people?'. And when the witnesses and the Advocates heard Rughumal addressing himself in such a manner, they did not mind how he addressed them!

Rughumal was very fond of using Latin words in his judgements like 'ab initio'. As I was inspecting his office, I came across the following order which he had passed in a theft case: 'The case is adjourned sine die.' The accused had remained in custody for six months before this order was passed as he could not furnish any bail. I was perturbed at the prospect of the accused languishing in jail as the order was six months old by the time I inspected the office. When I asked Rughumal why he could not decide the case, he replied 'This, Sir, is a sad story. I have been an ass.' The story was that a lame person was fast asleep in the upper storey of his house in Mirpurkhas. His wife and children were away attending a wedding in his village. He was awakened at midnight and saw a thief running away with his purse and watch. He got up, pursued him for a furlong and caught him eventually. The complainant's version was that he could not catch him red handed as he had thrown away his purse and watch in the bushes on the way. None of the stolen articles was found. The accused's version was that he was walking from the railway station to a friend's house when suddenly the complainant pounced upon him shouting 'Thief, thief'. He took the complainant to be mad, but his shouts attracted a large crowd and he was taken to the Police Station. The accused told Rughumal that the complainant's version was 'ab initio' absurd since he was a lame person and could not catch him in a pursuit. He requested the Magistrate to order a practical demonstration to test the veracity of his statement. Rughumal made the complainant lie in his bed and made the accused stand at a distance of a few steps and then shouted 'one, two, three'. By the time the complainant got up from his bed, the accused had rushed downstairs and when the complainant came down, the accused was not to be seen anywhere. Rughumal and his clerk too ran to trace the accused who apparently was a fast runner and was never found. I told Rughumal to decide the case since the veracity of the version of the accused had been proved and to acquit the accused 'in absentia'.

Richards was quick to see the comic aspects of court proceedings when serving as SDO, Amherst in Moulmein district. For instance, he had noted with amusement the solemn way in which a Burmese policeman was giving evidence for the prosecution in a case in which a man was being charged for having carnal relations with a cow. 'I measured the distance', he said, 'from the ground to the private part of the accused and then I measured the same distance to the private part of the cow, and they corresponded'. One of his special joys, however, was to read some of the judgements from his subordinate magistrates. He relates it thus,

U Daung Gyi's diaries and criminal case proceedings, which used to come to me on revision, were so great a source of amusement that I often kept a few of them for light reading at mealtimes, those halcyon hours when, pleasantly tired after a long march, one sat outside one's shack and felt the cool breeze blow through one. In later days when Burmese Civil Servants were better educated, one missed such gems as U Daung Gyi's translation of part of the complainant's disposition in a case of outraged female modesty. 'The accused', wrote U Daung Gyi, 'then pulled my peps for five bamboos lengths.' Or what blither rendering could there be of some heated words flung about in a village quarrel, 'I will cut you with dah in two pieces. I dare to poke with penis even to DC?'

It may well have been whilst reading one of his delightful criminal case records at breakfast time, when one of those sitting round me, watching me eat my breakfast, asked, 'Why do you read whilst eating, thakin? Are you bored?' To which a fat cartman put in a rejoinder 'As for me, I am too busy eating.'

FURTHER READING

The autobiographies of the contributors all have something to say on their work as magistrates, but there is a fictional treatment of the problems of court work which is well worth reading: Philip Woodruff (Philip Mason), *Call the Next Witness* (London 1945). A more overtly didactic treatment is offered by Penderel Moon, *Strangers in India* (London 1944), while Govindji Gopalji Desai, *Some Experiences of a Mamlatdar Magistrate's Life* (Ahmedabad 1906) provides a rare, if early, glimpse of problems encountered at a lowlier level. A standard work on the police is Sir Percival Griffiths, *To Guard my People, the History of the Indian Police* (London 1971). A rather different approach is provided by D. H. Bayley, *The Police and Political Development in India* (London 1969). The problem of communal conflict faced by so many district officers receives special study in G. R. Thursby, *Hindu-Muslim Relations in British India: a Study of Controversy, Conflict and Communal Movements in Northern India, 1923–8* (Leiden 1975).

CHAPTER 5

THE STRUCTURE AND INSTRUMENTS OF DISTRICT ADMINISTRATION

The district officer's title might vary from province to province, but the summary of his functions given by Donnison in Burma applied everywhere. 'He was the District Magistrate and in this capacity head of the magistrates in his district, and responsible for their work, and himself exercised special powers in virtue of his office. He was also, as readers of *Vanity Fair* will remember, the Collector. Lastly he was the Deputy Commissioner and in this capacity responsible for the general administration of the district.' It was this union of functions, this coming together in his person of authority in so many fields, from which flowed the dominance of the district officer in the structure of government and in the imagination of the people. But of course he did not work single-handed. Below the district came a series of subordinate administrations – the sub-division, the tahsil and the village – each with its own officers, and at district headquarters there was a considerable and experienced staff. Swann as SDO in Orissa neatly and modestly points out:

All this may sound as though I was a one-man band. This was not at all the case: my immediately subordinate staff, though small in number, were of high calibre, thanks to the good selection and training of the Madras tradition, and compared favourably with their equivalents in the north of the province. The clerical staff too were extremely competent: many of them were Madrasi Brahmins (like the District Officer), with an extraordinary capacity for visual memory, and what advantage they took – as I dare say they did of my ignorance of Madras procedures I shall never know.

Just how large and complex a supporting staff was to be found at a district headquarters can be seen from even the barest statement of the district establishment. One such list taken from Allahabad in the UP demonstrates the pattern prevailing in the northern provinces where the collector's kacheri was divided into two wings, one handling in the vernacular the records and correspondence of the revenue side, the other, using English, responsible for general and magisterial work. (In Madras English was used by both staffs.) The detail of the general and magisterial work was as follows: the English Office, with head clerk, judicial assistant, revenue assistant, record keepers and copying clerks; the Treasury Office, with head clerk, payment clerk, receipt clerk, pension clerk, personal ledger clerk, special clerk, vernacular accountant, cashier and assistant cashier, stamp vendor, money-tester and copying clerks; and the Courts Office, with readers or peshkars, revenue ahlmad (superintendent), judicial ahlmad and copying clerks.

The stamp-vendor listed here sold revenue stamps which were required on petitions and other documents as a form of fee, the money-tester checked the silver coinage in which revenue was still often paid, though paper notes were becoming commoner, while the copying clerks served as human duplicating machines. (Typewriters, like telephones, were still far from universal or welcome – as an Allahabad head clerk put it, 'We get words when we hold our pens.') In the Courts Office, which dealt with the work of the district officer as magistrate, the most important member of the staff was the peshkar, or reader. Not only did he act as clerk of the court, as Belcher has described, keeping the court record in Urdu while the district officer wrote a written summary in English, but he also accompanied the officer on tour and assisted him in many other ways. (In the Madras province he was called the camp clerk.) Another clerk on whom the district officer greatly relied was the nazir, or office manager, whose role as unofficial house-agent Midgley has described on his arrival at Muzaffarnagar station.

On the vernacular or revenue side of the collector's office records played a vital role. Settlement reports and records of rights in land were permanently maintained in collectorate strong-rooms since they were the best evidence of legal title. So, of course, were records from the magistrates' courts and the property deeds registered and maintained by the sub-registrar. Hence the battery of officials with titles such as record-keeper, arranger, copying-clerk and the rather enigmatic sounding bundle-lifter and weeder. The bundle-lifter was the man who took down and put back the bastas or bundles of connected files which were stored on the shelves wrapped up in squares of cotton cloth. The weeder was the record-room clerk who weeded out records of merely short-term importance. Le Bailly in the Punjab has a lively comment on him:

From subsequent service both in the colonial and home civil services I was never able to discover any equivalent to the Indian post of 'Destruction Moharrir (clerk)', whose task was to scrutinise the records of cases time-barred from appeal, and systematically to destroy all but one or two pages containing the names of the parties and the results of the case. A weekly report was required to be submitted of the number of files so dealt with, together with an explanation if the standard quota had not been reached, to my mind an altogether admirable practice.

Finally, attached to every collector's office or kacheri there would be an assortment of peons or orderlies, bhistis (water carriers) and sweepers. There would also be an indeterminate number, in all probability, of Umedwars or 'hopefuls', young men who had passed a qualifying examination and were now learning the pattern of clerical work by watching and helping those already appointed in the hope of a future vacancy.

The office staff just described was geared to handling the routine revenue and magisterial work of the district. Looking back to the thirties, to the early days of his career, Shukla comments:

Those days governmental activity was limited; administration did not touch the life of the ordinary citizen at many points. Many people could do without ever seeing or meeting a government official; they did not need his permission for undertaking so many activities. The reason was that during the Raj the State never developed into a full-fledged Welfare State, economic development was left to private enterprise and social justice was expected to be secured through the process of law.

Shukla adds, however, that the Second World War made a dent in that routine. The process of cracking the peace-time mould can be followed in the series of Handing Over Notes written by Arthur over the years to put his various successors in the picture. At Murree in 1941 the thumb-nail sketches he provided were of members of a traditional district staff – the intelligent, talkative but idle treasury clerk, the smart excise sub-inspector, the office qanungo on the revenue side of whom he notes 'Certain shop-keepers from Sunny Bank complain that he "insisted on a commission of four annas for each tobacco vendor's license sold".' By 1946 at Attock a civil supplies clerk has appeared, and at Multan in 1947 the office staff in-cluded a statistical clerk and a motor licence clerk, while the single civil supplies clerk of 1946 has become a separate department with a staff of a hundred and one under a civil supplies officer and a cloth distribution officer.

Appointment procedures differed from province to province, a mixture of examination and nomination. A public service commission was established at Delhi in 1926 to supervise recruitment and disciplinary appeals for the central government. But though Madras followed suit with a provincial commission in 1929, it was not until 1937 that commissions were appointed in the other provinces. However, the rapid expansion of the universities in India since the foundation of the first three at Calcutta, Madras and Bombay in 1857 coupled with the heavy unemployment in the depressed thirties, made it possible to recruit even university graduates as clerks. There were, however, complicating factors – particularly the jealous competition of Muslims and Hindus who viewed appointments through communal eyes, the demand from hitherto disadvantaged groups newly come to education, and the wish of the government to prevent particular groups with a tradition of service from entrenching themselves too firmly and exclusively in the district administration of particular provinces or areas. Martyn, in Bengal, demon-strates what problems in consequence arose:

At this time, and for many days before, appointments to Government posts were made on a communal basis according to a prescribed scale. If looked at from the point of view of efficiency it was a most unsatisfactory system. In fact I could fully appreciate the sentiments expressed by a hopeful candidate in the examination: 'Communalism has come like a broad scar across the slippery bosom of eternity.' Nevertheless, in the circumstances of Bengal, not to speak of India, such a system was the price that had to be paid if the Muslims and the Scheduled Caste people were not to be kept in a state of perpetual subjection by the more politically astute and entrenched Hindus. Nobody could, however, maintain that the working of the system did not present problems. Far from it. Thus a vacancy occurs in the Jessore Collector-ate in my time to be filled by somebody who is a member of a scheduled caste. The Government percentage for this category in the office was 15%. Our percentage, in fact, was 2%. The standard of education of those who appeared before me was poor indeed. One, for instance, was a school teacher from a small village school, who said that he was getting Rs26 a month and 'irregularities'. As I wrote at the time: 'Know-ing something of the irregularities of these schools I could understand what he meant. I expect he's lucky if he gets Rs15 a month, and that paid months late.'

I was able to make one concession to efficiency. I abolished the existing system by which the D.M./Collector nominated for clerical posts in the office: instead, I substi-

tuted a written examination plus an interview, thus ensuring that, initially at least, a
reasonable standard of competence might be expected.

Indian administration has been described as khagazi raj or rule by paper,
and certainly paper-work proliferated as administration grew more complex,
more statistical information was called for, more figures, more reports. From
East India Company days government had been one of record and report
and before the end of the nineteenth century enterprising Madras collectors
had established their own lithographic presses to produce their forms in
bulk and to duplicate their correspondence. And by the 1930s khagazi raj
was surely in full swing as Watson's amusing account of office routine in the
Central Provinces makes clear:

The DC was assisted by a clerical staff and a number of assistants, sometimes ICS but
mostly Provincial Service, the latter called Extra Assistant Commissioners. On the
general administrative side the main thing the assistants did was to sign routine letters
on his behalf. When anything so signed had to be published in the provincial gazette,
it always ended in print with '(Signed) Illegible, AC (or EAC), for Deputy Commissioner, – district'. The printer never attempted to read the signature, though it
would occasionally have been feasible.

To speed up correspondence we used a printed form of reminder, enquiring about
letters overdue for reply. It ended with the words: 'Your reply to this reminder
should be signed by *yourself* and not by somebody for you.' The idea was of course
that some subordinate might have suppressed the letter, and if so might suppress the
reminder, to cover up. Naturally this ending made the form too rude to use to an
officer of equal or higher rank; and there was a printed warning at the head of the
form against doing so. The form was naturally signed 'Illegible . . .', as above.

The DC of Amraoti, when I arrived, was the late Mr H. E. St G. McLenaghan. He
was rather slow, and over-conscientious, with paper-work, and had a very elaborate
system for dealing with it. Papers coming in from the district office for the DC's
attention were always flagged (so that they could be easily spotted among the connected papers in the file) with a coloured label headed P.U.D. (standing for paper
under disposal).

Mr McL. sorted the files out very carefully, according to the colours of the flags.
Yellow meant immediate, and received his attention quite soon. Red meant urgent,
and took a little longer. Green was not urgent, and took about two months. Often the
application was for stay for some proceedings; he would stay them pending orders,
call for a report with papers, and then reject the application after two months, and of
course not retrospectively. This was often in substance the best thing to do, though a
funny way of doing it.

He also used to write very long reports to the secretariat, for a reason he once
explained. If one sent a brief, concise, and clear report to Nagpur, someone there
would read it and then go through it with a fine-tooth comb to find some reason to
write back for further information and so put off dealing with it. But if one sent
20 or 30 pages they couldn't read it so quickly, and they would not want 20 more
pages.

For one district officer in Assam, indeed, fame came with a filing system:

I had been critical of the time-consuming method of keeping secretariat records and
the inefficient procedure for numbering correspondence. The Chief Secretary allowed
me to try to introduce a new system of my own though he smilingly said he did not
think I would be successful. Remembering how Kemal Ataturk had gone round
personally with blackboard and chalk, when he introduced the Roman script in
Turkey, I armed myself with similar weapons and persuaded the secretariat assistants
to adopt my scheme.

This filing system, which was adopted throughout the Province, and the compact desk which I designed are my only hopes for immortality, since thirty-seven years later, I hear that the one is still called the 'Hayley filing system' and each year many 'Hayley desks' are ordered.

Through this elaborate office structure and these no less elaborate files the torrent of paper-work flowed. Much of the work was routine, and went on with no more than an occasional check by the district officer, as Lloyd-Jones acknowledges: 'Then, as with all jobs, there were monotonous stretches of rontine. Fortunately the most oppressive tasks of a detailed nature were taken care of by a large clerical staff and the Collector was left with super-vision and inspection only.' Yet it was not always wise to rely upon office staff, easy though that was – the warning given by Shukla's Collector was well judged:

Mr. Acton would give me odd miscellaneous duties to perform. Once he asked me to inspect drug and poison shops in the town. When I asked how did I proceed, he advised me not to consult the *Peshkar* who would easily and obligingly produce an inspection note for me to sign, but to read all the concerned Acts and manuals, understand the whole subject, and then go and inspect.

Nevertheless much reliance had of necessity to be placed in the office staff, given the work-load of the district officer and the requirement that he should spend a considerable part of the year outside headquarters touring his district. Writing from Punjab experience, but nevertheless for most parts of India, Fearn makes the further point that British district officers were often compelled to rely on their senior subordinates because they them-selves lacked sufficient facility in the written vernacular:

All the land records and much of the 'revenue' business arising from disputes and transactions relating to agricultural land were recorded in Urdu. Even those European Officers who spoke the language fluently found difficulty with the written word, especially in manuscript. The D.C. Multan was no exception, and each evening when we were on tour I listened while he pronounced orders on a mass of minor revenue cases the details of which were read out to him by a formidable personage entitled the Head Vernacular Clerk.

Moreover it was the office staff which provided continuity. While district officers and sub-divisional officers came and went at an interval of two or three years at most – and those years broken by training sessions in early years and later by leave or by acting appointments while others were on leave – the superintendents and head vernacular clerks stayed in place, repositories of experience and local knowledge. Arthur, in one of his Hand-ing Over Notes, said of his Reader, M. Allah Baksh, 'He is intelligent, experienced, conscientious, courteous, and absolutely honest. He has a good knowledge of English, and a very thorough knowledge of the *Ilaqa* [area], and the Criminal and Revenue Law procedure. I have nothing but praise for his work and character.' Burma produced men of similar stamp. 'In my office', writes Donnison, 'I had a first-class Chief Clerk, well informed, extremely responsible, gentle and to the best of my knowledge, incorruptible.' This is high praise, but there is much testimony to the quality of the clerical staff – the quality of the drafts they put up, the 'impeccable English' of Madrasi clerks. Some corruption in the subordinate staff there doubtless always was, and during the war years of shortages, black markets, licences and rationing it certainly grew sharply, but happily there was also very considerable efficiency. Perhaps Woodford's comment upon his office clerks in Bengal may stand for all; 'Competent and reliable in their own spheres, a few lazy, debilitated or dishonest, and a few treasures of dependability, initiative and loyalty.'

If the collector in his district headquarters had a considerable staff at his disposal, he had an absolute army of subordinates in the district at large. They were needed. Each district was anything from the size of Yorkshire in northern India to twice that size in Bombay and Madras, and vaster still in Burma. Of the fifty UP districts though some, like the hill districts of Kumaun, had as few as 300,000 inhabitants apiece, others like Gorakhpur, as Radice records, might approach the three million mark. With such numbers it was necessary to split UP districts into four or even six sub-divisions. Alongside Radice's UP may be set Donnison's much more lightly populated Burma, if only to illustrate both the confusing variety of names and the basic underlying similarities. Donnison writes,

A typical district would be divided into three subdivisions, each of two Townships (an unfortunate name since these were in fact rural areas not towns at all). There would be Subdivisional Officers and Township Officers in charge, under the Deputy Commissioner, of these areas, each with a small office of some half dozen clerks and messengers. Subdivisional Officers were normally members of the Burma Civil Service. A few were members of the ICS who all started at this level.

The Burma Civil Service here mentioned was the equivalent of the Provincial Civil Service in India. Both were appointed by the local governments, not by the Secretary of State in Britain. From East India Company days there had been a distinction between the Covenanted Service – later ICS – nominated by the Court of Directors and the Uncovenanted Services recruited in India. In 1861 an Act entrenched that distinction, specifying those posts which might only be filled by Covenanted Servants. The growth of higher education in India, producing highly qualified men, made possible a division of the old Uncovenanted Service into Provincial Civil Services and Subordinate Services. It also produced nationalist pressure for wider access to the ICS. In 1892 a sixth of the ICS reserved posts were listed as open to Provincial Service officers of proven merit, and after the 1919 reforms, a fifth.

The subdivisional level was that at which the Provincial Services and ICS met, the newly arrived ICS man working together with the older, experienced Provincial Service officer at whose hands, indeed, much of his training was given.[1] Flack in Bihar, for example, was trained under such an officer –

---

[1] It is worth reminding readers that officers in charge of sub-divisions had many different styles. ICS officers were generally called Sub-Collector, Assistant Commissioner, Joint Magistrate, Provincial Service officers were called Deputy Collector, Extra Assistant Commissioner, Revenue Divisional Officer or Sub-divisional Magistrate.

'a good tennis player, billiard player, shot and in fact a fine chap of the old Mussulman school' – who had risen over the years to the position of SDO. When Flack was given his first posting he had another Provincial Service officer under him as a subordinate magistrate, Pandit Vibhutinath Jha, a Maithili Brahmin who 'spoke and wrote English, Hindi, Bengali and Sanscrit fluently'. Men such as these, often drawn from locally powerful landed and service groups, were a major support to district administration.

The sub-divisional officers might be resident and semi-independent in their charges, or attached to the district headquarters and so more at the disposal of the district officer, the pattern varying from province to province. In the Central Provinces independence, welcome in itself, was also financially rewarded as Watson records.

The S.D.O. of any of the six residents sub-divisions received an extra allowance of 100 rupees p.m. on top of his basic salary, and was treated as halfway between an assistant and a D.C. He was appointed [to his sub-division] by the government, whereas the non-resident S.D.O. was appointed by the D.C. (from the assistants that the government posted to his district).

The work of the SDO also varied from province to province. There was more magisterial than revenue work in Bihar, Bengal and Orissa where the land revenue demand had been permanently settled, and much concern in other provinces with the maintenance of land records, with revenue remissions in years of bad harvest and with the appointment, by delegation of the district officer's powers, of village headmen and accountants. But the SDO was everywhere omnicompetent within his own area, exercising magisterial, revenue and executive powers. To back him up there was a considerable and hard-worked clerical staff. 'The main donkey-work of the administration', in Flack's rather bald words, 'was carried out by about 25 clerks, peshkars and babus of various kinds and grades.'

Below the subdivision everywhere in British India except the permanently settled areas of Bengal, Bihar and Orissa, came the tahsil, taluq, or township, of which there would be one or two per subdivision, each containing up to several hundred villages. The officer in charge, the tahsildar, mamlatdar or township officer, had like the district officer a trinity of powers and functions. First came revenue powers, for it was at this level that the actual collection of revenue took place – permanently settled areas excepted. Revenue in cash or notes came into the tahsil treasury if there was no branch of the state bank available to receive it, and it was the tahsildar's responsibility to make sure that payments were up to date, using his process servers to recover revenue overdue. He was a second-class magistrate and had the duty of keeping the peace. Outside Bengal where land cases of necessity were tried by the civil courts, the tahsildar also had a varying jurisdiction in disputes over interests in land and land revenue, and with his deputy also dealt with changes or mutations in the land records when land was transferred as a result of mortgage, sale, gift or inheritance. The tahsildar was also required to tour and check the work of the village patwaris and headmen, to report on the state of the crops, to deal with agricultural disasters and report the degree of relief – eight annas, say, or twelve annas in the rupee of sixteen annas – as the case required.

As at superior levels, so in the tahsil there was a considerable office staff. There would be a land records office under a resident registrar qanungo; a sub-treasury, under the tahsildar's own charge, but with a staff of accountants and treasurers to handle the accounts of every revenue payer; a record room with its keeper; a judicial office with readers and clerks attached to the tahsildar's court, and also, of course, the head clerk and other clerks of the general office of the tahsil.

Finally, below the tahsil, at the village level came the last instruments in the government's hands, the patwaris or karnams, village accountants and record keepers, and the headmen or lambardars or patels – in staggering numbers. Kasur was one of several subdivisions of the Lahore district in the Punjab but the revenue staff, described by Arthur, for each of the two tahsils into which it was divided consisted of a tahsildar, six field qanungos, about a hundred patwaris and a comparable number of village headmen. With some two hundred and fifty districts in British India, each outside the permanently settled areas, equipped with its array of subdivisions, tahsils and villages, the total number of patwaris and headmen ran well into the hundreds of thousands.

The basis for the patwaris' or karnams' operations was the revenue settlement survey with its record of the village lands, their owners and cultivators, revenues and rents. The maintenance and constant updating of this mass of detailed information was the task of the village accountant, the patwari or karnam. With the settlement map as their base line it was these men who compiled the year by year domesday books of India. Thus, to look at northern India, in zamindari areas they kept up three main records: the khasra, an annual register, field by numbered field, showing the proprietors and tenants with the revenue and rent they paid and the crops being grown, irrigated or rainfed, with the areas under fallow; the khewat, a record of proprietors' rights in the village and the revenue they paid; and the khetauni jamabandi or record of tenants' rights, with the field each tenant cultivated and the rent payable. In ryotwari areas, the existence of cultivating subtenants was ignored so this last register did not exist. Because the field, not the holding, was the basic unit, the way in which the facts were ordered differed also, with very complicated classes of single and double cropped, irrigated or non-irrigated fields, with a consequently varying revenue due. The official, who was master of all this detail affecting the livelihood of so many people, was quite a power in the land, an essential instrument in the hands of the district officer.

The patwari corrected his records as changes occurred, whether in ownership or tenancy, each change being entered, properly attested by a superior official, in a mutation register. He was also responsible for forwarding a series of statements to the tahsil about the statistics of his village: the area sown, the adequacy of the monsoon rains, the harvest likely; the nature of the crops – how much wheat, millet or sugar-cane, for example; the area under fallow; the irrigation available; the pattern of landholding, tenancy and rents. The patwari and the headman, whose job was on the collection side, thus not only recorded and got the revenue in, but provided the detailed evidence of what was happening to village society in which they enjoyed a position of some status.

And even below them there was a further level, that of the hereditary village servants, as Symington with his Bombay experience explains:

Village servants were maintained and worked on a system which has survived till the present century. They were maintained in theory by a holding of land, hereditary and in perpetuity, free of tax or at a reduced tax, conditional on their performance of their customary duties. These included the daily attendance of a set number of men for any job that might crop up; the work of porters, guides and tent-pitchers for visiting officials; carrying and guarding treasure (especially land-revenue collections); the upkeep of footpaths; the removal of carrion (which, regrettably, they were driven by hunger to eat, and still did so in this century); waiting on the commands of the village-officers; and in general being at everyone's beck and call.

The village-officers the patel or headman and kulkarni or village accountant were also remunerated by the same system, a tax-free holding of land descending from father to son, in Maharashtra known as *watan* (to rhyme with button). But whereas their *watan* lands were reasonably big and good, the Mahars' lands – again I refer to Maharashtra, elsewhere there were other equivalent castes – were more often than not practically worthless. In spite of that they had to continue to provide the fixed number of men on duty; and since they could not survive on what their land produced, they subsisted on minute gratuities and scraps of bread doled out by the villagers.

In their number, too, should be included the village watchman, not a policeman, as Venkatachar records, but the policeman's

agent and ex-officio spy in the scattered villages. His chief duty was to report crime. Sometimes he was also the local registrar of births and deaths. The village watchman did his job for the magnificent salary of Rupees three per month when he was remunerated in cash. He could never be mistaken in the rural parts of UP in his dark blue shirt and red turban – the very embodiment of the might and power of the Raj in the eyes of his humble fellow villagers.

Dunlop brings all these actors on stage as he first saw them in Madras in their village setting:

I was met, when I arrived at my village, by the headman, and the karnam and some village officers escorted me to the choultry, next to the principal temple, in which were kept all the accountant's registers. I looked dazedly at the 'Adangal' [crop register], the survey maps, plotted boundary stones and unfamiliar measurements and crops as noted in the registers. I was shown births, deaths, water-rates, assessments for wet and dry, single and double crops, irrigation details and so on. Then I went out to the fields ... preceded by two Talayaris (village watchmen) with their long poles of office, my peon with his sash and badge behind me, my camp clerk and the 'karnam' beside me. The village headman (who spoke no English but always smiled) just a little in the rear, and 3 or 4 other village menials further behind ...

These were the instruments through which the district officer worked, the cast of which he was the actor-manager, without whom the show could not have gone on. They and the system they operated were 'the product of the Moghul idea of ordered bureaucratic authority – the "rule of rule" – which had standardized the norms specially applicable to the complexities of the administration and had induced a habit of work and built up a host of small traditions', as Venkatachar puts it. But they were also the products of the nineteenth-century revolution in government in Britain, whence the demand for ever more statistics, the growth in government functions and the steady pressure to push up the standards of literacy among office staff and to impose formal training even on patwaris and headmen. The pressure was resisted – there was stiff opposition and strikes by village officials in Madras for example – but standards were driven up, with an 'A' level expected of clerks on the vernacular side of the collector's kacheri, and perhaps a degree in the English office.

To higher standards and better training was added constant supervision. Every office, every individual, was subject to inspection and report. The Indian Civil Service Manual laid down that the collector should report half yearly on the 'character, conduct and fitness for public responsibilities' of his new assistant collectors. Once appointed they reported in their turn, as Rahmatullah describes, 'The Circle Officers submitted to me their tour diaries and Fortnightly Confidential Reports. These helped me to prepare my own Fortnightly Confidential Report...' and the process continued down the line, from SDO to tahsildar, tahsildar to field qanungo.

There was his own headquarters office for the collector or SDO to keep in hand – not taking too much on trust but, as Bonarjee evidently did, keeping them well on their toes:

There were, of course, precise rules on paper for the disposal and inspection of work, but the meticulous following of the rules never got one very far, since one could easily lose oneself in the jungle, and all the more so since one's subordinates were adept at putting up charts and statements for the edification of the unwary which were impeccable on the surface but not so innocuous underneath. I personally found that the indirect method produced far better results and greater efficiency than the mere following of rules. In India where time has always been one of the few things not elevated into an object of worship nor punctuality considered a virtue, an office could be made to function far more effectively by the simple process of the District Officer himself being punctual. Offices were scheduled to open at 10 a.m. daily, and example meant much, for even the most sluggish soul, to whom half an hour this way or that (especially that) meant nothing, would then make it a point of being in his place a few minutes before the arrival of the head of the District. Before starting one could spend a useful and salutary hour in looking over a few branches of the Office. The Pending References charts maintained by three or four selected clerks could doubtless be impeccable on the surface, but this could rapidly be checked by a quick examination of the files on the filing rack of the official concerned. A short round of the Copying Department, the duty of which was to issue on payment of the regulation fees copies of judicial orders and other documents, would put the whole branch on the perpetual alert. The fees for urgent copies were higher than those for ordinary, the normal time for the latter being anything from a fortnight onwards. If the proportion for urgent copies was abnormally high the reasonable inference was that excessive delays were occurring, since no one would wish to pay higher fees than were absolutely necessary for one's work. And there were lighter moments, too. Was the kacheri cat, for example, earning its keep? In the UP every district Office maintained a cat for the purpose of keeping down the number of rats and mice and reducing the damage done to files and papers, especially in the Record Rooms. If I remember aright, the Nazir (the Office Accountant) was given a specified sum on Government account every month for milk for the cat. It was always a moot point whether the Nazir actually gave the milk to the cat or whether he took it home for his children, and I never really investigated the matter since I always found both Nazir and cat seemed happy enough.

And then there were set piece inspections on tour: 'A kind of audit', as Donnison puts it, 'of the offices of one's Subdivisional and Township Officers. This again was a valuable thing; you came across all sorts of odd things that perhaps somebody didn't want to deal with – because he didn't know the answer, or the answer might be inconvenient to someone.' The form of such an inspection, in this case of the office of a mamlatdar (tahsildar) in the Bombay Deccan, has been described by Symington:

The office was a substantial affair physically, often built round three sides of a square, and also in terms of establishment which might number a score or so of subordinate officials and clerks. (A graduate clerk in those days was recruited on a pay of Rs 40, £3, a month. An Honours graduate got Rs 50, £3/15s.) The inspection was a solemn affair conducted annually in every *taluka*. A squad of inspecting officials and clerks commanded by the Collector's Head Clerk – himself of *mamlatdar's* status and a man 'on his way up' – would descend on the *mamlatdar's kacheri*, go through all his pending correspondences and other work; check the functioning of his Record Office, which served all the villages in his *taluka* as well as his own office; analyse the time taken to dispose of matters already decided; examine his magisterial files; count all the balances under various heads of cash, stamps, opium etc; inspect the sub-jail records – for every such office had three or four cells for under-trials and short-term convicts –; in a word check through the whole of his activities. The results of all this were written out at length in an Inspection Report. On the appointed day, his camp being now in the vicinity, the Collector would take his seat on the veranda with the *mamlatdar* beside him and go through the whole report item by item, usually well satisfied but sometimes not so well. The day or days thus spent I used to find enjoyable. It was an opportunity to discuss all manner of currrent affairs. And our subordinates were delightful people to talk and laugh with. Obviously the system gave scope for *sub rosa* understandings between the inspected and the inspecting staffs; but what system does not? Like most other functions of the administration it both worked, and also conduced to the protection of the poor against corruption or neglect.

Inspection, moreover, worked within a system in which precise written regulations provided a strong framework for action – some would say a strait-jacket. The old presidencies had accumulated very bulky volumes of standing orders, but even the younger provinces had their rule-books too, witness Maitra in Assam:

The three great codes of law promulgated in the last Century had put criminal justice in a set mould. The Assam Land and Land Revenue Regulation of 1889 laid down not only the principles but also the detailed application of the *Ryotwari* system and collection of land revenue. In the plains all cultivated land had been surveyed and mapped. Outside the area of laws, central and provincial, where the man on the spot may have been supposed to have some discretion, the Executive Manual (thank God one volume in Assam compared to eight in Bengal) laid down how to deal with all possible contingencies. How earthquakes (frequent in Assam) were to be judged and acted upon, whether knives and forks jumped on the table or the *punkha* overhead swung violently; on what scale rewards were to be given for killing a man-eater tiger and so on. Everything had been thought out and provided for.

But it ought also to be said that it was this very meticulousness, this precise direction which made it possible for the small handful of district officers to keep in steady motion the vast subordinate machine. The corollary of running it cheaply, with men of sometimes low levels of education, had always been to ensure that all problems had been foreseen and that answers were ready in advance.

The process of inspection was not confined to formal examination of records and stock-taking of office files. The administration also insisted that its officers, especially those on the revenue side should constantly tour – and preferably on horseback. With improvement in the road system the use of the car for touring became more common, a quicker method but more remote from the people and therefore somewhat frowned on. But though Maitra in Assam bought a car – 'a secondhand four cylinder canvas-topped Chevrolet' – he preferred an older (more splendid) means of locomotion: 'I revived touring by elephant and living in tents. In the winter this was great fun – breaking camp in the morning, sending the tentage by cart to the next point, and following it leisurely on foot or on elephant's back. At the end of two years I knew all the village headmen by name and sight.' The accessibility all touring officers were encouraged to maintain provided many bits of the jigsaw otherwise missing from the records. Bonarjee comments,

Every village was well aware of the people in the neighbourhood who made a profession of crime, and if a touring officer jotted down the names as he wandered around, he was in a good position to check them later with the charts and registers maintained in the Police Stations. If the names did not tally or if crime continued in an area where according to the crime chart preventive action had already been taken, it was clear that the records were being faked for the edification of easy-going inspecting officers and that the wrong men were either being put in the registers or being prosecuted or both. The Indian police were never above this kind of activity and I found it very satisfying to catch them out.

It was at the lowest level, in the village, where the records were generated which most vitally affected the individual landowner or cultivator, that the effort to secure efficiency and honesty was most intense. DC, SDO, tahsildar, field supervisor and register qanungos, and the Land Register staff all inspected the work of the patwari (and headman), most notably in his maintenance of the record of rights and mutations.

Given that in a single district, especially in ryotwari areas, the number of cultivators ran to many tens of thousands, and of fields to hundreds of thousands what could the district officer, himself subject to posting almost every other year, achieve by all this inspection of his staff? How good could he make the instruments in his hand? The amount of time available for thorough inspection was always being eaten into by the imposition of new tasks on the district officer, very markedly of course in time of war. Saumarez Smith in his departmental *Note on the Present Status and Duties of a District Officer in Bengal*, submitted to the government in 1944 drives home that point:

It would be an interesting though laborious task to compile from the various Manuals the many duties which are laid on the district officer personally. Most of them are simply disregarded, and with impunity, as the Commissioners are generally too busy (or too lethargic) to keep the D.M.s up to the mark. A few examples may be quoted:

(1) 'The Governor in Council attaches the greatest importance to thorough inspection by District Magistrates of the judicial work for the supervision of which they are responsible . . . the questions and remarks which follow are primarily intended for the use of District Magistrates. . .' (Manual for the Inspection of Departments under Magistrates, page 46.)

Then follow twenty pages of detailed questions on all aspects of magistrates' work. Most of my Magistrates' Courts have not been inspected for years, and when they were inspected this detailed questionnaire, which would certainly involve two days' uninterrupted work, was certainly not followed. Any idea of rapid justice in the criminal courts has long since disappeared. All one can say is that the great majority of Magistrates are still not open to bribes.

(2) 'The District Magistrate shall exercise constant supervision over the prevention and detection of crime, for the proper conduct of which he is ultimately responsible. An important part of his duty is to inspect the police stations of his district at regular intervals.' (Police Regulations, Vol. I, rule 31.) I undertook a campaign of inspecting thanas last cold weather, as it seemed a good way of getting to know the general lie of the land in the district. Most of them had not been visited by the D.M. since 1940.

(3) The Registration Department is one of the old-established departments, which is now allowed to go jogging along in the most dilatory manner, because the Collector (who is District Registrar) is not able to give much personal attention to the work. The Registration Manual prescribes 'a full inspection of the district headquarters office at least once a year'. I inspected it recently for the first time since 1937.

How well then could and did the system run? Symington in Sind recorded finding only one wrong entry at the end of his many miles of inspection tour by horse and camel. Yet he sounds dubious – 'This, I am sure, must prove something'. Hashim Raza was more certain of corruption in Sind where the lowest revenue official, the tapedar, wielded great authority since land revenue was paid only for cultivated fields and zamindars were ready to grease his palm if he would show cultivated land as uncultivated – as several successful prosecutions made clear. With Macdonald in Orissa it was the headmen, the sarbarkars who were totally untrustworthy – payments slow and declining – and he was early faced with the task of disposing of 'the more corrupt'. And for Bonarjee there is no doubt – all patwaris were untrustworthy to some degree.

The Patwari maintained a number of Records which were the basis of the Land Records system. Often the only literate man in the village, he would in addition write petitions and even private letters for the inhabitants for a small fee. For his official work he received the not very handsome average wage of RS. 18/20 per month, and was permitted to have a few acres of cultivation. Though cheap and reasonably efficient, as efficiency goes in India, the system was clearly defective. The Patwari had almost unlimited powers in his hand, or rather his pen, since he was in a position to manipulate the records in favour of anyone willing to pay him. Inspections could be, and were, made by a long string of inspecting officers from the Qanungo – his immediate superior, to the SDO himself. Indeed, even the District Officer could join in on occasion if the spirit so moved him. Nevertheless, every patwari 'got away' with his misdemeanours for some of the time at any rate, and much avoidable litigation, and probably some incorrect decisions in the Revenue Courts, were the direct result of the Patwari's all too human inability to resist temptation and to give way to the 'persuasion' of a well-to-do landlord or big tenant. Not that every patwari was unpopular, for not a few combined unscrupulousness with great skill in keeping on the right side of the majority of the people, and certainly with those who counted. In one of my Districts a patwari died worth, according to reliable information, some Rs. 20,000/– in cash and jewellery – no mean sum in the year 1934 for a man who, had he regularly saved his monthly salary would have taken a century to reach it. Yet there had never been a complaint against him. I never discovered the status into which he was reborn.

The problem was inherent in the system. Some measure of corruption, or of undue influence, in patwari and headman at least, had to be accepted as the price of operating the system reasonably cheaply. In the earliest days it was necessary to buy the support of those in the village who possessed power, knowledge and influence. Thomas Munro recognized this in Madras in 1817:

Where there is no village establishment we have no hold upon the people... Our situation as foreigners, renders a regular village establishment more important to us than to a native Government, our inexperience, and our ignorance of the circumstances of the people, make it more necessary for us to seek the aid of a regular establishment to direct the internal affairs of the country, and our security requires that we should have a body of head men of villages interested in supporting our dominion.

By the 1930s the British were more experienced, less ignorant, but as foreigners they still required, and had to bargain for, the support of men with local weight and influence. The village headmen, and many patwaris, came from dominant landowning castes or groups (as did the eighteenth-century English Justices of the Peace), who would accept low official pay because the real rewards, it was tacitly accepted, would lie in the increased authority and status which office provided, and an enhanced ability to injure their enemies or help their friends. In the nineteenth and twentieth centuries the government steadily sought to make headmen and patwaris more their officials, less those of the zamindars and powerful groups of cultivators, and more efficient and better trained. But if the terms of the bargain were altered a bargain remained. The purpose of the inspection was to keep men to their bargain, not to abrogate it.

Part at least of the stress upon touring, upon the district officer always being accessible to petitioners and callers, was that it enabled the government to keep a finger on the pulse of the countryside. At every point on the tour there would be mulaqatis or visitors to receive – as indeed there were at headquarters – and Shukla notes the wide social range from which they were drawn:

This was in the interest of the district officer, for he was expected to remain well-informed of the conditions in his district. Secondly, *mulaqatis* showed complete confidence in the district officer and related their most intimate family problems and sought guidance and help; especially, the widowed Ranis, indebted Zamindars and wards of the Court of Wards much depended on the sympathy of the district officer. Thirdly, the cultivators had unreserved faith in the power of the district officer to help them in time of distress and to protect them from oppression of the strong. They took for granted Collector's sympathy whom they called 'gharib parwar' (Protector of the poor).

It was not just information which the district officer hoped to secure from his visitors, timely warning about a failure of crops, growth of debt, or a riot brewing. He also looked for support in maintaining the established order, in keeping things running smoothly. The official district staff was one instrument in the DO's hand, the other was the small army of non-official collaborators. Le Bailly amplifies this point when he notes that one of the most onerous duties of a deputy commissioner was to

get to know the principal personalities of his district – not only of course his own subordinates – but the principal landlords and professional men and merchants – whose time and co-operation was as necessary to the functioning of the administration as those comparatively few officers who were paid for the job. British India was a poor country and could not afford any kind of expensive bureaucracy. It was fortunate therefore that there appeared to be an immense demand for social status which could be conferred in return for voluntary services. To keep in touch with these people DCs reserved three mornings a week when he was in headquarters in which he stayed in his personal residence to receive them. Interviews were usually about 10 minutes to quarter of an hour for each 'notable'. When on tour the DC was available to local notables for most of the day. Many of them accompanied him on horseback when making his inspections of the crops and the like.

The most common requests were for some kind of honorific title such as 'rai' or 'sardar' or 'khan sahib' depending on religion which title was acceptable – roughly equivalent to 'esquire' or a grant of a coat of arms in the past. Other requests were to be made a zaildar or an Honorary Magistrate (J.P.). Many of course did not aspire so high but sought the minor distinction of being a 'kursi nishin' which conveyed the privilege of being entitled to a chair in the presence of an officer. In fact one of course always offered a chair but many of the humbler – and always good mannered – callers preferred to stand in the presence of the DC: Other common requests were for jobs for a son or relative or to slander some hated neighbour on the opposite side of a local feud.

Le Bailly was here speaking from the Punjab, but the story was much the same in Sind, witness Hashim Raza describing the premier jagirdar of Larkana:

He contributed very liberally to War Funds and when I made out a case for the grant of a Knighthood to him, I stated that his presence was worth six police stations. Whenever my police were unable to trace an absconder and reported that he had moved to the Ghaibdero Jagir [estate], all that I had to do was to write a letter to the Nawab and the absconder was handed over to us within 48 hours! A knighthood was conferred on him ... the craving for titles kept many Zamindars on the right side of the administration.

Equally it was possible for the government to wield the stick of disapproval and loss of status and favour. 'Every Collector', Raza notes, 'keeps a book containing his remarks about the prominent personalities of the district, listing their virtues as well as their vices.' Rewards went to the one, but loss of a fire-arms licence or of darbari status went to the other. One sequence in the Larkhana book illustrates what might happen to zamindars on the wrong side of the administration: 'This Zamindar is a scoundrel. He needs to be crushed.' The second remark, recorded five years later read, 'I have crushed him'. The third remark written five years later still contained these inimitable words: 'Found him crushed'.

In Curtis's North West Frontier Province the manipulative pattern was much the same:

Although the Pathan had never been, like the Baluchi, a believer in a hierarchical society, he had hereditary leaders among the bigger landowners. It was upon this class, the Pathan country gentlemen, that the British rulers greatly relied. Social relations between them and British officers, whether serving in the 'Political' or with regiments doing their time on the Frontier, were cordial. All enjoyed field sports. Such Pathans were made honorary magistrates and were often in request to preside over Councils of Elders so long as the Frontier Crimes Regulations were in use. Their services were rewarded by titles and the grant of Jagirs (permanent appropriations of land revenue). There was consequently a broad target for nationalist politicians to shoot at – the alien and unbelieving rulers and their supporters, the Khans, the 'haves' of Pathan society.

Arthur in the Punjab provides a particularly detailed picture of his collaborators, their functions and rewards. His Handing Over Note for Murree thus describes a certain Government grantee or Inamkhar: 'Has worked extremely well in a quiet and conscientious fashion, giving consider- able assistance to the Police and Forest Departments', and of a retired qanungo: 'An important landowner with character and influence. He may not be absolutely honest but is worth supporting as he can be of good assistance to the administration', and of the suitably rewarded Honorary Magistrate: 'A rich Army Contractor and a loyal supporter of Government and has invested a fair sum in War Loans.' Later, in Attock district, 'remark- able for its loyal co-operation in the war effort', Arthur lists the grander rewards of such collaboration – one KCIE, one Knighthood, one MBE and two Khan Sahibs, together with eleven civil non-official grants of one square of land each, one landed gentry grant of two squares, seven special landed gentry grants and ten Jangi Inams or war awards.

The aid of the 'Government men' was not only sought in political or law and order situations – both Slater in the Punjab and Paterson in the Central Provinces called upon them for funds for much-needed hospital buildings, a little uneasy about this use of official persuasion but content in a good cause to use time-honoured techniques – 'the hint of a title here, the conferring of an honorary magistracy there, the publicity of a huge noticeboard on which donations were written up, with publicity in the provincial newspapers and so on.'

The use of non-official instruments of government was also practised in the towns; the threat of urban communal riots was everywhere met by calls upon the town magnates and group leaders for service on peace committees. And where the aid sought was forthcoming, reward followed. Shukla agreed to dine with the leader of the Muslim butchers, thus splendidly enhancing his izzat or status, if he would keep them all in order, while Williams in Rawalpindi made sure that when certain leaders who had helped rearrange religious processional routes scrutinized the next honours list they were not disappointed.

It says a good deal for the loyalty and imperturbability of the elaborate administrative structure in the districts that it successfully withstood three major efforts made by the Congress Party between 1919 and 1947 to subvert the established order. The allegiance of the non-official supporters of government at times certainly wavered. But at scarcely any point did the loyalty and efficiency of the vast army of the subordinate services suffer any noticeable collapse. Indeed Venkatachar writes, with the politically turbulent UP in mind, that the district administration showed no sign of visible deterioration until the last year of British rule. 'The developments on the political front', as he sees it, 'brought about mental adjustments rather than dislocation at the floor level of administration.'

FURTHER READING

Very little attention has hitherto been paid to the office staffs in the district, their numbers, recruitment, training and organization, though it is clear that head clerks, especially on the revenue side, must have been locally very influential men, given the constant changes of district officer which occurred. (Lines in his ten years in Bihar had fourteen 'principal appointments'.)

There is a very useful survey of the duties and organization of subordinate staffs, district, subdivisional, tahsil and village, by J. D. Shukla, one of the contributors, which though written from a post-independence viewpoint is of more general value: *State and District Administration in India*, Indian Institute of Public Administration (Delhi 1976). A more particular study of the patwari and chaukidar, which questions their effectiveness in one respect, but argues forcefully their power within village society, is by Clive Dewey, '*Patwari* and *Chaukidar*: subordinate officials and the reliability of India's agricultural statistics' in C. Dewey and A. G. Hopkins (eds), *The Imperial Impact, Studies in the economic history of Africa and India* (London 1978).

Much more attention has been paid, however, to the political and social aspects of district officialdom. One aspect explored has been the attempts to prevent particular sub-castes or communities establishing too strong a hold in particular districts, whether Brahmins in South India or Kayasthas or Bengalis in North India – or Anglo-Indians. (Such attempts might be made by the government itself or by a group or community in rivalry with one already entrenched.) Another aspect for study has been the power which officialdom wielded in rural society and the nature of the bargain struck with that officialdom by governments – Mughal as well as British.

The question of balance in recruitment is discussed in terms of Muslim versus Hindu in Z. Islam and R. L. Jensen, 'Indian Muslims and the public service, 1871–1915' in *Journal of the Asiatic Society of Pakistan,* IX:1 (1964), 85–148, and in a much broader way in W. C. Smith, *Modern Islam in India* (London 1946). Government alarm at Kayastha dominance in UP offices – and Kayastha alarm at the growth of competition from other castes, 'Every caste which receives even a primary education aspires to Government service and what was once the exclusive right of the Kayasthas is now shared by everybody', is touched on by Lucy Carroll, 'Colonial perceptions of Indian society and the emergence of caste associations', *Journal of Asian Studies*, XXXVII:2 (1978), 233–50, and the attack upon the Brahmin bureaucratic dominance in South India by A. Béteille, *Caste, Class and Power* (Bombay 1966).

On the power of the headmen, patwaris and the other district officials in their countryside the first major study was R. E. Frykenberg, *Guntur District 1788–1848* (Oxford 1965), then carried forward in time in David Washbrook, *The Emergence of*

Provincial Politics, the Madras Presidency 1870–1920 (Cambridge 1976), C. J. Baker, *The Politics of South India, 1920–1937* (Cambridge 1976) and in R. E. Frykenberg (ed.), *Land Control and Social Structure in Indian History* (Wisconsin 1969). An interesting side issue, the relationship between the revenue officials recruited by Government and those employed by the great landowners has been taken up for North India by P. J. Musgrave, 'Landlords and lords of the land: estate management and social control in Uttar Pradesh, 1860–1920', *Modern Asian Studies*, VI:3 (1972), 257–75 and for South India by C. J. Baker, 'Tamilnad estates in the twentieth century', *Indian Economic and Social History Review*, XIII:1 (1976), 1–44.

On the role of the 'notable', Washbrook, Baker and Frykenberg have all much to say, while for the North three interesting studies are: P. D. Reeves, 'The politics of order', *Journal of Asian Studies*, XXV:2 (1966); and 'Landlords and party politics in the United Provinces, 1934–7' in D. A. Low (ed.), *Soundings in Modern South Asian History* (London 1968); which look at the countryside; C. A. Bayly, *The Local Roots of Indian Politics* (Oxford 1975) looks at the town. The field, however, is rapidly growing; these represent no more than a sample.

CHAPTER 6

THE TEAM AND ITS TASKS

The prestige and influence of the district officer sprang from two features of district organization, one the intimate control which he exercised through the network of subordinate officials, from tahsildar down to village servant, and through those non-officials whose interest in stability coincided with that of government and whose social ambitions could be provided for from government patronage, the other his leadership of all the departmental services. Masterman sums up this second feature thus:

The District Officer (certainly in Madras) is essentially *head* of the District. He is not only responsible for the collection of land revenue, by far the largest source of provincial revenue, nor only the chief magistrate who, though he may not try many cases himself, has to review the judgments and sentences of all the subordinate magistrates in the district, but he is also head of all the other district administrative departments.

The District Officer in fact, with a jurisdiction greater both in area and population than the larger English counties does the work undertaken in England by the Chief Constable and by the County and District Councils in addition to his revenue and magisterial work.

There were in every district several officials responsible to a provincial departmental chief – to the inspector general of prisons, say, or to the surgeon-general, the chief conservator of forests and so on. But they were also expected to keep regularly in touch with the district officer about their plans, and, as Bonarjee explains, all were

at some time or other almost certain to call on him for advice, and quite often in difficult political or communal situations for help as well, the Forest Officer, for example, when adjacent villages illicitly grazed their cattle in his reserves, the Irrigation Engineer when his canal banks were cut, or the Health Officer when he needed assistance during an epidemic. During my time as Sub-Divisional Officer in charge of Lalitpur Sub-Division of Jhansi District, a severe Cholera epidemic necessitated my visiting a large number of villages in the company of the Tahsildar concerned and the Assistant Health Officer. Our purpose was to disinfect the wells and to inoculate as many people as we could persuade to undergo this treatment – treatment which fifty years ago was by no means popular. The Tahsildar provided the propaganda, I provided the moral authority of the Government, and the Health Officer provided the syringe. The combination of the three was quite successful.

It was naturally with the Indian Police that the district officer had the closest relationship. This was not merely a reflection of the fact that the ICS and IP were the two all-India services which had escaped provincialization under the Government of India Act of 1919, nor of the authority which the DO enjoyed over the police, specific though this was, as is clear from the *Note on the Functions of the District Officer* handed to the young Christie on arrival in Bengal:

Though the Superintendent of Police is responsible for the internal organization and discipline of the police, it is the District Officer who is ultimately responsible for the criminal administration of the area. He may employ the police as he thinks best for the maintenance of law and order and for the suppression of crime. The Superintendent of Police works in constant personal communication with the District Officer and consults him in all important matters. In cases of serious disturbance, actual or threatened, the District Officer assumes control.

It was rather, as Haig argues, that to speak of the district experience of the one without including the other would be misleading: 'It is not possible to think of the I.C.S. District Officer ... without thinking of the Indian Police (I.P.) District Superintendent of Police ("Captain Sahib Bahadur"). In this *team* the I.C.S. man was only "primus inter pares". Similarly with the gazetted subordinates of the District Officer and the S.P.' What this might mean in practice can be seen through the young and excited eyes of Arthur writing home about his first experience of city riot in Amritsar:

I have thoroughly enjoyed the last two days, and it has been extraordinarily useful experience for me. I have really been very lucky to have met with a riot within four months of my arrival in this country. These occurrences make you realise how much they depend on the British for Law and Order in emergencies. Jonah [Ivan Jones, the DC] had things taped ... the S.P. Durrant was also extremely efficient. This riot has really had rather a good effect as all the magistrates and Police officials have met together and got to know each other, and the sense of co-operation has increased enormously. The Police have been very efficient indeed.

Often teamwork was spiced with adventure. Georgeson in Madras was invited to a midnight raid with the police to compel payment of revenue by surrounding recalcitrant villagers and distraining their goods. This succeeded – surprise was complete. But what had been proposed as a swift dawn raid became a dragging day-long operation and a nightmare for his newly-married, anxiously waiting wife, since 'the Deputy Superintendent had told her all about the planned raid, saying that it should be great fun because the villagers had bows and arrows and, he implied, would use them with very little provocation!'

Teamwork, adventure, the pleasure which the company of another young Englishman offered in some otherwise rather lonely subdivisional posting – these were provided by the close links with the police.

Amraoti was not an attractive place in May. There seemed to be no redeeming feature and for the first few days I felt depressed and lonely. Some weeks later the place was brightened by the arrival from the hills of Neilson, the District Superintendent of Police, a man of great charm, perfect manners and lively disposition. From him in particular I learnt the supreme importance of good manners in dealing with Indians. I was to have much to do with him for here in the Maratha country there was considerably more trouble from 'civil disobedience' than there had been in the north.

Hyde's experience was certainly constantly repeated.

Yet close as relationships usually were there was also very often a touch of uneasiness too. Commenting on the close liaison between magistrates and police, Lane says 'such relationships would not be tolerated in a Western democratic society though I suspect that the French system of *Juges d'Instruction* comes somewhat near to it. We younger Magistrates were, of course, on familiar and friendly terms with young Police officers in the I.P. We were certainly not "in their pockets" or at their beck and call, but we shared the same experiences on riot duty and at other times.' The practical problems which arose from this closeness are neatly demonstrated by Belcher, describing his period as SDO, Kasur in the Punjab:

For most of my time the Superintendent of Police was Ronald Adam, with whom I naturally had to work very closely and fortunately was soon on very friendly terms. Weak administration had given most of the Sub-Division over to the depredations of the sort of 'robber barons' I had come across with Edward Eustace in Gurdaspur. These had had a long run and were men of far greater and more widespread influence than those in Gurdaspur, having in many cases through forceful or corrupt 'persuasion' of local officials, including the Police, achieved recognition from Government as respectable leading citizens and in some cases had even been appointed Honorary Magistrates. Henderson [DC, Lahore] decided to mount a determined campaign against these men, and since their power and influence was so strongly entrenched he persuaded the Government to post to the Sub-Division a sufficient number of particularly tough and effective officers as Magistrates and as Sub-Inspectors of Police in charge of the worst Police Station areas. The Sub-Divisional Officer to be in direct charge of the operation was my predecessor, Colin Macpherson, who set about it with great determination, and with the suitably reinforced official team succeeded in breaking the hold of the various villains over their 'baronies' and dispersing their gangs of bullyboys; the first and most difficult stage, as usual in such situations, was to persuade their victims that they could give evidence against them in safety.

The pendulum which had swung so far against the forces of law and had been dragged back with such energy and success, was now in danger of swinging too far in the other direction. The morale of the Police having been restored by the new tough Sub-Inspectors and the strong support they were automatically given by the District authorities throughout the special campaign, they now began to take that support for granted and to presume on it to the extent of virtually establishing a forcible regime of their own. That is not to say that they were feathering their nests – though human nature no doubt led some to practices of that kind – it was rather that they began to abuse their authority by employing improper methods of interrogation in investigations. There were never enough policemen to deal adequately with the volume of work in the average Police Station area – and the Kasur Sub-Division had always been above average in this respect; moreover the pay and conditions did not attract men of the highest intelligence. So when crimes had been committed their investigation tended to be by way of forced confession rather than patient interrogation and enquiry. This was often sought to be justified by the fact that local enquiry had indicated clearly enough who the guilty party was, but witnesses – or at least disinterested witnesses – were, as I have earlier explained, impossible to come by; hence the emphasis on securing confessions if at all possible. At all events, it was evident that serious abuses of police power of this sort were beginning to be indulged in.

That short cuts of this kind were being taken was brought to my attention quite early in my time at Kasur by a report of the death of a suspected thief while he was being held for interrogation at a Police Station. He had been a Christian and it was the local British Missionary who came to tell me a story, with many circumstantial details, of how the man had in effect been beaten so long and so unmercifully in an attempt to force him to confess that he had died. I sent one of my subordinate Magistrates in whose area of responsibility the Police Station lay to hold an official enquiry, at which the local Government Doctor gave sworn evidence that the man had died from congestion of the lungs leading to pneumonia; and although that condition could itself have been caused by excessive beating it was clear there was no real evidence on which it would have been possible to bring a charge home to the Police. In the face of this report I could not well act on my own suspicions, but Ronald Adam and I agreed that we must vigorously impress on all the Sub-Inspectors our determination to act against those found using violence to suspects or otherwise misusing their authority. This became one of the main themes of our touring visits to Police Stations – though we had at the same time to recognise the risk of undermining the morale of the Police or of doing anything that would open the way to false accusations against them and so allow the pendulum to swing once again in a dangerous direction. Perhaps our efforts achieved some success, though at the end of my time there we found it necessary to suspend a Sub-Inspector and recommend his prosecution for murder on facts very similar to those related to me by the Missionary. I later heard he had been acquitted.

Belcher has here touched on the great problem for the district officer in his handling of the police. They were often impelled to take short cuts in imposing or restoring law and order and a blind eye had sometimes to be turned to their methods. The young Cowley, freshly arrived in Rawalpindi from England, thought his DC Arthur Williams and the Police Superintendent a formidable pair, ruthless in their pursuit of law and order. He found them forestalling communal violence by a message 'that if there *was* any trouble certain people would be arrested immediately, and would be very sorry afterwards. At a later date some real political trouble threatened. The ringleaders were arrested the night before, held in jail on suspicion for the night, given a medical examination and a large dose of castor oil, then released. There was no trouble.' But at the lower levels the police were not merely too ready to use force, or fabricate evidence, but were often corrupt and oppressive too. Orr in Orissa, breaking a ring of money-lenders who were hoarding all the small change in Angul, issued instructions to the police inspector to prosecute the Marwari businessman caught in the act. 'To my astonishment the Inspector asked for an interview and tried to make me withdraw my instruction, showing me the entry in the police diary which stated that there was no case against the Marwari. I refused and when he persisted advised him that his behaviour was suspiciously partial.' Eventually, put under arrest, the Marwari entered a confession and went on to implicate the Police Inspector to whom he had paid a bribe of Rs 1000 to have the case against him withdrawn.

At a much more modest level there were pickings too. Hayley in Assam, much impressed by the intelligence of his chaprassi, offered him 50 rupees a month if he became his driver – as a chaprassi he earned only 12:

But he said this wouldn't suit him at all because what he was hoping to be was a village constable on 12 rupees a month. I pointed out that I would be giving him 50 rupees a month. He agreed about that, but said that he would make a great deal of money from extorting bribes once he was a police constable. However, later on he said that he was unable to become a police constable as the Assamese Superintendent of Police needed many bottles of whisky, and he was not able to provide these, so he was not selected as a village constable – nor as my driver, though for different reasons.

Yet on the whole did not the system work surprisingly well, given the small numbers and very limited resources of the Indian police? (A body as in Britain practically unarmed, though there were small contingents of armed police held in reserve.) Here is Radice's answer:

The Police were often bribable, but it was astonishing how well the system worked. In uniform these simple peasants forgot caste and local loyalties and carried out their orders. We all knew cases of half a dozen constables under an N.C.O. facing savage mobs and imposing order impartially. The main disadvantage of the system was that a really bad police officer in league with local despots could be most oppressive. It was here that good district and sub-divisional officers who knew their areas could keep the evil within limits.

How the whole machine was articulated is set out with great clarity by Maitra, on the Assam-Bengal border:

In the old Raj, keeping the peace was taken as an all-in job. There was the police to keep watch on the *badmashes* (bad characters), to investigate into crime and take criminals for trial to court. There was the magistrate to sit in court, to pass judgment ending, if found guilty, in fine or jail. In most serious crimes such as robbery or murder, after a preliminary hearing, he had to send up cases to the Sessions Judge. And lastly there was the jail to keep convicts in detention and release them when their time was over. (The civil courts, where litigation took place between one person and another, mainly over property matters, did not interest the executive administration of the district. That was the field of the judiciary headed by the District Judge who was answerable to the High Court.) Over all, and in fairly active charge of the whole operation, was the Deputy Commissioner or the Sub Divisional Officer. Theoretically this may be all wrong. The Judiciary, in the eyes of the theorist, should have nothing to do with the Executive. Similarly the true business of the jailer should be, according to the idealist, to fill all the deficiencies of the prisoner's mind and body – nothing to do with guilt or the sentence passed by court. The *Sarkar* in the old days set itself a much humbler goal, to keep the peace over wide areas, to punish the wrong doer and make crime unpopular. All this was done with an open system of public courts and police stations without any recourse to terror. During times of serious trouble there were lapses into detention without trial and trials in camera, but they were very much the exception.

There were periodical reports from the police regarding crime and also on the political situation, but the heart of the matter was the close and personal contact between the head of the magistracy and the head of the police. Local intriguers, and bad hats, who would have the administration weakened, took upon themselves by flattery, tale bearing etc. to create a rift between the two which wise officers took care to avoid. But the position was not easy.

Why personal relations were uneasy is set out by Donnison who, with perceptive candour, offers a police superintendent's view:

They were of course a particular, and particularly sensitive, aspect of the relations of the I.C.S. with all the other services. A deputy commissioner in a particular district might be very well liked, but the Service as a whole was not. It enjoyed better pay and pensions, could retire on full pension some five years earlier, and exercised more power and more responsibility. It was recruited from university graduates (Oxbridge graduates at that) and, by and large, from a higher social stratum. On formal occasions the I.C.S. took precedence of all other services. (This was all laid down in the Warrant of Precedence reproduced in the quarterly Civil Lists.) Add to this that some members of the Service (and still more their wives) were not devoid of a certain condescension towards those in other services, and it becomes clear why the I.C.S. were often referred to, with some jealousy and resentment, as the 'Heaven-Born'.

In the case of the Police, this was all exacerbated. The Police were recruited straight from school at the age of 19. The potential causes of friction were greatly increased because their responsibilities overlapped with those of the I.C.S., since both were concerned with the preservation of law and order. Yet their respective approaches were bound to differ. Police emphasis was on order – catching the criminal, and prosecuting and convicting him. This was important to the Deputy Commissioner too, who was responsible for the peace and quiet of his district. But he had other responsibilities. And although as Deputy Commissioner he was anxious to support his District Superintendent of Police, he was also District Magistrate and head of the magistracy of the district. In this capacity the emphasis was on law rather than order and he was required to act in a judicial manner and make sure that no injustice was done. This inevitably involved from time to time the throwing out of police prosecutions. Yet the ICS and the Police were the two services upon which depended the continued functioning of the other services, the ability of the ordinary man to go about his business unmolested, and the safety of the whole European population. If anything had to be done it was the police who had to do it, and the Police Officer who had to carry the can.

The district officer's relationship with the police was a very close one and a cardinal element in the successful performance of his functions as a magistrate in the broadest sense. With other departments working within his district the relationship was looser. In a rural economy, however, his revenue functions necessarily involved him in frequent contacts with the specialist departments concerned with the land. These were the forest department, the public works department (PWD) with its two major divisions irrigation and roads, and of course the agricultural department. Officers of all three departments were therefore expected to work in consultation with the district officer. Masterman makes the point: 'The Executive Engineer is responsible to the Superintending Engineer and the Chief Engineer for the upkeep of irrigation works, but it is the District Officer, in consultation of course with his local subordinate revenue officers, who decides when the sluices should be opened to let water into the seed beds and in what quantities.' (And he, it may be added, collected the water rates from the cultivators.) In Madras assistant collectors under training were always attached for short periods to PWD district officers and to district forest officers to learn at first hand something of their work. So Dunlop, in Madras, visited the Mettur Dam and its canal system with a PWD engineer and camped at the Mount Stewart Forest Bungalow in the high Anamalai Range, travelling through the forest on elephant back to inspect the plantations with a forest officer.

One of the main tasks of the district officer in his concern with forests was to help to protect the reserves of woodland, already vastly diminished by the advance of land hungry peasants, against encroachment, since the forests properly managed were not only a direct source of wealth as timber, but a necessary adjunct of agriculture – wood for ploughs and carts, a fodder reserve against famine years, and an essential barrier against soil erosion. Hyde in Berar reports how the struggle to preserve the forest was complicated by politics:

The population and the cultivation of the profitable cotton crop had greatly expanded, but one of the more unfortunate results had been the almost complete destruction of accessible woodland. There were left however still a number of what were known as *babul bans*, small areas of a hard wood, *acacia arabis*, useful for building, for carts, or for agricultural implements. These had either been preserved or planted and were protected as 'Reserved Forest' administered by the Forest Department. The villagers found any restriction irksome and although the preservation of the scanty remaining trees was for their benefit their resentment was exploited by the Congress, a major item in their 'Civil Disobedience' programme being the cutting down of the *babul bans*.

Happily a later posting to Bastar State, a hill girt valley in Central India, four-fifths forest, gave Hyde a more creative role. With a Parsi chief forest officer he was able to plan the scientific management of timber resources and to encourage the villagers to conserve and manage local woodlands themselves.

Forest and PWD officers were not only colleagues whose work was to be inspected and assisted, they were often welcome companions in smaller stations, to be joined on Christmas shoots or in summer swims, or in Orissa, in wartime, in the distilling of potent, unpalatable brews from bamboo shoots as replacement for peacetime gin or whisky. Lamarque in Madras also noted the general truth that:

Forest Officers and their staffs, probably because they led lonely lives away from 'civilisation', also tended to be characters. The Madura DFO's chief assistant, an Indian, was a man of sangfroid. Once, he told me, and I remember his exact words, in accents so well copied by Peter Sellers, he was in camp with Mr Wimbush, his DFO: 'it was night time, and I was sitting before a table in my tent. On my right was a Petromax lantern; on my left were my tapals (correspondence); I was about to sign my name on a letter when, out of the corner of my eye, I saw a tiger come into my tent and lie down behind my chair. What to do? (Pause). I signed my name'.

Other major departments with which the district officer was in contact were education and health, and the newer co-operation. From his Handing Over Note at Murree in the Punjab Hills Arthur shows how much time had to be made for these various supervisory duties. 'There are nine upper Middle Schools, of which I inspected all except the one at Ghora Gali. The model school [teacher training school] at Gulehra Gali under the inspiring leadership of the Headmaster, M. Abdul Hamid, is particularly good, and Montessori methods of teaching are being employed there in the primary class.' Of thirteen lower middle and thirty-five primary schools Arthur also inspected three and ten respectively. As he slightly sententiously noted for his successor's benefit, 'The inspection of schools, and the consequent encouragement of education is an important part of the S.D.O's duties, as the improvement of economic and social conditions in the tahsil depend upon the increased efficiency of education.'

Clearly, however, the self-importance of youth was matched by optimism and vision, for another letter home describes his hopes of radically enlarging the scope of the co-operation movement – in India basically a credit-providing institution not a purchasing or marketing one.

Another scheme which I have recently worked out and started in conjunction with the Cooperative Dept. is a scheme for the Cooperative Marketing of Fruit and

Vegetables in the Murree *Tahsil*. At the moment the *zemindars* are done down by
the Hindu *banyas* and don't get a fair price for their produce. We have set up collecting centres in various parts of the *tahsil*: the *zemindars* take their produce (fruit and
vegetables) to these centres, where it is graded and packed and then taken by lorry to
Rawalpindi, and there sold in the whole-sale market. The scheme started at the
beginning of August and is doing quite well. It may fail now for lack of sufficient
money and Government support, but it has tremendous possibilities and I shall bide
my time and, when in a position of authority, will try to introduce it throughout the
province. If Coop. Marketing could be properly organised and run by Govt., it would
mean the salvation of the *zemindars* in the Punjab, and in India if the scheme was
extended to India. I cannot understand why Coop. Marketing has not been done on a
much larger scale in England. Doubtless, it will be after the war. Of course, it is a
socialist measure pure and simple, but the Govt. of England after the war will be
purely Socialist.

Meanwhile Arthur had to be content with his position as President of the
Central Co-operative Bank and the influence which this gave him with the
existing 144 co-operative societies in the Murree Tahsil.

If the bias of development was rural, the towns were not ignored nor their
problems entirely neglected by the district officer. His role had become more
marginal, however, as non-officials took over municipal chairmanships and
Indian ministers, under dyarchy, took over the 'transferred' subject of local
government. In Burma, for example, McGuire's Yamethin District Council
was elected by the people:

It had a certain amount of autonomy, e.g. in public health, primary education and
minor roads. Its revenue was derived chiefly from government grants, auction and
license fees, and a cess on land revenue. It was lazy and inefficient, and a watch had
always to be kept on expenditure. Other people's money was easy to spend. I could
have wished that more of the members had come from the established merchants and
businessmen, but they were reluctant to come forward. However, for all its faults,
the Council was a useful training ground in the art of self-government. I intervened
rarely, and only when excesses, particularly of travelling expenses, became obvious.
No doubt there was corruption, and a lot went on behind the scenes which reached
me by hearsay. But the Council had this limited freedom and it was not for the
Deputy Commissioner to keep poking his nose in.

Bell, in Bengal, was only a nominated member of his District Board. Nevertheless he kept actively in touch with the District and the Village Union
Boards – 'praising and exhorting the members and presidents', as he puts it,
when on tour. 'The local dispensaries, supported by the Government and
the District Board were also visited and, necessarily, the numerous schools
for which, it must be said, there was great local interest, and always readiness to press for public support, and even to pay directly.' At the District
Board itself:

meetings were exceedingly lively, and I soon realised that the awarding of contracts
was a prime source of interest. There was an important matter for decision soon after
I joined – the award of a contract for metalling a good distance of the road to Tangail.
This had been granted and then revoked, and considerable efforts were made to try
and get my support for one side or the other. I helped the 'Tangail lobby' on the
Board, working with Abdul Hamid Chaudhuri, who was also the Local Board Chairman, and considered a 'Government man'. Another strong personality was Nurul

Amin, from Netrakona, who later after independence became the first Premier of East Pakistan.

The presence of such men is a further reminder that local government was now a 'transferred' subject – and that for politically ambitious men municipal office or district board membership was a stepping-stone and resource base for a political career. If, as Williams notes, there was 'much delay, inattention, nepotism and often misconduct' among committee members, they were all subject to pressures, having to reconcile the Government's insistence on reasonably efficient administration with the private claims of relatives and constituents and risk of exposure to [political] blackmail by the more exigent of these. . . .' He adds with retrospective understanding, 'we were perhaps too puritanical in condemnation of lapses and not sufficiently inclined to try to foster and encourage what was really a plant of alien origin.'

Usually the district officer had only a modest supervisory role to play in municipal affairs, though he was responsible for the management of nazul or government land in the towns or might find himself, as Mudie did at Cawnpore, a member of the Town Improvement Trust busy with slum clearance and redevelopment. Just occasionally, however, a more exciting opportunity came along, as it did to McGuire in Burma when he was Assistant Warden of the Oilfields:

Chauk was expanding, the oilfield drilling areas were spreading, and a festering cluster of houses to the north was in the way of drilling operations. Land was therefore acquired and the Deputy Commissioner, Magwe, and I, planned and planted in effect a new village of about 500 houses. Roads were made, latrines were built, standpipe water was provided by the Burmah Oil Company, and the house plots were made available for grants through my office. The plots were primarily for the aforesaid festering cluster. Eventually, after days of argument and persuasion, about two-thirds of the inhabitants were resettled. The remainder refused to budge, despite the clatter of drilling wells around them, until their houses and the whole area went up in smoke when the oilfields were destroyed during the war.

Chauk having become a town, a nominated Town Committee was appointed, with the townspeople and the oil companies represented and with a company doctor as honorary public health officer. There were two difficulties. One was a ghastly Municipal Manual which was supposed to be our guide. Originally a slim volume, it had grown to a couple of inches thick with hundreds of correction slips. It was quite incomprehensible, so we more or less made our own rules, which seemed to work satisfactorily. The second was the absence of a Sub-Treasury. My office was therefore used for the paying in of rates and all other monies received from the town. As it was a small and insecure timber and bamboo structure, and as receipts were at times considerable, it was an uncomfortable feeling to have so much loose money around.

A Bench of Honorary Magistrates was also set up, with members from the town and the oil companies. I was glad to see it, for it took most of the petty criminal work off my shoulders.

In the Punjab, however, the district officer was a more powerful figure, as Le Bailly explains, since 'quite independently of his position as Chairman of the District Board the DC held a supervisory position in regard to the other municipal bodies in the district. He was supplied with copies of their minutes and it was his job to make sure that they did not misuse their funds and carried out the duties entrusted to them.' Arthur certainly used the influence of his position to the full in securing the town improvements on which he had set his heart, as can be seen from this letter to his parents:

I want to stay in Campbellpur till I go on leave so that I can complete all my projects, which after initial difficulties are now making good progress and should be completed before the end of March. The drainage schemes (Rs. 75,000/– for Campbellpur and Rs. 20,000/– for Hazro) are about to start now – the funds have been provided, half by Govt. and half by the Municipal Committees concerned, and the P.W.D. expect to start construction next month. I have raised the money for the Sir Sikander Memorial High School at Basal (Rs. 50,000/–) and for the High School at Tamman (Rs. 44,000/–) – mostly from public subscription – and have arranged all the materials, and construction is due to start now as the contracts have been given. The Zenana Hospital at Pindigheb (Rs. 40,000/–) (for which Dick Slater deserves the credit) is now nearing completion. I have deposited the money (Rs. 7,500/–) as the public share of the cost of the installation of the X-ray apparatus in the Civil Hospital at Campbellpur and got Government to promise to contribute the other half, and the machine has been ordered from America. Having taken so much trouble with these projects, I naturally want to see them through.

Symington perhaps enjoyed the greatest scope of all, for he was appointed as Municipal Commissioner (Chief Executive Officer) of Bombay. He writes with real enthusiasm about his time as Municipal Commissioner:

I found it fascinating to study the working of the installations of a great city: to become a connoisseur of sewage, to be privileged to pull a fire alarm and time the arrival of the first engine, to hear the noise of the water-pipes as we followed the six-foot mains to their distant source by rail trolley. Even the refuse dumps, re-plenished by two train-loads a day, were not without their magic, when approached from up-wind. I fear I postponed *sine die* the visits I doubtless ought to have paid to the abattoirs and to the mortuary, not to mention its attendant incinerator; but our zoo, by contrast, was pure pleasure.

For all the relationships established by the district officer with officials of other departments or other bodies, the testing time was that of crisis and calamity, when team work became vital. With the police the testing time was usually that of major riots and disorders – with other services it might be famine, fire, flood, earthquake or cyclone.

'As I was leaving for court the telephone rang. "There is a fire in the city – near the Kacherie Gate" the voice said', and that was how Thompson on the North West Frontier was alerted to one of the most disastrous fires in Peshawar:

It was quicker to go off on my bicycle and that was easier to park. When I came in sight of the Kacheri Gate the fire was obvious, for flames were pouring out of a window on the fourth storey of a high house. A north wind was blowing the flames into the city and it looked dangerous. Dangerous it was, for in the few minutes it took me to get to the fire it had spread to the next house, and that was the beginning of the fire which destroyed a fifth of the city. Built mainly of sun-dried mud bricks held together by structures of timber on the lines of half timbered houses in Tudor England, the city was a ready-made bonfire only needing a strong wind to spread it. On the edge of the rising tide of fire I saw a tongue of flame race downwards along one of the wooden struts as if it was running down a column of paraffin. The city had only three fire hoses. I moved whenever I could from one to another of those hoses and to my great enjoyment directed the jet of the most powerful of them down a similar spread until the whole wall collapsed in the muddy waterfall. I must confess that I was still young enough to enjoy myself.

An immediate move had been to get the G.O.C. of Peshawar District to send us a squad of Sappers and Miners. Led by a young officer of my own age, they proceeded to blow up houses to the leeward of the fire. Unfortunately the principal result was simply to blow out doors and windows. Then the Sappers ran out of dynamite.

Another early move had been to call in the Frontier Constabulary, the first line of defence between settled and independent (i.e. tribal) territories. They provided a cordon beyond which there was a mob of sightseers who seemed to me more like a lot of cross-country runners waiting for the starter's flag, this time to race for the loot. And all the time there was the horrible feeling that a slight shift of the wind might sweep the fire roaring into the next door Hindu quarter. Suddenly I realised that the wind was shifting. Of all miracles it did an about turn and blew back exactly over the area it had just devastated. An adaptation of the Elizabethan quotation was appropriate, 'God blew with his wind – backwards'. In an incredibly short time the great fire had burnt itself out and I went home, not to bed but to my waiting court, – I had been exactly forty-eight hours on my feet.

When she had settled back home, ten days or more after the fire, my wife came down with me to see whatever was left of the fire. She still remembers the heat she felt through her thin shoes.

Even more disastrous was the Quetta Earthquake of May 1935 in Baluchistan. 'The city had been reduced to about two square miles of rubble and underneath were the bodies of some 25,000 of the former inhabitants.' That was to be Lydall's first Political posting – Under Secretary (Earthquake) – in charge of a scratch team of survivors, a schoolmaster, an engine-driver, a road-builder, a cobbler, a newspaper reporter and a chemist, working to restore the city and to provide relief to its inhabitants from the Viceroy's Earthquake Relief Fund. Here, however, there was no quick response, rather ultra-caution. 'After the earthquake the military, on medical advice, had sealed off the city for fear of infection', it was only months later that the first exploration began among the rubble. (One group which then did splendid work were the Punjab Boy Scouts who, as Cowley notes, had 'taken on the urgent task of removing and burying thousands of putrefying bodies'.)

Fire and earthquake were occasional visitations. But in eastern India flood and cyclone, and in Bihar and in the rain-shadow areas of the Deccan drought and famine were customary disasters, part of the gamble of life into which men were driven by pressure of population. The 24 Parganas District of Bengal, downstream from Calcutta, was delta country, old mud, new mud and swamp. 'Half of the Sunderbans', Bell explains, 'consisted of inhabited islands, the other seaward half, of islands in the process of emerging, government land (*khas*) to be colonised and embanked when clear above the highest normal tides.' Khulna District, east of the 24 Parganas, was similarly fringed with islands just rising from the delta mud. All were very fertile – and all hideously exposed to the cyclones of the Bay of Bengal. In 1941 it was Bhola, a Khulna subdivision, which was struck, as Bell relates:

Late in May there was a cyclone accompanied by a tidal wave, the biggest disaster which can affect the estuary area. The whole Bhola sub-division was affected, virtually all the houses being blown down with a high proportion of the supari or betel nut trees which were source of an important cash crop. In Bhola town, no building was left standing except the sub-divisional office, the civil courts, the sub-jail and the new district board dak bungalow. The sub-divisional officer himself with his family and others of his staff had to make do with makeshift accommodation in the dak bungalow, and then had to sort out themselves and the business of Government by various improvisations. Their worst task was the disposal of the dead bodies of men and cattle, the stench of bodies which had been exposed to the hot sun being overpowering. It happened that this cyclone coincided with the news of the sinking of HMS *Hood,* and the subsequent destruction of the 'Bismarck', and those events were more in my mind than Bhola until I returned to district headquarters. From then, relief work in the district was a first claim on my time. There was no reluctance on the part of the Government to provide money for relief in the district, and consider-able sums were advanced by way of loan, to the people who had land for security, and for relief works for the landless or the poorer cultivators – though such works were difficult to manage effectively in a Bengal monsoon. Some clothes were provided in the early days after the cyclone, and necessarily there was some free distribution of rice to the old and infirm and the fatherless and widows. Nearly Rs 20 lakhs was distributed in agricultural loans, and gratuitous relief was given to the value of almost Rs 4 lakhs, mainly in rice. Special house-building loans were made to non-agriculturalists to enable them to rebuild their houses. The agricultural department helped by buying seed in the unaffected parts of the district, and the public health department sent us a large extra staff to inoculate against cholera and enteric.

In 1942 it was the turn of the 24 Parganas, or rather of the seaward sub-division of Diamond Harbour to which Woodford had been posted with his young wife. Here, in November a cyclone swept in from the sea:

The muffled horizon was tinged a curious colour. The wind was rising and the flood tide instead of easing continued to flow. The storm cone had been hoisted. The Pilots' launch usually moored out there opposite the bungalow was apparently weighing anchor. I stood on my verandah ill at ease, watching this natural phenomenon, at a loss to know what if anything I should do. The wind rose that night to a regular roar, without any intermission, veering gradually. At dawn it was blowing a gale. I struggled out on foot to the north of the town from where I could see that the river *bandh* [embankment] had been widely breached and water was cascading into the fields. I made my way to the fort in which was installed a battery, a searchlight and, important for me, a telephone – still working! I told the DM of the flood and the near certainty that there would be generalised flooding in the south of the Sub-division, that emergency arrangements should be made forthwith. On his instructions I went straight to headquarters in Calcutta and together we called on (I think it was) Sen, Minister of Works. The Calcutta fire-fighting launch, with tanks full of fresh water was ordered to steam south. Wells would evidently have been flooded with brackish and polluted surface water. The despatch of teams of anti-cholera vaccina-tors was arranged. As soon as the high tide levels permitted the Colonization Officer would organise local relief work to repair the breaches.

I found some of the emergency wells, sunk behind earth ramparts against possible flood, still useful and people trekking towards them with receptacles of every conceiv-able shape and size. We had country boats, surprisingly numerous still, hauled high up on the beaches, cleaned out and filled with sweet water from the hoses of the fire-fighting launch. Rapid vaccination averted an epidemic. But loss of life had been serious. The Colonization Officer guessed a thousand in the Subdivision. One could only guess. On the Midnapur side, where the eye of the cyclone had passed conditions were worse and the death toll very high. For every person probably ten head of cattle were drowned. For many days thereafter the surface of the Hoogly was dotted with the dead beasts, travelling to and fro on the tide.

From rain and flood water to drought and famine, the precariousness of agriculture in India was often made evident. Kipling in his 'The Masque of Plenty' drew the ryot as a man, indeed,

'Whose life is a long drawn question
Between a crop and a crop.'

Cowley saw this vividly enough in Hissar, the Punjab district bordering the Rajputana desert where by 1941 there had been no rains at the right season for five years and famine administration had settled down almost to a routine. In the CP also famine was almost commonplace: posted in his first year to Jubbulpore, Hyde found outside the Circuit House 'a stone cross erected in memory of the officers who had died or been killed on famine duty during the disastrous series of failures which had devastated the crops between 1892 and 1901'. Almost his first duty was to review the need for further relief in the arid north-east of the district where partial crop failure had occurred. Then the whole area from the Satpura Hills northwards to the Himalayan foothills was hit by a quite unprecedented frost – one of Hyde's bullocks died of the cold, marching with his kit to camp:

The crops were in flower and these were killed by the untimely frost: though the actual plants were not killed they produced no grain. At harvest time crop experiments in which one harvested, threshed and winnowed a tenth of an acre, resulted in nothing but a pile of chaff. For the ordinary tenant cultivator and the village labourer it meant starvation unless help was given. For the district officer and his staff it meant first a detailed survey and assessment of the damage done and the needs in each area, including the suspension and remission of rents and land revenue, then the selection and organisation of relief works and the consequent necessity of ensuring that supplies of food grain were available. This last was a more difficult problem than it sounds to one living in a Western commercial economy; the whole mechanism for the flow of wheat, rice, etc. was geared to export, the cultivator's surplus product being sold firstly to the few local traders in towns and markets and then outside the province. There was little or no import; in normal times the villages were self-sufficient. There was no bulk storage adequate for the quantities of grain which if obtainable would have to be imported to make up the deficiency caused by the crop failure. The supply problem was partly solved by the importation to railhead of Australian wheat; but that of course took time.

Since the disastrous famine of, I think, 1867 with its shocking mortality, vigorous steps had been taken to have country-wide schemes for relief prepared and these had been formalised in a published 'Famine Code'. Every District had a programme of works planned for each area with details of where the famine camps were to be sited, staffed, supplied with water, tools, medical equipment etc. Most of the schemes were for road works: the construction and alignment of new or the improvement of existing roads, from metalled main roads through gravel secondary to village and forest earth roads, together with stone-breaking for reserved stocks of metal. Then there were water supply and irrigation schemes which included the construction of village 'tanks' and minor dams, but these tended to provide only for limited numbers for short periods, as did the few forest works, which could be undertaken.

A start was usually made with 'test works' involving a fairly stiff daily task of metal breaking and if people other than professional road workers came to these in large numbers it was an indication that there was genuine need for more relief, so 'scarcity' was declared and the first steps of the Famine Code put into operation. More works were opened, the 'task' was reduced, staff from all departments, particularly the Public Works and the Forest Departments, were drafted in and increased and detailed inspections were made starting with the worst affected and poorest areas. The object was to ensure that the old, the sick, the blind, the lame and those too young or otherwise unfit to work were kept alive and lists were made of those entitled to 'gratuitous relief' as the small dole was called. My visits to these villages where the aged and infirm were brought out for me to see, or into whose huts I went, opened my eyes to the reality and scale of poverty in the country. Often I was shocked at what I saw, and I was appalled by the vastness of the problem which has never been solved! However, our immediate job was to see that no one died from hunger and this I think we achieved. I do not remember having any deaths from starvation in the various districts where I worked.

Another special category for relief was 'nursing mothers' and I had to go round enquiring from the various young village mothers whether they could feed their infants adequately, and if not to put them down for free supplies of milk. This activity by a young man of barely 23 caused a certain amount of hilarity amongst my more frivolous companions, army and civil, in Jubbulpore.

But if there were comic moments, coping with famine was a desperate and exhausting business. Matthews, who joined the CP just a little later than Hyde, was quickly involved in famine work in Nagpur. The first famine task was to see people fed and to open relief works. But there was also the next farming season to prepare for, which meant replacing lost seed and working animals:

For such contingencies the Land Revenue Act provided authority for the issue to the cultivators of cash advances called 'taccavi' for seed purchase. These advances were recoverable in the following three years – assuming reasonably normal years. The distribution on the spot of these advances required a major effort and I shall never forget the three weeks I spent on this work. I issued forth *à pied* from H.Q. in the second half of April when temperatures were rising to well over the 100 mark and the hot winds had begun to blow. Apart from my bullock drawn tent carts there was a treasure cart loaded with an iron bound chest of which I had the key containing just over one lakh of rupees in coin. Two police constables armed with rifles accompanied the cart. The affected tract was seared and wilted by the drought and dust rose in clouds along the sunscorched cart roads. The foot journey across the glaring and shadeless landscape was far from pleasant. At pre-arranged distribution centres my tent was pitched and I sat at a camp table on a camp chair using the flap of the tent for shade. Applicants for seed advances had come in from the neighbouring villages and were marshalled before me villagewise by their respective patwaris – the senior official of the village. Each applicant was sponsored by his patwari who gave a brief statement on the applicant's holding, his circumstances and his credit worthiness. Not that the advances amounted to much – from Rs. 15 to Rs. 30. The application sanctioned, the applicant had his thumb pressed against a piece of inked blotting paper then against his name on the list retained by the Tahsildar in token of having received the money and the acceptance of responsibility to repay it. Although the applicants were dealt with with some speed it was often past midnight before the last applicant received his taccavi and the memory of the ring of light cast by the solitary hurricane lamp on the camp table lighting up the simple intent faces of those honest kindly people and the utter blackness beyond is with me to this day. So is the memory of those burning marches across the brazen landscape during which the skin peeled from my back in spite of the protection of my shirt.

The issue of taccavi after famine or flood was a matter for the revenue officials; the superintending of works or the repair of roads, bridges and culverts was one for the PWD; and campaigns to prevent epidemics sweeping through an enfeebled population was the task of the health department. Such epidemic control might require of the district officer the personal heroism of standing first in line to receive his jab from the hypodermic *pour encourager les autres*, or the posting of police to seal a border and prohibit movement, or, in Platt's Salem District, to isolate plague contacts after inoculation until the incubation period was safely over. A particularly interesting case was that experienced by Carleston in Guntur District, in the northern part of the Madras Presidency which is now Andhra:

There were outbreaks of Cholera in various villages, which were reported to me (on the prescribed form) with the information that the Health Inspector was carrying out inoculations in the villages concerned. However, the disease seemed to be spreading, I found, mainly as a result of people throwing corpses into the rivers, which carried the infection to the villages further down. The wells everywhere had been treated with potassium permanganate, and the villagers found the river water more palatable. The police had, therefore, to be brought in to prevent both these uses of the rivers, and a difficult job they had.

Villagers sometimes exercised some sort of quarantine against each other during cholera epidemics. News came to me of a small Madiga (depressed class) hamlet where there had been cases of cholera. The surrounding (caste) villages were preventing them almost from moving anywhere, with the consequence that they could not get to any shops or get food supplies or anything else. So we took food and paraffin there, and set up a temporary hospital. They were most grateful – above all for the paraffin, as they had been in darkness for some days, which made their suffering far worse. I later received a touching letter of thanks.

What Carleston noted, however, was that beyond prevention and quarantine nothing was done to help those who caught the disease:

Nothing was done for the patients. I learned that saline drip treatment could be effective if given in the early stages before dehydration had gone too far. So the American Baptist Missionary doctors organised a mobile unit to visit the worst affected villages and give treatment in hastily arranged temporary 'hospitals' – barns or sheds being used, as available, for this purpose. This was soon officially taken up, and Government mobile medical units were organised.

Azim Husain, visiting his own village in Jaranwala sub-division in the Punjab, found similar distressing evidence of health department neglect there:

I visited all the huts of the peasants and saw a boy lying on a 'charpie' (cot). I asked the reason and was told that he has been laid up for the last four months on account of a bad sore on his right leg. He was kept for two months in a civil dispensary in Jaranwalla and then sent away uncured and the parents of the boy were told to take him to a hospital in Lyallpur, the District headquarters, for further treatment. Civil dispensaries are supposed to be free but unless the attendant surgeon and the compounder get a reasonably handsome bribe they pay no heed to the peasants. In this case the paying capacity of the poor parents of the boy had come to an end and therefore they were asked to go. They had no money to go to Lyallpur and did not go there. They might have borrowed but they were told and believed that if they go to a hospital the leg of the boy was sure to be amputated, so it is best not to go. The boy had been lying in horrible pain for the last two months. When I asked them why they didn't do something about it, they turned round and said 'It is the Will of God and his Will must be done.'

It was in such cases, or in emergencies, that the voluntary agencies came into their own – the Scouts and Guides, members of the Seva Samiti or, as Carleston related, missionaries. The medical work of missionaries was everywhere welcome – some individuals indeed achieved an India-wide reputation, witness the little ditty recorded by Lydall about Dr Henry Holland:

> Put a needle in his hand
> Cataract will flee the land.

Just how Dr Holland came to be so immortalized can be understood, perhaps, from Barty's account of him at work at Shikarpur in Sind:

For about six weeks every cold weather, the district bungalow at Shikarpur was given over to Dr. Henry Holland (later Sir Henry). He ran a Mission Hospital in Quetta where he won a world-wide reputation as an eye specialist. Each year he would bring a party of doctors and nurses down to Shikarpur to treat people from all over upper Sind. Rows of brushwood and straw huts would be built in which string cots were installed for the patients. Relatives came to feed and tend them. Then a marathon session would begin, with cataracts being flipped out like shelling peas. Sir Henry had an idea that the prevalence of cataract in Sind may have to do with the dusty atmosphere or the muddy water. Primitive though the conditions of this field hospital were, the liberal use of strong disinfectants seemed to be effective, supported no doubt by the natural immunity of the patients.

Curtis, at Tank in Waziristan, was no less impressed by the work of three women missionaries there, of whom he offers a delightful portrait:

They had set up their hospital to care for women, particularly Mahsud women. It remained open from September to the end of May by which time all tribal women had sought refuge from the heat in their native hills. They made no attempt at conversion. To do so would have invited assassination. But a chapter of the gospels in Pushtu was read in the wards daily. To this no Muslim could take objection as Jesus (Isa) is reverenced as a great prophet by Islam, a compliment which, sadly enough, is not reciprocated by Christendom. The Ladies were greatly respected and they could drive their mission van along frontier roads without fear of ambush.

The physician and surgeon was Dr. Maidie Shearburn. Her slight figure, blue eyes, and fair hair gave her a totally misleading appearance of fragility. She was a skilful surgeon, so greatly esteemed that the Mahsuds asked for a Men's Ward to be opened. To it desperately wounded men, casualties of tribal conflict, would be borne, to be saved if their arrival had not been unduly delayed.

Dr. Shearburn gained special fame for providing women with new noses. In the lower ranks of society it was the practice for a husband who suspected his wife of having taken a lover to cut off the end of her nose. This solved the lover problem and did not deprive the husband of his wife's services. (If a man had any pretensions to gentility he killed an erring wife.) Dr. Shearburn evolved an operation by which surplus flesh was gradually transferred to the patient's face and eventually to her nose. She was able to choose a becoming shape. I cannot say to what extent the operation improved the woman's looks because I was never allowed into the Women's Wards. But it was a popular operation so I suppose it did.

The Hospital Matron was Miss Vera Studd of the missionary–cricketing–City of London family. On her rested the running of the hospital, and the training and disciplining of the Pathan girls who had to be taught nursing. She had a fine command of Pushtu and had been a member of the team responsible for the Pushtu version of the gospels, a task admirably carried out.

The Administrator was Miss Ethel Hadow. The hospital had to be economically managed and much of its food and other supplies was grown on the little farm attached to it. Miss Hadow was the daughter of a clergyman and with her white hair and rubicund complexion looked like an XVIIIth century parson.

The missionaries were also very active in education, and had played a most important role in South India – Carleston comments upon the fine independent secondary schools in Bangalore, Roman Catholic (St Joseph's), Anglican (Bishop Cotton's) and Methodist, for boys and girls – and in Bengal and the north eastern hills, of which Bowman writes appreciatively.

But despite this good work, educational and medical, and the fact that very often it was to a mission hospital that the district officer turned when wife or children fell ill, the relationship of the district officer with the missionary was an uneasy one. As a proselytizing body missionaries introduced one more religious division into a country already, in the official's eye, too much so divided. Moreover the various Christian missions did not always work harmoniously among themselves, free of sectarian feeling and nor, it must be said, did missionaries see eye to eye with officialdom in social and political matters. Missionaries as well as Congress attacked government excise policies as an encouragement or condonation of the demon drink, their work with low castes upset that hierarchy in the countryside which officials often accepted and used, and missionaries such as C. F. Andrews showed themselves sympathizers with Congress rather than the Raj. Perhaps district officers were always a little put out by the presence of rival claimants to authority and allegiance in their territory!

This official ambivalence comes through very clearly in Belcher's account of his service in the Kasur sub-division of Lahore:

Missionaries were an interesting feature of District life; and not always an unmixed blessing to the District Officer. On the whole the chances of converting to Christianity members in good standing of the Muslim, Hindu, or Sikh communities were pretty slim, so those whose aim was conversion had usually to concentrate on those of low social standing, the lowest castes or outcasts among the Hindus, and those on the comparable fringes of the other communities, whose life was harshest and whose adherence to their established religious group weakest. These naturally tended to include in their numbers the petty thieves and other minor criminals, and one of the paths to successful conversion was for the Missionary to take up their cases and demonstrate a special influence on their behalf with the District authorities. This was sometimes attempted with indiscreet, or at least indiscriminate, zeal – all the more because of the rivalry for converts that seemed often to exist between the missions from the various branches of the Christian Church. These ranged from the sandal-shod Belgian Catholic fathers who lived almost as simply as their flock and were often to be seen cycling cheerfully in their rough cassocks along the hot dusty dirt paths in the remoter areas, to the Americans or Canadians living with their families in houses made comfortable with many North American comforts. Besides these there were some admirable medical missionaries, among whom I remember especially a remarkable and devoted group of Finnish ladies who lived and worked in the Gurdaspur area; some of them came from remote villages within the Arctic Circle which they were only very rarely able to revisit.

The problem which the missionary posed was sometimes obvious enough – as when Jehovah's Witnesses began touring the Roman Catholic quarter of Bangalore with loud speaker vans, blaming the Pope for starting the War, a habit which Carleston had to stop in order to prevent a riot, or when missionary work in the Lushai Hills led to revivalism among the Christian tribal people, 'when its subjects "spoke with tongues", danced wildly, and worked themselves into a state of hysteria in which they could be dangerous' as Bowman reports. Christie, just across the border in the Chittagong Hill tracts, gives the other side of the picture – 'My Lushais claimed that they had migrated to avoid the attentions of missionaries in Assam, who insisted on making them wear trousers and topis [pith helmets] although they preferred their home-woven plaids and feathers in their hair.' McGuire in the Kachin hill country of Burma voiced a more diffused concern at the disruption which conversion might cause. 'We had the American Baptist Mission, the Bible Churchmen's Missionary Society, and the Jesuits, all as it were competing for the souls of the Kachins. There was the possibility of families being divided against themselves, between animists and Christians of one sort or another.' If McGuire felt unhappy about the process of conversion, Orr in Orissa quite positively disliked it. He was full of praise for the mission-run zenana hospital for Indian women at Berhampur, and for the cheerful acceptance of a life-time of self-denial by Spanish Jesuit priests who had left Spain as young men to spend their lives in Orissa, and indeed to die there without ever returning home. But it is clear that he was totally out of sympathy with the assumptions underlying much missionary work in India:

One of the effects of British Imperialism in India which I always considered to be among the least creditable was the encouragement given to Christian missionaries to proselytise their religion. It seems to me presumptuous in the extreme for any religion to claim that it is 'better' than any other, and when it comes to proclaiming that a particular sect such as Baptist, Jesuit, Church of England, Church of Scotland is again 'better' or 'truer' than the others the situation becomes ludicrous. I have no objection to, indeed I applaud, Christians who because of their religious convictions are prepared to devote their lives to healing the sick or teaching the poor. If they restrict their activities to these services they should be welcome in any community; but when they also preach that the religious bonds which provide the cultural base of that community are false or mistaken, they negate all the good they have done and ultimately destroy the community. This process was seen most dramatically in some of the tribal communities in the Agency Areas of Orissa. The animist beliefs which had enabled these primitive tribes to survive into the 20th Century still as coherent and strictly-ordered social organisations, were discredited and dislodged to make way for the extraordinary and equally irrational notions and dogmas of the Christian missionaries. But the new set of beliefs instilled by the missionaries proved to be an inadequate substitute for the old set under which the community had thrived. Social and moral values suffered. Statistics in Berhampur showed, after the establishment of a Christian mission, that the crime rate, venereal disease and prostitution all increased. On one occasion in 1945 I visited a village (not in the Agency Area) which was described as a Christian village and where there had been some outbreaks of violence between Hindus and Christians. When I arrived there the villagers assured me that in future everything would be fine, as they had held a public meeting at which they had decided to reject Christianity and revert to Hinduism. I commended their decision and assured them that I would discourage any attempts by the missionaries to win them back again. On my way back to Berhampur I called in at the mission headquarters and gave them my news and views.

The same ambivalence was to be found in relations with the European business community in India. Their overall significance in the Raj is very pungently put by Maitra, in whose province of Assam they were of course a more pervasive and powerful element than was usual:

Whatever advance was made in the political or administrative field, there was hardly any change in the basic colonial economic pattern of the Raj till its last day. In fact it may be argued that the stagnation in economic field led to excessive importance being given to politics and the capture of power. The administration especially in the Punjab, was all for the *kisan* and all against the native *bania* but could say very little against the British bania.

If the Assam Government had taken a vivid interest in the country and the people it was a thing of the past. The thing that really mattered was the tea industry. The importance of this industry in a backward agricultural province may well be imagined. The tea companies were mostly British owned. Nine out of ten of the Managers were Scots. The industry was well organised in local 'Circles' of the Indian Tea Association [I.T.A.]. The 'Circles' in their turn were grouped into district Associations of Assam Valley and Surma Valley. The I.T.A. had its apex at Calcutta. The planting industry was represented in the provincial Legislative Assembly by several members. In my time they were led by an ex-I.C.S. man from Bihar, Hardman by name – a switch over from public service to private sector which became a flood after Independence. The Governor kept close touch with senior planters and stayed with the Superintendents of some of the bigger tea companies like the Jorehaut Company and Bishnunath Tea Co. The bungalows of these *burra Sahibs* were very large and very comfortable. The planting group in the Assembly kept very close to Government House. During the war, tea plantations supplied a large number of labourers for the building of military roads like the Ledo road and the Kohima road. Government of Assam sometimes corresponded directly with the Chairman or Secretary of the I.T.A. branches at Dibrugarh and Silchar. I was two years Deputy Commissioner at Silchar and saw a lot of the local I.T.A. secretary Nobby Clark who was very proud of his decoration C.I.E. (Companion of the Indian Empire), and behaved almost as if he was the Government of Assam. In Assam, particularly during the war, the I.T.A. was an *imperium in imperio*.

Bell's comments on the planters he knew in Siliguri, below Darjeeling, are less acid – indeed he is sympathetic to the young planters, hard hit in 1932 by the world recession, and of their seniors writes, 'I may have started my stay in Siliguri somewhat apprehensive about my relations with the planters ... on reputation, not quite my type. However I came to be on good friendly terms with the garden managers whom I met, and particularly with the more senior or publicly active of them who served on official bodies.' Nevertheless he too notes the power they exerted, connecting the existence of very good roads in the district with the strong European planter representation on the Board.

Elsewhere in India it was with such industries as iron and steel, coal and cement, or up-country cotton mills that the district officer was most in contact – often over strikes or labour disputes. The railway, coal and iron town of Asansol in Bengal, or Raniganj nearby with its paper, ceramics and aluminium works, with 70,000 mine workers and another 70,000 in industry are cases in point. On them Woodford has this to say:

The greater part of the labour force (for coal, iron and steel) was recruited by labour contractors outside the province. The SDO was concerned with their, relatively so poor, living conditions, their health, their inter-communal quarrels, and their quarrels with the management and with the native Bengalis of the villages near the mines and factories; concerned also with the growing interest and initiatives of the Government of India. One felt that Asansol was an important productive region for India at war; one also had many friends among the managements and this made social life more interesting; yet, on the whole, the sense prevailed of living in an industrial world which had not enriched the lives of workers, in which few cultural affinities between workers and villagers had been established, in which living conditions of workers in their *dhowras* [slums] were poor and without any aesthetic quality.

I asked myself whether the time would ever come when ordinary labourers, coolies and cultivators would be able, like clerks, to buy a little more cloth, a little more kerosene and some sugar, an umbrella, gym shoes, perhaps even a bicycle. The circulation of money had increased in Asansol – to the advantage of big landholders, wholesale merchants, contractors and, no doubt, industrial management. Meanwhile the controlled distribution from my office of opium took place as it had always done. The scent of opium would drift from the villages in the evening. At least there was the occasional luxury of the opium dream.

Meanwhile it was the task of Woodford, as District Officer, to preside over the Mines Board of Health:

Almost all the mines were represented. Financing was by a minute cess on coal tonnage. Dr Sen, a grey, faded, bald-pated, stooping, bespectacled, ageless gentleman, who lived next door but one to me, was the executive officer. He commanded a few inspectors and vaccinators but he did not see his mission in ambitious terms: the means were small. Only one of the mines delegates on the Board (Evans of Turner Morrison Co.) was openly ready to support a proposal for a considerable raising of the cess. Sanitary and living conditions in the coal field remained primitive. Dr Sen's surplus energy flowed into charitable work in the town. But things were destined to change. A Mr Young was sent out from England as Coal Commissioner with the Government of India. He was concerned mainly to increase production which also involved arrangements for supply of housing and rations to workers whose attendance was regular. The Government of India, perceiving that productivity is related to health and welfare, set up a new institution for the Bengal and Bihar coalfields financed by a much bigger cess on coal production. Dr Sen and the members heard with surprise and mixed feelings how they had been outflanked; the new Welfare Commission would be undertaking malaria control, and would establish a hospital and a new township specially for colliery labour! Evans, the exceptional mine manager, smiled and so did I.

For Woodford it was the contrast between the living conditions of European management and Indian labour which jarred; for Watson and Dunlop it was the manners of mine manager or box-wallah (businessman) – who 'spoke to the labour force in a rather basic jargon, akin to what was called memsahibs' Hindi. The word *balari* (bloody) was much used' or who proved a 'blustering, swearing type of Englishman' – which grated; but to others the offence was the businessman's assumption that fellow Britishers in the ICS would take his side even when that conflicted with the good of the people in his charge. In Bihar, for example, with its industry, mining and the great steelworks at Jamshedpur, district officers like Lines could find themselves involved in difficult labour problems and not seeing eye-to-eye with management. Similarly Solomon, at Hazaribagh, when a strike broke out in the Giridih collieries, 'as chief Magistrate in the sub-division, [I] tried to hold a balance between Government (of India) as employer and the workers. I fear my detached attitude was not to the liking of the Colliery

Superintendent. . . .' And at Madura in Madras, where the second biggest cotton mill in the world, that of A. and F. Harvey Ltd, employed 15,000 workers, a similar situation arose when they came out on a strike with which Lamarque was involved:

Predictably enough, the new Congress Government was sympathetic to any workers' grievances, especially when the employers were European, and so it behoved any European collector to tread very delicately. A firm hand with the strikers was likely to be deprecated.

These difficulties were illustrated shortly after my arrival. The Madura Mills remained closed for some weeks by reason of a strike. Eventually the management decided to re-open the Mills, but with a reduced work-force. At this, Westlake, under instructions from the Congress Government, issued an order under section 144 of the Criminal Procedure Code, prohibiting the re-opening of the Mills for a month, on the grounds that the opening was likely to lead to a breach of the peace, since the strikers would picket the Mills and try to prevent the other workers entering. It was the first time such an order had ever been issued against a management, and was sharply criticised by the Europeans, as improper interference with the management's legitimate rights.

Coupled with this uneasy tension between support for European business interests and concern for the Indian worker went some uneasiness in social relationships too. There was perhaps a certain disdain for the stuffiness of senior management circles in the metropolitan cities. Lamarque's comment on Madras is brief but tart: 'like Calcutta, though to a lesser extent, its society was dominated by the European businessman, who, with a few notable exceptions, tended to be narrow politically and quite unprepared for change'. The district officer might show, as Lydall did, a cheerful enough acceptance of the planters' boisterous, hard-drinking style, but coupled it like Lamarque with a clear awareness of intellectual superiority.

The last important group with which the district officer was in regular contact was that of his seniors in the ICS, the commissioner and the provincial and central secretaries. Commissioners sometimes seemed rather shadowy figures, fifth wheels on the car, men honourably retired from real work in the district. Martyn, however, had a clear part for his Commissioner to play:

In my experience I did not see the Commissioner in the role of either an initiator or as a co-ordinator. I saw him as the one to encourage. In fact he was particularly valuable when he was on my side in the perpetual warfare that I was waging in an attempt to obtain 'justice' out of Government on every front – not only in matters directly affecting law and order but also in the fields such as Education, Public Health, Irrigation and Agriculture. And here it was always a battle to know how to get the officers of these specialised departments to visit you (for each D.M. thought of himself as the only pebble on the beach). Thus in May 1937 the Deputy Director of Agriculture visited me in Jessore Town. He had come down for one day only, without giving any proper warning: I wanted him to come down for a week and go on a long tour with me.

With the Secretariats staffed by men from the districts who in most cases would return to district work, relationships might have been expected to be easy, but curiously they were not always so, as Midgley on appointment to a Civil Defence Committee of the UP discovered:

Micky Nethersole, Commissioner of Lucknow, objected to the presence of an officer as junior as myself at the centre of the Provincial administration. He protested to the Chief Secretary. I was a mere dogsbody but Nethersole thought I ought to be out in the districts. District Officers in general despised Secretariat wallahs. In particular to seek a post in the Government of India, except as a final stepping stone to a Provincial Governorship, was regarded as a sort of treachery.

Just as the Districts despised the Provincial Secretariat in Lucknow, so the Secretariat in Lucknow despised the Imperial Secretariat in New Delhi. For instance, we ran our own peculiar form of rationing. The Government of India had appointed a Rationing Adviser seconded from the Ministry of Food in Whitehall. He came to Lucknow and instructed us to conform to the model scheme which had been introduced with his approval in Bombay. We simply told him that we wouldn't. He didn't believe we couldn't, but we didn't. Our independent ways were not disapproved of by the Governor, Sir Maurice Hallett. The Governor once sent for me to complain about some elaborate directive I had sent round to the districts. I said I had only précised some even more elaborate stuff from the Government of India. 'Government of India', he said, 'what do they know about it?'.

This bloody-minded attitude was healthy. It promoted practical administration and discouraged red tape. At the same time, the fact that key posts from the Government of India downwards were staffed by the ICS kept a sufficient reinforcing thread running through the whole fabric. You never quite knew that you might not find yourself receiving in one capacity the instructions or criticisms you had issued in another. The sense of unity in the service was further fostered by the pay structure. Pay was graded according to seniority in the service rather than by post. Governors and High Court Judges were an exception, but even they drew the standard £1,000 per annum pension which applied to all. Ambition tended, therefore, towards getting the right job and doing it well rather than towards promotion for its own sake. The District Magistrate in a tough post like Cawnpore was as happy as any of his colleagues enjoying the fat of the land in Lucknow or Delhi.

The antipathies between province and centre were in part the natural consequence of the great diversity of India which made it difficult to plan for the whole and yet to accommodate regional difference. But the tensions which developed between district officer and provincial secretariat could scarcely all be attributed to geography. Slater offers one possible line of explanation which has considerable plausibility:

Could inadequacy of communication have had something to do with the perennial antagonism between District Officers and the Secretariat? I was never able to find a satisfactory explanation for this phenomenon. At first I thought it was a time honoured joke: that convention required the District Officer to rail at those numskulls in Lahore. But it went deeper than that: there was often real bitterness. This might have been understandable had the Secretaries to Government been a race apart, with no direct experience of district administration. But they were not. With regular transfers between Headquarters and the field there should have been no obstacle to comprehension. Yet somehow the gap was never bridged, the feeling of 'them' and 'us' persisted and there were few files that did not carry their quota of acrimonious exchanges.

Despite this unfortunate tradition few district officers seem to have disliked their period in the secretariat, though not all were found to have the aptitudes – financial for example –which were required – and nearly all were impressed by the high quality of secretariat staff. Listen, for example, to Martin at Patna extolling 'the immensely active secretariat staff of intelligent and hardworking clerks, collecting and collating "necessary papers", drafting letters, consulting other departments, and always exerting a firm and infinitely polite pressure to see that the officials above them conformed to precedent'. Or to Midgley at Cawnpore:

The war brought to an end an age of leisure and dignity in the transaction of Secretariat business. All files had hitherto been printed for the archives. This was carried out with such precision by clerks not always fully familiar with colloquial English that I once found in print the marginal annotation 'balls' over the initials of Frank Mudie. A distinction was made between official and demi-official correspondence. Official letters began 'I am directed' and demi-official letters 'I am desired'. L. P. Hancox was brought in from Cawnpore where he was District Magistrate, to run Food Supply and Rationing. A practical administrator he bypassed the system by beginning all his letters with 'I am directed/desired to state as follows': He then wrote what he had to say in unconvoluted prose.

Secretariats were permanent and perhaps slow-moving celestial bodies – governors flashed across the district officer's sky in rare and sometimes eccentric orbit. At intervals most districts would receive a governor's visit – even the most out of the way. Christie perched in his bamboo jungle above a loop of river in the Chittagong Hill Tracts in 1935 thus had His Excellency Sir John Anderson descend upon him:

Sir John was nothing if not thorough. He had discovered that no Governor in living memory (if ever) had visited the Chittagong Hill Tracts. Governors' visits to districts were usually brief, seldom for more than one day; but to make up for past omissions Sir John decided to extend his visit to the Hill Tracts to nine days, and to bring with him a party of one hundred, including his staff and their wives and domestic servants. He proposed, during this time, to hold a Durbar in Rangamati and to tour around 'visiting the interior'. This was, of course, a great honour but rather a severe strain on the resources of a backwoods district, and of its multi-purpose Deputy Commissioner. The Governor began his visit with an embarrassing act of unpunctuality, by arriving at his first halting-place inside the district four hours before he was expected, so that I was not there to meet him and his fleet of launches. Security was the reason for this change of plan without warning; and considering Chittagong's record of terrorism, it was justified. More embarrassment was to follow when the Governor's party consumed in one day the store of eggs calculated to last them for three. This was the only occasion when I had to send the Chittagong Hill Tracts Armed Police into serious action, with orders to collect from the villages round Rangamati one thousand eggs by nightfall.
But the visit was a success. The Governor showed a well-informed and sympathetic interest in our affairs, and I survived his searching cross-examinations on subjects ranging from administration to natural history. We showed him as much of the 'interior' as we could in the time available. For this purpose we built separate camps of bamboo houses, complete with triumphal arches and banqueting halls, between which the Governor and his party progressed in state, with the assistance of twelve elephants, who were paraded every morning after breakfast to salute His Excellency with upraised trunks.

Orr in the Agency Area of Berhampur in Orissa did his best, for his part, to impress his Governor at what was the last durbar in the province, in 1945. To be displayed to the great man was a village, boasting both dispensary and school, perched on a plateau precariously approached by a fine example of the PWD engineers' skill. The aim was to arrange with the sub-assistant surgeon (or 'sub-assassin') for a not too ambitious display of skills in a dispensary 'analogous to a cottage hospital which had to function without electricity or running water', and for the school-teacher to put on a pro-gramme 'to show the children at their best without inhibiting him from asking for additional funds', while the Governor's party was to be conveyed safely up and down the road labelled after its builder *Arunachalam's Folly*. There was also a tribal dance in the evening for Sir Hawthorne and Lady Lewis performed by Saura women who 'wore no clothing above the waist and coloured beads below and had a ready greeting and uninhibited smile'. Orr and the Governor's secretary Robert Swann were watching the dancing line – 'displaying a fascinating variety of breast movements, shapes and sizes (we agreed that at least they were all well-developed) when Lady Lewis leaned across to Robert and said: "They're awfully small aren't they?" Robert's thought processes seized up . . . Lady Lewis said again: "They are small, don't you think so?" I came to the rescue. "I've never seen a tall Saura", I said, "even the men are never more than about five-and-a-half feet."' Finally there was the durbar proper – speeches and a ceremonious exchange of token gifts. 'The gifts offered to the Governor were acknow-ledged by him touching them and returning them to the donors. The gifts given by him were lengths of white silk cloth. It looked very good quality, and at a time of universal rationing of all textiles it was greatly appreciated by the recipients.' 'Goodwill radiated on all sides', so Orr recorded, 'and the British Raj seemed safely set for another hundred years.'

Maitra, however, was less sanguine about the magic purveyed by gover-nors, and has this comment to make on the four whom he met:

In Government, whatever its form, the tone is set by the men at the top. Assam was no exception and everybody looked up to HE the Governor.

These four men, all ex-I.C.S. must have had different backgrounds, but the com-mon factor was that they had climbed to the top of their profession after 30–40 years of service, when they were ageing and fairly tired. They and their wives were going to enjoy their time as Their Excellencies, living in that delightful English country house like Government House at Shillong with its retinue of liveried servants, A.D.C.s and everybody in sight *salaming*. They were not going to spoil the fun by looking into reality too closely or raising controversial issues. They had known nothing about Assam, and in the course of their long ascent to success had left the dust and grime of district work years ago, and proved their worth as Secretariat hands ending up finally at Delhi or at one of the major provincial capitals.

Perhaps it is right to redress the balance a little with another of Orr's Governors of Orissa, Sir Chandulal Trivedi, whom he came rather un-expectedly to serve as Secretary:

Sir Chandulal Trivedi was not one to let grass grow under his feet, or anybody else's feet. I had to report for duty at Government House immediately and there I dis-covered Sir Chandulal's demonic appetite for work, which unfortunately he assumed was the normal attitude of his subordinates. From my first day in Government House I worked like a slave, and very often felt that I was treated as one. Sir Chandulal was too intense and too absorbed in whatever he was doing to waste time trying to be nice. He was coldly analytical, brilliantly diagnostic and his decisions were quick, succinct and nearly always right. These were not qualities on which he could build popularity, nor did he expect nor desire it. He was supremely efficient, and when his mind was not occupied by some official problem (which was seldom) he showed thoughtfulness and kindness for others. But at work he could be brutally censorious, callous and offensive. I was at the receiving end of all his moods, and developed an interesting duality in my reactions. I built up an intense antipathy on the emotional front, but an equally intense admiration and respect on the intellectual front for his ability.

FURTHER READING

There are histories of all the major services with whose officers the district officer came into contact, but two co-operative studies provide the easiest approach to any further study of the team and its task. Sir Edward Blunt (ed.), *Social Service in India* (London 1939 and 1946), with chapters on agriculture, medicine and public health, education, industrial labour, co-operation, voluntary effort and social welfare was specially written for ICS probationers and is a good formal survey. L. S. S. O'Malley (ed.), *Modern India and the West* (London 1941) is more concerned with the inter-action of India and Europe, and is often admirable within short compass. It adds to Blunt's work chapters on the law, on missionary activity, on economic development and on the progress of women, as well as surveys of Hinduism, Muslim culture and regional literature and drama.

CHAPTER 7

PLEASURES AND PAINS

A reader who has progressed to this point in the book might think that the district officer was some sort of dedicated automaton who had subordinated his private life utterly to the needs of the job. Indeed living as he did under constant public inspection, particularly when he was on tour or in camp, he had of necessity to be something of an anchorite or possibly even a stylite. The position of the district officer inevitably called for a degree of detachment. He was a man apart by virtue of his job. But in addition it was advisable for him not to become too identified with, or beholden to, individuals or specific groups of people in the district. There were always people about who might capitalize on a real or imagined relationship with him in order to further their own ends and this could be damaging to the reputation of the district officer. Ray recalls that 'dining out with zemindars could sometimes be a pleasure – but not always so – and this had its pitfalls, since the acceptance of too much hospitality from a particular individual could lead to the rumour, possibly fostered by himself, that he could influence you in official matters. One sub-division maintained a very private file, handed down from one incumbent to another with a list of those people with whom it was desirable to dine only once.'

These were problems common to both British and Indian officers. There were other problems too. In a country of deep communal divisions between Hindu and Muslim the Indian officer had to overcome any difficulties caused by the fact that he was most probably a Hindu or a Muslim himself. It was obviously easier to remain impartial in some communal dispute if one was neither. The Indian officer might in any case find himself working far from the province of his birth and, such being the variety of India, in very unfamiliar surroundings. Venkatachar notes the differences between the UP and South India where he was born:

The caste system was not so rigid as in the Brahmanical south. The presence of a Muslim elitist class and rich land-owners in the countryside was a new experience. Muslim influence was in evidence in tastes, ideas, attitudes, manners and decorum among the upper middle classes in towns. While the educated South Indian had a passionate devotion to English language and culture, the educated class in the UP used the English language as a necessary tool for administration. Cultural pride was reserved for Urdu, even Persian.

Conversely, Faruqui, a Muslim who had been born in the Punjab, encountered in Nasik district, Bombay, what he describes as 'anti-Muslim prejudice':

The Marathas having fought the Moghuls and nearly seized the throne of Delhi once were still anti-Muslim. They considered themselves a martial race which could have ruled India had they not been defeated by the Muslims in the fourth battle of Panipat and had the British not taken advantage of their set-back to seize power in the sub-continent. They still dreamt of the military conquest of India.

But despite all the cultural and religious differences that might make an Indian feel something of a stranger outside his province there probably was no lonelier official than the bachelor British sub-divisional officer living at his headquarters some distance from the district centre. Lamarque gives a good description of the isolation and austerity of his life in a Madras sub-division:

Sivakasi was in fact a particularly remote and unsophisticated spot. My house was a large, stone-built, isolated affair, a mile out of the town, and much too big for a bachelor. Ramnad (Ramanathapuram) district tended to be flat, parched country, inhabited by the Chettiars who, being an enterprising and quick-witted people and seeing no future in cultivating their indifferent land, tended to emigrate in their youth to Burma and Malaya where they made their fortunes in business, mostly money-lending and then returned to Ramnad in their old age. Madura (the district head-quarters) was about 40 miles from Sivakasi, but in fact I very seldom went there. For one thing I was kept too busy. Sivakasi was notorious for its high crime rate, stimulated, so it was said, by an all-the-year round hot, dry climate, so there was a great deal of court-work. Amenities were few in Sivakasi. There was no electricity, and only a tiny club. In fact, one can quickly get used to paraffin lamps and the 'Petromax' which gave brilliant illumination, at least when there are servants to do the lighting and servicing of the lamps. I possessed no refrigerator but a curious box called an 'icy-ball', the mechanics of which I never understood. This could store ice for a period, but could not make it. My nearest neighbours were a detachment of armed police and I would be woken by reveille on their bugles, a romantic sound in that remote spot. Two British sergeants were in charge, but otherwise there were no Europeans in Sivakasi. The nearest was a Dutch couple 15 miles away, and I would visit them occasionally. Otherwise as I recorded at the time, rather smugly, I was happy to be alone with books, work and the radio for company.

The loneliness sometimes experienced by British officials and noticed by several of them troubled the Indians, with their close and extensive familial connections, much less. Gupta, indeed, recalling a leave taken in the hill-station of Mussoorie, some distance from Bengal where he was serving almost suggests the reverse: 'all my brothers, sisters and brother-in-law came and stayed in the bungalow I had hired for the season. We had three small children aged below four and the strain of running our house for so many was terrific. We had plenty of recitations, music and picnics.'

Like Lamarque many contributors confirm that the 'job-satisfaction' was usually, though perhaps not always, great enough to dispel or at least minimize the effects of isolation. Haig felt that 'to a greater degree than I think is the case in the U.K. – except possibly in the highest ranks of the Home Civil Service – our job took complete precedence over other things'. Haig was a bachelor throughout his time in India, and he evolved a life-style which enabled him to undertake a punishing programme of work and play. 'Within two months of landing in India', he writes, 'I discovered what was for me an optimum method of sleeping, namely 4 to 5 hours a day. This produced immediate and very deep sleep and was to some extent geared to a regimen of a ride (on duty or as a hack) every morning and "sweating exercise" every afternoon. What was thus set up was a sort of unvicious circle; the exercise and long day produced the deep sleep which, being short, provided plenty of time within the 24 hours for work and other activities.' An illustration of the routine he was able to manage, at least in the cold weather, is given in this extract – quite a typical one – from the camp diary he kept for the year 1935 while serving as SDO in Agra district (UP):

Friday November 22.
Off at 6.30. By car to Saintha and then ride to Bhilantpur enquiry (6 miles). Stop at Achnera, and back 8.45. Tahsil inspection 10–12.30. Practical test for gun licence-holders 1–2. Court work 2.30–5.30. Peshi [hearing petitions] 6.30–7.30. Run on canal bank – 2 fast 660s (the second in 1.35). Files 8.30–11 p.m.

Bachelors were of course in a minority, and though it had been the custom in earlier days that British officers should not get married until the end of their first tour a number began to flout that convention in the 1930s by going out to India married. This shared initiation into the joys and hardships of Indian life probably strengthened and deepened more relationships than it loosened and dissolved. Woodford, who travelled out in 1940 with his French bride, describes his first year in Rangpur (Bengal) 'as a prolonged honeymoon. We had a minimally furnished bungalow of our own beside the tank (pond) and nothing better to do than watch and learn, and she to set up her easel and paint the passing show of India on the roads and at the water-side. Bee-eaters dived to and fro across the lawn; hoopoes dug their beaks into it and displayed yellow and black crests through the warm bright winter.'

But early marriage for all its satisfactions and solaces was not without snags for those still on a junior's pay. Fowler in Burma writes:

A young married officer found it rather a struggle to furnish a house. When you were senior enough to be allocated a furnished residence in the civil lines [housing area for government officials] most of the essentials were provided by the Public Works Department, but as an Assistant Commissioner in most stations in Burma you had to lease and furnish a house in the town. When my wife first arrived we lived in a house lent to me by one of the river pilots who was away on leave, but later we moved into a large teak house which was eminently suitable but rather bare. I remember that my wife had to use a packing-case as a dressing-table and a wire stretched across a corner of the room as a wardrobe. We had camp beds and small mosquito nets tied to tiny frames fixed on the end of the beds and at that stage we did not aspire to a refrigerator. We could buy beautifully made furniture from the district jail, con-structed to my own design by long-term prisoners who used to take a delight in adding rather lovely carved panels where the design permitted. But I had to calculate my monthly budget carefully before I ordered anything, and we used to estimate a large round of drinks after tennis at the club to be worth a chair which we badly needed. The Chinese grocery used to do all its calculating on a rapidly-clicking abacus, and after a large weekly order we used to await the result of this deft addi-tion with trepidation.

Hope went out married to Madras in 1938. He and his wife prepared a note on setting up house in India and sent it to the India Office who under-took to make copies available for others 'taking the same bold step of going out married' – to use the words of the India Office official gratefully acknowledging its receipt. Hope and his wife had a net amount of about Rs 500 a month to live on (£37.50) taking account of a private subsidy of £10 a month to supplement official earnings. Among much good advice in the Hopes' note was the suggestion that married couples should take a supply of medicines when they went out: 'Eno's, cascara, Dettol and iodine are all useful and along with ordinary first-aid appliances and Carter's Little Pills for the staff who will require to be dosed from time to time are about all you are likely to need.' As an indication of the prices obtaining in 1938, the Hopes bought a fairly complete inventory of locally-made furniture and carpets for about the equivalent of £65. But their car, a four-year-old Ford V8, was proportionately a good deal more expensive at £80.

The contributors to this book are the husbands, and ideally the wives who shared so many of their husbands' experiences should be quoted too. Fortunately we have one account of touring in Sind and Bombay from Mrs J. B. Brown, whose husband served in those two provinces before the Second World War:

More than a year ago, my husband in his capacity of Collector and District Magistrate was in charge of a district in Sind, a land of sand and desert and terrific heat, in the north of the Bombay Presidency.

I arrived out from home accompanied by my two small children and their nurse, in the beginning of October and after several weeks in which to unpack and settle in, I set off touring the district with my husband. Our procedure when the touring season began in November was as follows: After chota-hazri at 6.30 a.m. on a delightfully cool crisp morning, we set off, on horse back or camel back or by car for our first camp, from 20 to 30 miles distant. Most of our servants, and our kit consisting of carpets, tents, beds, pots and pans, tables, dishes etc, not forgetting a large wooden box with the children's toys had gone on the night before, by baggage camels. Our cow and calf also accompanied this moving establishment, the cow walking, the calf riding in a bullock cart because the Indian servant firmly believes that no cow will give milk unless it sees its calf before it. The children went in the car which was loaded up with the remainder of our kit, namely, bedding-rolls, picnic basket, water bottles, thermos flasks etc. Often our road lay along the top of a bank alongside of a dried up canal bed, with desert stretching on either side as far as the eye could see, and with an occasional clump of trees and cultivated land, denoting the presence of a village. On nearing our destination we were met by Zemindars on horseback, the head man of the village and others, welcoming us with garlands and bouquets drenched in sandal-wood scent.

We then arrived at the *dak* or government bungalow, which is often surrounded by a well kept flower and vegetable garden and found everything in ship-shape order. Tents had been erected for extra bedrooms, and breakfast and hot baths awaited us. We then settled down for from 3 days to a fortnight and then proceeded to our next camp. Near many of those camps excellent duck shooting could be had, and sometimes muggers (crocodiles) were found lying on the river banks. Friends from headquarters sometimes came for duck shooting and by putting up extra tents, accommodation was provided for them.

In the cool of the mornings and evenings the children went for walks with their nurse and a puttee-wallah, whose duty it was to scare off curious dogs, buffaloes and villagers.

The children and their toys occasioned great interest amongst the villagers, many of whom had never seen a white child before. One toy in particular, a duck that waddled on wheels, aroused great curiosity and crowds would follow it, whilst my small son aged two proudly pulled it along on a string.

Sometimes our camp consisted entirely of tents. One large tent, well furnished with camp kit including a wood-stove, made an admirable sitting room, two others did duty as bedrooms and a fourth an office. The servants slept in small tents whilst a grass structure with a built up earth fireplace served as a kitchen. Our drinking water had often to be carried a great distance as that near at hand was salt and brackish. Of course it and the milk were always boiled before using.

Our evenings in camp were quiet and uneventful. If numbers permitted we sometimes played bridge, but more often we lay in long camp chairs before a wood fire and read books from the library in Bombay, or magazines from home, and listened to the unceasing creak, creak of bullock waggons which moved by night.

Touring accompanied by his wife seems to have exposed the officer to an even greater degree of friendly but unblinking curiosity than he would have experienced on his own. This seems certainly to have been the case in Burma as this account by Fowler illustrates:

Provided one's wife did not mind rough touring Moulmein was ideal for a young married officer. There was enough social life to make it a gay enough place, even during the first part of the war, and two or three times a month we set off with our cook boxes, bedding rolls and our Burmese lugalay and Mugh cook, either along the rivers by launch, or down the red laterite roads through the forest. Sooner or later we had to transfer into bullock carts or onto village ponies, occasionally into sampans, and our camp homes were often in dak bungalows or headmen's houses with their teak floors beautifully polished with coconut husks; occasionally we stayed in remote field huts built on stilts with large bamboo grain containers underneath on which the children of the household would lie much intrigued and watching our every move. One of our tour centres was half a day's journey up the river Ataran, and often as our steamer made its slow progress against the stream, through the sound of its paddles we would hear the singing of a party of Karens, going down to Moulmein for some American Baptist gathering. The sound of their voices swelled as the steamers drew near and the effect was unforgettable. We used a forest bungalow on the Ataran. It was built on tall stilts on the river bank and a low bund was thoughtfully provided to the little hut at the far side of the compound. Sometimes during the monsoon the flood water rose far above this and then a boatman in a dugout canoe had to be pressed into service; but the whole thing was conducted with such decorum that my wife managed with no great embarrassment. Meanwhile, my wife and I had been touring the district extensively, and had soon developed a great liking for the agricultural population and had got to know my Subdivisional and Township Officers. Here I would like to pay her a tribute of appreciation for being an excellent D.C.'s wife, bearing long marches with fortitude, and not unduly disturbed when, on one or two occasions, she discovered that inquisitive eyes were peering through the mat walling of our shacks whilst she was taking her bath in a tin tub. Among her various district activities were the formation of a troupe of Girl Guides and taking her place at numerous semi-official functions such as tea parties (at which we were usually accorded the honour of being given two cups of tea, one on each side, at the same time) and practising on the Burmese lady guests her incipient knowledge of their language, at which she had begun to take lessons. She also judged fat babies at Agricultural Shows which my Officers arranged at all the Townships.

As Richards notes he and his wife found any hardships on tour constantly eased by their admirable Burmese servants.

We were, too, most efficiently looked after by our domestic servants, for whom we formed an abiding affection in particular for Nang Zing Yaw the Kachin, Ko Sein our Mugh cook who was to die in one of the Shwebo bombings, and dear old U Aye Maung, then about sixty, who always managed to turn out excellent meals on tour within half an hour of arrival in camp. I can see them all now so plainly as they toiled across the parched, harvested paddy-fields in a cloud of dust behind the bullock carts which carried our kit.

The loyalty and ungrudging service of Indian servants provided a constant background to the ups and downs of district life of nearly everyone, bachelor or married, and whether they were a small army out on tour or just one or two. Cowley's bearer was selected for him by the wife of his first DC at Rawalpindi in the Punjab. This is his tribute to him:

Madar Baksh was a gentle, likeable little Muslim of about 40 who attached himself to me with a quiet efficiency which developed, as we grew to know and trust each other, into a devotion to my interests that was restrained and undemonstrative, but absolutely dependable. He was to be with me all my service. One of the hardest things in losing India was to lose Madar Baksh, but at least I was able to get him a safe and sure post, and corresponded with him until his death in 1974. He had to employ a letter-writer for this. But he was 'the friend of my friends, the enemy of my enemies', the perfect butler, valet and cook.

But among the pleasant, sometimes idyllic moments, there were harsher and more anxious times too. In the days before the introduction of antibiotics and with medical facilities of only a primitive character outside the larger towns health could be a major worry. Slater was accompanied by his wife when he did his settlement training in Jhelum district of the Punjab. They lived in a small village two thousand feet up in the Salt Range.

It was a very beautiful place, but in Arcadia you need to be fit, and Barbara's health began to cause concern. The nightmare that followed was one of the occupational hazards of the service. It could happen to any district officer living in the back of beyond with no private transport other than a horse, hopelessly inadequate communications and access only to the most limited medical facilities. But it happened to us, and it nearly ended tragically. Barbara fought stoically against head-aches, sickness, lassitude, making light of a condition far more serious than was suspected. Salvation came from the British community working the salt mines in Khewra at the foot of the mountain. Alerted I forget exactly how – if not by smoke signal, by something not much more modern – the Manager sent up his estate car into which Barbara was loaded, bed and all, and in which we crept the fifteen hair-raising miles of mountain road to the plains below. Khewra was in the twentieth century. I was sure she would respond to nursing and proper hygiene. She didn't, and emergency arrangements had to be made to get her to the British Military Hospital in Rawalpindi where meningitis was suspected. It proved otherwise and the crisis passed, but not before she had permanently lost the hearing of one ear.

Bringing up a family of four boys in the North West Frontier Province presented special security problems for Curtis and his wife, Decima.

The Mahsuds were much impressed by the fact that I had four sons. 'Tsaloor Zamin, Tsaloor Toopakoona. Four sons, four rifles,' I remember an old Mahsud malik say musingly. 'You will be a powerful man in your own country'. Tank was not an ideal place for children. One had always to bear in mind the possibility that they might be kidnapped. When I went on tour I wore, as was the usual practice for Political Agents, a service revolver and ammunition belt. It hung in a cupboard at Tank. Putting it on I noticed several rounds were missing. It occurred to me that the elder boys might have taken them and as they had been making charcoal in an earthen oven they had built, they might have had the idea of putting a round in the fire to see what happened. My wife had a talk with them and, although they both steadfastly denied knowing anything about the missing rounds, she was not certain they were telling the truth. The loss of service ammunition was such a serious matter that she felt justified in listening outside the bedroom door after she had said good-night to them. The elder boy urged the younger to agree to his telling their mother the truth. The younger replied tearfully, 'You know he said he would cut off our heads if we told anybody'. This was Decima's cue for a re-entry. After much crying the truth came out. One of my Mahsud orderlies had bribed them with sugar-cane (we had noticed that they always seemed to be chewing it). The problem now was to secure the return of the stolen rounds from the orderly and arrange for his transfer to another post without his losing face. I handed the matter over to the Assistant Political officer. He took his time but eventually the missing rounds were returned and the orderly was found a place in the tribal police. This was generally agreed to be as satisfactory a conclusion as could be expected in Waziristan.

By the middle of April it began to be very hot, and it was time for Decima, Nanny and the children, not to mention the two dogs, to move to cooler climes. The exodus to Kashmir was no small undertaking. The family travelled by armoured lorry to Kalabagh on the railway. They had to start before day-break as they had to go through the Bain Pas on the Bhitanni hills while the frontier constabulary pickets were in position. On one occasion there was a loud explosion, the lorry stopped and everybody took cover. Decima imagined that they were being held up. It was an anti-climax to find that it was only a burst tyre.

After a night in the train they arrived early in the morning at Rawalpindi. Here they embarked on a hired bus for Kashmir. A night had to be spent at a rest-house en route and they did not reach Gulmarg until the evening of the second day. Decima and the boys finished the journey by riding ponies up the final hill and Nanny and the baby followed in a rickshaw. It was a strenuous journey. The family did it altogether four times.

But of course the official and private pre-occupations of the district official did not, and could not, stand in the way of his playing his part in the institutional aspects of social life in India. These revolved largely round the clubs which ranged from racially exclusive institutions in the bigger centres like Calcutta, Madras and Bombay to friendly little tennis clubs in small up-country stations where the touring officer was only too glad to have the chance of a game of tennis and bridge with the taluk officials and the local professional men. Raza recalls that in Bombay the Assistant Collector's Manual specifically stressed the need for ICS officers to play a full part in club life:

Even though you may be shy of thrusting yourself among comparative strangers, make a practice of going to the club regularly, it will probably rub off some unsuspected corners of your personality to your lasting benefit. Even if you should find the society at the club uninteresting, you have, in virtue of your position, to fill a place in the social life of the station, and to do your part to amuse and entertain the other residents, who may not have your resources of culture and interests. Golf, tennis etc and bridge are valuable aids to getting to know your fellows.

Raza started his career in Ahmednagar, a large military station in Bombay, where the British Brigadier was the President of the club and the Collector (an Indian) the Vice-President. The latter put Raza up for membership, and on election, he found himself the only Muslim member.

In some places where there was a resident British commercial community, more or less permanently settled there for their working lives, the club was the focus for social life in a way in which it was not for the more transient official. Midgley describes the club at Saharanpur (UP):

The Superintendent of Police and I were the only European members of the district administration, but there was a small British community in Saharanpur. This comprised the European staff of the tobacco factory, the paper mill and the Remount Depot. All met together at the station club, together with those Indians who had adopted English social habits, for tennis, the occasional game of billiards and, of course, the reviving chota peg. There is nothing like a long whisky and soda, thirst quenching, restorative, easy on the liver and inducing a mild intoxication as the evening proceeds for promoting social intercourse. The variety of background and experience, the smallness of the gathering, focussed, as it were, under the sweep of the fan, induced a flow of reminiscences. This was the world of Somerset Maugham. There were small dreams – hints of liaisons – comedies (I remember the delicious triumph of a young lady, formerly somewhat despised as nanny to a captain's family in the Remount Depot, returning as no less a person than the wife of the Director of Remounts himself on an inspection visit). The flavour of social life was more concentrated by the detachment of the English section of the community from local events. Although we in the service sometimes laughed at the British business community for their racial snobbery and faulty Hindustani, I did not notice that they excited any hostility. To the tolerant Hindu, 'we, the Sahib log, were just another caste'.

Lydall describes the club in the tea-growing country at Lakhimpur in rather similar terms:

The club was basically a planter's club though it also welcomed the local government officials. There was no actual colour bar. An Indian medical officer who took over during my time automatically joined the club. For the educated Assamese, mostly pleaders, an evening drinking whisky and playing billiards with tea-planters would have held no attraction. They had their own well-established and very different social set-up and their wives were in any case in purdah. It was otherwise in the case of Indians leading a western-style life in Bombay and Calcutta and of the officers of the Indianised 16th Cavalry who could not be full members of the Peshawar club though they were members of the Cavalry Club in London.

It was in such cases that unhappy awkwardnesses might occur, such as that which Husain met with when invited to tea at a Lahore club by his Settlement Officer (Sir) George Abell:

One day he asked me and Hamid to have tea with him in the Punjab Club, where he was staying at the time. We arrived at the appointed hour but were told by the man at the desk that Indians were not allowed in the Club and we left quickly and quietly, leaving our cards. The next day Abell called us at the Settlement Office and profusely apologized and expressed his indignation at the existence of the rule debarring Indians from entry into the club. He assured us that he would try his best to have the rule changed. I don't recollect when the rule was changed but I do recollect that both of us, knowing Abell, had no rancour or ill feeling about this incident.

Such incidents were very much the exception and rarely happened outside the provincial capitals. Indeed Masterman, who started his service in Madras in 1915, takes issue with Leonard Woolf who described the Club (in Ceylon) as 'the centre and symbol of British imperialism . . . with its cult of exclusiveness, superiority and isolation'. 'I do not think', Masterman writes, 'this is quite true of up-country clubs in India. There was discrimination of course, but it was not a case of discrimination on grounds of colour. It was a question of status.' He goes on to recall that at the Palamcottah Club at the headquarters of Tinnevelly district, while an Indian officer of an All-India service was elected to membership, another of a provincial service was not, and there was much argument whether the status of a Briton who had been sent to the district to recruit labour for the tea estates of Ceylon was such as to justify admission. Later, when Masterman became a member of the Board of Revenue, he saw very nearly all the up-country clubs in the Presidency. 'None of them discriminated against Indians as such, but the members were predominantly officials, and as the services became more and more Indian-ised, so the number of Indian members increased.' Masterman goes on to describe the Palamcottah Club

the best of the smaller moffussil (up-country) clubs. There were good tennis courts and a golf course of sorts on the sandy maidan round the club totally devoid of grass on which prickly pear grew luxuriantly and provided a formidable hazard. Once Sayers (the District Superintendent of Police), tried to organise polo on this maidan, though none of our mounts, except Sayers', was very much like a polo pony. I recall the Forest Officer coming to the field for our first practice on a very large ungainly-looking animal which looked round for a minute or two, decided that polo was not his game and galloped straight back to his stable taking his rider with him. We never saw them again on the polo field.

Club life in Burma with its smaller stations and more relaxed ways seems to have been a less formal affair than in India. Moreover, as Donnison points out, 'Burmese women enjoyed a status and freedom unknown in India and rare in Europe. The Burmese were cheerful and outgoing with a mischievous and irreverent sense of humour – they laughed readily and not only at other men's misfortunes.' Such people were by nature clubbable, and Wallace describes the family feeling that existed between all the officials, regardless of race, at the up-country station of Pakokku with its small club:

I got back from tour on Christmas morning (in 1933) and breakfasted and dined with the Flux family (executive engineer, Public Works Department). My young Burmese Assistant Commissioner under training, who was staying with me, came too. Five of our company had gone up to Mandalay for Christmas. The remaining nine of us were entertained by the Fluxes, three Burmans, two Anglo-Indians and Chinese and one European – a very happy family party it was. The absent contingent had sent us a wire from Mandalay on Christmas Eve 'Greetings to those holding the fort'. When they returned a few days later, they brought cold stores as Christmas presents, butter, cheese, bacon and sausages. On 28th December the itinerant government chaplain turned up, we get him about one week in six, and held a Christmas service. As DC I read the lessons.

In some provinces the ICS arranged their own social functions which were known as ICS weeks. Bowman describes the annual ICS week in Lucknow, which already seemed to him, 'an interesting survival of Victoriana':

In my first year, I received an invitation to stay at Government House. A visit to Government House in ICS week involved a considerable amount of baggage. One had to take white tie and tails, black tie and dinner jacket, lounge suits and casuals, to cover the various social events. A good supply of stiff collars was desirable, as they often wilted in the heat of the dances and had to be changed. I was allocated one of a row of tents in the spacious gardens of Government House, a luxurious tent, with all sorts of amenities, including electric light, its own bathroom and my name on a board outside. ADC's directed one's activities and saw that one was correctly dressed and put in the right place in the order of precedence for meals. There was a formal dinner party with the Governor, Sir Harry Haig, and Lady Haig. There was an afternoon at the races, when HE and Lady Haig made a state entry in an open carriage driven up the race track and escorted by troopers in colourful uniforms with lances. There was the formal ball at Government House where the military appeared in dazzling mess dress, the civilians wore white ties and gloves and tails and any decorations they happened to possess, and the women vied with each other in the elaborateness of their hair-do's and dresses. HE and Lady Haig made a formal entrance down a red carpet, preceded by the Military Secretary and ADCs in uniform. There was the less formal but more romantic ball in the Chattar Manzil, the ornate palace formerly inhabited by the women-folk of the King's of Oudh. Etiquette was *de rigueur.* Everything carried an aura of the great days of the Raj, when the stamp of Victorian upper-class society was set on the British in India, and convention ruled with a firm hand.

Belcher records that rather similar arrangements operated in the Punjab:

From my relative solitude in Lilla, I particularly appreciated the traditional Christmas week in Lahore. The official Christmas break lasted a full week, from Christmas Eve to New Year's day, on the theory that with distances between family home and duty station being so great for most of the Indian officers and staff, no lesser period would enable them to celebrate the holiday adequately with their families. Perhaps a somewhat specious theory, but one of its more agreeable aspects was that it allowed a great part of the Punjab ICS cadre, necessarily leaving a few to 'mind the shop' in the districts, to gather together in Lahore for a week of individual and collective reunions. These included an annual ICS dinner given by the Governor, and naturally also a round of the sorts of gaieties – parties, music, race-meeting – that in the rest of the year were absent from the lives of those living and working in the smaller and remoter districts. Though there was no distinction made in all this between the Indian and the British members of the service, and the Governor's dinner, as I remember it, was well attended by both, the Lahore week tended to be more a British than an Indian occasion. This was no doubt partly because it was a Christian festival, and partly because the Indian members could in fact use the break to visit their families in other parts of the province or elsewhere in India, whereas for the British members their British colleagues collected together in Lahore had, as it were, to do duty as their family for the Christmas festivities.

Raza spent a most pleasant week in Poona in September 1935, designated as ICS week, Poona being then the summer capital of the Bombay Government:

This used to be an excellent get-together of members, their wives and children and was particularly welcomed by the junior members of the service who got an opportunity to meet their seniors in a relaxed atmosphere. I was agreeably surprised to get an invitation to stay at Government House during the week. I learnt later that this privilege was conferred on me because I was the most junior member of the service of that year. We had a couple of sessions under the presidentship of the senior-most member of the ICS, to consider service matters. We participated in golf, tennis, billiards and bridge tournaments. We tried our luck at the famous Poona races. The highlight of our celebrations was a cricket match between the Governor's eleven and the ICS eleven, which was followed by a white tie banquet and ball at Government House. The Governor of Bombay at that time was Lord Brabourne. He and Lady

Brabourne made a most charming pair, handsome and considerate. Lord Brabourne captained his team, and his performance both as bowler and batsman was commendable. In fact he was largely responsible for the victory of his team over the ICS eleven. The week was rounded off by a seven course dinner at the Poona Club.

Apart from what was available in the clubs, and that was limited, recreation in the districts was largely a matter for improvisation. The commonest activity was probably shooting, for which many parts of India provided at that time, but possibly now no longer, an abundance and variety of opportunities unmatched anywhere in the world. Most people did their shooting casually after a day's work in camp or getting up early on a Sunday morning to go after duck or snipe; but Rahmatullah brought a distinctively methodical approach to his sport as his account of shooting a crocodile in Murshidabad (Bengal) shows:

My Murshidabad memories include the bagging of my biggest crocodile – most easily, comfortably, and as if by appointment. The Ganges was full of crocodiles, and once in the course of several decades it overflowed its banks and its strong currents pushed out crocodiles in the adjoining ponds and low-lying areas or inland lakes known as 'jheels'. I received information from a villager in the course of a tour of the interior of the district, that a huge crocodile basked regularly on a tiny island of sand in a small lake very close to the road. He said that the slope of the embanked road was thickly wooded and provided excellent cover and I had only to get down from my car, walk down the slope and shoot the crocodile from only 50 feet or so on any day exactly at noon. I at once issued my tour programme which said, 'Leave Berhampur by car at 11.30 a.m., shoot crocodile en route at 12 noon, proceed to Jiaganj and inspect Union Board etc. and return to headquarters by 3 p.m.' I found the information about the crocodile correct in every detail. I had my Mauser 315 and also my double-barrelled shot gun with 12 bore 'Rotax' bullets which for all practical purposes converted a shotgun into a most powerful rifle at close range. I preferred to use my shotgun and placing a couple of 'Rotax' bullets into its barrel, moved down the roadside slope in perfect cover and sat down nicely at the edge of the lake at a place where I could just see the white neck and gullet of the crocodile. Only a single bullet did the job. The crocodile turned turtle and was dead. A villager swam to it with a rope and made it float down to me. Its skin gave us a ladies' bag, shoes and wallets.

Hunting in the foothills area of Gorakhpur in the UP, though successful enough, had rather an unexpected impact upon Shukla:

One part of my sub-division provided ideal ground for shikar (hunting). I was fond of hunting the deer, for it provided the sport of chasing them over a wide area. Once I encircled a herd of deer with half a dozen elephants. The elephants closed in but the herd disappeared behind long grass and bushes. As we gave up hope, the leader of the herd raised its head to see if the danger was over, I shot him at once and he fell dead. We then proceeded to the spot. All the members of the herd had run away, but one doe stood by the side of the dead deer and continued to look at me unafraid even though I had a gun in my hand. Her sad and reproachful look I still remember, as if she was saying that I had done her grievous wrong, having killed her mate for no fault of his or hers. This scene made such an impression on me that I gave up hunting except that of birds.

Over in Sind, however, the main sport, as Barty describes, was either duck on the lakes and marshes or driven partridge:

Sometimes, if the mail failed to arrive, or if there were few petitions and no criminal cases, we would go out with our shotguns and walk up a few partridges for the pot. At some camps, one of the local zemindars would organize a full day's shooting, either partridge or duck. The Shahbunder subdivision of Karachi district abounded in *dhands* (lakes) where thousands of duck from Northern India and even as far away as Siberia gathered in the cold weather. Tamarisk bushes provided ample cover in which little platforms were built for the guns. There was no system of shooting only at the morning and evening flights. The local belief was that if you did that the birds would just fly off to another *dhand* at the first shot. So shooting would begin about 11 a.m. when the day was warming up, and the theory was that by then the birds would be too lazy to fly high or to go away elsewhere; instead they would foolishly mill around the same *dhand* at a convenient height. It certainly seemed to work out that way. Before sunset you would be brought back to dry land in a punt with your bag and there would be a counting and sorting of birds. Many Zemindars kept game books in which the details of every shoot were recorded. Shovellers and other less popular birds would be distributed to the beaters, each shot would keep what he wanted for himself and his servants and the balance would be sent to hospitals even as far away as Karachi. On an organised shoot, partridge would be driven, not walked up, and instead of taking one's own picnic lunch, the host would provide a curry lunch washed down with beer. Acceptance of such hospitality was allowed although it was not easy to repay it, but one had the consolation that, in Sind, such Zemindars were owners of hundreds or even thousands of acres, were wealthy men, and in the course of conversation could provide you with a lot of useful and interesting information about your district and its inhabitants.

At Monghyr in Bihar, Flack was able to shoot from the comfort of a launch on the river Ganges:

Captain Drummond had a pilot launch about 50 feet long, and he cruised up and down his stretch of river checking on sand-banks, 'chaurs' (islands formed by alluvium) and general changes in the river. These matters he had to report to his company. On Sundays, he would take six or seven friends for a trip. The entertainment offered included pink gin, beer, occasional duck-shooting, crocodiles (the fish-eating gharial of the Ganges) and surf-boarding behind the launch. As you could fall off the board two or three miles from land, a crewman stood in the stern with a life-belt ready to throw. The launch would then turn round and pick up the surfer and life-belt, after about five minutes. Geese, duck and other birds used to migrate south from Siberia, and one Sunday on the river, I had my rifle, a grey lag flew over and a friend fired drawing only slightly ahead and brought it down from 100 feet, the shot of a lifetime.

Burma probably had an even greater abundance of game than India. Richards remembers that in Henzada snipe-shooting could be had within a mile of the town centre. But Henzada's chief attraction was Allentaung, literally the hill of Allen, a former Deputy Conservator of Forests:

This was an area of thickly forested country on both sides of the Arakan Yomas. Extensive stretches of grassland broke up the bamboo and mixed jungle, and the whole area was a natural grazing ground for game, large and small. Here were elephants, bison, deer and all the lesser species in abundance. Gibbons called from the trees, and I rather think it was here that I was given monkey curry for breakfast and found it so good that I asked for a second helping. Not that I shot the monkey myself – I always used to get out of that one by saying that shooting a monkey always brough the British bad luck.

Richards points out that success with the gun could add interest and

variety not only to the working day, but to the chicken and rice diet, which
was all that the touring officer could otherwise expect:

What marvellous dishes they were – those snipe slightly roasted and seasoned with
a squeeze of lemon and tabasco sauce, and what better to eat than a Burmese
jungle fowl, or at Christmas in camp, a fine peacock – nowadays, I believe, protected
as the National Bird of Burma but still, no doubt, illicitly poached by the village
gun-holder.

The classic Indian equestrian sports of tent-pegging and pig-sticking
were to a large extent the pursuit of the Army. In the Punjab tent-pegging
was the more popular and Slater describes his introduction to the sport:

It was one of the younger maliks (land-owners) who initiated me in the art of tent-
pegging, which was to the people of Attock what rugby football is to the Welsh.
A buccaneering rumbustious character, he was frowned on by the rest of the family
and lived on his estate some miles from Pindigheb. Here one hot summer evening
when Barbara was in the hills, I took my horse for tent-pegging practice. It was
thirsty work calling for copious refreshment afterwards. That night I went to bed
with my riding boots on. But my tent-pegging improved and I was soon to hold my
own with the aces of the district, eventually winning a major competition under the
benevolent eye of the Punjab Premier, Malik Khizar Hyat Khan, himself an Attock
man and a devotee of the sport. Tent-pegging was not only enormous fun, it conferred
a prestige which no amount of solid administrative virtue would have earned. I owed
a debt of gratitude to the dissolute malik which he never showed the slightest sign of
expecting to be repaid.

Pig-sticking was a sport practised more frequently by earlier generations
of ICS men than the last one, but Bowman was able to try his hand in Agra
district:

The Gunners in Agra were a pleasant friendly crowd, and I spent a good deal of
time in their company. They were enthusiastic pig-stickers. When I acquired a mount,
they persuaded me to joint the Agra Tent Club and I was introduced to the excitements of hunting the wild boar. Looking back at it, I am deeply conscious of the
cruelty and horror of pig-sticking; but at the time it was fascinating, challenging and
blood-stirring. There were large areas round Agra with long grass and scrub jungle
interspersed with wide stretches of open country. Pig abounded in this country and
were a constant source of annoyance and danger to the cultivators who welcomed
our activities as long as we kept clear of their cultivation. Most of the hunting was
done in the area round Fatehpur Sikri. The ponies and spears were sent out the day
before the hunt, along with the club huntsman mounted on a camel. Members of
The Tent Club went out in the evening in cars to a suitable spot in the jungle. The
Gunners usually gave me a lift in their Mess car, an enormous yellow Rolls-Royce
tourer of pre-1914 vintage. We slept in blankets below the car which had a high
clearance. After breakfast at dawn we arranged heats and joined the line of beaters,
waiting for the shouts which informed us that the pig had broken cover. Then a
dash at full gallop through the line and on into the jungle, with the pig scurrying
and jinking ahead of us. Sometimes we got him, sometimes he got away, but always
it was a thrilling, irresistible feeling compounded of excitement, blood-lust and sheer
exuberance in galloping. After a morning of hunting we would return to Fatehpur
Sikri, the ponies in a lather of sweat, and would sit in the shade of the palaces,
regaling ourselves with beer and sandwiches. Crude and cruel it undoubtedly was; but
it was an experience of an age-old traditional sport which it would have been hard to
find anywhere else in the world. One of the fascinations of pre-war India was that it
allowed one to participate in ways of life long since abandoned by the western

world. At times, one was back in the Middle Ages. To anyone with a feeling for the historical it was a unique privilege to be part of a way of life such as our fore-fathers must have led. Perhaps it affected us to some extent.

The commonest relaxation took the form of sports and games which were available everywhere, tennis, swimming or hockey for example. In Bengal, Bell reports that the younger administrators and police officers played football and hockey not just for enjoyment, but to cultivate friendly relation-ships with the people in the difficult aftermath of the terrorist campaign in the 1930s. The most remote taluk headquarters had a tennis court. Cultural and intellectual pursuits, except for the reading of books despatched from lending libraries in provincial capitals and the writing of occasional verse, are mentioned less frequently. Ray argues that opportunities for the develop-ment of cultural interests might have been greater if the probationer had been taught something about Indian culture instead of 'having to pick it up as he went along'. But probably the increasing pressure of work, intensified by war-time tasks, made it difficult for either Briton or Indian to emulate the scholar administrators who, in a former age, had played such a notable part in the discovery and preservation of Indian archaeology and culture. Hyde, as Dewan or Prime Minister of Bastar State, was acting in this older tradition when he was able to take steps to preserve thousand-year-old temples from the encroachments of the jungle or remove, for safe storage, statues mouldering in the villages. Midgley for a time in charge of the area which included the deserted Mughal city of Fatehpur Sikri, was less enthusi-astic about archaeology: 'This became a burden when M. S. Randhawa, our scholarly Collector, decided to mark his tenure of office by writing a history of Agra – subdivisional officers to provide him with the first drafts.'

The district was not always the best place to study the performing arts. But Narasimham in the Madras Presidency was able to pursue his interests in Carnatic music, and Solomon was introduced to the complications and fascinations of Indian dancing when he was taken by a provincial service colleague to witness the Sankirtan, that ecstatic Hindu religious group dance, at the temple in Deogarh in Bihar, and if the more exotic cultivation of the senses is to be included, then surely Rahmatullah's initiation, at Murshi-dabad in Bengal, into the art of mango tasting must rank high:

I feel that no account of Murshidabad can be complete without recalling its fantastic 'Mango-Dinners' which the landed aristocracy gave during the hottest season of the year. It was customary for them to invite the District Magistrate at such annual functions. I had to accept invitations to some of them. The party was held in exquisite sweet-scented gardens on lush green lawns. The decorations on such occasions made the entire place look like some fairy land. Rajas, big landlords and members of their families clad in ultra-white 'dhuti Kurta' of the finest muslim drenched in perfumes from Paris and Ittar from Lucknow sat in swings with fan-bearers behind. On my arrival, amidst fan-fare, they all stood up, the bands played the national anthem and I was treated as a representative of the Crown, escorted to a dais, lavishly decorated. The attending guests were called one by one and presented to me by the host Rajas. The ceremony over, I was led to the main banquet table to take my seat on a special chair, The Raja's own throne! The guests then took their seats at the banquet. Mangoes were served first in small slices, as their names were announced. As many as 125 varieties or more were thus presented to the guests, for Murshidabad was famous for such a large number of varieties of mangoes being grown there. It was a job tasting 125 slices. I stopped at 10.

Throughout the mango season I received samples of the best varieties of mangoes grown by the Rajas, Maharajas and others of the landed aristocracy. The name of the mango as well as the time at which it was to be taken, was marked clearly on each and every one of them. The hour so marked was not infrequently midnight or a few hours past midnight, for lovers of mangoes took them at all hours of the night! The markings were done by experts who knew at what hour a particular mango in his hand would be just ripe and taste best.

The presence in India of so many tribal peoples, of the caste system and of a variety of religious sects, meant that many district officers became amateur anthropologists in the ordinary course of their duties. Hayley, however, was a trained anthropologist and when he was serving in the Jorhat district of Assam he was able to make a study of the distinctive religious institutions to be found on Majuli Island on the Brahmaputra river, said to be the largest river island in the world, and to use this as subject for a doctoral thesis. Here a fifteenth-century Hindu religious reformer had established a number of religious houses called 'Satras', rather similar to Buddhist monastaries, housing their disciples without any of the caste distinctions common to Hinduism.

Perhaps for many, the deepest satisfaction of all was the beauty of the countryside, the forests and hills in particular but not excluding the changing aspects of the unending plains, a strange mixture of magic and monotony. Kashmir is, of course, one of the world's beauty spots and was always a favourite place for a break in the hotter weather. Cowley, who was transferred from ordinary administrative work in the Punjab to become the province's youth organizer, describes an unusually strenuous expedition in Kashmir with some of his Indian friends and his dog, Pluto.

Latif, Qureshi and I took a party of twenty students to Kashmir. We took a lorry from Rawalpindi up the familiar Jhelum Valley road. At Domel we stopped to drink tea at a cafe built above the river. A large Tibetan mastiff was sleeping in the sun outside and I edged Pluto carefully past him. As we came out, however, the dog woke up and growled. Pluto was out of my hand and at this huge dog in a flash. No one dared interfere once battle was joined. As usual it was scarcely a battle. With sharp tugs Pluto dragged his opponent backwards until suddenly with one vicious tug they both disappeared over the edge into the river below. That separated them. Pluto was soon back shaking water all over us and we hurriedly departed. Around the corner we caught a last glimpse of the other dog standing forlornly on a rock in the middle of the river. So once again I climbed up through the forest to Tragbal. This time we went on – over four miles of snow, with patches of purple primula Kashmiriana, blue gentian and yellow rock-rose. Far ahead the white spire of Nanga Parbat showed for a time above the clouds. There is a rough stone hut on the 12,000 feet pass, for there have been some bad accidents here – one autumn storm killed a whole train of three hundred mules and their drivers. As we came down from the pass we turned a corner and stopped in mingled horror and amazement. A mule had perished there, and around it were four fearsome birds, the size, it seemed of ostriches. They were Himalayan griffons with a wing-span of 18 feet. As we rather doubtfully approached they took lumbering steps to one side and watched us pass as though sizing us up for a future meal.

The hill-sides were covered with silver grey artemisia. Down the Kishen-ganga river were willow, dog-wood and wild apricot trees, with patches of blue iris and some very tall 'white-hot pokers'. A plumbeous redstart flew across the river. The party set off to climb the Kamri Peak at a height of 15,000 feet:

The final obstacle was a narrow knife-edged ridge of snow. At 2.00 p.m. we were gazing entranced at a vast solitude of icy peaks etched in black and white, the valleys completely lost to view at this height. Less than forty miles to the north, soaring above the cloud with the whole of the west ridge and the eastern shoulder visible was Nanga Parbat. We examined it with hungry eyes. Some day, perhaps.... A pair of Alpine swifts circled round us, tails vibrating, and a few dark sparrow-like birds – Stolicka's mountain finches. Occasionally, from deep in the valley, and mellowed by distance, floated the lonely call of the cuckoo.

Cockburn had the same feeling of space and remoteness as he describes a moment in northern Burma:

One reward to those who tour in these parts is the feeling of peace and quiet. One clear December day I was on a saddle 8,000 feet up on the border with Yunnan. As I looked west, I could see across successive mountain ranges to the high mountains on the Indian border one hundred miles away; as I looked east I could again look over successive ranges to high mountains one hundred miles into China.

No single final summing up is really possible, and few contributors served long enough in the ICS to be able to assess the pleasures and pains of the career to the full. Yet perhaps Lloyd-Jones's verdict on a nine-year stint does sum up district work in words with which many would agree:

The narrative of my career in India will, I hope, convey the feeling of satisfaction I obtained from district work. I felt I was doing something worth-while and at the same time my faculties were kept at full stretch. I cannot claim to have always been happy in my work; the climate in the hot weather and rains I found trying and my health suffered for a time mainly because of too long a period without home leave. Then as with all jobs there were monotonous stretches of routine. But generally there was enormous variety in the work which developed my interests and tested my abilities to an extent that I have never experienced since.

Or, as Hubbard recalls, in verses entitled 'ICS (retd.)' published in *Punch*, 19 April 1950, describing a ride of inspection one Punjab morning.

> I know that the world was on my shoulders
> And for just this reason my heart was light.

CHAPTER 8

TRIBES AND ISLANDS

District administration was nowhere without colour and variety as Christie shows. A note scribbled to his wife when they were in the Chittagong Hill Tracts in 1934–7, 'If you want to see a tiger, just step down to the office compound for a moment, and bring the camera with you.' Yet every province could offer occasional postings which broke the regular district mould or which were more colourful and exotic than usual. Some such postings were accidents of history late acquisitions like Darjeeling in Bengal, perhaps, which could not be assimilated to the normal provincial pattern. Others were tribal tracts of mountainous or forest country, often an anthropologist's paradise, too poor to sustain a full administration and requiring a simpler system of customary law. North-west and north-east there were military frontier zones, while all across India lay a patchwork of princely states, of all sizes, largely independent in their internal administration but subject to the paramountcy of the British Crown. After some years of district work it was possible for a few to obtain selection to the Political Service and so to a regular career on the frontier and in the princely states. ('Lean and keen for the Frontier, fat and jolly for the Princes', as the tag went.) There were also occasional secondments from the district to deal with short-term administrative problems in these areas – the settlement of tribesmen on some newly-irrigated tract of land, say, or the minority of a ruler – which could come a district officer's way. What was common to all such postings was a sudden, welcome break in routine, the need to learn something of a new local language and pattern of society, and greater freedom of action for the officer concerned.

Officers serving in the frontier regions in the tribal territories and in other provinces in the backward, mountainous agency areas were known as political agents, or agents, and were responsible directly to the Governor-General or Governor, thus escaping from the formal administrative structure of the district. Bell notes that the whole Darjeeling District was excluded from the operation of the Montagu-Chelmsford reforms of 1919 and Orr that the same was true of the tribal Agency areas in Orissa: 'the British legislators believed that it was necessary to afford their inhabitants special protection against exploitation by more sophisticated sections of the population. Tribal law and custom were strictly observed and the Agency Regulations, which superimposed the British concept of justice and law, were carefully devised to reinforce rather than to substitute the tribal laws.' It was thus a paternalistic system which put a concentration of authority into the Agent's hands. He was often very much out on his own, both literally and metaphorically, as Georgeson and Downing, working in adjacent

Agency Tracts of Madras – Chicacole and Bhadrachalam – make clear:

The country [Chicacole] is a tangle of mountains, thickly covered, except on the highest peaks, with jungle. All this jungle is pervaded by a smell which, at the time, I had never met anywhere else, that of the creeper lantana. When, not having smelt lantana for sixteen years, I again smelt it in the Queensland hills, it invoked, as nothing in the meantime had done, my tours in the Sowra country.

Metalled roads penetrated only the fringe, as far as the foot of the hills. All communication beyond that point was by earth roads. There was no wheeled traffic, except for a few bicycles owned by some prosperous residents. The earth roads, which were more elaborate than was necessary for walking, were designed for elephants. The making of earth roads and of rest sheds, except for skilled supervision, and the carrying of Government officers' luggage was a liability of the inhabitants. They paid no taxes of any kind, even being allowed to ferment and distil liquor for their own consumption without excise duty. Their contribution to the administration was to carry out all unskilled labour within their area. This, of course, left a great deal of public expenditure on the Agency to which the inhabitants made no contribution, of which the salaries of the Government officers were an obvious example. But the arrangement, though fair and accepted by the inhabitants as such, was, by the time at which I first saw the Agency (1932), making the Government uneasy as smacking of forced labour and small payments were made for all work done. The bissoyis [headmen] were, however, still required to find the necessary labour. They presumably did so according to a rota, but the arrangements were left to them. All touring was on foot. The alternatives were elephants and *dholis*, chairs lashed to poles and carried on the shoulders of four men. The Government, however, strongly disapproved of the use by its servants of dholis: and, indeed, no healthy person, unless very indolent, would prefer being so carried to walking. Some old-fashioned Indians, however, thought it more dignified. Luggage was carried either by elephants or by parties supplied by the bissoyis. Marches were generally from the headquarters of one bissoyi to those of the next, an easy walk averaging about ten miles.

When a Government officer was touring, it was the duty of the bissoyi whose area he was leaving to provide carriers to take his luggage to the next halt. The bissoyis were, of course, under no obligation to provide carriers for non-officials, who had to make their own arrangements with them. Very few had occasion to travel in the Agency and in fact I never met any in the Parlakimedi hills except a missionary, a young Canadian woman of great courage who, almost alone among people from outside the area, knew the Sowra language well. Her touring depended on the good will of the local bissoyi and it sometimes happened that, having arrived in a place with carriers provided by the bissoyi of the place from which she had come, she found the new bissoyi unhelpful and had great difficulty in getting out again. She cheerfully accepted malaria among the conditions of her work.

For Downing, too, progression on foot was the usual mode within the Agency Tract – or in one corner of the Nugur plateau by hands and feet up ladders permanently fixed in the hillside, but since the subdivision was traversed by the Godavari river, in his case there was an alternative, as he explains:

The other way of touring, when there was enough water in the river, was by the houseboat with which I was provided. This was perhaps the most delightful method of touring imaginable. Fir six months of the year, the houseboat lay at its mooring at Rajahmundry below the Ghats, but when the rains came in June, it was harnessed to a launch and brought up the river and I could embark on it and cruise up and down the length of my territory, tying up whereever there was work to be done or it seemed a pleasant spot to spend the night. A good deal of this houseboat touring was, in fact, done from Rajahmundry because it was the practice for three months in the summer when the river was at its height and surface communications in the Agency almost non-existent to move the Special Assistant Agent's office down to Rajahmundry from where I paid periodical river trips to the Agency to deal with arrears of court work and the periodical sales of liquor shops.

It was a somewhat lonely existence. One great standby was being able to have books sent to one from the excellent library of the Madras Literary Society. In my evenings at Bhadrachalam, I got through a great deal of serious reading which I should hardly have had time for anywhere else. But there was little social life and the only other Europeans in the Agency were two missionary ladies about thirty miles from Bhadrachalam at Dummagudem where, among other activities, they ran a lace-making school for Kaya girls. The senior lady, Miss Clara Wallen, was Australian and had lived at Dummagudem since 1902. I believe she had not been out of India since before the First War, but she had a worldwide circle of correspondents to whom she sent lace from her school and was, in every way, a delightful and stimulating personality. At that time, however, I did not find the loneliness oppressive. I enjoyed the sense of independence and responsibility.

The obverse of the isolation of the district officer in the Agency Tracts was his power of independent action in the many fields of which he found himself in charge. Downing writes,

The ordinary civil courts had no jurisdiction and, as Special Assistant Agent, I combined the function of Sub-Judge with that of Sub-Collector and Joint Magistrate and had power to try civil suits – fortunately very few as I never understood them – and I also had the power of a District Education Officer, Collector of Excise and Commercial Tax Officer, besides being ex-officio Chairman of the Agency District Board in which capacity I corresponded with myself as Sub-Collector, though I never quarrelled with myself and reported myself to the Board of Revenue, as one of my predecessors was alleged – probably apocryphally – to have done!

In spite of my multiplicity of functions, I was not overburdened with routine court or revenue work. The Kayas were honest and unlitigious people who seldom came into conflict with the law. Almost the only crime they committed was murder, usually as a result of a quarrel following a drinking bout as they were great consumers of palm toddy. Once the deed was committed, they invariably gave themselves up and made a confessional statement. I once had an accused murderer staying in my bungalow for twenty-four hours waiting to make his confessional statement as is was considered advisable to keep them out of police hands to ensure that their statement was made without intimidation. In fact, Kayas were virtually never convicted of murder. A plea of diminished responsibility was inevitably accepted and a relatively light prison sentence imposed.

Probably what gave me most satisfaction in the Agency was the sense of having the power to take action for the benefit of the people in my jurisdiction and actually see results flowing from one's own decisions. I had my own public works budget which I could spend as I pleased. I drew up my own roads maintenance programme, I could give a village the money for a new well and visit the village in a few months' time and see the well in operation. I found that most of the rural schools existed in name only. It was difficult to get teachers to go to the remote villages and often they never went near the schools at which they were supposed to be teaching, except when they heard that the Special Assistant Agent was about to visit them. I was able to find the money to establish a boarding hostel near Bhadrachalam where Kaya children could receive board and lodging while they attended school in the town. I still have the silver trowel with which I laid the foundation stone and which I received the authorization of the Madras Government to keep. I wonder if the hostel still exists.

I also had the satisfaction of feeling that I could, in certain ways, influence the framing of Government policy as far as the Agency people were concerned. For example, the Madras Board of Revenue had decreed that no new permanent assignments of agricultural land should be made until after the war in order to reserve land for men serving in the Armed Forces. This was a reasonable policy in most areas, but it made no sense in the Agency where for years we had been trying to wean the hill tribes from their traditional practice of shifting 'slash and burn' cultivation with its concomitants of deforestation and soil erosion. The Kayas and Reddis were regarded as totally unsuitable for military service so that there were virtually no ex-service men's interests to be considered. I put these considerations to the Board of Revenue, who accepted my recommendation and exempted the Agency areas from the operation of this particular order.

In all the jungle tracts, the main form of agriculture was 'slash and burn' cultivation (jhuming) of the hillsides, coupled with the cropping of the small areas of alluvial soil in the stream beds. Christie describes the system particularly vividly:

Jhuming suited the nomadic instincts of the hillmen and their carefree, indolent way of life. It was an easy, but wasteful form of cultivation, and, as the scope for unlimited movement became restricted, one of diminishing returns. The jhumias lived in bamboo houses, built on stilts and thatched with bamboo leaves or coarse grass, which, with the permission of the local headman and the co-operation of neighbours, could be put up in three or four days. There were no land disputes or boundary problems: the family lived above, in a single room with an open platform, and the pigs and chickens below. There they stayed for three, five, seven years until the land was exhausted or the urge to move again came upon them.

Every January or early February, they cut down the bamboos or other jungle in a patch on the hillside. This was allowed to wither and dry, and in early April they set fire to it. For a fortnight or so, there were bonfires all over the hills and the air was full of smoke and bamboo ash. When the first rains fell, in the middle of April, the whole family, men, women and children, would go out on the hillside and dig holes with the handles of their daos in the rain-softened, ash-covered soil. Into these they threw a handful of mixed seed, of paddy, cotton, millet and various vegetables, not forgetting a few cockscomb and marigold flowers to add colour to the crop. It was a cheerful social function and there was plenty of singing and laughing while they worked.

Thereafter, the work of the jhumia was normally easy. He only had to keep his jhum weeded and wait for results. Obediently, each crop came up and ripened in its season; first the paddy in August and September, then the millet and vegetables, and the cotton in November. The short-staple cotton was a valuable cash crop, in demand for mixing with long-staple varieties from other parts of India. Some was kept for the family loom and the rest was taken to market where the price he could get determined the degree of ease with which the jhumia could live for the rest of the year. The establishment and regulation of markets was an important responsibility of the Deputy Commissioner, for the convenience of the hillmen and also to ensure fair terms of trade. The jhumia would have got a better price if he had sold his cotton ginned – that is, after removing the seeds – but it was too much effort. He rated prosperity in terms of ease, two good meals and a pot or two of rice or millet beer a day. He was a great drinker and maker of songs, and a keen hunter of wild pig and barking deer, with a gun if he could afford it, otherwise with spear or traps. But the accumulation of wealth was an idea foreign to him, except in the form of silver rupees for necklaces to adorn his wife and daughters, and if these were hard to come by, there were orchids in the forest and marigolds in the jhum.

Easy as it sounds, jhuming was an uncertain form of livelihood. Late rains or drought could ruin a whole crop and, at rare intervals, the bamboos might flower and die, the seed attracting hordes of rats who would eat every grain of paddy growing in the jhums or stored in the granaries. At such times especially, the simplicity and thriftlessness of the hillman needed the protection of authority from the wily trader or money-lender from the plains.

It should be added that the plainsman also needed protection from the activities of the jhumias. Christie, as an ex-officio Port Commissioner of Chittagong, was made very aware of 'the damage and expense caused to Bengal's second major port by unrestricted jhuming in the Karnaphuli valley when silt from eroded river banks was washed down in the monsoon and kept two dredgers continually at work to clear the narrow harbour mouth'.

The revenue system in all the Agency Tracts was simple, at times almost non-existent, and collection, as Christie explains, was non-regulation to match:

My Bengali predecessor had been a sick man and unable to tour regularly so that Government dues had not been collected for nearly two years. The jhum tax was assessed on each household, with a commission for the Chief, if he troubled to earn it and did not line his pocket in other ways; the plough rent was assessed by area on the few settled farmers. Both taxes were simple and light, but no one will go out of his way to pay a tax. I must go to collect it, and the arrears, myself; but to sweeten the pill, I must offer some attraction, and turn each local collection into a gala day. Sometimes it was the police band, often it was the police elephants, but most successful of all was the Deputy Commissioner's wife who, dressed in khaki shirt, shorts and topi, could easily be, and sometimes was, mistaken for the Deputy Commissioner himself. There were occasions when the enthusiasm for this exhibit was such, when her real identity was established, that I had to draw a circle round her in the dust and say 'Thus far and no further' to inquisitive village women who had never seen a memsahib before and were intent on exploring if she were white all through. So the money came rolling in and no Government could be niggardly with grants in the face of such unlooked-for prodigality.

Revenue touring could be combined in the Chittagong Hill Tracts with training of the Hill Tracts Armed Police, grown slack and ill-disciplined over the years, and with what Christie describes as 'the usual work of reviewing gun licences, settling boundaries and appointing village officials.' More excitingly, there might be the organization of a kheddah to capture the wild elephants whose beautifully graded tracks, milestoned with their droppings, provided such good routes through the bamboo. Christie writes,

I had been getting reports of serious damage to crops by wild elephants on the edge of a reserved forest. It was really the business of the Forest Department to keep under control the fauna which they sheltered, but for some reason they were unwilling that year to arrange a kheddah – the capturing of elephants in a stockade – so I decided to do it myself. I read up all the manuals and literature on the subject, and engaged a kheddah contractor from Chittagong. On this first occasion, I paid the price of experience. The contractor had other more profitable work on hand, and postponed my kheddah until too late in the season. Very few elephants were caught, but the contractor pocketed his fee.

By the following year, I was wiser. The contractor tried to economise by building a stockade with thin walls and hoped to discourage the elephants from charging it by means of vicious spikes pointing inwards, concealed under bamboo leaves. This was not in the Queensberry Rules: I made him remove the spikes, build a double wall and make small openings through which we might rescue any very young elephants caught in the drive before they were trampled by the herd in the stockade.

The operation itself was skilful and exciting. For days, a large herd had been manoeuvred gently towards the wings of the stockade which were of lighter construction, stretching far into the forest. At the same time, the tuskers of the herd, which are troublesome and dangerous in a kheddah, were being gradually separated from the females and tuskless males.

On the appointed night, I was sitting on a platform above the stockade. The silence was eerie, broken only by the distant 'sawing' of a leopard. Suddenly, about a mile away in the forest, all hell broke loose. With yells, gongs, crackers and flaring torches, the herd was stampeded, driven between the long wings into the stockade, and the trap was dropped. The pandemonium and wild trumpeting within were fearsome. The terrified animals tried to charge the walls of the stockade, but could not get their shoulders to it as a trench had been dug round inside. We managed to rescue two small elephants through the openings. Next morning, the herd was quiet, but restless. Water and fodder were passed through the openings, but were not touched.

Then Lal Bahadur's turn came. The trap was raised and, with his brave mahout astride his back, toes behind each great ear to act as rudders, Lal Bahadur entered the stockade and trumpeted a challenge.

'Now, my pearl, my darling, carefully, go carefully', said the mahout in elephant language.

One stout-hearted old lady accepted the challenge and came forward. The rest made way as if to allow room for single combat. There was a short, fierce tussle with trunks intertwined, but Lal Bahadur's tusks were too much for her. She turned, and he chased her round the stockade, belabouring her with his trunk.

A few days later, the captured elephants, who had meanwhile accepted food and water, were brought out one by one and tethered, each beside a trained elephant. The process of indoctrination had begun.

We caught thirty-six saleable elephants, a profitable catch for Government and for the contractor. I had the pick of the bunch for the police, and chose an eighteen-year-old youngster to replace the pensioned Daisy. Within a fortnight, the new recruit had learnt to obey simple commands.

Kheddah operations were as rare as they were thrilling. But preparing programmes of inoculation against cholera and smallpox and the giving of simple out-patient medical care were experiences shared by most Agents. Medical aid, as Christie records, was indeed one of the most appreciated gifts which they could carry into the remote villages of the hills:

Earlier Deputy Commissioners, according to the tales I was told, seem to have governed by magic. Tom Lewin (Tong Loyn in Moghi, Tangliena in Lushai) was an expert conjuror and had allowed himself to be shot at ten paces by a muzzle-loading gun – from which he had palmed the lead bullet, and substituted a wax one – to demonstrate the invulnerability with which Queen Victoria had invested him. More recently, C. G. B. Stevens, a victim of terrorists in Comilla soon after he left the Hill Tracts, had regaled his audiences with card tricks. I could not match these feats, but my portable gramophone gave some entertainment and, perhaps more usefully, I was compelled to become a kind of witch doctor or medicine man. These villages were several days' march from the nearest hospital or dispensary and wherever I camped, the villagers brought their sick for me to cure. I took with me a medicine chest, and some of its contents were included for 'magical' as well as medicinal properties. The symptoms, in most cases, were a headache or a stomach ache or an open sore. Aspirins might relieve the pains, fruit salts frothed and bubbled impressively and permanganate crystals would incarnadine the water with which I bathed the sores. Malaria being endemic, quinine could do no harm, nor mentholated cough lozenges, and their bitter-sweetness was acceptable as a potent charm. In most cases, I urged, without much confidence that my instruction would be heeded, that the patient should go or be carried at once to the nearest dispensary. Their faith was touching. When I visited the villages again, I was told of the cures which had resulted from my unqualified treatment, but never of the failures. In between their panacea, I knew, was an opium pill.

From Christie's Chittagong Hill Tracts, a line of hills runs north to the mountain gorges where the Brahmaputra breaks through from Tibet into India and the Irrawaddy and Salween into Burma. Along this border land were a further series of Tracts – the Naga country, which Bowman describes, and so north to the Sadiya Frontier Tract at the very top of the Assam Valley where Lydall served as Assistant Political Officer. But the same pattern was repeated over the border in Burma – in the Lushai hills, or in Shwegu where Cockburn, to his evident pleasure, was posted. For Shwegu District, as he relates, contained two Kachin Hill Tracts, one on each side of the Irrawaddy, inhabited by Kachins, totally different from the plains Burmese in dress and most other ways:

The Kachins, together with a considerable number of other smaller tribes and ethnic groups, live in the extremely mountainous northernmost three hundred miles of Burma, as well as over the border in Yunnan. They had been on the move southward for some long time, but had been stopped by the British conquest of Upper Burma in 1885. My Kachin Hill Tracts represented one of their southern outposts. Unlike the Burmese, the Kachins were animists and very many had been converted to Christianity; they were a fighting race too and provided many recruits for the Burma Rifles and the Burma Frontier Force.

The vast mountainous frontier areas of Burma were almost entirely the responsibility of the Burma Frontier Service and not the I.C.S. so I counted myself lucky to have any Kachins in my charge and set off to visit them as soon as I could – in December 1939.

The country was much wilder than anything I had come across in Burma before. Instead of the bullock-cart, my kit was carried by elephants, instead of a Government bungalow or a Headman's house, I slept in a tent in a jungle clearing. I knew that wild elephants and leopards were common in the area and there were even a number of tigers so I did not sleep any too well my first night, but after that I settled down. I was interested to note that when we stopped to pitch camp each afternoon, the first act was to cut down a tall bamboo from the jungle and, using it as a flagpole, hoist the Union Jack. No one on the plains of Burma would ever have thought of doing that!

The path I was following – the only one indeed – ran along the foot of the small mountain range and all the Kachin villages were at the top. So each morning I had to leave my camp and scale three thousand feet to the village I wanted to visit. The Kachins, as befits hill-men, used paths which I found unbelievably steep and, although I was reasonably young and athletic, I was worn out by the time I reached the top – never has rice beer tasted better! The Kachins here lived in small villages made up of a few long houses occupied by complete families; thus, one day was enough for me to spend in each village trying to deal with any subject or complaint which any individual wished to raise. They were a law-abiding people and the journey to the SDO's office was very much too far to be worth making so they seemed quite willing to wait for an annual visit. Their problems were the usual ones of crop failure, trouble with elephants, health and so on; their complaints were over the ownership of property, of crops and so on.

They seemed to me to live at all times not far from the poverty-line. They had just a few pigs and fowls and what the jungle would provide. There was no level ground to allow for normal cultivation of rice and they seemed to know nothing of terraced cultivation; instead, they would burn and clear a stretch of hillside and sow hill rice there. After taking one or two crops, they would repeat the process on another piece of hillside and so on. This was known as taungya cultivation and was practised throughout the mountain areas of Burma. It was inefficient because yields were poor; it was unsatisfactory because it destroyed good trees, replacing them with a growth of bushes, and allowed the good top soil to be washed away by the rains, but against this, there was a virtually unending supply of hillsides available.

It was the custom for each Kachin who came to see me to bring a gift, normally a chicken or three or four eggs, so when, in late afternoon, it was time for me to return down the hill to my camp, I always had an embarrassing supply of gifts which I could neither refuse nor leave behind without causing grave offence. However, the local duwa (hereditary headman or chief) and other village elders always accompanied me to my camp so we had many available porters.

After supper, the arrangement was always that we gathered round the camp-fire and talked for hours – the Kachins would willingly have talked all night; we covered any subject from village hygiene to the war in Europe. I have never felt more humble than when, at the end of such a day, the local duwa, at least twice my age, would thank me for coming, saying that although I could only come once a year, my visit was something they valued greatly for I came as a father and helping them on a great variety of subjects.

I spent Christmas at a Christian Kachin village at the far end of the mountain range. This was peacock country so I had roast peacock for my Christmas lunch instead of roast turkey. Much to the villagers' delight, I bought a pig and a lot of rice and entertained them all to a Christmas meal of pork curry eaten from banana leaves.

It was a tangle of remote and difficult hills which sheltered the Kachins in Burma. Similar country was also found, however, in a broad band across central India. To the east, in the Madras Agency Tracts, this harboured the Sowras and Kayas; further west, in Bastar State, came the Muria and the Bison Head Marias (so called from their magnificent dancing head-dress incorporating bison horns) and, on the mountain fringes of the Bombay Presidency, the hunting Bhils were found. Symington was deputed to investigate the progress of the Bhils, while Hyde was appointed Dewan to the Maharani Prafulla Kumari Devi of Bastar, the last princess of the ancient Kakatiya dynasty.

Bastar as a State came under the ultimate control of the Foreign and Political Department, but Hyde, though merely seconded, had very wide powers, and equally wide responsibilities. In consequence he found the work very satisfying and creative. Even a brief recital indicates the extent of the matters over which he was in a position, as chief executive of the State, to act. He was able to initiate and achieve substantial improvements in communications, in forestry, agriculture and animal husbandry, and in the health services. In the social field he was able sharply to discourage an objectionable form of labour bondage for debt. And for the welfare of the tribespeople, which was a special concern, nothing was more satisfying than the medical work he encouraged – and nothing more appreciated:

There was one service the tribespeople appreciated above anything else the State could do for them and that was medical treatment, especially of the prevalent disease of yaws. They did not want schools where they were taught in an alien language (Hindi) usually by a Hindu teacher who was an unwilling exile in the, to him, un-congenial jungle. They wanted freedom from interference in their tribal way of life, a minimum of taxation and occasional festivities where they could dance, sing and enjoy a drink, but they really did want medical help. Early in my Bastar days, I decided to give priority to medical aid, to step up the provision of drugs, particularly the specifics for yaws, the German drugs neo-salvarsan and sulph-arsenol. This painful and disfiguring scourge was widespread amongst the aboriginal villages; it was contagious and often affected whole families. I also decided to increase the number of touring dispensaries so as to get treatment to as many of the more remote villages as possible and where the touring doctor could follow up cases which had been treated in the hospitals and permanent dispensaries. This was necessary because the rapid clearing up of the symptoms after one or two injections, which seemed miraculous to the tribespeople, led to their returning home too early before the completion of the course of treatment and so to relapses.

Following the example of my predecessor, Grigson, I would take a doctor out on tour with me; when the word went round, he would be fully occupied at every camp giving injections to the numbers of yaws patients who flocked in from all the accessible villages. After some experience of this and seeing the benefits it brought to the tribesmen, I first increased the budget provision and later gave the Chief Medical Officer *carte blanche* to purchase all the drugs he needed for the yaws campaign so that the staff would no longer have to restrict inoculations after the allocation had been exhausted. As most of the aboriginals, particularly the Marias, did not want to enter the hospitals as in-patients, when the new hospital was built we added a special covered shelter where they could camp with their families, light their fires and cook their food; this became very popular with the tribespeople coming in for yaws treatment. The campaign was so successful that I had hopes of being able to eradicate the disease throughout the State and even beyond its borders as we found patients coming for treatment from across the border in British India. It was, however, so very widespread that when I left, we were still treating vast numbers.

Over in Bombay, Symington was not only appointed to review the working of Government measures for Bhils and other tribal peoples, but was also involved in another specialist assignment as Criminal Tribes Settlement Officer. He assisted and briefly took over from O. H. B. Starte who had made his life's work the redemption of 'tribes and groups, often nomadic, who by heredity and tradition were criminals. Robbers, cheats, murderers, highwaymen, coiners, sneak-thieves, confidence-men, each tribe according to its guild and craft'.

To cope with a situation in which whole generations of children were brought up in the assumption that counterfeiting or housebreaking was their proper and only way of life, the Bombay Government had passed a Criminal Tribes Act. This identified the Criminal Tribes, provided for registration of men of those tribes who had a criminal record and for their surveillance, and, if necessary, required them and their families to live in a Criminal Tribes Settlement, the aim being, as Symington notes, to train them to earn an honest livelihood:

First, the settler was obliged to work for his living; reciprocally, the Department was obliged to find work for him to do. For this purpose, Starte and his team of equally devoted settlement-managers slowly built up good relations with mill owners, factory managers, railway officers, forest officers and other employers up and down the country in whose neighbourhood settlements were established. Secondly, the settler was required to support his family and to send his children to school. He was given a large plot in the settlement and helped with materials to build his house; and there, he and his neighbours, who were also his caste-fellows, lived their lives in conditions as far as possible similar to those in a village. Tribal affairs were dealt with by caste *panchas* (committeemen) and were not interfered with, provided they did not conflict with good order.

Registered settlers were required to attend roll-call morning and night, and at night to remain inside the settlements, some of which had perimeter fences. By day, they went to the town to work and were free to go about as they liked; but plain-clothes guards kept watch on the liquor shops and on the bazaars – to see that settlers only went there to *buy* things.

Besides industrial settlements, there were agricultural and forest-working settlements; anything that might help a man to a stable and normal way of life was tried.

After a period of good behaviour, a man's attendance at roll-call would be excused and he could move out of the settlement proper to an adjacent 'free colony'. Eventually, the last step was taken; his registration under the Criminal Tribes Act was cancelled and he was a free man. He would probably elect to continue in the free colony – to which indeed many men who had never been registered at all resorted of their own volition – which finally became a suburb of the neighbouring town.

A member of a Criminal Tribe who wanted to be a free man was required to have faith in himself and his ability to enter the ranks of honest society. And in officials, as Symington adds, what was required was a very large dose of faith and optimism and the knack of knowing true from feigned reform.

The 'crims' were generally very nice. They were always charmed to show off their skills. A V.I.P. visitor would smile in disbelief when warned that he would have his pocket picked while he stood there. The smile would change when one man handed him back his note-case and another returned a silk handkerchief to his wife. In dealing with their requests, one needed to be even more of a psychologist, or, preferably, a mind-reader, than in the usual line of service. When Hanmant Naik Ramoshi (*naik* – gand leader, in the Army, a corporal), once the leader of a notorious band of robbers, asked me for a pass to visit and attend to the lease of his fields, what did he really want to do? Dig up stolen property? Acquire some more? Pay off an old score? When I believed him, I did him much harm. He slid all the way down the worst kind of snake, and had to start again at square one.

And when five Haranshikaris said they *must* go on a long journey to get their hunting-nets exorcised since a nameless enemy had put a spell on them and they could not catch game any more, what was one to think? Naturally, I did not disbelieve them; indeed, I would have liked to know where to get my own gun exorcised as it had been bewitched for years; but could I honestly take the risk? If the treatment of the hunting-nets were to coincide with two or three housebreakings in the same neighbourhood, I could picture very well the caustic pity of the local Police Superintendent as he discussed the matter with me.

Misjudgements might have appalling consequences and backsliding could be thoroughly disheartening, but, as Symington records, the settlement system, given time, did work,

When I took over, the population in settlements and free colonies were eight thousand and five thousand five hundred respectively. The corresponding figures for my last year in India (1946) were four thousand five hundred and nine thousand five hundred, and illustrate the steady, if slow, accomplishment of our purpose. [Later Symington was given responsibility for the working of the Bombay Children Act which provided for the setting up of children's courts, remand homes, approved schools and a probationary service.]

If history drew the map of British India, nowhere did it do so more quirkily than when it added chains of islands off the west and east coasts of the continent. To the south-west of India run the coral islets of the Lacca-dives – the Laksha divi or 'hundred thousand isles' – and the Maldives. The latter, all but the northern island Minicoy, belong to Ceylon, the Laccadives plus Minicoy, were administered by Madras, an Inspecting Officer being deputed from Malabar district to them. Carleston describes these islands and a typical tour of inspection:

The Islands, whose inhabitants depended almost entirely on export of coconuts and coconut products for their livelihood, were governed under a special Regulation covering both civil and criminal justice. Subject only to the Madras Government and High Court, the Collector of Malabar and the Inspecting Officer were the supreme authorities. Each island had an Amin in control with a karnam (accountant and secretary) to assist him. Since there were no police, the Amin's authority had generally to be firmly upheld. It was an offence to disobey any 'reasonable order of an Amin'; specified offences included 'failure to assist in landing or drawing up a boat' and 'failing to attend when called upon to assist in protecting coconut plantations from the ravages of rats'. Rats were the prime pest, living on the coconut trees, moving from tree to tree and devouring the coconuts. Rat hunts were obligatory, and I held one on each island during my stay. Some of the Melacheris, the landless, tree-climbing class, climbed a group of trees, frightened and shook off the rats, which were then killed with sticks by people on the ground, very often on the way down (the hunters being quite expert in their timing!) and at any rate soon after. The islanders were expected to hold such rat hunts regularly, and the Amin had to keep a register showing the number of rats destroyed at each. But the islanders were lazy and registers could easily be faked. So they were ordered to keep the dead rats' tails for production before the Inspecting Officer. I had the job of counting rats' tails – 1,550 in one island, said to be the produce of two years' rat hunts. Some looked more than two years old. I had to ensure that the tails were effectively destroyed in my presence after counting lest they should be preserved for a future count!

Litigation was the favourite 'recreation' of these simple people. Nearly everyone had a petition of some sort, this being necessary to 'keep up with the Joneses so to speak. I soon began to ask each petitioner what was in his petition, and in quite a number of cases he did not even know. The petition-writers had been busy and were ready to provide the matter as well as the language of a petition! My cases included complaints against Melacheris (the tree-climbing poor) for wearing sandals or shoes, and in another island for carrying umbrellas – all of which was against Island tradi-tion. Melacheri Lib. was on the move; but for the sake of law and order, and for economic reasons too, changes had to come gradually. So, as a compromising first step, I permitted the wearing of shoes and sandals and the carrying of umbrellas by the Melacheris for weddings and on festival occasions. The Islanders were frequent visitors to the mainland, Calicut in particular, coming in their odams (large sailing vessels) to sell their coconut products and take back supplies of grain and other food etc., and not least to pursue their litigation at the Collector's office.

Minicoy differed in many respects from the other islands. The population was Mahl, as in the Maldives, while that of the Laccadives was Moplah to a man. Fishing was the main source of income – not to mention wrecks from which the Islanders supplemented their income from time to time. Many of these Islanders worked as 'lascars' on ships and had travelled considerably, bringing home all sorts of mementos, for example expensive and elaborate tea sets! There was a lighthouse on this island, generally visible on the voyage between Aden and Colombo. It was manned from Ceylon. Relations between the Islanders and the lighthouse people were never very good. There was some leprosy, and those suffering from it were, by mutual consent, restricted to a sort of settlement in the north of the island. 'Snake-boat' races and dancing were the island sports.

The eastern islands, the Andamans and then to the south of them the Nicobars, are a reminder of the days of sail. They were acquired during the search for staging posts on the India–China run and for a naval base open in the SW monsoon for operations in the Bay of Bengal when Madras and Calcutta were closed to sailing ships by stress of weather. They lie on an arc from Burma to Sumatra, but are directly administered from Delhi. Neither group shows any racial or cultural affinity with India, the Andamans being originally inhabited by stone-age Negrito tribes, the Nicobars by a Polynesian people. Thickly clothed in rain forest, linked by coral reefs and mangrove swamps, the cluster of islands [main settlement] was very beautiful, as Paterson recalls,

There was a vividness of colour, there was a clarity of light, there was the colouring of the sea and there was a sparkle about the whole place that was rather a joy after the somewhat dusty plains of the Deccan and the Central Provinces. The D.C.'s house – polished hardwood with enormous windows to let in the sea air – was a lovely house with a lovely garden stretching out towards the sea, bordered by two superb lines of casuarina trees and with marvellous views out to Ross Island and to Ritchie's Archipelago.

The reasons for a British presence in this tropical paradise had been various. Port Cornwallis, named after the admiral brother of the Governor-General of India, was an eighteenth-century naval base on the north of the island to cover the Bay and the passage into the China Sea – superseded first by Penang and in the nineteenth century by Singapore. A little later, a new settlement was established by Lieutenant Blair on South Island to prevent the activities of the aboriginals as wreckers or pirates, and this became the modern capital, Port Blair. A struggling foothold, it owed its development to the Indian Mutiny of 1857 for, as Paterson explains, a decision was taken that some of the mutineers should be exiled to a penal settlement to be created near Fort Blair.

Somewhat later still the advent of Christian missionaries to the islands in the 1880s and 1890s, drawn by reports of unredeemed souls 'black, naked and untutored', had unfortunate effects on the indigenous negrito population. Brought from their jungle habitat to Port Blair they quickly succumbed to the diseases of civilization and were virtually decimated. Twenty years later the survivors moved back to their native jungle, although it was a pitifully small band that was so restored to their original life.

Finally, from the early 1900s, as Paterson explains, a revolutionary change occurred in the administration of the penal settlement.

All convicts who came to the Andamans were volunteers, the attraction from their point of view being that, subject to good conduct, they earned a somewhat greater remission than they would have if they had served their sentences in an Indian jail. From the point of view of the administration, two conditions were imposed. First of all, that all convicts who came to Port Blair were serving long sentences and secondly, that they were not habitual criminals. The result was the most remarkable mix-up. There were Pathans from the North-West Frontier, Punjabis, Sikhs, Sindis, Bengalis, men from Southern India, Moplahs, Tamils, and men from Burma. There was no part of India that was not represented and somehow or other, this astonishing mixture had to live together. (The remarkable thing was that it worked and there was very little trouble indeed. There were some differences.) The Pathans did not like the Punjabis very much; the Sindis and the Sikhs rather hated each other and, in general, the men from the North of India had a somewhat condescending attitude to the Southern Indians and to the Burmese, but, considering what a polyglot mixture of race and religion the place was, it was quite remarkable that there were extremely few incidents.

The large percentage of convicts who came to Port Blair were murderers. They were men who had escaped the death penalty because of provocation or some other mitigating circumstances. The administrative arrangements were fairly simple. On arrival, a new convict spent three months in jail to give the administration a chance, however slim it may have been, to see if they had a homicidal maniac on their hands. At the end of three months, the new arrival was allotted to what were called convict stations that fairly closely resembled Army barracks. These were established at various points round the harbour and provided a very considerable labour force for maintenance, construction work, development work, work on the ship when in harbour and a labour pool for various departments of the administration. The men were paid the rate for the job and each barrack had a Jemadar, equivalent to a sort of Sergeant Major, responsible for the behaviour and conduct of the men living in that barrack. Their hours of work were laid down and, apart from the time they had to spend on work, the rest of the time was their own, except that they had to be in on time for roll-call in the evening. They did their own cooking, they did their own purchases, they bought their own clothes, there was no convict uniform. At the end of two years, subject to good conduct, the men could ask for their families to be brought from India to Port Blair at Government expense, provided the men themselves could find accommodation for their family although there was, if I remember rightly, a limited number of Government quarters.

Perhaps even more striking was that at the end of three years, again subject to good conduct, a convict could elect to become what was called a self-supporter. In other words, he could leave the barracks and set up in his own trade or profession and earn his own livelihood. The result was that garage mechanics, shop keepers, the hairdresser, carpenters and so on were as likely as not to be convicts. To take a couple of random samples of how this worked out in practice. In my own household, the second bearer was a Burman, a most immaculate and charming person who was serving a sentence for murder. My two gardeners were convicts and so were the four orderlies attached to me, of whom one was always on-duty at the bungalow in case of emergency. As another example, if I remember rightly, the crew that manned the round-the-harbour ferry service, including the Serang as skipper, were all convicts, and they really were a first-class lot.

But to come back for a moment to the convict stations. Each station was in charge of what was called a jailer, Anglo-Indians to a man. There were only eight of them and one of them was in charge of the jail and each of them carried, I think, a very heavy responsibility, but they really were very good at the job and I would like to pay tribute to them. They had a clear understanding of the general line of policy that was being pursued. They knew the men in their charge and, as I was to find, they had invariable capacity to cope with whatever situation with which they might be faced. The administrative structure for handling several thousand convicts would, I think, have made the Mandarins of the Home Office shudder, but the point was that it worked.

Paterson's instructions when he took over as DC were to keep discipline light, to move out the subversive Bengali political terrorists who were upsetting the convicts, and to provide constructive work and extra-mural activities to improve the quality of living for the convicts and the population as a whole. This last instruction Paterson set about fulfilling by trying to extend cultivation, by sports of many kinds for the convicts and even by baby shows:

I also organised an agricultural and crafts show, including a baby competition, and chucked in a certain number of sporting events for good measure. This proved a very considerable success and practically the whole population of Port Blair turned out on the day. There was a destroyer in at the time and I was standing somewhere at the back of the crowd with one of the Naval Officers, and he said to me, 'How many of these would be convicts?' I am afraid I could not resist shooting a bit of a line. I said, 'Well, perhaps two or three thousand', in my most casual voice, 'of whom perhaps two-thirds are murderers.'

More seriously, Paterson also co-operated with the Forest Department who operated on a considerable scale:

The reserves of timber in the jungle were very large and some of it was first-class timber indeed. I think it must have been a forest officer's dream job since it covered the whole range of forest activities from felling, extraction, transport to the mill, milling and, eventually, marketing and, of course, the question of forest conservation work. For felling and extraction, they used a quite considerable herd of elephants. [Radice records of his arrival in Port Blair, 'Among our fellow passengers were a number of elephants brought to work for the Forestry Department. These were lowered into the sea on arrival and swam happily ashore...'] The timber felled was extracted to a central point for loading onto a light railway which ran by gravity down to some point where it would be picked up in one of the Forest Department ships or towed as a log raft to the saw mills.

Finally, Paterson made the occasional visit to the Nicobar Islands, coral islands in the true South Seas pattern, running a long way further south to within a hundred miles of Sumatra. Dutch pirates, French Jesuits and the Danish East India Company had successively made contact with the Islands. Britain annexed them during the Napoleonic Wars, relinquished them, and in 1869 again took over control – from Malay pirates led by a deserter from the Royal Navy. Typically, the Islands lay within the diocese of the Bishop of Rangoon and it was on his advice that a resident Assistant Commissioner was selected – a man called Scott who, with his wife, agreed to take on the job. Of these we hear:

They were not missionaries in the pure sense, but both had, I think, deeply religious convictions and they and Richardson (a Christian, educated Nicobar man) were the main driving force in the slow process of educating the Nicobarese gradually into the ways of civilization. Money was not in use in the Island and the few traders who were allowed to trade there were very closely controlled. The system was a pure barter one. So many pairs of coconuts for a length of cloth or some salt or whatever was required. At some stage in his career, Scott had been a first-class footballer and one of his early means of contacting the Nicobarese was teaching them to play not only football, but really first-class football, and Scott used to make a little bit of money on the side whenever a destroyer or cruiser turned up by placing bets in the wardroom on a Nicobarese victory at any football match arranged with the crew of the ship.

It was here, on a last visit in January 1940, before his return to the Central Provinces, that Paterson saw, on the Post Office hut, a clear-cut notice which said, 'Next collection, April 1940'.

No further cry from the lush forests and palm-fringed coral beaches of Andamans or Nicobar could be imagined than the other special tract in which many officers served, the Political Agencies of Baluchistan and the North West Frontier of India; what Murray, with eyes still green from a posting in Assam, described as,

A savage desert of gravel plains and cruel mountains, stunned by heat in the summer and swept by bitter winds from the snow-covered heights in winter. It was 'Boys Own Paper' country with villages of fortified houses where outer walls were blank except for loopholes and stout doors, and the towers rose like miniature skyscrapers, neighbour seeking to overlook neighbour in order to have the upper hand. A parched and sparsely-peopled tract of inhospitable mountain desert, scanty of produce, whose beasts of burden were the camel or the ass, whose inhabitants went always armed to the teeth, ready to commit or suffer outrage, bold, brave, cruel and dangerous, ruled by the laws of the Koran and the blood-feud.

The district officer had entry to this world through selection for the Foreign and Political Department of the Government of India. The Viceroy himself held this portfolio and he vetted applicants personally. ('The Viceroy, Lord Wavell, looked us over one at a time. He was laconic and regarded me wordlessly across his desk. I wished to look him in the eye', Murray recalls, 'but was not sure which eye was good and which was glass, and so looked at each in turn.') Those who went to the Frontier as Politicals had all had district experience in some other province. But unless they were posted to the five settled districts of Hazara, Peshawar, Kohat, Bannu and Dera Ismail Khan, little of their experience would find any direct application. In the North West Frontier Province beyond the settled districts, and in Baluchistan, the Political Agents 'managed' but did not administer the tribal areas under their jurisdiction.

In Baluchistan, where feudal states such as the Khanate of Kelat survived, tribal chiefs and elders had considerable influence which could be used in the control of the tribes, either informally or by their presence as members of jirgas or tribal councils. In Waziristan and other parts of the NWFP, however, there were no rulers or chiefs, but rather a fierce belief in his own worth of every individual tribesman. Curtis happily describes this individuality as 'the dictatorship of the proletariat expressed, not in the tyranny of the few, but in the license of the many. It was not anarchy, but it was nearer to it than any European could comfortably go.' Here the whole tribe was involved in decision making.

In both Baluchistan and the NWFP local policing was left largely to the tribes themselves. In the same way all crimes and disputes in which frontier tribesmen were involved were dealt with under the Frontier Crimes Regulation by the tribes themselves. The different social structure of the two areas led, however, to marked differences in the way the system worked. Curtis, at Nasirabad in Baluchistan, in describing the jirga system in operation demonstrates the impact of social hierarchy:

The magistrate framed issues and then referred the case to a Council of Elders under the presidency of a named individual. The Jirga had some resemblance to the old

English jury, but it was not selected at random. Less important cases were referred to a Jirga nominated by the magistrate from a list of persons of standing and established character. This was drawn up partly in accordance with tribal custom and partly as a result of discussion. More important cases were put before the standing Jirga of Nasirabad which included all the notables of both east and west tahsils.

Jirgas paid no regard to the Code of Criminal Procedure or to the Indian Evidence Act – a codified form of the English and Scottish Law of Evidence. No pleaders were allowed to appear before them. They followed their own procedure. If they found difficulty at arriving at the facts – which was not often – they would administer oaths. A Baluch tribesman did not easily forswear himself, and that he should do so, swearing by his Tumandar's (Chief's) beard, was quite unthinkable.

Their methods of business were informal. Passing by the courtyard of the tahsil where a Jirga was going on, I have seen in one corner a group of grey beards huddled round a huqqa, enjoying a smoke and a chat; another bespectacled elder absorbed in a vernacular newspaper; yet another deep in conversation with a witness, while the remainder could be discerned in the midst of a small crowd, every one of whom appeared to be in full cry.

At the end of all this, they would give a coherent account of what they thought had occurred, what the relevant tribal custom was, and how they thought the matter should be dealt with. All this would be recorded in writing by a clerk detailed for the purpose.

The magistrate was not bound to accept the Jirga's findings or recommendations, but he could not come to a contrary conclusion. If he was not satisfied with the report, he could refer the matter to a Jirga of higher standing. The supreme Jirga was the Shahi Jirga of Baluchistan which included the leaders of all the tribes of the province.

In Waziristan, however, there was no question, as Lydall saw, of hierarchies of elders and leaders:

These Jirgas were not the Councils of Elders which I had known in Loralai (Baluchistan), but a collection of an entire tribe, sitting on the ground in a semi-circle many rows deep and tending all to talk at once. At the centre point of the semi-circle would sit the Political Agent, the Assistant Political Officer and/or myself, trying to make ourselves heard. The handing over of offenders would be demanded, failing which tribal responsibility would be enforced, hostages would be taken or rifles deposited as security.

That tribal responsibility was accepted by the individual tribesmen followed from the situation of the tribe 'as a society united by a common aversion to its neighbours', as Curtis puts it:

Tribal society is designed to stand the shocks of war. It maintains a discipline superior to other forms of society. The life and property of the individual are at the disposal of the clan. He must make peace or war in accordance with the general will which is arrived at in open discussion to which every tribesman may make his contribution. The clan, on the other hand, is answerable for the behaviour of its members. In a society where public business is decided without the aid of letters, the tribesman learns to speak lucidly, persuasively, and often wittily.

Each tribe or clan maintains an account, as it were, of profit and loss, not only in matters economic, but also in matters of 'ghairat' (self-respect); and that account must be kept in balance. Nowadays, money is often the solvent of a debt; but it is a kind of paper currency, the validity of which may always be questioned. The gold in tribal transactions is life. This is the basis of the blood feud, that terrible institution in whose shadow most tribesmen pass their days, never entirely 'defended from the fear of their enemies' – to use the phrase in the Anglican Prayer Book – and obliged to devote to security, to a new rifle or a taller tower resources which might well have been deployed in the development of their country. However, it can be argued that in a country where there is no Government to enforce sanctions on those whose conduct is injurious to others, the blood feud spares as much life as it destroys. The fear of provoking a feud to be the curse of generations of his descendants must give a man pause.

This was certainly the case in Baluchistan where, Curtis argues, the tribesman's object was to seek such a settlement that the injured party's relations would not consider themselves in duty bound to pursue the matter further, and thus to avoid further feuding and disorder. Curtis adds, however, there was no evidence that the people of Nasirabad envied their Sindi neighbours their police, pleaders, magistrates' and judges' courts.

In Baluchistan there was no police force. Instead there were levies produced by the different tribes who served a term and were then replaced. Their equipment consisted of a coloured pagri and a Sam Browne belt. They were expected to come with a mount, usually a Baluchi mare, a gallant little breed characterized by pointed ears which almost met over the animal's head. They provided their own weapons, a sword, a shot-gun or a flint-lock. There was a reserve of magazineless Lee Enfield which could be issued in emergency. However Baluchi custom accepted a duty to support the ruler and to turn out a pursuit party much as our ancestors were obliged to join in a hue and cry. It was also accepted that a community which failed to do its duty might equitably be called upon to pay a collective fine.

In the NWFP the same rough system applied. Emerson describes the position in the Wana or South Waziristan Agency:

Being transborder territory, the laws of British India did not, in general, apply to the Mahsuds, and a system of tribal and territorial responsibility was enforced by the Government and accepted by the tribesmen. Offences occurring beyond the occupied forts and the roads, between tribesmen, were not regarded as our concern, but if a crime was committed in our enclaves or on the roads, the tribe in whose territory the crime had taken place was expected either to produce the offender or be punished themselves. As it was contrary to the Pathan code of honour, to hand over anyone, except in very special circumstances, the tribe usually paid up.

If the Jirga did not acknowledge responsibility for an outrage and make reparation, then some measure of compulsion was applied by the Political Agent. That pressure might be economic or military and be exerted through various instruments of control. One approach to the problem presented by the frontier tribes was to encourage them to integrate economically with the settled districts. The administrative border was, therefore, an open one which, in the winter months, would be crossed by tribesmen bringing down produce – notably of timber – for sale in the plains. They were, in effect, hostages for the good behaviour of the tribe, and *barampta* – the arrest and detention of tribesmen of an offending tribe found in India – was a traditional instrument of control. Again, a system of allowances existed, twice yearly payments for good behaviour distributed to tribal leaders. This Curtis describes:

During the summer, I went from Scouts' Post to Post paying half yearly allowances. The system had its merits as it reminded one, periodically, of the personalities and problems of life of each clan. The P.A. had his own rooms in each post, but I used to mess with the one or two Scouts Officers in residence. If I had a day to spare, I used to go out on gasht with them. They moved fast over steep and rough country and I was always anxious lest I let the good name of my service down.

The second payment he made from his winter base for South Waziristan at Tank:

As I looked at the tribesmen, I would see a striking display of nose, beard and whisker. But more formidable than these features would be their eyes, which gave, at best, a cold, at worst, a cruel expression to their faces. The elders of the tribe (Pushtu Spingerai, literally the white bearded) would be prominently seated. At the back would be the kasharan – the young men – noisy and excitable, but occasionally reduced to silence by some sour comment from an elder. Distribution of allowances was followed by general discussion. All the old grievances were trotted out. The contribution of the A.P.O. [Assistant Political Officer] at this stage was invaluable. He knew the details of every case and would come up with the one aspect of it which the tribesmen had found it convenient to forget. It was important to keep the discussion friendly and never to score off any tribesman so as to make him a laughing stock. Bad enemies might be made that way. When a tribe had offended and was unrepentant, it was possible to stop tribal allowances.

Again, there was a system of tribal police, known as khasedars. They had no uniform and provided their own weapons. They manned posts along the roads and their primary duty was to aid the Scouts in keeping the roads open. They also escorted political officers when they moved about tribal territory. While it was unlikely that the khasedar would do much to defend one, his very presence was a protection. An ill-directed shot hitting a khasedar might provoke a blood feud.

Khasedari brought in about seven lakhs of rupees yearly to the Mahsuds. This sum, and various contracts for roads and the like could be put in jeopardy by contumacy.

But there was also a very mobile military arm which the political agent could bring into action, the various bodies of Scouts – the Tochi Scouts, the South Waziristan Scouts – Pathan corps some thousands strong, recruited mainly, but not exclusively, from the settled districts and officered by selected British and Indian officers and responsible to the governor, not to the army commander. They occupied forts strung out along the roads leading to the major garrisons of regular troops such as Wana, Razmak, Bannu or the Khyber. How these were employed to deal with various levels of tribal offence is thus described by Lydall:

The villages of the offenders might be rounded up by a Scout gasht (patrol). As an example (to quote from North Waziristan Weekly Political Summary for the week ending 7 June 1938) 'On June 5th, the Commandant, Tochi Scouts and the Assistant Political Agent were returning in the latter's car from Ambor Shiga when a bomb exploded under them near mile forty-six, ruining the off-front wheel of the car. Accordingly, the Scouts gasht, on their return from Ambor Shiga, rounded up the neighbouring villages and arrested thirty-five men, including several bad characters. Next morning, a Hamzoni Daur Jirga were informed that they would be fined five hundred rupees – unless the culprit and adequate proof were produced within ten days. The same evening, the real culprit – one Mir Shaid Khan Umarzai – was produced by the Maliks.' The Scouts Commandant, Felix Williams, had been much affronted by a bomb being put where he might run over it. I, on the other hand, was irritated because, having put my tribal chauffeur in jail for murdering someone in pursuance of a blood feud, I had to change the damaged wheel myself.

More serious cases of bad behaviour called for larger scale reprisals. A military column would advance into the territory of the delinquent tribe and try to bring them to battle before they faded away. They would then 'exert economic pressure', which involved, for instance, blowing up agricultural water-channels which had been built with Government money and encouragement. Either Bacon or I would accompany the column and we would be supported by a handful of tribal representatives.

In the most serious cases of delinquency, when a whole tribe was involved – as when, in my time, the Madda Khel Wazirs were harbouring the Faqir of Ipi – and when military activity had produced no change of heart, the R.A.F. would be brought into play. The whole area of the tribe would be proscribed. A few days' notice would be given, after which planes would fly over the proscribed area and bomb any sign of life. This was, of course, a form of blockade rather than of belligerence; nevertheless, Government got a bad name internationally for 'bombing peaceful civilians'. But at least it was more effective than military operations, besides normally killing nobody on either side. One or two small areas called sanctuaries would be indicated into which the tribe would crowd, abandoning their homes and what agriculture and grazing they might have. Neighbouring tribes would be forbidden to harbour them under threat of being proscribed themselves and altogether they would suffer sufficient hardship, especially in winter, to encourage them fairly rapidly to send a Jirga to negotiate a settlement.

Even in the hills, in tribal territory beyond the administrative border, not all aspects of civilian administration and development were left behind. The open border encouraged trade, and road building not only gave employment to hundreds of tribesmen, but encouraged the growth of trade. What could also be done was to encourage education, as Curtis records,

I was always encouraged when Jirgas asked for help with education or with schemes to improve the productivity of their land. My allotment for financing schools was small and was soon exhausted, although the tribesmen asked for minimal help with the payment of the salary of a school master and the purchase of equipment. Government were curiously unresponsive when asked to increase it. However, some of the clans accepting that it was unlikely that they would get help from Government during the war, set up their own schools. The financial commitment was not heavy. They had to pay a school master, but that was not a well-paid profession in India; a room had to be made available, and slates and books purchased, but no furniture was needed as the little scholars sat on the ground. I have seen in such an establishment a few little girls – a welcome sight – but they were always withdrawn at eight years of age. This, of course, was only primary education. At this time, a number of sons of maliks attended the High School Dera Ismail Khan where they boarded at a hostel managed by the C.M.S. Thence some made their way to Peshawar to the Edwardes' College or Islamia College for an university education.

And when possible, he relates, schemes for land reclamation were also introduced, difficult though these were.

They either involved embanking land in the bed of a torrent to protect it in time of spate; or making a karez (an underground water-channel in the construction of which certain tribes from Afghanistan are skilled); or making a surface irrigation channel. Obviously, money could not be granted without ascertaining whether the project was practical, and whether it was being spent for the purpose for which it was granted. That meant that some officer must have access to the site under tribal protection – a matter not lightly to be undertaken by a tribe since it presented their enemies with an opportunity to make mischief.

However, both Curtis and Emerson made considerable excursions into the hills to view spots where wire-netting reinforced embankments might be thrown across the streams to embank land and provide irrigation, relying on tribal laws of hospitality.

'During the whole of my trip', Curtis comments, 'I never once felt uneasy about my safety. But when I heard the evening call to prayer and realised that I was the only man paying no heed to it, I had a feeling of cold isolation.'

FURTHER READING

It is interesting, in the light of the major effort made since independence by the governments of India and Pakistan to integrate the tribal and frontier area peoples, that district officers seem to have accepted without comment the alternative British strategy of shielding them from outside social, economic and political pressures. The one obvious continuity from the pre- to the post-1947 period is in the equivocal attitude of district officers towards evangelization. There is an extensive anthropological literature on tribal India and an equally large literature on the North-West Frontier. The following are a relevant sample:

C. C. Davies, *The Problem of the North-West Frontier* (Cambridge 1932), is a straightforward narrative of the development of frontier policy, and Sir Olaf Caroe, *The Pathans, 550 BC–AD1957* (London 1958) provides a vigorous survey by a man who was Governor of the NWFP, and F. Barth's admirable *Political Leadership among Swat Pathans* (London 1959) offers an effective social analysis.

Stephen Fuchs, *The Aboriginal Tribes of India* (London 1977 and India 1973) is a solid general survey with a full bibliography. Two distinctive approaches are C. von Fürer Haimendorf, *Morals and Merit* (London 1967) and F. G. Bailey, *Caste and the Economic Frontier, a Village in Highland Orissa* (Manchester 1957) which are both written with verve. For central India there are a series of books by Verrier Elwin, including *Leaves from the Jungle* (London 1936) and for Bastar State, *The Muria and their Ghotul* (Bombay 1947).

On the Indian Political Service as a whole there is the comparatively recent study by T. C. Coen, *The Indian Political Service, a Study in Indirect Rule* (London 1971).

CHAPTER 9

BURMA – THE LOST PROVINCE

As the Montagu-Chelmsford Report 1918 said: 'Burma is only by accident part of the responsibility of the Governor-General of India. The Burmese are as distinct from the Indians in race and language as they are from the British.' Yet up to 1937 Burma was governed as part of India and only at that late date did the separation take place which recognized the marked differences between the two countries. In the following pages these will be illustrated from the experience of ICS officers who served in Burma. Elsewhere the voices of Indian members of the service have been heard. That there are no quotations from Burmese members is an indication of the degree to which the present regime in Burma has sought to isolate itself and impose censorship on communication with the outside world. Burmese members were not invited to contribute, and if they had been, would probably have considered it more discreet not to do so. In any case Burmans began to come into the service at a later stage than the Indians, and consequently there were fewer with much experience or seniority by 1947. Unfortunately the outstanding Burmese member, U Tin Tut, was assassinated in 1947, having retired from the ICS to enter independence politics.

The marked cultural and political differences that led to separation meant also that the ICS in Burma lived and worked in a setting totally unlike India, even if the actual nature of the work they did was much the same in both countries. Historically much of Burma had been under British rule for a far shorter time than most parts of India. Culturally, as Donnison notes, 'there were not the extremes of wealth and poverty of India. There were no maharajas or wealthy industrialists – on the other hand there was not the grinding poverty.' Burmese women enjoyed a status and freedom unknown in India and rare in Europe. Moreover, since most of the inhabitants were Buddhist, religion contributed to social homogeneity where in India it often divided. There was not the endemic Hindu-Muslim religious bitterness and there was for all practical purposes no caste. Cockburn emphasizes the significance of this religious factor:

One cannot write of the villages without a reference to Buddhism. In the villages its influence was entirely for good. The religion gave the Burmese a standard of behaviour, the monks gave an example. In every main village there was a Buddhist monastery and here every child came to school – as a result there is virtually total literacy among the Burmese. In the cities the position was rather different for many of the younger monks had little to do other than involve themselves in political protests of one sort or another. Buddhism was the main provider of entertainment for the villages also in the shape of pagoda festivals. They had their religious element but there was always a fair-ground also with a variety of food-stalls and gambling stalls. Most popular of all was the *pwe*, a stage play put on in the open air, and full of nicely vulgar doubles-entendres, which usually went on all night, the audience coming and going as it suited them.

Though there was much regional variety within Burma, Richards attempts a summing-up of the Burmese character as follows:

They were an easy-going, laughter-loving community with whom it was easy to be on good terms. Few of them lacked a marked sense of humour. It was not in their natural make-up to adopt a rather cringing, suppliant attitude towards those whom they recognised to be their superiors. They were great supporters of the stage. They excelled in parody and burlesque, bringing the house down with their imitations of what they thought amusing about the way the Britisher dressed, ate, talked Burmese and generally conducted himself. They took off the accentuated penuriousness, meekness and love of money displayed by the Indian, the guile and commercial acuteness of the Chinese.

Though, perhaps, he lacked the application and dogged perseverance of the Indian, the Burman would work industriously and competently when he had to. But there was that volatility in his nature that, after a long and tedious bout of labour, he must suddenly, without notice, take a day off and see his girl friend. He saw little object in doing more work than was necessary. Unlike the Indian, he rarely saved, but spent his money without much thought for the future. The Burman was quick to wrath...

I think I am right in saying that Burma had more murders than any other province.

The volatility of the Burmese was not without effect upon the district officers who served in Burma. 'I think that some of all this rubbed off on us', Donnison remarks, 'Taken together I think that all these factors contributed to an easier and more relaxed atmosphere and in consequence of this, a less remote and starchy attitude amongst European members of the ICS.' The fact that Burma was in many areas lightly populated meant that

the population of districts were correspondingly less – a large district might have 700,000–500,000, most had less, some very much less. As a result of this lesser size of districts in Burma Civil Stations were also smaller. In smaller stations there was less temptation for Europeans to remain aloof, indeed if they did they might find themselves with no social contacts at all.

Moreover, although Burma might constitutionally form part of British India, historical and geographical factors had always made this a remote and isolated province, and Donnison argues that this, too, contributed to the less formal atmosphere of district work and life.

Before the days of air transport it was a three-day sea journey from Rangoon to Calcutta. The Viceroy was not resident in Burma – we were therefore spared vice-regal pomp and circumstance. There was in peace-time no army presence in Burma comparable to that in India. Postings of Indian civilians from Burma to the Government of India were rare. Accordingly there was not the same ossifying weight of history and tradition as had built up in India.

The remoteness of Burma and the many ways in which it differed from India meant that as the prospect of substantial advances towards some form of self-government for India drew closer and assumed form with the despatch of the Simon Commission to India and the holding of the Round Table conferences in London the issue of Burma's relationship with India also became more urgent. The original intention of the Simon Commission had been to concentrate constitutional change at the provincial level, leaving the centre untouched. But Indian pressure – including that from the Viceroy Lord Irwin – and the need to involve Princely India, led to plans being made for some devolution of authority at the centre too. Such a move was given some impetus by the appearance of overt Burmese nationalist feeling expressed in an abortive rebellion in 1931–2, which Wallace describes, parallel to the civil disobedience movement of those years in India. It was at this point that the possibility of separating the Government of Burma from that of India took shape. The approach to separation and the manner of its achievement have been set out by Donnison:

A general election held in 1932 was fought on the separation issue and the result was an almost solid, if very surprising, vote *against* separation. First thoughts and speeches on assembly of the new house did not bring much light. But gradually it became clear that while Burmese opinion, as had been expected, favoured separation in principle, it wished, as a matter of tactics, to defer this until after Burma had derived the maximum political advantage from continued, albeit terminable, association with India. The British government was not prepared to give Burma the option she desired of contracting out of the India government when she thought this might suit her convenience and decided that in view of the pledges given that separation would not prejudice political progress, the wishes and the welfare of the Burmese people would be best met by immediate separation. Separation was 'forced' upon Burma and accepted with a sigh of relief. There was no audible criticism, and the issue passed straight out of politics.

From his experience as an SDO in one of the two sub-divisions of Minbu district on the western side of the Irrawaddy river, Wallace confirms that:

Little heat was engendered by the election. This does not mean that there was not some wild speaking (on the anti-Separationist side) notably by some young men up from Rangoon in April 1932 (two of whom, U So Thein and Thakin Ba Sein, later in different ways were to cause great trouble over many years to British and, later, independent Burmese Governments). We had reports of inflammatory approving references from the platform (not from So Thein or Ba Sein personally) to the killing of Subdivisional and Township Officers in India and to bloodshed being the only way of gaining political salvation. Such references moderated when it was observed that speeches were being taken down in shorthand.

Richards, too, ran into some anti-British feeling at Henzada in the early 1930s. When U Saw, a well-known political fire-brand, went round the district calling for 'the expulsion of the "British dogs of foreign despotism" who should be "kicked into the sea",' Richards arrested him. A year or two later Richards met U Saw again, but this time he was a Minister paying an official visit to Tharrawaddy where Richards was then DC:

I had been waiting a bare five minutes when a chuprassee came and asked me to go upstairs. U Saw, at once, offered me a chair, and the first thing he said to me was, 'Well, Mr. Richards, I hope you have forgiven me for what happened at Henzada', which shows that even the worst men, among whom U Saw would certainly merit a place in any 'Newgate Calendar' of Burma, have at times their generous impulses.

Despite these Burmese political manoeuvrings separation took effect on 1 April 1937. In the words of Donnison:

I doubt whether this in itself made any appreciable difference to the life of an officer in the districts. At headquarters in Rangoon it meant the assumption of new functions that had hitherto been the responsibility of the Central Government of India. These included such matters as foreign affairs, defence, monetary policy and coinage. New departments of government were created to administer these. In addition between the Government and those directly concerned with the assessment and collection of the revenue, there were interposed two Financial Commissioners, a kind of Board of Revenue. Each of the Commissioners had a Secretary who was in charge of the office. I came to be Secretary to the Financial Commissioner responsible for what had originally been central government revenues, mainly Customs and Income Tax.

The Government of India Act 1935 not only provided for the separation of Burma from India, and for the creation of new provinces in India such as Sind and the North West Frontier Province. It also greatly altered the relationship between the bureaucracy and the politicians, putting an end to dyarchy and entrusting all the portfolios of the provincial governments to a cabinet of elected ministers. Burma did not escape this phase of political evolution, as Donnison records:

But what did make a considerable difference to the administration, both in Rangoon and up-country, was that separation coincided in time with the grant to the Burmese of a much greater instalment of very real self-government, indeed it was the same Act of Parliament that wrought both these changes. At the headquarters of Government there was a fundamental change in the relations between civil servants and their ministers – the latter had a very real measure of power. And as ministers realised this they were not slow to interfere in the districts also for party or purely personal reasons.

In the pre-war period nationalist politics in Burma seem to have attracted less notice than parallel developments in India. The leaders were little known outside Burma and the issues were sometimes parochial. But the pressures were there, as McGuire noticed in Myitkyina in 1938–9:

Although the district remained quiet, I became increasingly aware of the rising tide of nationalism. The House of Representatives was pressing for early self-government as a condition precedent to full support to the war effort. This of course could not be conceded, and the Governor made it clear that our first concern was to win the war. The political parties responded by becoming more vociferous, and I was soon given some idea of what I should look out for. The main parties were the *Myochit*, led by U Saw, the *Sinyetha*, led by Dr. Ba Maw who later became President of the puppet regime under the Japanese, and the *Dobama Asiyayon*, a sort of Burmese National League of fairly recent origin whose members called themselves 'Thakins' or 'Masters'. The *Thakins* needed watching most, as their resolutions and speeches were violently anti-British. Among them was U Aung San, later to lead a select gang into Burma along with the invading Japanese and still later to become Premier, at the end of the war. Most of the leaders were University graduates.

What was significant, of course, was that after separation there would be little more than two years of peace in which change could work itself out and less than five years before Japanese invasion engulfed Burma. The time scale in Burma was thus considerably foreshortened, making comparisons with Indian experience less relevant.

It would be useful, therefore, to consider those aspects of district work which were peculiar to that country. Burma was rich in minerals, particularly in oil, mainly found in Upper Burma along the Irrawaddy. So a district officer might find himself as McGuire did, under the rather splendid title of Warden of the Oilfields, superintending the operations of three big British oil companies, a smaller Indian concern, and some twenty-four Burmese families operating shallow hand-dug wells. He was in general administrative charge of the oilfields and controlled the issue of prospecting and mining licences, collected the government's royalties, protected the oil-bearing sands from damage, investigated accidents, intervened in labour disputes and kept a general eye on the whole industry.

If oil production was largely the preserve of the industrialized Burmah Oil Company, a giant on the Burma scale, the extraction of jade, a more romantic if, in the aggregate, less valuable mineral was in the hands of small-scale enterprise. McGuire, before becoming Warden of the Oilfields, had been DC at Myitkyina in the far north of Burma and writes:

West of Mogaung, and a day's march into the hills, were the jade mines. They were unique in that part of the world and produced some highly valued jade. They were not extensive but large enough to accommodate a fair-sized community of Chinese, who had almost monopolised the area since the days of the Burmese kings. The Chinese were industrious and expert craftsmen and had built up an extensive trade. The mines themselves were a mixture of jade-bearing surface stones of various sizes, mostly in and around river beds, and of shallow mines of rock. Outwardly a jade-bearing stone is rough-skinned and, to the ignorant, very like any other stone. The expert Chinese, however, knew the difference. When they picked up a stone which they thought would hold jade, they would scrape or file off a small section of the skin. If it was a jade stone, the jade would become visible. They would then sell it to the traders. Sometimes they would leave the stone as they found it and sell it blind. A lot of bargaining went on with the traders, also mostly Chinese, before deals were completed. The stones eventually found their way, some to Rangoon and Mandalay, but most of them to China for manufacture into ornaments, necklaces, bangles, rings and so forth. I saw one stone, the size of a football, with its window opening on what appeared to be translucent, apple-green jade and therefore of the highest quality. The lucky owner estimated its value ex site at a lakh of rupees, about £7,500. No stone, large or small, was disregarded. Not all the jade was green, there was a variety of colours, but green predominated.

I visited the jade mines several times, not only for sight-seeing but also to ensure that there was no trouble and that royalties were paid. Technically the area was within the domain of the local Kachin *duwa*, or chief, but in fact it was left to look after itself. There was no cause for worry on communal issues. No doubt there were quarrels and fights, but there was no serious crime.

We had to turn a blind eye to the Chinese addiction to gambling. It would have been too expensive to expand the administration to enforce the gambling laws, and in any case I doubt whether the Chinese would have submitted patiently to the process. Also, as the mining area was an entity on its own, tucked away in the hills, gambling did not attract either plains Burmese or the impoverished Kachins. So the Chinese gamblers in effect took in their own washing, and we were content to leave them to it.

Opium was a problem, but no large scale smuggling was brought to notice, nor was there evidence of addiction spreading to the plains. Here again it would have been administratively impossible, without considerable and expensive preventive staff, to enforce prohibition.

Two other largely overlapping problems special to Burma were those relating to the presence in the country of considerable numbers of Indian immigrants and to the opening up of Lower Burma to the cultivation of rice for export on a massive scale. Burma being overwhelmingly Buddhist, escaped the religious tensions created in India by the rivalries of Hindu, Muslim and Sikh. But it did not escape racial tensions between Burmese and Indians, as Cockburn discovered as a young magistrate in Mandalay in 1938:

On this occasion the riots were country-wide and the Burmese were attacking Indians. There were large numbers of Indians throughout Burma and, unfortunately for them, they were disliked and despised by the Burmese. They were disliked as foreigners and because many of them, as money-lenders, had acquired amounts of land from Burmese who could not repay their debts. They were despised because many of them did work which the Burmese thought too heavy – dock coolies – or too unpleasant – sweepers or rickshaw wallahs. For these and other reasons there was always trouble ready to erupt.

In the same year Richards, who was then DC Tharrawaddy in the lower delta country, saw violence erupt:

Riots broke out in towns all over Burma, with indiscriminate slaughter of Indians, men, women and children, whether they were Mahommedans or Hindus, accompanied by burning and destruction of shops and houses owned by the Indian population and the looting of bazaars where they sold their wares. As one would expect, Tharrawaddy was one of the districts most affected and firing on rioters and looters had to be opened on several occasions. Slashed and battered bodies of men, women and even children lay about in several of the towns. I was constantly on tour, travelling from one scene of disturbance to another, and it was the most harrowing week I have ever spent in my life, not excepting some of the scenes of carnage in the First World War.

Once violence had been contained the Government of Burma appointed a committee of enquiry, to which Donnison was appointed as secretary.

To cool off tension, and ascertain the facts, the government set up an Inquiry Committee under a High Court Judge, Mr Justice Braund. His committee of four included two Burmans, U Khin Maung Dwe and U Po Han, and two Muslims, Senator Rahim and Dr. Rauf. After hearings in Rangoon the Committee decided to continue its inquiries in the districts affected. As most of these were in the delta or along the Irrawaddy, the Committee, at my suggestion, decided to tour these areas in the Burma Government launch *Irrawaddy*, a large, comfortable, and imposing river vessel used by the Governor for riverine tours. There was accommodation for the six of us and our office, and also for a cook and staff whom I engaged. The obvious advantages of this arrangement were that we had comfortable accommodation, that we were spared the difficulties of making arrangements for our considerable party at all the places we visited, and that we could work as we travelled. The less obvious but greatest advantage was that the members of the Committee lived together, without dispersing nightly to their different backgrounds and pressures, and came to know each other extremely well, and, I think, to trust each other in a way that would not otherwise have been possible. That the Committee was able, against all expectation, to present a unanimous report was due in the first place to the personality, charm, and determination of our Chairman, but in the second place, I would guess, to our six weeks of living and working together on the BGL *Irrawaddy*.

The findings of the Committee were that the riots had been deliberately sparked off by political opportunists in order to embarrass, and if possible bring down the subsisting Ministry, making use for this purpose of an anti-Muslim book by Maung Shwe Pi that had been published a good many years before without then causing offence. But the situation in which the riots were possible had been created by three factors.

1. Unsatisfactory conditions of land tenure – half the agricultural land of the country was in the hands of non-agriculturalists most of whom were Chettyars (Indian money lenders).

2. The Indian Question – Indians had an excessive share in the economic life of Burma and in the Services, their gains were remitted to India, having made their pile they returned to India.

3. The Marriage Question – the difficulties that arose from marriages of Burmese women with foreigners but particularly with Muslims.

The ill feeling between indebted Burmese peasants and Indian money-lender-landholders was shown to be one of the key underlying causes of the unrest. The Burmese Ministers set out to deal with this by a new tenancy act, 'a complicated piece of legislation', as Wallace describes it, 'produced in a hurry, enabling the Government to fix a "fair rent" for agricultural holdings. There was much to be said for it, but it was of course a very hot potato politically (particularly so because much of the Lower Burma paddy land was owned by Indians) and its sudden introduction without enough time for preparation threw a very heavy burden on the already heavily over-worked Subdivisional and Township Officers and on the Deputy Commissioners.' Little time for the measure to defuse the situation was given, however, before the Japanese attack upon Burma drove many of the Indians – landlords and labourers alike – to flee back to India.

At no point did the experience of the district officer in Burma differ from that of his counterpart in India more radically than in his direct exposure to two military campaigns of the Second World War. Burma was in a multitude of ways a very distinctive province in which to have served – with its oilfields or jade mines, its rice-bowl delta, its Buddhism and love of theatre. Yet for district officers in India a transfer from Muslim Sind to Maratha Bombay, from the cotton tracts of the CP to jungle-girt Bastar, provided contrasts of regional personality scarcely less sharp. But while in India war meant primarily organizing a country serving as a base for fighting outside its borders for every district officer in Burma war was an engulfing nightmare. Of the total ICS cadre in India few were ever within sound of gunfire, but of the tiny handful of the Burma service, two became prisoners in Japanese hands, nine, including two Burmese, lost their lives as a direct result of the war, and three, faced with the destruction of everything they had worked for and the betrayal of the Burmese by British failure to defend the country, took their own lives. Losses occurred to a degree unknown in India in other services also.

For many months after the outbreak of the war in Europe there was a rather unreal period in Burma as there was in India, though one of great personal anxiety. The war thereafter drew closer to India's western borders, but it was over two years before the onset of war in South East Asia. Meanwhile in Burma first steps had been taken in the control of food prices, collections for the War Fund and the creation of an information service.

Wallace at Moulmein had, like others, to requisition land for barracks and air-strips and had to establish an observer corps like the Home Guard of which Woodford speaks in Bengal. McGuire, as Warden of the Oilfields, also found ARP (Air Raid Precautions) added to his district duties:

We also brought in air-raid precautions, and here I had to be careful to explain to the townspeople that when they heard the sirens they were not to be frightened, we were only rehearsing. My Burmese S.D.O., both then and to the very end, was first class in keeping the people calm. The precautions included masking all the oil-rig lights with bamboo sheeting and preparing for a black-out to be enforced if we were given air-raid warnings. The Burmah Oil Company also provided a light aeroplane to fly over the oilfield and town in a mock air-raid.

But McGuire was also occupied with more elaborate preparations made as the Japanese threat became more menacing:

The Government took the realistic view that if the worst should happen and the Japanese invaded and over-ran Burma, the oilfields and refineries would have to be destroyed. To advise on denial the Government brought in a British expert, Mr. W. L. Forster, who came to Yenangyaung and, with the oil companies fully co-operating, proceeded to draw up comprehensive plans for denial. Secrecy was essential, for it was easy to visualise the possible effect on the oilfield labour and on the civil population once rumours had started to spread. I doubt whether the secrecy was absolute, but to our relief there was no disturbance or panic. Perhaps this was so because the war was still remote and the Japanese had not started to move. I think too that the confidence of the people remained unshaken when they saw us – Government officials and the oil companies – going about our business as usual and enjoying our usual recreation. All the trappings of peace were still there, and were seen to be there.
   In the middle of 1941 defence exercises were held throughout Burma. They involved the armed forces, the Military Police and the Frontier Force, the civil officials and the civil police and, in the oilfields, the British personnel, all of whom had by then been enrolled in the Burma Auxiliary Force. A British Army Major was attached to my office for the purpose. The exercises were aimed at bringing all the forces, army and civil, into a state of readiness.
   Then, on 7th December, 1941, came Pearl Harbor and the start of hostilities by Japan. The invasion of Burma began on 11th December, 1941, at the southern tip of the country. On 23rd December Rangoon had its first air raid, with heavy casualties. On or about 10th January, 1942, the Japanese advanced in force across the Siamese border, towards the river Salween and on to Rangoon. On 3rd January, 1942, I received instructions through the Governor from the G.O.C., Burma, that in the event of it becoming necessary to give up the oilfields through enemy action, the oilfields were to be totally denied to the enemy.
   In the oilfields denial preparations, already well advanced, were speeded up. The oil companies, with Mr. Forster, who was assisted by a section of the Royal Engineers, prepared the charges for blowing up the storage tanks and vital installations, including the power station. Most of the producing wells were made ready for being junked, e.g., by dropping into them tubing and cement.

For Wallace, DC at Moulmein towards the north end of the long narrow Tenasserim Division, the threat had long been very much closer still, for the Japanese had moved into Indo-China when France fell in June 1940 and had been reported at Maesod airfield just over the Thai border. Wallace recalls:

After Pearl Harbor and the simultaneous Japanese invasion of Malaya, everything hotted up. I remember that we were much concerned (with our knowledge, for instance, of the nearness of Maesod) with blocking open spaces where aircraft or parachutists could easily land. Bamboo spikes came into this. We had several air-raids on Moulmein, fortunately with few casualties because most people except essential workers had already left the town. The Indians had made for Rangoon en route for India. The indigenous population simply melted into the countryside, a phenomenon that recurred all over Burma, unexpected, but most welcome. In a land of villages and small towns few indigenous families were without links with the countryside. But one had to keep essential staff if one could. Some of them, especially Anglo-Indians and Anglo-Burmans, were very brave.

During January 1942 individual thrusts westwards to the coast were made by the Japanese farther south and the Subdivisional Officer at Victoria Point (Naiff) and the Deputy Commissioner at Tavoy (Fishwick), both members of the I.C.S. were captured. (They were interned for the rest of the war.) They had stayed at their posts instead of trying to get away because of orders that in the event of invasion Government officers must stay put and carry on with their jobs for the sake of the people. This instruction had been drafted with European conditions in mind. It was, of course, quite unsuitable for European officers in Asia in face of an enemy like the Japanese who interned all Europeans for the duration as soon as they could lay hands on them. This was before our turn came in Moulmein. On 20th January the Japanese launched their main attack on Burma over the frontier east of Moulmein.

Wallace hung on to the last moment at Moulmein with a skeleton staff, maintaining as good a flow of information as possible, fire-fighting, paying out three months' salary to the District staff, burning files and documents and finally evacuating the local jail staff and convicts, who had been kept as war labour for as long as possible, to the adjoining district of Thaton. It was here that Donnison joined him, sent down from Rangoon to help in the evacuation of his old district. Of this period he writes,

There could obviously be no general evacuation of the population of a district. Towns, however, as the war approached, evacuated themselves. By far the greater part of the inhabitants left for the jungle, or for remote villages where perhaps they could stay with relatives, taking what they could with them. The towns were left bleakly deserted until such time as the war had moved on, when, doubtless, life revived fairly soon under Japanese occupation.

The task of the Deputy Commissioner as war approached his District was to keep the administration working for as long as it could be of use to the Army. Since many functions of the administration came to a stop, as parts of the District came under enemy control and as communications broke down, there followed a concentration upon essential services. This meant that it became possible to allow those officers to go who for good reasons wished to leave, generally because they had families in the neighbourhood to look after. Volunteers were called for to remain and man the essential services. These were mostly Europeans (if there were any), Indians, or Anglo-Burmans – it was, naturally, the Burmans who had local family responsibilities, and whose families could not escape to safety in India. Persons recruited locally for service only in the District, such as the lower ranks of the police, clerks, village headmen, naturally remained in their Districts, which were their homes, and where they had their families, and disappeared to remote jungle villages when the time came.

The circumstances of a DC when his district was invaded by the Japanese Donnison jotted down in these terms:

There was the straight-forward danger from bombing or other enemy action. There was a great lack of information about what the enemy or one's own forces were doing.

There was a total absence of instructions from above – one had to take all one's decisions oneself. I have been reminded that at about this time the Governor broadcast a statement authorizing all officers of the administration to exercise, if need be, any of the Governor's powers.

Postal and telegraphic communication broke down. There was virtually no telephone system outside Rangoon, and what there was ceased to function.

Transport was a problem. The railways continued to function for a time but ultimately came to a stop.

I don't quite know how food came to us. Markets closed. Some servants ran away. But Indian servants saw their best hope of getting away to India in staying by their employers. My own servants were Burmese but stayed unhesitatingly with me until I sent them away. In Thaton someone cooked and produced meals for us.

In the later stages of the campaign the heat was at its greatest.

There was anxiety about wives and families who had to be got away from front line districts and sent to India. This was by no means easy. And having achieved it it was sometimes very difficult to find out where they had got to.

There was great exhaustion.

Above all there was a heavy burden of responsibility which had to be borne alone, unsupported by a command and administrative structure such as there was in the army – responsibility to keep the administration going as long as possible both for the army and for such members of the public as remained (I am thinking of hospitals), responsibility to meet the army's requests for information and supplies, responsibility to take away to safety at the last possible moment those of one's subordinates who wished to go.

And finally it was entirely one's own responsibility to make one's way to India – there was again no organisation to lean upon.

Another special feature of the withdrawal through Thaton district is set out by Wallace:

After leaving Amherst, I was put in charge of the adjoining District, Thaton. In this District was the large quarry-jail of Mokpalin. It was working hard producing material for airfields further back in Burma. As we were on the Japanese side of the Sittang Bridge the staff and the convicts were very jumpy and would have cracked if we had not hit on the expedient (which was kept dark from higher authority) of keeping one train for evacuation permanently standing by in the sight of all. This enabled the Superintendent to hold his men until the last moment. I mention this as an example of the sort of thing which necessitated personal visits by the Deputy Commissioner to keep up confidence. Another example was the maintenance of the air-raid warning system throughout the length of Thaton District. With the fall of Moulmein this had broken down. We managed to get it going again for the benefit of Rangoon on the other side of the Gulf of Martaban.

Among our 'Invasion Instructions' was one to 'deny boats, carts and motor transport to the enemy'. This sounds fine until you try to do it. The boatman, the carter or the car-owner hides up his means of livelihood in creek or jungle as soon as war approaches the District and you have neither time nor staff even to begin a process of search. The only way to get a reasonable proportion of such means of transport destroyed, which we employed in certain areas for special reasons, was to offer a good price for the article and send what trustworthy officers could be spared to selected centres to advertise the fact they were paying cash. If word got round quickly that the price was good, results were quite satisfactory. But it was an expensive business.

The time for accounts and audit was fast passing, however, and, as Fowler recalls, money was no longer what it had been:

I was told to go to Shwebo on the other side of the Irrawaddy and to burn the un-issued stocks of ten and five rupee notes of the Reserve Bank of Burma. These had been sent up from Rangoon in some fifty packing cases, each one containing about fifty bundles of a thousand notes. The only way of destroying them in secure conditions seemed to be in a furnace and we were fortunate in finding a convenient rice mill with a co-operative owner who was prepared to help. The furnace had a funnel on top that normally fed the husks that came down a shute from the mill wheels. Instead of the husks we fed the furnace on bank notes and the only problem was that we had to stop occasionally when the steam pressure needle got to the red line which showed that the boiler was producing too much steam. I had the help of a Burmese operative from the mill who passed the bundles up from the cases so that I could drop them into the hopper. He thought it was madness to burn money like that and pleaded with me to spare just one bundle for him.

Meanwhile McGuire, as Warden of the Oil Fields, was preparing for a bonfire on a grander scale:

Rangoon fell to the Japanese on 9th March, 1942, and with it went the loss by demolition of the Syriam oil refineries. Our forces had begun their withdrawal and were now dependent on the oilfields for their supplies. (Right up to the time of denial the army was supplied.) I was delighted and relieved that the townspeople remained calm. The civil offices, including my own, the Treasury, the Magistrates and the civil police continued to function and the bazaars remained open. Inevitably there were signs of collapse when the hordes of refugees from Rangoon and lower Burma came pouring through Yenangyaung in vehicles of all shapes and sizes. The bazaars then closed, but even so to my knowledge there was no looting or civil commotion. The villagers quietly submitted to the destruction of a number of their houses to ensure a clear way for our troops when they came through.

I was more actively concerned in the evacuation from the oilfields, for which I requisitioned a large steamer, with a flat on each side. It was kept ready, with steam up, some way down river away from prying eyes, including those of the army. It was fully provisioned by the companies.

Early in March 1942 it was clear that the British forces were fighting a steady withdrawal northwards and that the oilfields were coming under threat. On 12th March, therefore, I ordered the steamer to come alongside and the evacuation was begun. I stayed throughout the night while non-essential personnel with their wives and families embarked to proceed to Singu, a village on the west bank of the Irrawaddy, 20–30 miles north of Mandalay. The evacuees [mainly Indian] would then go on foot through the Shwebo district, across the river Chindwin and then on *via* Imphal to India. The steamer, with its two flats, left at dawn carrying from 4,000 to 5,000 evacuees. The number was excessive, but the commander stopped each night, allowing passengers to cook their meals on shore. Another steamer, with two flats, left Chauk on 17th March with about 1,750 evacuees on board.

About this time the European wives and families, including my wife, were evacuated by air from Magwe. We were only just in time, for on 21st and 22nd March the Magwe aerodrome was heavily bombed and rendered unserviceable.

Timing now became vital, and the greatest credit must be given to the Corps Commander, General Slim, for his accurate judgement throughout. On 30th March we heard that Prome, 30 miles to the south was under attack. I was given the E[vacuate] signal for the Thayetmyo district. All oilfield labour made their way up river. This was followed, on 1st April, by the D[estroy] signal for the installations between Thayetmyo and Minbu. All were thoroughly destroyed.

In the evening of 14th April I received the E signal for the two remaining groups, Yenangyaung, Chauk, Lanywa and Yenangyat. All Indian oilfield labour then embarked and all were taken safely to Singu.

There were left in the oilfields the denial teams, all of them British, the Resident

Geologist, the Controller of Petroleum, and myself, together with the denial officer and his Section of Royal Engineers. I gave instructions to the civil officers and the civil police to destroy their records and to leave. Some of the Treasury was taken by lorry up north, and I still wonder what became of it.

In the evening of 15th April I received the 'D' signal for Yenangyaung except the power station. [This was transmitted to the companies.] Throughout the day and night wells were junked, workshops and offices were destroyed, machinery was smashed, and the oil tanks blown up. We had the spectacular sight of the main tank farm, with its large number of tanks containing millions of gallons of oil, shooting up in flames to well over 500 feet.

The denial teams, along with myself and my colleagues, left for Chauk on the 16th. That same night, 16/17th, the Japanese infiltrated into the north of Yenangyaung. On the evening of the 19th the denial of Chauk, Lanywa and Yenangyat was completed. The denial teams made their way inland to the west and India.

The last word may go to Cockburn, who was one of a number of Burma ICS called up for military service and who therefore saw the campaign from the army point of view:

I must, however, pay a tribute to the Burmese people. The war, they felt, was no business of theirs and they could very willingly have done without it. Nevertheless during the first six months of 1942 while the Burma Army retreated northwards pursued by the Japanese the people of Burma remained sympathetic and helpful to us; they were bewildered and frightened but never treacherous. This was the experience of I.C.S. colleagues winding up the administration of one district after another as the Army was pushed back. It was the experience of individual soldiers and small units as well as large. We could move anywhere in a district without interference of any sort.

There were two other tasks of this period of retreat which fell to the district officers. Donnison was involved in the first of these, liaison with the Chinese Kuo Mintang troops from Yunnan, offered by Chiang Kai-shek, which moved down from the north to cover the Sittang Valley. His task and that of his team was to arrange supplies for this force and ease relations with the local population. But after their hard-fought action with the Japanese at Toungoo, the Chinese lost heart and pulled out. As they did so they plundered the country – 'in the case of the Chinese to live on the country was the officially recognised method of supply'. There was little to be done to secure supplies for them as the railway ground to a halt, and little protection could be offered to the villagers against them. The other disintegrating army which district officers had to help as best they could was that of Indian labourers and cultivators fleeing to India. After the bombing of Rangoon on 23 December 1941, which caused several thousand casualties (largely Indian) the first mass exodus had begun on foot over the Arakan Yomas towards Chittagong. In February and March 1942 Richards was sent to do what he could for this pitiful flood of humanity:

They came in a seemingly endless stream, the young and the old, the healthy and infirm, men, women and children, leaving scores to die along that *Via Dolorosa*, victims of cholera, debility and despair. Here were old men who had probably not walked even a mile in many years, setting out on a journey of a hundred miles to Mother India, women with great, hulking children on their backs, many so weak that they could barely struggle along. Some of the dead we burned, others were hastily buried in shallow graves. Though food supplies were established along the route, they were insufficient to deal with the numbers involved. It would have been far better if they had stayed.

Wallace records the same problem in Pegu – the heart-breaking problem of 'crowds of Indians, mostly cultivators, setting out on the long trek to India. One had to do one's best to help them on and, at the same time, keep them from getting in the way of our troops.'

Those troops would soon be treading on their heels, together with the civil administrators from the districts, setting out to walk to India across the still higher hills, the Lushai and Naga Hills, to Imphal and in Richards's case to Dibrugarh in northern Assam. From his final report submitted after arrival in India it is possible to follow McGuire on his march out of Burma. On leaving Myitkyina he and his party went by car to Maitawng, 102 miles along the road running north from the oilfields to Sumprahum. On 16 May they set out on foot over the Dara Kyet pass for the Hukawng Valley leading to the Naga Hills:

The Dara Kyet is a steep climb and a severe test of strength in bad weather. The first inkling of trouble ahead was at Naiting, which was deserted except for evacuees. Not a Kachin was to be seen, nor any domestic animal or bird. All edible commodities had been looted by earlier arrivals and the Kachins had fled in fright. One of the worst features of the evacuation was the haphazard trek of Indian native soldiers armed with their rifles and ammunition ... With a few notable exceptions, British officers preferred to help no one but themselves, to ignore the men and make their own way out as quickly as they could. Civil officers, again with exceptions, were just as bad. It was altogether a disgraceful exhibition of rotten morale and it was no wonder that the native soldiers – and for that matter most of the comparatively small number of British soldiers on the route – became increasingly aggressive and difficult to control. The result was that large numbers of undisciplined troops made their presence felt at each village by shooting off their rifles, killing the village pigs and chickens, rifling the granaries and, in some cases reported to me, robbing Kachins who were unlucky enough to meet them. Further on, when provisions became scarce, there was wholesale looting of any *taungya* (hill cultivation) where ripe crops or vegetables could be found.

For so long as the weather held, the roads in the Valley were excellent. But heavy rain which began on the 17th May and continued for several days, put an abrupt end to comfort. The Valley is so flat that there is practically no drainage. The road surface is either loose cotton soil or clay crumbled into thick dust by motor or cart traffic. The first heavy rains turned these roads into quagmires. Where cars could not move, carts got stuck and evacuees on foot could only progress by shuffling along the edges, clinging to the jungle at the sides and floundering in soupy mud from ankle to thigh deep.

Maingkwan, when we arrived there, was a scene of desolation. I am informed that it was looted on the 8th May by Sikhs and Punjabis of the Frontier Force, assisted by some British Tommies, this too in defiance of the local civil official, of an evacuation officer and of two British military officers, who apparently could no nothing against a numerically superior and desperate rabble. Chinese troops, a few days before our arrival, completed this bad work. We found nothing left of our carefully prepared food dump except rice, which fortunately was in such quantity that a goodly balance remained. All our tinned milk, tinned foods, sugar, etc., had been taken.

This disaster had a serious effect on the food situation and was the direct cause of much suffering, if not of many deaths. All these evacuees could now hope for, between Maingkwan and the camps on the Assam side, was rice, plus such provisions as could be dropped by planes. The only places suitable for planes were Shingbwiyang and Tegap Ga on the Burmese side.

In the Hukawng Valley, at Taihpa and at Yawpang reached on 21 May, McGuire and his party stayed a week to join with other civil and military officers in establishing a measure of control over looting and the operation of the ferries:

Not the least important part of our work at Taihpa and Yawpang was the removal of corpses. The villages were rapidly becoming uninhabitable. At Taihpa by means of a flat rate and at Yawpang with the assistance of Captain Stapleton, Burma Frontier Force, and some Chin troops collected by him, also using one house as pyre and thus bringing in the Kachins to save their village, we were able to complete this unpleasant task. Corpses in villages and along the route were a ghastly sign of the hardships of the journey. There were hundreds of them, increasing in number as the road conditions worsened and the trek over the mountains to Margherita took its toll of weakened constitutions.

By 31 May, McGuire had reached Shingbwiyang, the last village of any size before the hills began:

Shingbwiyang was a welcome haven for the hordes of hungry evacuees. Civil officials were there and several Army officers on their way through stayed on for one or two days to help. Captain Stapleton organised his Chin troops to guard the ration godown [warehouse] and to assist in the collection and distribution of food and medicines dropped by plane.

There was an unpleasant incident the evening before we left Shingbwiyang. About 200 Chinese, the advance party of a large detachment, arrived and made straight for the food godown, obviously in order to help themselves. We forestalled them by posting extra guards. Then they returned to camp about a mile away, where they arrested my Kachin Taungok, Kawlu Ma Nawng, who happened to be the most influential Kachin official in the Valley. They took away his kit and his revolver before releasing him. Then they had the effrontery to try and use this arrest as a bargaining counter in the hope of obtaining food. It took some hours of strenuous argument to ensure the return of the Taungok's property. Eventually, the Chinese got no food – there was insufficient in any case – and were advised to make their way back via Yawpang, where we agreed that they could have half the balance remaining of the rice stored there. I gather that they did not take this advice.

We left Shingbwiyang on the 5th June in heavy rain. The weather had broken in earnest two days previously. Small streams were already swollen and a particularly nasty one had to be crossed, I think eight times, with the water waist high at the beginning and breast high at the end.

Of this stage McGuire says:

The trials of the Hukawng Valley roads were nothing to what now had to be faced . . . One particular climb of about 4000 ft. was nothing but a steep scramble up so many mud-clogged steps which never seemed to end and which took a heavy toll of the less robust. Evacuees could only make slow progress and many suffered great distress by having to camp out in makeshift shelters and by exhausting their provisions through having to go slow.

We arrived at a hamlet a mile above Tagap Ga on the 8th June. That evening the weather cleared and a plane arrived to drop food at Tagap Ga. Stapleton and I, with a few troops, hurried down the hill to see what we could do. We arrived just after the plane had finished and found sepoys and many others who possessed weapons, particularly Sikhs, looting the provisions and preventing other evacuees getting anything. Then followed a hectic half-hour while we tried to recover some of the bags and to restore some semblance of order. I had some critical moments in one house filled with Sikhs, who refused to part with their loot and seemed prepared to do violence to me and to the Havildar (Indian sergeant) with me. It was useless attempting to use our revolvers, in fact we were seized and were only released when it was made clear to them that armed troops were on their way to help us. Outside, Captain Stapleton came up against a gang returning with several bags. One of them not only refused to part with his loot but so obviously made as if to attack Stapleton that, after adequate warning, Stapleton was compelled to shoot him in self-defence.

Heavy rain then made it impossible to drop supplies on Tagap Ga for some days:

The food question quickly became most serious ... Almost all the evacuees had consumed the rations issued to them at Shingbwiyang. The principal diet – in many cases the only diet – was of bullocks or buffaloes that had died of exhaustion or had barely escaped that fate by being shot.

On 13 June a few days' break in the monsoon began. But the planes which dropped food also dropped messages that the onward road was impassable as the Namying river was in monsoon spate, that the relief camps established by the Assam tea-planters were to be withdrawn and that the refugees should return to Shingbwiyang where more food would be dropped. The news spurred everyone, however, to push on before it was too late:

Everyone packed up and streamed down the hill to the river. A good many managed to get over that day. The remainder crossed next day, the 17th, and the day following. We estimated that ... about 2,500 persons must have crossed. It was a difficult crossing, as the river was about 250 ft. wide and a good 5 ft. deep in the middle, with a swift current. A rope which had been dropped some time previously had broken and was useless. But sturdy Indians nobly helped people by carrying to and fro bamboo poles to which evacuees clung as they struggled across.

On 17 June, with the main route believed to be impassable, McGuire and Arnold and a few Chin troops set off along by-ways, guided by a Naga chief, to warn the Indian authorities that this large party of refugees was attempting to get through:

It was a journey of nightmare climbs and leech infested jungle. No stream was crossed without a perpendicular and scrambling climb down and up a steep cleft. The first range of mountains was close on 6,000 ft., the Pat Koi range was a close second. Each village halt was about 3,500 to 4,000 ft. up, reached by a switch back mountain track. But apart from the strain of mountaineering and the curse of leech bites, our tour was most interesting. The Naga villagers could not have been more hospitable. Our Naga Chief was magnificent, we certainly could not have made the journey so comfortably, if at all, without him. The track was not one of the best and at times was hardly distinguishable from the surrounding jungle. But at any rate we were spared the mud and corpses of the main road and we were able to eke out our rations now and then by a chicken or some eggs.

We took eight days from Tagap Ga to Tirap. It was a pleasant surprise to find it was an official camp, especially as we were greeted by a European with most welcome tea and biscuits. Our pleasure and relief were increased when we learnt that the rest of our party had been able to get through via the main road ... [which] was apparently in a dreadful state owing to mud and to steep ascents, but was not entirely blocked.

Our news of the extra 2,500 came just in time, as the relief organisation was intending to close down on the 30th June. This organisation, run by the Indian Tea Planters

Association, was a magnificent show and deserves the fullest recognition for saving many hundreds of lives by setting up camps stocked with food and medicines and by voluntary work in most arduous conditions. As soon as news came through of this extra 2,500 there was no other thought but to carry on, in spite of difficulties over getting coolies and of adverse monsoon weather. Thanks to the I.T.A. the great majority of the 2,500 got through and the percentage of casualties was much smaller than I had anticipated.

The next day McGuire reached Margherita on the railway, and went straight into the Assam Oil Company hospital at Digboi, where, in his own words, 'we spent some days recovering from a miscellaneous assortment of complaints which included semi-starvation, exhaustion, malaria, leech bites and boils... We can sum up the whole story by saying that it might have been worse.'

Once recovered McGuire reported to Simla for further orders, as did the other district officers as they struggled through. Wallace relates what happened to him when he did so:

I went up to Simla where my wife was and where the Governor of Burma, with a few senior officers and a nucleus Secretariat were establishing themselves, and was appointed Defence Secretary to the Government of Burma.

As was remarked to me, 'Defence Secretary, Burma', seemed an odd title for my post since we had no Burma left to defend. In fact, there was a vast amount of work to be done in relation to the Burma armed forces. But my real work was concerned with various parts of Burma which in fact still were under British control, or at least not under Japanese control. These were bits of the extreme north of the Akyab District in Arakan, the Arakan Hill Tracts, the Chin Hills, the Naga Hills, the Hukawng Valley and the Putao Subdivision (Fort Hertz) in the extreme north of the Myitkyina District (Kachin country). Some of these areas later on were temporarily occupied by the Japanese; some never were. There was in fact all the time, however attenuated, what might be called a 'Frontier Areas Administration'. In the Chin Hills we had administrative officers continuously as late as the spring of 1944 when the Japanese made their unsuccessful push to take Imphal and Kohima and for a time our officers moved out with the Army. These officers were invaluable to the Army that stood between the Japanese and India because they knew, and were known to, the local people. The soldiers were strangers. These Burma officers mostly lived on the country to start with. They were of course cut off from their normal sources of supply in Burma. They were supported by, and worked closely with the Army, but they were not yet automatically 'on the strength' as it were and a makeshift Government of Burma supply organisation for meeting some of their wants from India was set up under a Burma High Court Judge based in Calcutta. There was a great deal of improvisation of this sort in the early chaotic days. These men on the frontier were the Burma District Officers of the time.

The Government of Burma in exile was also planning for the future, as McGuire records:

We were in Simla from 1942 to 1945. The Governor, Sir R. Dorman-Smith, set up our various Departments and had with him Sir Paw Tun, Prime Minister at the time of the evacuation, and his Finance Minister, Sir Htoon Aung Gyaw. We also had several of our Burmese colleagues. Plans for reconstruction were prepared by each Department and comprehensive reports, with draft despatches, went to the Governor for submission to the Secretary of State. A Supplies Department was also created, with the vital work of co-ordinating the provision of supplies estimated to be needed on our return.

Meanwhile the military authorities had insisted that, while active operations were in progress in Burma for the recovery of that or other countries from the Japanese, administration must be military. A picture of what was involved in being a District Officer under military administration is given by Cockburn:

In August 1944 I was transferred to the Civil Affairs Service (Burma) with my Army rank of Major and posted to Myitkyina District in Burma. CAS (B) was, in fact, the military Administration for Burma as it was reconquered from the Japanese.

Myitkyina District was in the first district in Burma to be reoccupied. It covered the most northerly and mountainous 200 miles of Burma with Assam to the West, Yunnan to the East and Tibet to the North. In terms of the war with the Japanese it fell within the sphere of the Chinese troops who had been regrouped and retrained by the Americans in India. On 17th May, 1944, Myitkyina airfield was seized by American forces; Chinese troops were then flown in so that they could take Myitkyina itself some four miles away. In fact this took them until 3rd August, and by that time Myitkyina town had been razed to the ground, only five houses remaining habitable.

The problems facing us in trying to re-establish an administration in Myitkyina district were unusual and very different from peace-time experience. I will try to list some of the main ones:

1. There was as yet no through road from India so the troops were maintained wholly by air. This put a tight limit on the number of Civil Affairs officers who could be allowed in as well as on the essential supplies which could be flown in.
2. The Japanese had not bothered greatly about the needs of the local population. There were shortages of everything, particularly rice, cloth, blankets, warm clothing, salt and agricultural implements. We ourselves for some time had only Army lavatory paper for correspondence, court cases, etc. There were 45,000 in need of relief supplies.
3. While the re-establishment of law and order demanded the re-establishment of a Police force with the minimum delay there were several additional handicaps:
   (a) The Chinese troops, although rationed by the Americans, still reverted to type and looted villages and smuggled what they could back to China. Each of us Civil Affairs Officers was at some time held up or pursued by Chinese troops.
   (b) There were a number of Chinese deserters who formed armed gangs and terrorised wherever they could. Two of our small number of Civil Affairs officers were murdered by them and a third was lucky to escape.
   (c) The Kachins in the hills had resisted the Japanese most bravely and at severe cost. On the other hand the Burmese and Shans on the plains had, perforce, accepted the Japanese administration and, the Kachins believed, had informed against them. So as the Japanese retreated the Kachins saw their opportunity of taking vengeance.
4. The American Commanding General 'Vinegar Joe' Stillwell disliked the British. This was often reflected in official attitudes although individual American officers could not have been more friendly and helpful.
5. By the nature of the terrain there were few roads in this vast district and naturally there were few vehicles available to us. The railway line which ran from Myitkyina south had been left without a single serviceable engine by the Japanese. So communications were not easy.

Having listed the difficulties I must make it clear that there were tremendous advantages too. In the first place the people were delighted to see us back. Myitkyina is mainly a Kachin district, the Kachins had remained incredibly loyal to the British and as a result had suffered grievously from the Japanese. But the Burmese and

Shans in the southern plain had also found the Japanese cruel and overbearing and concerned not at all with their welfare. Besides this we were starting from scratch in a disaster area and virtually anything we did was of benefit. We were, too, able to get on with the job without any seniors breathing down our necks or asking for explanation or justification. In our own small way we were pioneers. The air force too did a marvellous job in flying in our supplies, in spite of their other priorities, and in free-dropping them at places other than Myitkyina. Finally jeeps fitted with railway wheels ran an excellent mini-train service south from Myitkyina.

We set up our headquarters in one of the surviving five houses in Myitkyina. The house was built on stilts so with bamboo matting we turned the down-below open part into four offices. We lived above sleeping three or, when necessary, four to each of the two bedrooms.

The house had previously been the Japanese officers' brothel (or possibly one of them) and the ladies' names were in Japanese above each door. The half-dozen ladies involved – all Koreans – were caught a few days later and seemed very happy at this end to their involvement with the Japanese. As soon as the military situation permitted we were also able to establish Civil Affairs Officers in two other small towns 30 and 50 miles from Myitkyina. In addition we were able to build a small hospital in the compound of our Myitkyina headquarters, using bamboos, the plant of innumerable uses. Not far away the officer in charge of the police established himself, a police station, a lock-up of sorts and, very quickly, a police force.

We had, of course, responsibilities towards the military. We acquired land, timber, bamboos and so on when they needed them. We recruited whatever labour force they required. We provided local information of whatever sort was called for and smoothed out any misunderstandings between the troops and the locals. The better we did our job for the military the better they were pleased and the less they harassed the local population.

On the civil side we could only make the first beginnings in re-establishing an administration. Our priorities were to establish that the Government was back and in charge; to maintain law and order; to provide and distribute essential supplies; to encourage the maximum effort by the locals to help themselves in agriculture and in other ways such as salt production to give one example; to contact and register ex-Government servants of all sorts.

The most effective way of establishing that the Government was back was to get around and be seen and heard. On tour I seemed to talk or listen unceasingly. I had much to tell the people in terms of advice, encouragement and, indeed, orders. They too had much that they wanted to ask for, complain about or just tell me. Among the Kachins there were many tales of persecution by the Japanese and also of risks taken to help British soldiers from Wingate's first Chindits to escape. On the plains the Burmese and Shans told of bombing raids always, they said, hours or even days after the Japanese had moved on. Everywhere I found a great welcome and also much variety; I chased a gang of Chinese deserters who were known murderers – luckily perhaps I did not catch up with them! I caught some salt smugglers on a jungle track and a poppy-grower elsewhere in the jungle. Salt was always in rather short supply in some northern areas – in peace-time I had come across a market where salt was used as currency – and since it was non-existent when we returned we had to fly in large quantities as well as encouraging the maximum output by local salt-boilers.

To maintain law and order included the setting up of criminal courts. We were only able to at this stage try the most serious cases but there were a number where individuals had taken advantage of the Japanese presence to settle old scores, even by murder.

Although I had been a pretty inexperienced civilian magistrate I now found myself empowered to give any sentence including the death penalty and I did sentence to death one man who had committed more than one murder. All the cases we tried had to be sent back to Delhi for review by the Judicial branch of CAS(B).

As soon as we set up headquarters in Myitkyina and whenever we visited any sizeable village on tour Government servants reported in considerable numbers. They all hoped for re-employment but with our skeleton staff and administration this was not possible yet. A few were taken on and the rest were registered so that we knew where they could be found and could make some check on what they had been up to during the Japanese occupation.

While we worked to re-establish administration in the far North of Burma the Japanese forces were being steadily pushed south. So it was no surprise when in April 1945 I was posted as Senior Civil Affairs Officer in Bassein district. This district was 700 miles south of Myitkyina in the extreme South West of Burma and would be my first independent charge.

Before I could get there, however, I was put on a special job. WSW of Rangoon were the three district of Pyapon, Maubin and Myangmya, known collectively as 'The Delta'. Their land mass had been formed over the centuries by silt brought down by the Irrawaddy so they were flat, very fertile and heavily populated. Their links with the rest of Burma were entirely by water. As all the main fighting in Burma centred on the main North–South trunk roads these three districts had not been fought over. In addition as the fighting approached Rangoon they had been evacuated by the Japanese who would otherwise have been cut off.

Thus for some weeks these three districts had been in the unimpeded power of roving well-armed bands of the Burmese National Army, an army which had fought along with the Japanese and had then revolted and fought with the British against the Japanese. It was not known whether they would now oppose the arrival of a British Military Administration, possibly by force.

This was the problem to which I and an ICS colleague were required to find the answer. We toured the three District Headquarters in two MLs of the Burma Navy, going ashore at each one. At each landing, and particularly the first, we were ready for anything. To our pleasure we were not only not opposed but actually welcomed and a return to law and order instead of marauding bands was positively welcomed. So I reported accordingly and made my way to Bassein.

As district officers returned to their old haunts there were cheerful scenes of reunion – from Fowler's old dhobi flourishing an approving, if three-year-old, chit from his wife, from the ecstatic Burmese, nearly all in ragged clothes, and covered in scabies who welcomed Richards back to his old district, or from the more formal welcome parties which Wallace met with at Moulmein. But, as Fowler describes the scene at Moulmein, the task of building up the administration, virtually from scratch, was a formidable one:

The town was in a sorry state. After the Japanese withdrawal to their surrender area dacoits had had a field day. They were attacking houses and pedestrians in daylight and boats on the Salween were regularly boarded and the occupants robbed. Murder was rife and no doubt old scores were being settled. The police and the administration generally had scattered and sought safety in the countryside. Japanese occupation currency, the only legal tender in recent times, was lying in the gutters and blowing about as so much useless paper. We got the keys to the treasury and in the strong room we found the floor covered with silver and gold ingots which the Japanese armies had carried with them as loot and only left when they could not carry them any further. Some bore the marks which we later were able to identify as used by a mine in China. The area covered by these depredations was indicated by the presence there of the G.C.M.G. insignia bearing the names of the Governors of Hong Kong and Singapore. There were also many rather sad lockets with hair and photographs framed in them. All these were sent up to the custodian of Enemy Property but I fear that the original owners would not have been traced in many cases. Clearing up this desolation and confusion was the first post war task of the district officer. Within days the police and junior administrative staff were reporting back for duty and we soon had law and order re-established. The Roman Catholic nuns and fathers had kept their schools in being and they were only too eager to start education going again. There was great relief and enthusiasm as schools were re-opened and the young were able to restore a measure of order to their lives. Medical services were in great demand and one of my first concerns was to drive out to a leper colony which I used to visit when I was there as subdivisional officer. I found some of the people I had known in rather a poor state. The Japanese had not provided them with the modern drugs which they had used before the occupation to arrest the disease and the leprosy had become active again. Their condition generally had deteriorated and morale was very low. I promised them I would get them some drugs although I had to warn them that I did not know quite what was available. Their faces brightened and when I was able to return in ten days' time with all the drugs they needed, which 17 Div. had flown in, they were overjoyed.

The war with Japan ended on 15 August 1945, and on 16 October 1945, the Governor of Burma and his civil government resumed responsibility for the administration of Burma, except for parts of Tenasserim Division along the western edge of the Malay peninsula which came under civil administration on 1 January 1946. Elections were held in Burma in 1946 resulting in an overwhelming victory for the Anti-Fascist People's Freedom League. In January 1947 the British Government accepted the principle of full independence for Burma, as it had done for India, and an interim government was set up with Aung San as Prime Minister. Finally, on 4 January 1948, Burma became independent and chose to leave the Commonwealth. The history of those years, like the history of the corresponding run-up to independence in India, cannot be compressed into a page or two. But something of what it was like to live through them at the district level emerges perhaps in the following reflective accounts.

Wallace, back at Moulmein, comments:

I think it is worth noting the deep and at first subconscious change that had taken place in my feelings about Burmans and Burma between 1942 and 1946. This is of no importance in so far as it related to me personally, but in so far as it was typical, as I believe it was, of other British officers also and, in reverse, of most Burmans it had importance. In 1942, even during the long retreat, I never felt other than completely confident in my dealing with Burmans. I spoke the language, I got on well with them, I was a senior officer in the administration (though I do not think I consciously thought of myself in such terms). In 1945, when we returned, the atmosphere was changed. Friends were glad to see one back, British arms had triumphed, but the old unquestioning confidence had gone – on both sides. We had been driven out of Burma. The Burmans had seen this happen. In the trite phrase, things could never be the same again. From very soon after the first fine flush of enthusiasm succeeding our return it became clear to me that we had returned to a different Burma. But so long as one was part of a military administration, even though performing civilian functions, the direct comparison with our pre-war feelings was lacking. When however I became a civilian in January 1946 I began more fully to recognise this change in mutual attitudes and by the time I went on leave in March 1946, I was very conscious of it.

Cockburn, by now Deputy Commissioner, provides a final survey, a summing up tinged with sadness of one district officer's experience in Burma:

Hanthawaddy was an unusual district. Its district headquarters were in the Old Law

Courts building in Rangoon but no part of Rangoon was in Hanthawaddy district; thus the district headquarters lay outside the district. The district consisted of all the land from immediately south of Rangoon to the sea stretching for some 30 miles or so to both the East and the West of the Rangoon river. The district was cut off from Rangoon by water and, perhaps because there was no road link, the inhabitants were in the main simple cultivators and fishermen and there was surprisingly little political involvement.

The pattern of work and the problems were very much as have already been described; maintenance of law and order, collection of revenue, criminal cases and so on. I toured as much as I could, now having my own launch and crew, and found the villagers as peaceful and welcoming as ever.

We did have some trouble, however, with the Communists. Their honeymoon period with the Government and with the Nationalists had ended and they could see that they were now losing the fight for an effective share of political power in independent Burma. They were anxious, therefore, to create what trouble they could. In Hanthawaddy district their support was insignificant and all I remember them doing was a little 'forcible ploughing'. They would go to a village as far as possible from a Police Station and, with the help of some local villagers, would start ploughing a field of some absentee landlord. By the time word had been sent to the Police and some police had arrived they would have moved on. It was a pretty pointless exercise which never gathered any momentum.

As Burma moved towards Independence life in Hanthawaddy – and indeed in the country generally – remained pretty peaceful and the Interim Government with U Aung San as Prime Minister clearly had the support of the vast majority of the populace. On 19th July, 1947, however, a shattering event occurred which could well have upset the whole peaceful transition. On that day I was out on tour some 20 miles South West of Rangoon when news came that U Aung San and some of his Cabinet Ministers had been murdered. I had my launch with me and I made all speed for Rangoon fearing that what would follow would be either rebellion against the Government or civil war. I arrived in the early evening and found Rangoon quiet and under curfew.

It appeared that two men carrying concealed sub-machine-guns had managed to break into the Cabinet Room when a Cabinet meeting was in progress. They opened fire immediately killing the Prime Minister, five other Ministers and two officials – one of them the young man who had taken over my post in the Secretariat. They had then fled. The authorities acted very quickly; the two gunmen were arrested and, as a result, U Saw, the instigator of this plot, was also arrested. U Saw had been Prime Minister of Burma in 1941 and had been interned when he tried to obtain Japanese backing against the British – this was before the Japanese had declared war. Events had now moved power away from him and his plan was to arrange the murder of U Aung San and his Cabinet and to seize power himself in the resulting chaos. It was possibly quite a close-run thing but he failed because the authorities were able to destroy his plot very quickly and totally. The position throughout the country was controlled also for the same reason and because it was clear to everyone exactly where the guilt lay. Nevertheless things were on a knife-edge for some days at least.

Sometime in November 1947 all British officers in district jobs were brought into Rangoon and spent the last few weeks before Independence working in the city. I was, I think, the one exception. As Deputy Commissioner, Hanthawaddy, I already lived in Rangoon so there was no need to move me; I was, however, replaced by a Burman as DC and became instead Assistant DC. This suited me very well. I was relieved of responsibility but drew my normal pay and was able to continue touring right up to the end.

The end came on 4th January, 1948. My wife and I were among those on the lawns of Government House early that morning to see the Union Jack lowered for the last time. The Governor – Sir Hubert Rance – then drove down to the docks and boarded the cruiser which was waiting to carry him off. We lesser fry had to wait for a week in an independent, friendly, celebrating Rangoon until the next regular sailing of a ship for England.

As I sailed down the Rangoon river for the last time and looked at my own district of Hanthawaddy I was deeply sad. In spite of the war and all the tragedy and hardship it brought with it my time in Burma had been particularly happy and I would not have missed the experience for anything. I liked the country and had been lucky enough to see a lot of it; I liked my Burmese colleagues who were intelligent, friendly and easy to work with; I liked the common people whether headmen or simple villagers. I considered that my job as a District Officer could not have been bettered in what it offered – variety and responsibility among friendly but not subservient people.

As I look back I should like to think that Burma received as much from me in particular and from Britain in general as she gave us, but I cannot think so. No matter how much we liked the country and the people – and everyone of us liked them greatly – we could not avoid being the alien representatives of foreign conquerors looking as different from the Burmese as we manifestly were. While I appreciate that attitudes were different in the nineteenth century, the fact remains that we were in Burma because without true justification Britain, a Great Power, fought three wars against Burma, a tiny country in comparison. This to me remains shameful.

The fact remains too that it was the presence of Britain in Burma which ensured that the country was, in the 1940s, fought over twice in a Great Power war with which the Burmese had no direct concern. If this is not shameful it is at least a most unhappy outcome of our presence there.

FURTHER READING

For those who wish to learn a little more about Burma as a province and country two works can be recommended: F. S. V. Donnison, *Burma* (London 1970) is an excellent general introduction and J. F. Cody, *History of Modern Burma* (New York 1958) has a useful bibliography.

On the war in Burma S. Woodburn Kirby, *The War against Japan*, 5 vols (London 1957–69) is the official study of operations in Burma, for which the companion volume is F. V. S. Donnison, *British Military Administration in the Far East 1943–46* (London 1956). Geofrey Tyson, *Forgotten Frontier* (Calcutta 1945) looks at a particular period, the 1942 evacuation from Burma, from a more Indian and civilian viewpoint. Philip Woodruff, *The Guardians* (London 1954) provides a short study on the work of the ICS in Burma in the war period, as part of his larger study.

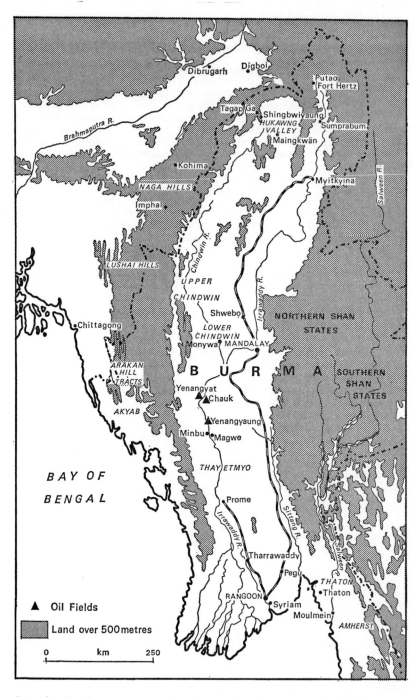

Map showing the escape routes from Burma. Based on maps in F. S. V. Donnison, *British Military Administration in the Far East*, HMSO 1956.

CHAPTER 10

ORDER AND POLITICS

And now in prison I had ample leisure
To spin and muse, in short indulge my pleasure
The while came news from city, town and village
Of riot, slaughter and tumultuous pillage

Violence reigned, and I expressed my sorrow,
For each day's violence, promptly on the morrow!

From The Saint and Satan
a political satire by S. Solomon

Attempting with conscious rashness to sum up in a phrase the period between the two world wars in India, Gorwala has this to say: 'The state during this period is best designated "The security state". Its primary attention was devoted to the maintenance of order and the enforcement of the due processes of the law.' There certainly were other aims, justice and some measure of economic development for example, but the maintenance of order was seen as a major task, and indeed as a major test of a district officer's quality and efficiency. Yet the instruments of coercion, had coercion been desired, were remarkably meagre. Public order, as Donnison saw, 'in the last resort depended on the loyalty and competence of the police force under its British and Burmese or Indian officers. Short of calling on the military, this was the only force, both in the organisational and the physical senses, at the disposal of the Deputy Commissioner.' Yet the police were few, ill-equipped and largely unarmed. This was the UP as Radice saw it:

As for the Police, here too everything was done on the cheap. Each district had a Superintendent of the Imperial Service, of whom in the thirties about half were Indian. The main work was done by the Police Station Officers (Thanadars) of whom there would be thirty to forty in the average district. In each Police Station there would be twelve to twenty civil police. The only firearm was the Thanadar's revolver and a few old muskets kept securely locked up in the Thana. I believe that at that time there were only two important countries in the world where the civil police normally went about without firearms – Great Britain and India. The normal weapon of the Indian policeman was the lathi or bamboo staff. Had it not been for the fact that the population had no firearms, save for a few carefully controlled sporting weapons, and for the generally peaceful and civilized character of the peasants, such a thrifty and weaponless policing would not have been possible.

However, at district headquarters there was a body of usually about two hundred Armed Police, a semi-military corps, who were employed as Treasury guards and for emergencies, such as Hindu-Muslim riots. Their weapons were .410 smooth-bore muskets which usually fired buck-shot. Unfortunately, as usually happened, these weapons were not used until a mob was at close quarters and thus fatal wounds were inflicted. Automatic weapons were unknown and, until the Second World War, mechanical transport, radios or even, in most places, the ordinary telephone were not available.

These were the exiguous forces within the district which had to deal with village affrays, assaults and dacoities, with hooliganism in the towns, with industrial unrest and communal violence. As Martin tersely puts it, in Bihar 'one Sub-Inspector with perhaps a dozen constables was responsible for preventing and suppressing crime in an area of often as much as 100 square miles'. Beyond that, says Venkatachar, 'The rest of the district officer's authority was made up of judicious management; some bluffs and cajolings, a few confidence tricks thrown in.'

Some of the problems to be dealt with were those to be found in any peasant society, quarrels over land or water and, in a countryside which was a patchwork of unfenced fragmentary holdings like the open fields of the medieval English village, quarrels over grazing or over crops at harvest time. Bell in Bengal saw two crops always ripening to harvest – one of rice, the other of affrays and litigation.

In the difficult interwar years of world depression there was added, more-over, an intensifying agrarian unrest as tenant and landlord each sought to shift on to the other the fixed government revenue demand, which grew steadily more burdensome as prices fell. Mudie at Allahabad in the UP reports a startling instance in 1930:

There was considerable agricultural distress and the zamindars were pretty hard put to it to pay their revenue, even as reduced in accordance with the reduction in tenant rents. One day, eleven Mahommedan zamindars came to tell me that they were very frightened of what might happen to them. I reassured them as best I could and shortly after that spent a weekend riding round their villages. All seemed quiet, but a few days later, a man came in to tell me that all eleven had been killed by their tenants.

The same depression hit industry and unrest manifested itself in the Indian industrial workforce, which politicians were beginning to organize. Here was a further problem for the district officer, as Carleston in Guntur, Madras records:

Tobacco was the principal crop of the district, and most profitable. At Chirala there was a large factory belonging to the Imperial Tobacco Company and also a 'Criminal Tribe' Settlement (run by the Salvation Army), from which it drew much of its labour. Some Congress lawyers from Guntur had organised a Union among these workers and formulated certain demands, but the Management would not deal with the Union, which had not been officially recognised. The leaders therefore called a strike, which was partially successful. The Commissioner of Labour (T. G. Rutherford) and I tried to bring the parties together but without success. Meanwhile, as the signs seemed threatening (and on the advice of the Commissioner of Labour), I called in a platoon of the (armed) Reserve Police from Guntur and stationed them in the town, a little distance from the factory, and out of sight, as a precaution. A police guard was put on the factory and I spent most of my time in the vicinity. One afternoon a very large crowd gathered, I believe intending to prevent those who wanted to from going or returning to work, and even to attack the factory. The crowd had gathered on the railway line, which passed near the factory, and soon began to pelt the small (but armed) police contingent guarding the factory with metal from the railway embankment. The crowd was warned to disperse, but the violence increased, being whipped up by some agitators in front. Finally the police opened fire and killed two young men in front who appeared to be inciting the crowd. At this the trouble very quickly subsided. The bodies of the two young men were recovered and later taken for post-mortem examination. We patrolled the town during the night but there were no further incidents. Next morning, to my surprise, the whole labour force trooped peacefully back into the factory and resumed work as if nothing had happened.

This took place under a fairly new Congress Government and it was a bit uncertain what their attitude would be, since some of their supporters had been involved. A full-scale judicial enquiry was set up under Mr Justice Horwill (a judge chosen by the Chief Justice). The Union and the strikers, who had pressed for the enquiry, eventually produced no evidence, though their case had been that the police fired when the crowd was running away and that the two men had been shot in the back. The latter contention was disproved by the medical post-mortem report. The findings of the Court justified the action taken, and blamed the trouble on the lack of leaders among the crowd, the 'Union' leaders having disappeared at the first sign of trouble. The Congress Government (under Mr C. Rajagopalachari) accepted the verdict, but used the occurrence to insist in future that all concerns where there were even partial strikes should remain closed (by magisterial order) until the dispute was completely settled.

At much the same time Martyn was handling a strike of 60,000 jute workers from the vast mill complex along the banks of the Hooghly, and in Bihar Solomon was peacefully settling the first major strike in the State collieries at Giridih. Five years later in May 1935 a strike against wage cuts would end in violence and arson – 'the five years intervening', Solomon noted, 'had seen a great increase in the solidarity of labour in India'.

But for every district officer the most difficult form of disorder to handle was that which had or could be given religious or communal overtones. In India caste, sect and religion provided the strongest social bonds, satisfying the deepest emotional needs but also providing access to jobs and other quite secular benefits. Conflicts which could be given a religious guise were therefore especially serious. Numbers of these lay within a single religious community – in Lucknow, capital of the UP, many conflicts were between Shias and Sunnis, minority and majority segments of the Muslim community. The conflict, as Lloyd-Jones notes, was as much social as religious, but the religious colouring gave it a dangerous universality:

The old ruling class of Oudh had been Shias and this sect were intent on preserving their traditional rights and privileges as against the more numerous and progressive Sunnis. The periods before the main Islamic festivals – Mohurrum was an especially difficult time – were occupied with anxious negotiations in an attempt to reduce the occasions for friction and riot. The cardinal rule was 'no innovations'; all processional routes and public religious celebrations had to be exactly as on previous years and as established by precedent. At the festivals themselves I had to spend many hot and weary hours accompanying processions and waiting at police outposts in case of trouble. Despite our precautions, several disturbances occurred in my time, usually when some element or other was determined to cause trouble, and some of these were serious when after the usual 'lathi' charge had proved ineffective, firing had to be resorted to with fatal casualties.

There could also be conflict amongst Hindus – in South India particularly where temples and monasteries were very wealthy and a share in or control over their resources was a very valuable thing. Georgeson, posted to Conjeeveram (Kanchipuram), found the annual temple 'car' festival a terrible headache – car being the word used to describe the massive wooden-wheeled structure, the vehicle of the god, whose image was dragged on it round the streets

so that as many people as possible might see the god, or, to be more accurate, be seen by him. Cars are a feature of the Vaishnavite Hindus; that is, that one of the two main divisions of Hindus whose special worship is of the god Vishnu. The temple at Conjeeveram belonged to the Vaishnavite sect that followed the teachings of Ramanuja. But there was rivalry between the two sub-sects of his followers: the 'Tengalais' ('Southerners') and the 'Vadagalais' ('Northerners'). I forget which was which, but the theological difference was that one held that God holds the soul as the mother cat holds its kittens ('the cat holds') and the other that the soul clings to God as a baby monkey clings to its mother ('the monkey holds'). I do not suppose that many zealots understood the difference. What they did know was that one painted the trident-shaped caste mark which orthodox Vaishnavite men wear on the forehead with the outer prongs vertical and joined by a rounded base ('the U-marks') and the other painted it with the outer prongs converging on the centre one between the eyes ('the Y-marks'). The rivalry was due not to *odium theologicum*, from which all Hindus are completely free, but to conflicting claims to the performance of various parts in the service of the temple. These had been laid down precisely by courts, but relations became very tense at the time of the car festival and during it the town was heavily policed. It was therefore the policy of the Government, if possible, not to post Hindu magistrates or police officers to jurisdiction over Conjeeveram, and certainly never Vaishnavites.

However it was tension between Hindus and Muslims which was and long had been the major cause for concern. Where one community was very much smaller than the other, as in Madras and the NWFP, the problem was a minor one, but there were few districts in which the approach of one of the great religious festivals did not cause anxiety, as Bonarjee relates:

Communal peace, always delicately balanced at the best of times, became most precarious during the four great religious festivals – two Hindu and two Muslim – which spanned the year, and now was the time for local elites (if they deserved this term) to compete for local power and influence by the simple process of working on, and working up, religious differences as such. This last was not a difficult matter when one community reverenced the cow and the other regarded that usually mal-treated animal as an item of food and at *Id* an animal for religious sacrifice; when one community regarded the Peepul tree with reverence and the other sought to lop its branches in order to provide easy and clear passage for the tazias at Muharram; when at the Hindu harvest festival of Holi it was customary for lighthearted revellers to spray all and sundry with coloured water of various hues, and a Muslim after a good sousing would call on his friends to avenge the insult; when in the face of Muslim objections to the playing of music before mosques at prayer time, a Hindu procession, say during the Dussehrah festival, would choose just that place and time to halt with its band in full blast. Quite apart from what might be termed the normal and regular possibilities for strife, it was impossible to foresee all the snags that could arise at any time in a country so adept at producing the unexpected. Both the political and communal problems and their results were especially trying for Indian officers. All festivals in my eyes were a great nuisance.

Reflecting on the perennial communal problem, Shukla argues that it was the British concern to be neutral and fair between the two communities which was the basic error; what was needed was an authoritative pronouncement:

If during the early period of the Raj, the British had applied general principles to these problems, the situation might have been rationalised. For example, regarding the cow-slaughter they could have taken up the position that it was a civil right of everybody to eat what he liked and those who ate beef could kill the cow. On the other hand, they could have ruled that every country has its traditions and as there was a strong sentiment against cow-slaughter in the country there should be no cow-slaughter; people could eat the flesh of so many other animals. But this might have seemed like siding with the Hindus against the Muslims, because Shah Waliullah, a Muslim divine, had proclaimed that cow-slaughter was an Islamic practice. But the British did nothing really to solve the problem. The same happened with music before the mosque.

The situation differed from place to place and separate detailed arrangements for every place were laid down and recorded in the Police Station registers. No deviations, changes or innovations were allowed. And the whole thing was supported by pro-hibitory orders under Section 144 of the Indian Criminal Procedure Code and a contingent of police, headed at more important places by a magistrate.

How to deal with communal tension and violence was an issue which each district officer had to work out for himself, in the light of local circumstance. In Jabalpur, in the CP, a town with a long history of communal discord, Paterson opted for the strong arm and preventive strike:

I did a lot of thinking about this communal situation and, rightly or wrongly, I came to the conclusion that the answer was a really strong hand to put an end to trouble before it really grew into anything serious. A clash when it did come was during the Mohurram Festival and towards the end of the festival the Mohammedan procession got totally out of hand. I had had a detachment of the special armed police posted to Jabalpur for the Mohurram period and Ozanne, Superintendent of Police, and I managed, with the help of the city Superintendent and the use of considerable force, to get the Mohurram procession outside the immediate boundaries of the city. In the city itself I issued an order imposing a curfew and the police proceeded to enforce this as rapidly as possible. When we had got the city more or less quietened down we sent an extra detachment of armed police to join the force holding the riotous pro-cession on the outskirts of the city and said that the magistrate should let the proces-sion come into the city and disperse. It did not, of course, quite work out as one had hoped and the procession proceeded to run amok, burning and looting and destroy-ing cars, and eventually, I think largely to prevent themselves being overrun and after the usual warnings, the police opened fire.

The casualties were three killed and ten wounded but I reflected that compared with the casualty lists of the past three years this was a relatively small total. But it had involved the use of police and the use of arms, and on the basis of the report which I sent to Nagpur, the Government decided that a judicial enquiry into the handling of the whole episode should be held.

This seemed to me quite reasonable that one should be answerable for one's decisions, and in due course a judge held an exhaustive enquiry into the whole circumstances of the riot. His report came down fairly heavily in our favour in the sense that the mob had, as it were, asked for it and nothing else could really have been done to stop the situation and prevent the city really going up into serious rioting all over the place.

After further thought I came to the conclusion that probably the best answer was to produce a fairly overwhelming show of force before anything happened. Strictly speaking, the use of troops in aid of the civil power was supposed only to be brought into effect if the situation was getting beyond the control of the civil authorities. But the Brigadier agreed that, although it wasn't quite according to the book, if I wanted a show of force he would be prepared to put a Company or a couple of Companies at my disposal.

I only used this offer twice. Looking back I think there was no doubt that the policy paid off since for four and a half years, bar one small incident, we had no other rioting and no casualties.

Others relied rather more on influence, on 'managing' the leaders of the communities, and on keeping crowds good-tempered – as did Midgley's experienced police officer by having sweetmeats and cool drinks ready to distribute if tempers soured or anger flared. One cheerful account of such tactics, in this case at Muharram at Sasaram in Bihar, is provided by Martin, summoned to action by a telegram from the Sub-Inspector of an outlying township:

This Sub-Inspector had obviously been greatly drawn during his youth by the majesty of Shakespeare's diction and had often delighted me during some rather dreary dacoity cases by his references in court to 'vaulting ambition' and 'loathsome cankers'. This time the telegram message was direct and ominous. 'Hindus of Nokha feeding fat the ancient grudge against Muslims. Come quick. S. I. Nokha.'

The particular trouble had been caused by a vigorous neem tree which grew in the courtyard of a Hindu temple situated on the route on which the local Muslims were accustomed to take their tazias. To the Hindus all neem trees are holy, and one that grows in a Hindu temple even more so. When in the course of years its branches started to cast their shade over the road the stage was set for conflict. In order that the tazias should follow their traditional route it seemed essential that the branches of the neem tree should be cut. Now Hindus could be seen every day cutting branches off neem trees for every conceivable use from firewood to disposable toothbrushes. But to do this to oblige the Muslims and make smooth the path of the Mohurram festival was another matter entirely.

Martin's predecessor had got round – or under – the neem tree problem by lowering the road at that point. But the neem had grown and in the road bedrock had been reached. Martin arrived to find an ugly situation:

From the predominantly Hindu countryside peasants were beginning to move into the little town on the rumours that the Muslims were defiling a sacred neem tree. At the spot itself there was the Muslim procession halted at the bottom of the ditch, the tazia bearers holding their poles straight up as high as they could. Never were they going to dishonour the memory of Hasan and Hussein by lowering the tazia below its maximum height to accommodate a Hindu neem tree. In the night air there had arisen a kind of low humming roar. The SI was silent, meditating perhaps upon the need to stiffen up the sinews and summon up the blood. To force the procession through would almost inevitably lead to a damaged neem tree and an immediate riot in which the outnumbered Muslims would stand little chance. But to force the procession back to follow another route would not only contravene standing instructions but would lead to endless accusations of bad faith on all sides and make the task of ensuring peace next year almost impossible.

Martin's answer was personally to climb the tree, rope the overhanging branch, and with a silent prayer to pull it upwards. 'All Hindu ears were waiting for the tell-tale crack of a sacred neem twig; the Muslim tazia bearers were standing almost on tiptoe defying my efforts to get the branches clear of their poles.' But the branch did bend and the procession went through. As for the next year, Martin continues:

The Babu Sahib of Garh Nokha, a local Hindu landlord, had for long let it be known that he would not be averse to the title of Rai Bahadur. My successor let the Babu Sahib know that a solution to the problem of the Mohurram festival would be a prerequisite to such long overdue recognition of his services to the community. Now the Babu Sahib, as befitted the biggest landowner in the area, owned two elephants. By some mischance their mahout omitted to feed them for several days before inadvertently letting them loose, the neem tree represented one of the few visible sources of nourishment that met these hungry animals and whilst a neem tree is indeed sacred to the Hindus, Ganesh the elephant is a true god and can do no wrong!

What both Paterson and Martin in their different ways were seeking to prevent, the ugly horror of full-scale communal rioting, is illustrated from Barty's experience at Sukkur in Sind. In most parts of Sind Hindus were few, one or two shopkeeper-moneylenders, very vulnerable and so subdued. However, in larger towns like Sukkur, Hindus were in sufficient numbers to feel able to look after themselves and even to be provocative, marching, bands playing, past a mosque, and thus the Sukkur riots began:

Peter Cargill and I were quickly recalled from tour and put in charge of a patrol of Punjabi Muslim armed police. At Oxford and later, I had often wondered how I would feel and behave in such a situation. To my surprise, fear did not enter into it. Sindhi Muslims were not recruited into the army. They therefore lacked the discipline and training which would have made them more effective rioters. The most lethal weapons they possessed were hatchets, whereas we had firearms. I do not suppose that Peter and I were in any real danger at all. On one of our patrols, after dispersing several groups of yelling trouble-makers, I suddenly realised that Peter was no longer with me. Turning back a short way, I saw him disappearing alone down a side street waving a huge revolver over his head and shouting 'bugger off' at a little mob in full retreat. His platoon of police quickly picked up the phrase and found it worked like a charm.

No news was coming in of what was happening in the district, but rumours were rife. I was particularly worried about Shikarpur for which I had a feeling of special responsibility. With a population about the same as Sukkur's, it was much more vulnerable to arson, being a densely packed old town criss-crossed by narrow lanes, too narrow even for one car, let alone a fire engine. The whole place, tinder dry in that climate, could have burnt down in a night; and fire and panic could result in appalling casualties. Eventually the District Magistrate and DSP agreed to my taking two lorry-loads of armed police under the Muslim Deputy Superintendent of my sub-division and an Anglo-Indian sergeant.

Shikarpur was found safe but tense – 'the Hindu community was terrified, and swaggering young Muslims were looking for an excuse to start something' – but the arrival of a company of Indian infantry made possible the regular patrolling needed to maintain order in the town. But the outlying villages had also been affected. On the drive to Shikarpur Barty had found the Hindu houses of one village burnt, the shops looted and many dead, and had just been in time to prevent a similar disaster in another: 'We could clearly hear shouting from a village – soon we could make out the glow of flames leaping. We debussed and approached the village rapidly on foot. A number of Muslims were busy setting fire to shops and houses, looting and encouraging each other with shouts of "kill, kill".' They were dealt with, but for many nights thereafter Barty was regularly out with a busload of police patrolling the countryside – 'they were slow, bumpy, dusty and cold journeys over the rutted earth roads' – until order and confidence were fully restored in his sub-division.

All the ordinary problems of law and order were increasingly complicated, however, by the intrusion of politics, both constitutional and extra-constitutional. The Government of India Act 1919 at the provincial level had by the device of dyarchy devolved limited but real power and patronage upon the elected politician. In consequence, though the franchise was a restricted one, a more thorough organization of political parties and constituency politics had occurred. Political leaders in the towns had established links with the men and groups with weight in the countryside; the politician as well as the district officer now had his finger on the rural pulse, could put the needs of the countryside to government, and could offer rewards to loyal supporters. Under varying degrees of official supervision, local politicians had also taken charge of the self-governing municipalities administering the towns and the district boards in the rural areas. The district officer had to learn to share power with the politician. Moreover, the civil service itself was changing: since 1924 there had been no British recruitment to the professional and technical All-India services except the police, and more Indians were entering the ICS. The result was immediately noticed by Hyde when he first arrived in the CP:

When I joined in the late twenties, the provincial government was already largely Indianized, a fact that few people in India or Europe realized. The cabinet presided over by the Governor, Sir Montagu Butler (the father of 'Rab'), consisted of two ministers from the elected Legislative Assembly and two nominated members, one of whom was an Indian. An Indian, Mr Tambe, had recently officiated as Governor, and of the five Commissioners of Divisions, the senior ICS administrative posts, two were Indians. Amongst the half-dozen posts of Secretaries to Government I think three were held by Indians; and the Deputy Commissioner of Nagpur, the provincial capital, was an Indian who later became Governor of Orissa.

Venkatachar argues that an irreversible shift of power occurred between 1919 and 1935: 'The politics of mediation between the people and the government had shifted from district to provincial level. The politician now stood forth as the mediator and had displaced the district officer. Except for the rural conservative landlords and the oldfashioned gentry, people knew where the source of power now lay. The decline in the influence of the collector's position was visible.'

In one sense, indeed, a shift of authority was a positive aim of the 1919 Act, intended in Venkatachar's words 'to involve Indians in the business of government so that mere opposition to British rule might be blunted'. Sir Geoffrey Ramsden praises Sir Montague Butler, Governor of the CP, in just such terms: 'He was very astute politically – especially when he persuaded Tambe, and later Raghavendra Rao, to join his Cabinet and criticise and attack from *within* instead of attacking from without.'

But in the same years many politicians operated outside the constitution, challenging the authority of government. The 1919 Act got off to the worst of starts. The illiberal Rowlatt Acts were passed, the sometimes violent Indian protest against them was met by the counter-violence of General Dyer at Jallianwala Bagh, and that in turn by the non-co-operation movement led by Gandhi and the Congress leaders. Since, at the same time, Indian Muslims had been outraged by the Allied dismemberment of the Ottoman empire, Muslims and Hindus came together in a concerted anti-government campaign. Ultimately the non-violent boycott of government institutions called for by Gandhi ended in disorder and violence, and Hindu-Muslim unity foundered in recrimination and communal strife. Nevertheless more people had been personally involved in politics than ever before, the consent of the governed had briefly been withheld, authority had been repeatedly challenged and defied. The district officer's position had thus been subjected both to sap and assault at the same time.

The Liberals, the anti-Brahmin Justice Party in Madras, the country Unionist party in the Punjab, all worked the new constitution. But the Congress party boycotted the 1920 elections and fought the 1923 elections, in which they made a good showing, either to refuse office or to take it and wreck the constitution from within. This negative or hostile political stance did not prevent the 1919 Act being worked, but it did sour relations between officialdom and Congress, the greatest of the Indian parties. It was easy for the district officer to see Congressmen as enemies and to seek allies among the old established, rather 'feudal' loyalists of the countryside, or the urban Liberals, or the Muslims. The very tersely set-out views of Haig in the UP, which he believes were widely shared, exemplify this tendency:

Our main responsibility was the maintenance of 'Pax Brittanica' (law and order) inside a unitary system of Government.

We were against Congress, who were trying to chuck the British out. We tended to regard with favour those Indians whom we considered 'loyal'.

Partly on account of this we had a slight tendency to favour Muslims – who tended to be scared of Congress – against Hindus.

When the next round of constitutional reforms began in 1927 the same unfortunate cycle was repeated. Any Indian welcome for reform was buried under anger at the appointment of an all-white Simon Commission to review constitutional progress. When the Viceroy Lord Irwin then clearly defined the goal as Dominion Status and invited Indian leaders to a Round Table Conference in London to share in working out a new constitution, Gandhi chose to oppose government rather than accept, using the common anger against the Simon Commission to unite a party otherwise divided into radical and moderate wings. He called for another campaign of civil disobedience and opened it by his own long, theatrical march to the sea at Dandi to make illicit, untaxed salt. In the course of the year some hundred thousand persons, following his example, courted and received prison sentences for breaking the law – many of them women, who now entered politics in an unheard of way and number.

Whether these dramatic confrontations advanced India's cause more than the skilled presentation of her case by the Liberal, Muslim and Princely delegates to the first Round Table Conference in late 1930 is uncertain. What is clear is that civil disobedience revived in many district offices the emotions first aroused during non-co-operation in the 1920s. During the Parliamentary debate upon the Act of 1935 which embodied the reforms which had been thrashed out, Clement Attlee urged the Commons to deal with the forces of a modern India, a living India, not the dead India of the past, in other words to deal with Congress. But it was the actions of that Congress under Gandhi's leadership which made it so difficult for the district officer to see the future in Congress and so easy to seek support from an older India. This emerges very clearly from Symington, then at Ratnagiri on the coast south of Bombay, who had first-hand experience of civil disobedience of the Salt Act:

In 1930, aged 26, in common with the great majority in the Service, I was not at all opposed to the idea of Indian independence. I thought it was intrinsically desirable. But, while accepting its certainty and desirability, it seemed obvious that those major aspects of the scene were being adequately attended to by Secretaries of State, Viceroys, and squads of Privy Councillors and politicians of both races.

That being so, I could see no good reason for people to go round breaking the law – especially in *my* district.

I did not mind amateurs going to the seaside and making a few handfuls of horrible salt as a demonstration. That was on a par with making speeches, and I unsportingly refused to oblige anyone by arresting him. But when we heard that more ambitious law-breakers had raided the Shiroda salt-works and got away with some hundred-weights of the stuff, the Police Superintendent and I thought we would have to try and stop them. But we still did not want to make arrests.

One Saturday night in the middle of May I got word from the Bombay Police that the southbound steamer, the *Kamlavati*, was crammed with *satyagrahis*. They were on their way to Vengurla, to reinforce our own local demonstrators. An all-night drive got me to Vengurla in time to be rowed out to meet the incoming steamer early on Sunday morning. There I instructed the Captain Sahib not to land any passengers, and handed him an order to that effect written out in longhand on an odd piece of paper to show to his superiors. Possibly because he was of a different faith from his customers, political as well as religious, he agreed with every sign of delight and I departed quickly, supposing my mission to be accomplished.

Symington goes on, of course, to record that though the satyagrahis were refused permission to land in Goa, at that time Portuguese, from where they could have marched on the Shiroda saltworks, he forgot that the ship called at Vengurla on its way back to Bombay. A second long row out to the ship and further instructions to its captain were therefore necessary before this civil disobedience was finally frustrated.

The somewhat schoolboy humour with which the discomfiture of the satyagrahis – added to by the steamer's corkscrew gait – is recounted does not conceal the hostility which Symington felt. He adds a comment to his story:

The mainspring of the thinking of the Congress seems to me to be epitomised in a single phrase of Gandhi's in *Young India* in January 1930. '*They* [i.e. the British]', he wrote, '*only respect those who are prepared to pay an adequate price for their own liberty.'* Some may say that was a glimpse of the obvious. But would they be right? Could it not, more realistically, have been a disastrous misreading of the situation?

There was an arrogance in the attitude of the Congress not only towards the British but towards their own countrymen, an untenable claim to speak for all India with their single voice – for Liberals, for Untouchables, for Muslims – regardless of the other parties' explicit rebuttal of that claim, which finally destroyed half of what they were setting out to achieve. In the end, the price they made India 'pay for its liberty' was not only 'adequate', but grossly excessive.

Many other district officers record with cynical amusement the routine acts of minor disobedience of the law, often signalled in advance, designed to lead to martyrdom in the cause of freedom. Watson in the CP thus records the search of a Congress Party office:

The party secretary watched our proceedings with obvious signs of unease, but he probably was not altogether pleased when we left without arresting him. Jail was a recognised qualification for political office in the future. There was a young man in the district who, I was told, would have paid 10,000 Rs (£750) to be arrested; but he was too timid to give any cause for arrest, and his IQ was far too low for a political career.

But some were not belittling but bitter – witness Hyde's account, also written in the CP in the 1930s, of Congress agitators. Several of the leaders were of low character, he says, and the tricks they used to manufacture 'atrocities' were revolting. He particularly disliked their use of women in demonstrations in the hope that they would get injured or be arrested, and one instance he witnessed where the police were tricked into striking an agitator who proved to be blind.

Gorwala describes the agonizing, energy consuming results of being trapped in such a situation:

The weary tales of accusation and counteraccusation, the fixing of responsibility, on occasion, over the excessive use of force, the lengthy enquiries, the constant reports to government by telegram and letter, sometimes even by telephone, the answering now and again of charges of unpreparedness or overpreparedness, the deep-seated indignation at being accused of fomenting the very trouble one had been most anxious to avoid.

For all district officers anxious to sustain a fragile structure of order and an efficient district administration, such destructive political agitation must have been hard to bear. Beyond that reactions varied according to the seriousness of events. In one aspect civil disobedience in 1930–1, like non-co-operation in 1920 or the Quit India movement in 1942, was a deliberate attempt to unite in a national cause a great diversity of more local hopes and grievances. The response was therefore patchy. In Hyde's CP the elaborate preparations to protect Europeans when Gandhi was arrested in April 1931 proved ludicrously overdone. But there was real violence elsewhere, as far apart as Chittagong in eastern Bengal and Peshawar on the North-West Frontier.

In Bengal violence was a recrudescence of earlier terrorist activity and it culminated in a dramatic raid upon the armoury at Chittagong. Martyn gives the flavour of those days:

The few months at Chittagong were notable for the fact that, for the first time in my service, I came face to face with the implications of terrorism. Bengal, to a greater extent than any other Province, had a tradition of terrorist activity. The reasons for this were various. It did not help that the Hindu gentlefolk were avid for education while the chances of such scholars obtaining white collar employment (the only employment they would touch having regard to their family background and status) were meagre indeed. It was not for nothing, too, that the Temple of Kali, the Goddess of Destruction and perhaps the most popular figure of the Hindu Pantheon in Bengal, was in Calcutta. In such circumstances it was not difficult to see why a wrong under-standing of the meaning and implications of freedom (at least from our point of view) would lead to violence and be given religious backing.

Up to date the murder of John Peddie in Midnapore, the fact that L. G. Durno (my first D.M. in Nadia) had been shot at in Dacca and lost an eye in the process, or that deaths had resulted from the armed raid on Writers' Buildings and the murderous attack on the Police Armoury in Chittagong had simply been news. Now I found myself buying my own revolver and meeting, on arrival at Chittagong, the gunman who would accompany me wherever I went.

In Peshawar on the other hand the outbreak was quite unexpected. There the Pathan nationalists, the Muslim Khudai Khidmatgaran (Servants of God) or Red Shirts, who were allied with Gandhi and Congress, seized the city and held it for four days. The loss of the provincial capital rather un-nerved the Governor, but the coup was unplanned and the city was soon brought under control – 'a child, astonished by its own tantrum, returning to the security of nanny's hand', as Thompson puts it.

Thompson perhaps underplays both the cultural and emotional antipathies to British rule upon which the civil disobedience movement and regional nationalism could draw, and the economic distress caused by the onset of world depression. He does, however, note that an enhancement of revenue demand when Peshawar district was re-settled had caused a grievance which the Red Shirts played on (the same agrarian discontent was exploited by the UP Congress under Jawaharlal Nehru's leadership, which threatened non-payment of rents by the peasants). He also catches the unforeseen opportunist quality of the event.

Nevertheless civil disobedience was over by 1932. A new Viceroy, Lord Willingdon, had rejected Gandhi's claim to be spokesman and mediator for the Indian people, outlawed Congress, seized its assets and banned proces-sions. But these moves were only successful because public support for civil disobedience had already been eroded; people did not want to see economic life disrupted or a major breakdown of law and order. Gorwala as an Indian serving the Raj may speak defensively, but he voices a widely held view of the way politics had been going:

Their aim was often the paralysing of government and the general administrator was called upon in the name of patriotism to resign, either as a protest or as an aid to paralysis. The general administrator did not believe government could be paralysed in this fashion. Even if it could, it would be against the real interest of the people to attempt it. For the result would be not self-government but anarchy, than which any government was obviously to be preferred.

The Muslims had largely stood aloof from the civil disobedience of the 1930s, and the more the Round Table Conferences and Parliament got down to the details of constitutional advance, the more anxious they and other groups became to enjoy the tangible gains which co-operation with government promised. Moreover the government had itself been active in rallying moderate support, using its well-established ties with the notables of the countryside. The Punjab was not a Congress stronghold, but Le Bailly's account of the pattern there was not without parallels elsewhere:

In the Punjab Congress propaganda had mainly affected the urban shopkeeper class, a class obviously unpopular with the great majority who earned their living by tilling the soil or by herding cattle. At the same time the continued deepening of the trade depression convinced many traders that civil disobedience was bad for business. In the circumstances the civil disobedience campaign in the Punjab at least was something of a damp squib.

In the Montgomery district the centre of Congress activities, such as they were, was the flourishing market town of Okara about 20 miles from headquarters on the road to Lahore. On several occasions some of the notables approached me with the advice that if the Okara Congress and its demonstrations were left to them they would soon cease, but scenting something irregular I gave them no encouragement. Eventually it came to the point that throughout British India Congress demonstrations were only occurring in cities like Bombay and in Okara (population perhaps 10,000). The Punjab Government therefore wrote to enquire why they still continued in Okara? On this my very experienced Commissioner wrote saying that he was satisfied that I had been doing 'all that the law permits'. I took the hint and told the local notables that I accepted their advice and Congress demonstrations thereupon ceased.

In Bihar, however, Congress and the peasant movement were strong and the government had to be correspondingly active in mobilizing loyalists. 'To counter the Congress campaign', writes Solomon,

Government encouraged District and Subdivisional Officers to rally all those who could be counted to withstand the popular tide. Aman Sabhas (Loyal Assemblies) were formed all over the country and I threw myself wholeheartedly into the campaign. A special feature of our anti-Congress propaganda at Giridih was the regular issue of our Aman Sabha bulletins, which were eagerly awaited and read by friend and foe alike. We were unsparing in our onslaughts, on Congress and Mahatma alike.

In the Bombay Presidency Hashim Raza noted the special effort made to retain the confidence and support of the peasantry:

W. W. Smart, Commissioner, Poona Division, was very keen on village uplift and called for periodical reports to ensure that steps were being taken to improve the lot of villagers. The main point which he made in his circulars was that to improve the economic condition of villagers was a vital necessity and that a contented peasantry was a bulwark against political agitation.

But by far the most elaborate effort to elicit loyalist support and to prepare it for the post-reforms period of provincial autonomy was that made by Hailey, Governor of the UP. Venkatachar, as DC of Gonda, and then as UP Provincial Rural Development Officer was well placed to observe events in the run-up to elections in 1934, and he writes with a rather mordant pen:

The feudalism of the land system came under attack by the Congress no-rent campaign. A dangerous era of political activity affecting the interests of the landlords had already begun. Hailey had no use for the old policy of being the protector of the Oudh nobles. He wanted to stir them to protect themselves against their own destruction. Under the coming reforms, government authority will not be there to protect their interests.

Hailey's plan to help the landlords to organise themselves for protection of their interests was politically astute. He reorganised the court of wards department which was a strong arm of district administration in the management of taluqdari [major landlord] and zamindari estates during the period they were under the control of government. He took it out of the management of the Board of Revenue and placed it under the charge of a newly created President of the courts of wards who was assisted by an advisory body of landlords.

Under his guidance, the 'Pioneer' of Allahabad was required to further the interests of the landowning and other conservative groups. The 'Pioneer' of Kipling shifted to Lucknow in a new *avatar* [incarnation]. Its finances came from the rich landlords and the court of wards.

Hailey took bold steps to use the district administrative machinery to promote his ideas of a stable party in the countryside. He made speeches all over the province, emphasising the importance of the landlords as a class and their responsibilities to direct rural politics.

The district officer was intimately involved in working out the Governor's policy. At the headquarters of the government, there was a Director of Publicity. The district publicity officer – an officer of the Provincial Civil Service – carried out under the general supervision of the district officer the programme and directives received from the Directorate. Sometimes, directives even came from the Chief Secretary.

The district publicity officer arranged meetings in the rural areas. He had the assistance of publicity vans and films on rural health and sanitation to propagandize rural uplift. The campaign hammered away the idea that improvements in villages will redound to the credit of landlords. The district officer presided at some of the meetings to lend prestige to the campaign.

Besides propaganda, two small rural improvement centres were launched, near Gonda. One was called *Meri Umed* (my hope); the other was a model housing colony on Crown land. Both were financed from the court of wards.

But the efforts of government, in Venkatachar's experience, did little to stir into activity landholders who preferred to lean upon the dwindling authority of the district officer:

Their customary and social link with the peasantry was weak, much of it eroded. By nature indolent and pleasure-loving, they had hosts of inefficient and rascally servants to manage their affairs. They never met their tenantry. They lived in a world of make-believe that the tenants were loyal and would obey the behests of their lordly masters.

When the ban on Congress was lifted in 1934, it was the Congress workers, cycling through the countryside, spreading the message that Congress rule would reduce tenant rents and stop taluqdari oppression, who won the support of the peasant. Congress success in the November 1934 elections to the central legislative assembly demonstrated that.

From March 1935 therefore new efforts were made, through the British Indian Association – 'a trade union of the Taluqdars' – to form a loyalist party to fight the elections when provincial autonomy was introduced. Venkatachar became Provincial Rural Development Officer, touring extensively as a liaison officer between the district officials and the Government at Lucknow, and organizing meetings with his Minister Sir Jwala Prasad Srivastava. 'These divisional meetings ostensibly for purpose of giving impetus to development work, were avowedly political rallies for furthering the cause of the National Agricultural Party. Srivastava was the driving force behind the party.'

But government influence was not enough to tip the balance in favour of landlords who, Venkatachar argues, 'had no idea of countering the mass leadership of Congress. They had no tactics to mobilize the vote of their own peasantry. Like the old liberal leaders they were afraid of the masses; they could not be induced to face a mass gathering.' At the provincial elections in 1937 the National Agricultural Party won only a handful of seats and Congress took office with a substantial overall majority.

The disastrous electoral result was the end of Zamindars and Taluqdars as a force in the political life of the Province. The Collector of my Aligarh days was then in Lucknow doing election work. Reflecting on the results of the election, he remarked to me that it was the beginning of the end of British rule as it was hitherto thought that Congress had some influence in the urban areas and over the urban intelligentsia; now, it had convincingly demonstrated that it held the rural area in its grip. What was astonishing, he added, was that Congress played the game and won on rules set by government.

The rules referred to were those embodied in the Government of India Act of 1935 under which India was governed until independence in 1947. The Act introduced full provincial autonomy under Indian ministers, and the prospect of a federal centre in which Princely India would have a share of the seats and in which Indian ministers would share with British counsellors the portfolios of the Council of Ministers, though this latter part of the Act did not come into force. Given the continuing Indianization of the ICS and the Indian Army the Act implied the replacement at every level of the system of bureaucratic control by one of informal influence. The task now was to make sure, as far as possible, that those who came to power under the Act would be willing to maintain the British connection. The district officer as an administrator had now to learn to work with politicians – and to acquire some of the skills of the politician himself.

For the district officer, however, the first consequence of the passing of the Act was that he had to supervise elections in which many more had the vote than before, including women in some number and peasants and artisans who might often be illiterate. Georgeson up in the hills at Coonoor, in Madras, relates the system devised:

Each candidate was allotted a colour, the national parties having the same colours throughout the country. Thus the Congress had yellow: its opponents complained that this gave it an unfair advantage because saffron was associated with marriage and they alleged that women who didn't know one party from another were led to believe that in voting for the yellow they were voting for the success of their marriage.

In the polling station was a screened booth containing for each candidate a box of the colour allotted with a slot on the top. On the side of the booth furthest from the entrance the screen had a horizontal rectangular slit. Beyond that a clerk sat watching the slit, through which he could see the ballot boxes and a few inches above.

The voter, after the name was checked with the electoral list, was asked if he or she understood what had to be done and told the procedure. He was then given a card, went into the booth and put the card in the box of his choice. The watcher behind the screen could see the hand put the card in the box and his function was to check that the voter did nothing irregular to the boxes.

I was polling officer in charge of a station situated in a remote part of the mountains some distance from my headquarters. I went there on the previous evening, slept on a camp cot in the village school, which was being used as the polling station, presided over the polling from 7 a.m. to 6 p.m. and then took the boxes to district head-quarters.

This election at Coonoor, which helped to return a Congress government in Madras, was uneventful and unsophisticated but, thanks to the long political experience of Bengal, Martyn's election in Jessore was a livelier, more practised affair:

The elections were on a communal basis – some seats for Hindus, some for Muslims, some for the Scheduled Castes. We were the recipient of many instructions from the Provincial Government and the detailed administrative work was admirably handled by an efficient Deputy Magistrate who knew he had my full support. After the elections he shared with me his relief that I had not breathed down his neck and how strengthened he had been by the knowledge that no attempt to get at him, through me, would succeed. The sort of difficulty that might so easily have arisen was highlighted by a visit by a Namasudra (Scheduled Caste) candidate shortly after I had joined. After the usual courtesies he *a* wanted the polling booths, selected by the Deputy Magistrate, to be re-sited to suit himself, and *b* threw out hints that 'the Government officers' were against him. He got a flat refusal on *a* and, when challenged on *b*, hastily withdrew his insinuations.

The electioneering campaign of the numerous candidates followed the pattern beloved by some politicians in every age and clime. Thus the Chairman of the District Board (who became a Minister following these elections) was alleged to have promised a tube well in every village – leading the more innocent to believe that the chronic water supply problem of the District had been solved. The Muslim voters in one area were informed that their prayers flew upwards and could not reach Allah unless they had a good representative in the Council who could plead for them!

The 1937 elections ended with Congress enjoying clear majorities in the largely Hindu provinces of Madras, Orissa, Bihar, and the CP and UP. After a short period of indecision they took office in these five and also in Bombay with a little outside support, while in the NWFP the Red Shirts took control. Muslim coalitions took office in Assam, Sind, Bengal and in the Punjab where the Unionists continued strongly in power. At the centre, since the federal structure was not yet in being, there was no such transfer of power. For most Indians, however, and for the district officers, it was the provincial changes which were significant, as Maitra points out:

The failure to capture power at the centre by Indian politicians was not so important as one might think, so far as British India was concerned. It was the provincial Government which kept the peace through police, brought up the wrong doer before the court, collected the land revenue, looked after the sick in hospitals, provided for schooling of boys and girls, arranged relief during famine and so on. For all practical purposes, it was the provincial Government that meant *Sarkar* in the eyes of the common man.

What happened when new hands grasped the levers varied from province to province and district to district, for, as Maitra argues, it was not so much the letter as the spirit of government which altered when the new ministries took office. He offers two personal experiences:

In Mangaldai in Assam while I was trying to keep the Muslim immigrants from Mymensingh district in Bengal from encroaching beyond the line set apart for them, Mr Abdul Matin Chowdhury, a Muslim minister from Bengali-speaking Sylhet, came on tour. He suggested that as a Bengali I should sympathise with the Bengali immigrants and not deal too strictly with their encroachment on land kept reserved for the Assamese. Of course I knew that the minister's harping on the Bengali sentiment was insincere. A Muslim Leaguer, his real object was to increase the number of Muslims in Assam. The incident brought to me face to face the spectacle of a high Government dignitary asking me, in pursuit of his own sectional interest, to disregard the declared policy of Government. I told Mr Chowdhury politely that I was posted to Assam not as a Bengali but a member of the I.C.S.

Sometime later it was the Chief Minister himself with whom Maitra brushed:

A Muslim trader of Silchar had cornered the firewood market with the ultimate result that dead bodies of Hindus, which are customarily cremated, remained unburnt. Being empowered at the time by the Defence of India Rules, I impounded the firewood from the iniquitous trader. The latter approached the Chief Minister through the local Muslim League M.L.A. (Member of the Legislative Assembly) to have my order cancelled. Sir Saadulla sent me a telegram to hold my hand and to meet him in person on a certain day. My reaction was to sell the firewood at a reasonable rate to various people who wanted it particularly at the burning ground. Then I sent a telegram to the Chief Minister that, knowing his well-known views on black marketing, I had anticipated his wishes. When I met Sir Saadulla and told him that I had already sold the firewood to deserving parties, he was livid with rage.

In Saran district in Bihar, home ground of one of the Congress ministers, Kemp had a rather similar experience:

The Congress ministry were great interferers in the day-to-day administration of the districts and in Saran district in particular. With so many of their henchmen in the villages the Ministers lacked no sources of information or requests for favours on which the District Officer was required to report and often to act in the manner indicated. Generally however one managed to avoid a clash, without having to compromise too much on principles.

But were the complaints raised by the district officers about the working of the new political system justified? They themselves used government patronage, in a discreet and gentlemanly way, to keep administration running smoothly. Politicians seeking support from new, inexperienced voters had of necessity to make it clear that the giving of electoral support would be rewarded.

Maitra describes the politics of Assam as 'lawlessness from the top', and he clearly dug his heels in against (undue) ministerial influence being exercised within his district. Martyn in Bengal was perhaps more understanding, arguing that the difficulties under which the ministers in his province worked were immense and 'the reasons (and perhaps the justification for their behaviour) were at least discernible, if not always acceptable'. To start with the ministry was a coalition; staying in office – and, for the Muslims, giving their co-religionists a fair crack of the whip, was all that held it together. Their team was an uneasy collection of individuals too:

Fazlul Huq, the Chief Minister and leader of the Peasants' Party was an orator, not to say demagogue. With enormous support from the Muslims of E. Bengal he was unstable and unpredictable – the despair of his friends and hardly the one to reassure the Hindus, official or otherwise. Nevertheless he had endearing qualities. When the news reached the Cabinet Room that Lord Brabourne had died that morning in Government House, it was Fazlul Huq who abandoned the meeting in tears. The rest of the Ministry was a combination of Hindus, non-Congress but without any real political base, two Scheduled Caste Ministers (neither of whom cut any ice), and the Muslims. The most outstanding was Khwaja Nazimuddin of the Muslim League. After him the most prominent was Huseyn Shaheed Suhrewardy. He had strong labour/mill affiliations and was a politician to his finger-tips and beyond. There was also the Nawab of Dacca who was in charge of Agriculture.

Such was the Ministry dependent for office on supporters in the Assembly many of whom were highly communal in outlook and hungry for the loaves and fishes of power – power which, they felt, had been denied them by the better educated, more politically astute Hindus. And finally they faced a consistently and unrelentingly hostile Press. A democratically elected Government without a Press to put across its point of view was an uncomfortable experience.

It is against such a background and the hostility of many, including Government supporters, that the Police Budgets had to be pushed through the Legislature. As Nazimuddin explained at a meeting early in 1938 with the Chief Secretary (Hogg), the Inspector General of Police (Farmer) and the Commissioner of Police (Colson): the troubles that the public have gone through, the tradition of centuries and the general attitude of the people 'all combine to make the lower ranks of the Police disliked and feared by the public'. No wonder the Ministry had to put all their proposals to a Party meeting before submitting them to the Assembly itself.

It would be wrong to think of the Party meeting as a gathering of administrators/legislators sitting round a table. Rather, as I described the scene at the time:

'You would have been astonished at the Party meeting – some sit round a table, others walk about or stand talking in a corner. Complete chaos and babel. When I looked in Tamizuddin – one of the Ministers – was on his feet haranguing the Party in Bengali, as if he was in Hyde Park. The noise was deafening. Nazimuddin doesn't mind the Assembly, but he does fear the wild men of the Party and rightly so.

'The Party house – 47 Gorachand Road – at the back of beyond, very difficult to find and very disreputable when found. It is used as the living quarters by a number of members who come in from the mofussil. Nothing is clean and we wouldn't stay there for a moment. The Party meeting was attended by 30–40 members in very much undress apart from the Ministers who did turn up in workaday clothes, except Fazlul Huq who appears in slippers, shirt etc. at the slightest provocation.

'It was most enlightening. To get the Party point of view, they look at the communal point of view; some of them were absolutely unreasonable and wanted to down the Hindus by exalting the Muslims on every occasion. Shouting was the usual method of addressing the meeting. Many of them attacked Nazimuddin in a most direct way. He had to promise to look into this, that and the other.'

In the end Nazim won his point.

In Bombay, too, Ministers had something of the same problem in handling their party supporters, as Symington records, but a much stronger ministry could act far more decisively:

It was a momentous occasion when, in the month of April, we came under the rule of the Party which had been agitating against the British *raj* for more than twenty years. But, if anyone at the time expected dramatic and revolutionary changes, he was in for an anticlimax. Our new Government had enough sense and experience to realise that nine-tenths of its work would lie in the field of day to day administration, and that spectacular reform must be a fringe activity.

Its most novel and characteristic measure was the introduction of Prohibition. This brought with it, in addition to the loss of revenue, the usual concomitants of evasion and bootlegging; but they never became in India the menace that they had been in America, and I cannot honestly aver that it did not benefit the population at large. We foreign addicts, along with the aboriginal tribes, were given a special dispensation to meet our congenital weaknesses.

One feature of the early months of Congress rule was objectionable, and embarrassing to the new Government. Every petty Congress committee, regional, district, or village, not to mention their secretaries and chairmen, assumed it had somehow acquired official status and could give orders to local officials. This quickly grew into a nuisance; and firm action was needed, and was taken, by the Congress High Command to squash it.

So far as I personally was concerned, the work of my department went on without interference or interruption. My minister was K. M. Munshi, and I found him an excellent man to work under. Other members of the Cabinet were the Prime Minister, G. G. Kher, a pure-hearted, indeed sentimentally inclined Gandhian if ever there was one; Morarji Desai, upright and austere, the enemy of drink, gambling, horse-racing, and most forms of pleasure; and Doctor Gilder, a Parsi heart specialist.

Like the other Congress governments elsewhere and at other times, our Government was committed to agrarian reform, debt relief, and all kinds of social betterment, which of course included that fine old catchword 'the removal of Untouchability'. It was they who passed the Harijan Temple Worship (Removal of Disabilities) Act. But since its provisions were only permissive – i.e. temple trustees were *enabled* to declare their temples open to Harijans [Untouchables] if they thought fit – the Act was little more than a gesture. In other ways they were able, having regard to the realities of their political situation, to do no more than we were doing already to help the Harijans.

In the Punjab the transition was simple for the Unionist Ministry which took office in 1937, since it built upon the long and successful experience of the Unionists under dyarchy. In Madras, however, where the Justice Party had been in power since 1920, the Congress Ministry was new to office. As Lamarque says, its assumption of full provincial powers was a landmark on the Indian road to self-government:

But it was not an easy transition for the permanent officials. The Congress ministers were committed to independence for India, impatient for results, and suspicious of their officials, particularly of the British of the older generation. Some of them, notably Rajagopalachari himself, were cautious and wise, a few, like Dr Subbaroyan, were anglicised, but there was a strong radical and left-wing element, ready to exert every possible kind of pressure on others. Small wonder then that, as I recorded in letters home, Brackenbury looked tired and harassed and worn. He was finding the training of Ministers in government as being the art of the possible a very difficult task, though he was quite prepared to go along with their ideas where, as he saw it, matters of principles were not involved.

Masterman saw the Madras Ministry from the inside as he had been posted from the district to be Secretary to the Ministers of Health and Education, Subbaroyan and Dr Rajan respectively. He writes:

The position in the Secretariat as a whole was peculiar, almost bizarre. The Ministers were totally inexperienced in administration or the ways of government, even Local

Government, whereas the Secretaries – all British at that time – had 20 or more years of district and secretariat experience, and were the same men who a few months previously had been putting these same Ministers and their like in jail!

It was said that we ran the government. I do not think that is quite true. No one could run Rajaji [Rajagopalachari]. We did of course have a good deal of power inevitably owing to our greater experience and succeeded I think in putting a stop to some of the wild schemes of the Ministers without causing great offence. In minor matters our views generally prevailed, but in major policy matters the Prime Minister was supreme. In these matters he more often than not agreed with the Secretary as against the Minister concerned. He told me once that he had much greater confidence in the judgment of his British secretaries than in his Indian colleagues. It is therefore truer to say that the government was run by the Prime Minister and the permanent Secretaries.

It was Rajaji who was responsible for the success of the Congress Government in Madras and it was more successful and efficient than in most other parts of India. His office room was always darkened and he himself wore dark glasses. One was confronted with a small, rather frail looking figure, sitting huddled up in a chair, but his brain was astonishingly alert, even when he looked half asleep. He was refreshingly straightforward in what he said to his Secretaries.

But the fact that the 1935 Act was working in the provinces and the realization that power and patronage was passing into ministerial or party hands from those of the ICS became a cause of alarm to minority groups who seemed excluded from power. Muslims in Bombay or the UP, Hindus in Bengal or the Punjab, and Sikhs in the Punjab too all felt a new uncertainty about their future. The communal problem with which district officers had so long grappled was increasingly a political problem too.

The refusal by a victorious Congress to form any coalition with the Muslim Leaguers and Nehru's campaign to appeal over the heads of the League to Muslim voters sharpened political antagonism. Muslims had long taken comfort in the thought that in a federal India, such as the 1935 Act had envisaged, Muslims would be in a dominant position in several provinces, including Sind newly separated from the Bombay Presidency. Now they began to speak of separate homelands, of Pakistan. This may still have been only a bargaining point, as Downing believed, but the idea of partition had been floated. And since the League had done only moderately well in the 1937 elections, it was necessary to rally Muslim support so as to convince government that the League, not Congress, spoke for all Muslims, and this meant that Muslim fears and sense of separateness had to be played upon. Lane at Faizabad in the UP met some of the men who would orchestrate fear of Congress among Muslims.

One of these, the Raja of Pirpur, often visited us in camp or took us for shooting parties or invited us to dinners. He was a cheerful extrovert who loved shooting and country life, but he was already strongly imbued with Muslim League politics and ideas. He spent hours talking about the iniquities of the Hindu-controlled Congress and the superiority of Muslims to Hindus.

His name would be on one of the two reports produced by the League on the oppression of Muslims by Congress ministries and high-handed Congress party workers. These reports, true or false, sharpened antagonisms and helped swing Muslims behind Jinnah. The outbreak of the Second World

War served only to increase the polarization between the supporters of Congress and the Muslim League.

On the same day, 3 September 1939, that the British Prime Minister declared that Britain was at war with Germany, the Viceroy Lord Linlithgow announced that India also was at war. There was no prior consultation with Indian leaders, and when in October the Viceroy outlined the Government's aims he could say no more than that Dominion Status for India was the goal, that Indians would be asked to help frame reforms to that end after the war, and that meanwhile a consultative group representing the major parties and the Princes would be formed to assist the Indian war effort.

To Lane in Lucknow, and to others, this seemed a very unimaginative appeal to India:

It did seem to me then that most middle-class Indians were prepared to back and help Britain wholeheartedly in the war *if only* some generous political gesture had been made by Delhi or Whitehall. My letters home were full of scorn for the Viceroy, Lord Linlithgow, whom I roundly accused of lacking imagination. A great many of the remarks I made then were no doubt naive and based on very slender evidence: but I must say, with hindsight, that I am still of opinion that India could have been handled more tactfully at the outbreak of War and that if it had, the response might well have been generous.

In fact, however, neither the League nor Congress leaders had offered their unconditional support, and before war had been declared the Congress Working Committee had ordered the provincial governments to be ready to resign rather than assist in the war preparations of the British Government. Congress would fight for freedom only if offered it herself. When Linlithgow offered so little, so late, the Congress provincial ministers were asked to resign and by 15 November all had done so. Direct rule by the Governors, assisted by ICS Advisers, took their place.

The Government of India was content for the moment to make no further move but to concentrate upon the war effort. But there were other reactions as Raza, serving in Sind, sets down:

When the Congress Governments submitted their resignation, Mr. M. A. Jinnah instructed Muslims all over India to observe a Day of Deliverance. This was done with great enthusiasm. The gulf between Hindus and Muslims was widening rapidly. Several communal riots took place resulting in bloodshed.

On March 23, 1940, the All India Muslim League, meeting in Lahore, passed a resolution demanding formation of Muslim States in the North East and North West of India when the British withdrew from India. This resolution is popularly known as the Pakistan Resolution.

But even after the fall of France in June 1940 Linlithgow promised little more than had been offered in October 1939, though Indian leaders were invited to join his Executive Council. He did, however, recognize League claims to the extent of declaring that power would not be transferred to any Indian government whose authority was denied 'by large and powerful elements in India's national life'.

The reply of the Congress leadership was to launch a limited civil disobedience movement from October 1940, a means of satisfying party militants and of applying mild pressure on the government. District officers once again found themselves dealing with Congress volunteers, as Symington in Bombay records:

After two years of successful if unspectacular rule the Congress reverted to its old function of agitation and obstruction. In the early months of the war this took the form of a succession of small processions demonstrating against help towards the war effort. Volunteers were allocated their day of sacrifice. When it dawned they began to walk round the streets with slogans and banners that said 'Not a man! Not a rupee!' In due course a police-officer would go out and collect them; and later, after refusing to pay a fine in lieu of imprisonment, they were hauled off for a few weeks in jail. It was a rite which the sensible Congressman could not afford to miss.

It was the pressure of war, however, rather than that of the politicians which finally compelled the government to reconsider its attitude of no change during the war. Pearl Harbor in December 1941, the fall of Singapore in February 1942 and of Rangoon in March – these led to the despatch to India by Churchill of the Stafford Cripps Mission. The offer conveyed was that of an elected constituent assembly to be set up as soon as the war ended. This would draw up a Dominion constitution, which Parliament undertook to accept even if it chose to secede from the Commonwealth. The one proviso was that any province objecting to the new Union constitution might opt out of it. For the interim, an enlarged Viceroy's Executive Council containing Indian leaders would act as far as possible as a war cabinet.

The offer came very near to being accepted by both the major parties despite the possibility of a piecemeal Pakistan which it seemed to offer. It was, however, because of the limited powers of the Indian Defence Minister in the proposed Executive Council or Cabinet, and the absence of collective cabinet responsibility – which if agreed would have given the Congress members of it a dominant role – that Congress eventually rejected the offer. Rejection was followed on 7 August 1942 by a Congress demand that Britain 'Quit India' immediately and by the threat of mass civil disobedience if it failed to do so. (The Japanese by now were on India's very borders.) As Gandhi told journalists 'this is open rebellion'. On 9 August the Congress leaders, including Gandhi and Nehru, were arrested. There followed attacks on an all-India scale against railways, the post and telegraph systems and government installations. In the eastern UP and in Bihar particularly, but in some other places too, there followed for district officers the greatest test of their ability to maintain law, order and the structure of government since the Mutiny of 1857.

No area escaped some tremor, some shock waves, even though the epicentre was in the middle Ganges valley. Faruqui, for example as Collector of Thana, had enjoyed having the amenities of Bombay so nearby, but in 1942, when Congress launched the Quit India movement, he had cause to regret the city's proximity:

The movement gave no pretence of non-violence. It was openly violent and terroristic.

In this critical revolt, proximity to Bombay city was a handicap to me. The movement started from Bombay city and when the British Government pounced upon the law-breakers, they easily escaped into my district which had a long common border amongst jungles and hills. I had violent trouble everywhere. What is worse, it was not possible to get police reinforcements from the provincial reserve force as Bombay city itself and other districts also had their own troubles. My personal handicap was that the head of my own police force of the district was an extremely Congress-minded and anti-British Parsi officer. What is worse, he was a pessimist and a defeatist by temperament, if not by design. Every morning he would brief me on the situation throughout the district. And he would take such a gloomy and pessimistic view of things (with remarks like 'we are finished. The situation is out of hand' and so on) that when he left me my nerves were shaken and I used to feel completely demoralised and lost. How I survived the daily dose of defeatism and pessimism, I do not know. It was a special grace of God that I did.

Across in Madras Narasimham in Devakottai also had a rough time of it. He had to send his wife and young daughter to Madras to be with her parents and had himself to move from his bungalow to the police station where there could be round the clock protection, which was a singular irony since for a while he had been suspected by the CID of being a Congressman himself! He had to patrol his sub-district by armoured car and to his evident distress had several times to open fire and witness people being shot and killed.

Delhi, the seat of government, was not immune either. On the arrest of the Congress leadership a hartal or general strike was engineered which, Le Bailly argues, was not spontaneous indignation. Buses were burnt, property severely damaged and Indians wearing Western clothes were singled out for attack. Here, however, quick action prevented any serious breakdown of law and order. Le Bailly himself sallied out with an armed section of police against the mob, his own duty being to declare it an 'unlawful assembly'. He was met with such a hail of stones and bottles from the defiant crowd that the SP had to order five rounds of deliberate fire. 'Firing into the air was strictly forbidden – the reason being that the mob could not know that apparently ineffective fire was deliberate and would rapidly counter-attack and might well overwhelm the police.' Mounted police using lathis at the trot then completed the dispersal of the mob.

In the eastern UP the disturbances were more serious, but Mudie, Chief Secretary to the Government, had been warned by a Muslim talukdar that this was a danger area, being rather unattractive to British officers and so neglected. Mudie had therefore made sure that there was a British collector or superintendent of police in each district there, failing only in Ballia. When the rioting began it was contained within ten days or so, Mudie downing his secretariat pen, borrowing a shotgun and visiting the districts himself to ensure prompt action. At Benares, Mudie adds, the Collector 'rather resented my intrusion – and told me so'. Lane, assistant to Finlay, the Collector concerned, saw events at Benares from ground level:

It was fairly obvious to us that the Benares Hindu University was a focal point for planning sabotage and the violent dislocation of communications to the Army fighting on the North-East frontier. All the districts in the Benares Division were seriously affected and all Magistrates and Police Officers were heavily involved. In Benares itself I was deputed with a posse of mounted police to halt and turn back a large mob that was actively engaged in pulling down telegraph poles in the city itself and pre- paring to advance against Government property. Finlay was a fine and experienced District Magistrate and it was not long before we had Benares itself under control and the University closed down (though many of the students had by this time dispersed to lead gangs of saboteurs in neighbouring districts).

In the districts of Ghazipur and Ballia, however, things were very different. Police forces were small and distributed in outlying 'thanas'. The mobs, led by students, attacked and destroyed Government buildings and even the police stations themselves. In central Ghazipur the police held out and defeated their attackers but in Ballia, where the District Magistrate was foolishly weak, the mobs were able to capture every police station except one and to wreck and destroy numerous Government buildings, including even Seed Stores. The U.P. Government sent a senior Com- missioner with special powers and a force of armed police to the affected area and in about 15 days the rioters were dispersed and the districts of Ghazipur and Ballia were brought again under Government control.

Ballia had the appearance of territory over which a battle had been fought. The people were thoroughly cowed and apparently expected condign punishment. My main job was to assess Collective Fines in the villages and areas where the worst offences had been committed, and such was the state of panic in the District that this took very little time indeed. I did my best to calm exaggerated fears and to get the administrative machine working normally.

For some considerable time my views on India, on the prospects of Indian indepen- dence and my relationship with Indians, particularly Hindus, became almost 're- actionary'. I was revolted by the atrocities reported in Bihar, and the atrocities I actually knew of that were perpetrated in some places in the Benares Division by mobs attacking police or stray Government servants. I was disgusted at the wanton destruction of property and above all I was fiercely angry at the obvious attempt to cut communications to the Army in the North East and thus make it easier for the Japanese to invade India. This change of feeling did not make me any less friendly to my Indian colleagues and private Indian friends, but I grew very cynical about Indian politicians, both local, Provincial and National.

It was in Bihar, however, that government was most thoroughly subverted during the riots of August 1942. This, as Martin says, was 'a dyed in the wool Congress province':

The landlords who formed the richest and most influential grouping in the province were united only in a recognition that to survive and prosper they would have in the long run to make their peace with the Congress Party; and much the same feelings influenced the members of the provincial services, particularly the magistracy and the police, who formed the great part of the administration. The average Bihari, though a tough and dour character, was not renowned for martial valour, and there was no tradition of service in the pre-war Indian Army which might form a nucleus of deter- mined loyalty to British rule.

Orr was in Patna, the capital of Bihar, when on 9 August 1942 the Congress high command was arrested. Orr relates what followed:

When the 10th August dawned, letter-post and telephone no longer operated. With dramatic suddenness and meticulously precise planning the Congress Party had over- night disrupted every form of communication (except the radio) not merely between Bihar and the rest of India, but between Patna and any other district headquarters, and even within districts and sub-divisions. While telegraph and telephone wires were cut, electric cables (which looked very similar) were left intact so that people could still enjoy the benefits of electric light and fans. Main roads were made impassable by the destruction of bridges or simply by digging deep trenches across them. Fish-plates were removed from railways and no train could travel more than a mile or so in either direction. The stultification of all centralised Governmental administration was complete. Control passed over to the individual district and sub-divisional officers who simply had to cope as best they could with this sudden, universal and un-precedented emergency. They had however the written instructions of the Internal Security Scheme to fall back on, and all Europeans were collected together into the 'keep' areas to await relief. Fortunately Gandhi's preaching of non-violence was heeded, at least initially, and there were very few killings. There were however two tragic incidents which brought home to us the danger and ugliness of the people's mood. The first was the murder of two young R.A.F. officers who had been travelling by the Punjab mail train between Calcutta and Delhi. The other incident was the murder of a Sub-Divisional Officer in Aurangabad. He was an Anglo-Indian Officer of the Provincial Service and he was tied to his office chair; files and furniture from his office was stacked around him; kerosene was poured over him and the whole lot set alight.

In Patna the 'Keep' area covered the entire New Capital, which included Govern-ment House, the Secretariat, the High Court, and the residences of almost all the Europeans. Patna City was strictly out of bounds. The only possible method of com-munication was by messenger. The Governor had with him in Government House only a very small team of helpers. In Patna he was completely cut off and he knew nothing of what was happening in the rest of the Province. But there was from the outset one small consolation; for a steady stream of information flowed in to Govern-ment House from Patna's Old City area. This information was brought to me person-ally by my own A.R.P. staff. It told us of meetings of Congress Party members and some of their plans for substituting their own administration in place of the British, not only in Patna City but throughout the Province. It was from this source that we first learnt how universally successful the insurrection had been in Bihar.

News also began to filter in from the districts. By the second week the Military were able to send out patrols to add to the flow of information. Reinforcements were requested from Ranchi, and plans were being prepared for the gradual recovery of control. The reinforcements which set out from Ranchi had to travel by road as the railways were still out of commission, and their progress was slowed by the detours and river crossings necessitated by the destruction of bridges and culverts. It took them almost a week to reach Patna. Their arrival signified the end of the siege and the beginning of the re-conquest of territory where the Government had lost control. It was a slow process and one which inevitably did little to enhance pro-British sentiment. Control over the last 'thana' was not effected until February 1943, six months after the emergency began.

The Bihar risings were viewed by Orr from the beleaguered centre. By Martin they were seen from the district, from the southwestern periphery. His sub-division, Sasaram, was important as the point where the vast sandy bed of the river Sone was crossed by the direct rail route and, 'potholed and bumpy as it was, by the only all-weather road for vehicles from Western India to Calcutta, already in constant use by convoys of military vehicles'. A major effort was made here against communications:

The riots were led by younger members of the Congress Party assisted by students from Patna University and by the older boys of the local High English Schools. The aim in Sasaram was to make the railway inoperable by burning the railway stations and signal boxes and organising gangs to remove lengths of railway lines. In rural areas the local police stations were the object of attack and in subdivisional head-quarters the object was to demonstrate the powerlessness of the local officials to maintain authority. A more sinister aspect was the presence in many areas of quite large numbers of professional criminals who normally earned a somewhat precarious living by means of violence and robbery, and who quickly saw the possibilities in a wholesale breakdown of law and order.

In a letter to an old Oxford friend serving in the UP Martin then tells his personal experience of what was only too clearly a period when he was in great personal danger. The first news received was that 'a large mob had commandeered a train from Arrah and were coming to Sasaram along the light railway destroying all the stations as they went along and looting the cash'. Then boys from the school invaded the Civil Court; when the police were ordered to clear them out 'the Hindu constables became engrossed in contemplation of the infinite', while the police havildar explained that 'if we attempted to open fire on the mob we should all infallibly be killed – he had discussed the matter with his friends and they were all of the same opinion'. Martin retired to the treasury, armed with a revolver, where the guard un-accountably had expressed their determination to remain at their post and open fire on anyone who came near. There he waited, a scene like a re-run of the Mutiny in 1857:

As the sounds of excitement in the town became louder along came a detachment of soldiers from Arrah, in the good old melodramatic style, and much to my surprise. I thought the crowd would now abate its ardour but oddly enough it didn't. We had quite a lot of trouble arresting some students and then a largish crowd went off to the station to burn a military petrol dump. We went off after them in a lorry with 12 soldiers and the subaltern who was in command. We got to the station all right but couldn't disperse the crowd. When we tried to get back we found that they had put a barricade of bullock carts across the road and were lined up on either side to pelt us with stones. So we had to dismount and remove the carts while the others covered us with fire, which was necessarily at close range. We went on and on firing without really getting the crowd to move out of the way. One of them got up near enough to give the officer a crack on the head with a lathi before he shot him with his revolver. Altogether we had to fire 43 shots before the truck could get through and they were still pursuing us closely when we did get away. The subaltern told me that the situation was 'militarily untenable' (he was rather a pompous young man). We only had 20 men including 4 stretcher-bearers and if the crowd attacked us again, particularly at night, we shouldn't be able to stop them. I was getting all ready to pack up and wondering whether to take the gramophone or all my books, when along came another eleventh hour deliverance. A whole regiment puffed into the station along the main line.

Sasaram is now the headquarters of the Beds. and Herts. Battalion, very tough guys, having broken out of Tobruk and beaten up the Vichy French in Syria among other things. The general effect though has been to pacify the place pretty thoroughly. We also had a visit from the Military Police, Punjabis who don't care much for Biharis at the best of times, who burnt two or three villages near where the main line and the road had been damaged, and shot all the inhabitants who ran away.

I don't know what the damage was in your direction but it has been quite thorough here. The main line via Patna has been completely wrecked and won't be working properly for 4 months. The main line via Sasaram is now working in a chaotic kind of way without any signals. North of the Ganges has been the worst area. Altogether quite a lively time.

By the end of 1942, even in Bihar, normality had returned, local officials had recovered their nerve, the police were busy dealing with crime rather than subversion. District officers, having mastered their own feelings, were trying to heal the wounds and dilute the hatred created by the process of restoring order among the local population. Attention could be turned again to tackling the grave and growing problems of a war with the Japanese which had now lapped over onto the soil of India itself.

FURTHER READING

The literature on the politics of this period is very extensive indeed. The works suggested here provide general introductions and useful bibliographies – an entry into a large field.

B. R. Tomlinson, 'India and the British Empire, 1880–1935' in *Indian Economic and Social History Review*, XII:4 (1975), 339–80, and 'India and the British Empire, 1935–1947', *Indian Economic and Social History Review*, XIII:3 (1976), 331–52, are two broad answers to the question, what was the place of India in the Empire. To these may be added his *The Indian National Congress and the Raj, 1929–1942* (Cambridge 1976).

R. J. Moore, *The Crisis of Indian Unity, 1917–1940* (Oxford 1974) looks at the period through the eyes of British policy makers and establishes the constitutional framework within which change took place.

B. B. Misra, *The Indian Political Parties... to 1947* (Delhi 1976), provides a long sweep, scholarly and comprehensive, from a third perspective.

Three volumes: Ravinder Kumar (ed.), *Essays on Gandhian Politics, The Rowlatt Satyagraha of 1919* (Oxford 1971), especially Kumar's introduction and D. A. Low's study of the Government of India's reaction to the 1920–2 non-co-operation movement; D. A. Low (ed.), *Congress and the Raj. Facts of the Indian Struggle, 1917–47* (London 1977); and C. H. Philips and M. Wainwright, *The Partition of India: Policies and Perspectives, 1935–47* (London 1970), serve to demonstrate the enormous variety of political response across India in the period up to 1942.

On the special problem of the Muslims P. Hardy, *The Muslims of British India* (Cambridge 1972), is particularly clear and helpful. With it might also be mentioned Aziz Ahmad, *Islamic Modernism in India and Pakistan, 1857–1964* (London 1967). Stephen Oren, 'The Sikhs, Congress and the Unionists in British Punjab 1937–45', in *Modern Asian Studies*, VIII:3 (1974), 397–418 adds the Sikh dimension.

CHAPTER 11

THE IMPACT OF WAR

The Second World War was a catalyst of change in the politics of India. It proved no less so in the administration and economy of the sub-continent. But once the immediate shock of the announcement of a state of war had died away – some panic buying, some sharp increases in prices, the activation of the procedures laid down in the War Book and the toilsome decyphering of messages the gist of which had already been gathered from BBC bulletins – India settled back to normality, to a phoney war made doubly unreal by distance. Ever since the Munich Conference men had been bracing themselves for the onset of total war with Hitler's Germany. But to Bell, Settlement Officer at Dinajpur in Bengal, as to others, expectation was falsified:

All officers on leave or on leave preparatory to retirement had been recalled to duty when war was imminent, and I was reconciled to staying in India until the end of the war. One of my letters says that I can expect to come home in time for the unveiling of the war memorials. But by early January, I was told that there would be no objection to my going on home leave to Britain. So with India showing so little signs of war, I stayed on at Dinajpur until the middle of March and completed my Final Report. There were more men in uniform in Calcutta, but in Dinajpur the only sign of war had been an immediate price rise, following the general reaction of the business community: I noted that the price of cow dung cakes had risen from 3 to 4 pice for 20. So on 29 March I left Calcutta and, travelling by flying-boat from Karachi, I arrived at Poole on 4 or 5 April. I have always been glad that I was in England in the summer of 1940 – able to feel the atmosphere of a country really at war, and to share the emotions of my own people. Perhaps, also, not to have had to show to Indians an air of confidence which might not have been quite genuine.

To most district officers, however, the relief of sharing in the experience of war was denied. Instead there was frustration and anxiety as Barty records:

It was during my second period of hot weather leave in Karachi that we heard of the outbreak of war in Europe. Although long expected, it still came as a shock. As the weeks and months went by, it was equally disturbing how little a state of war affected the province and its people. There was a feeling of frustration and helplessness at being so far away. Soon after returning to Sukkur, I wrote to the Revenue Commissioner applying for release to serve with the Indian Army. The reply was a firm 'no': but he kindly went on to explain the reasoning behind what was a decision of the Government of India in relation to the I.C.S. and, for all I know, other civilian services. Apparently in the 1914–18 war, the Government of India agreed to release some members of the I.C.S. for military service provided they were sent back alive at the end of hostilities. As a result, those who were recruited and given commissions spent the war in clerical jobs in India (so the story goes). When the second world war was imminent, it was decided not to repeat this mistake. It was also foreseen that overseas recruitment would soon dry up, and that in total war, new departments of Government and the vast expansion of others would be required. All this was expected to place a great strain on existing resources of trained civil servants. Very few of us were therefore allowed to slip the net and get into uniform.

But after the early months when no one could imagine what the war would mean for India, then still caught in the timeless cycle of hot weather, monsoon and harvest, suddenly war drew close. In May 1940 the German armies thrust through Holland and Belgium into France. By 2 June the last of the British forces had been picked up from the Dunkirk beaches, three weeks later Italy entered the war, and before the end of June France had surrendered. In the summer and autumn the Battle of Britain was fought out in the air. By September Italian forces under Marshal Graziani had advanced along the North African coast into Egypt, poised for a push to close the Suez route east. India was suddenly very directly involved as a source of manpower, of military supplies, and of war finance.

At this time one or two ICS officers with flying experience were released, when the shortage of fighter pilots was most acute. Thereafter although for everyone anxiety mounted, and the urge to action intensified, no others were allowed to go. Bowman tried resignation from the ICS, which was refused, and even travelled to Pondicherry, where the French had declared for De Gaulle, in hope of joining the Foreign Legion. His dreams of Beau Geste, of kepi, blue coat and desert sands ended prosaically, however, in a posting as District Magistrate to Bareilly.

There was soon plenty to do in the districts. By the end of 1940 the 200,000 men of the peacetime Indian Army had been increased to 430,000; that would be doubled again in the next twelve months, and again or nearly so by the end of 1942, the total growing to about 2,250,000 men by the close of the war in Asia in 1945. Initially the work of recruitment of this new army was largely confined to the northern India of the traditional 'martial classes', to districts such as Rawalpindi and Jullundur, to which Williams was successively posted in 1939 and 1940: 'In the Rawalpindi countryside the tradition of military service was strong; military pensions from the First World War amounted to about six times the land revenue; and this new war brought men flocking to enlist.' In other areas encouraging the flow of men would be a major preoccupation:

Certainly the promotion of the war effort imposed extra work on the administration, and in Jullundur this took the main form of encouraging the flow of recruitment. The Sikhs were undoubtedly a martial race, but the war had not brought the same large flow of volunteers as had been seen amongst the Muslims of the north-western Punjab, and the civil officers of the district had to second the efforts of the Army's recruiting staff. I tried to attend as many recruiting meetings as possible, rewarding the headmen of villages where response was good, and enquiring closely into the circumstances of those where it was not. The interest later taken in their own domain by the Sikh Princes had a welcome effect, but eventually one heard that a sinister argument was being used to encourage Sikh recruitment, namely that as the end of the war might see the withdrawal of British rule it was prudent for Sikhs to acquire the military training which would be so valuable in the inevitable communal civil war.

In Lucknow, as City Magistrate, Lloyd-Jones's involvement in recruiting was even more direct:

I was civilian recruiting officer for the armed services. I paid early morning visits to the recruiting office where I would find a dozen or so youths lined up. After weighing and measuring them to see that they reached the physical standards laid down, I would pass them on to the Army. One of the Congress leaders during the War, Mrs Pandit, I think it was, was being questioned by an American newspaper reporter who asked how it was possible to recruit a volunteer army of over two million men, if India was so hostile to British rule as Congress alleged. He received the glib reply, 'Rice soldiers'. Of course, there was a mercenary element; our paid recruiters received 5 rupees for each recruit brought in and part of this sum no doubt went to the recruit. Also it would be idle to pretend that the young men came forward through an ardent love of the British Raj. The inducement to enlist was that which is common everywhere; to see the world and broaden horizons. Few men from our area actually went into combatant units, they were required for the ancillary and technical services. Hence there was an opportunity to learn a trade and acquire a skill which would be useful in peace time. Such recruitment meant no discredit on anyone's part.

But, as Belcher records, the task of the district officer did not end when the new recruit had been inducted:

With the German attack on Russia in June 1941 and their subsequent giant strides to the East, and even more with Japan's entry into the war in December, the possibility that hostilities would directly affect India began to seem decidedly real; in consequence new tasks began to fall more heavily on the Provincial and District administrations. Already the involvement in the Middle East campaigns of the Indian Army had affected the Rawalpindi District from which recruitment had always been high; it became necessary in order to maintain the morale of the servicemen overseas to take special steps to look after the problems of their families at home. This led to a decision that any Commanding Officer should correspond directly with the Deputy Commissioners of the Districts from which his men came about any complaint about their home affairs which he thought merited attention. The result in Rawalpindi was a very substantial flow of correspondence of this kind – and on the allied question of the genuineness of requests for compassionate leave – and I was asked to take on the task of dealing with these 'military petitions' as an addition to my other duties.

But there was much of human interest in these petitions. The knowledge that a serviceman could through his CO have a direct line to the senior civil officers in his home District was not only some comfort, and in genuine home difficulties some compensation for his own absence from the scene. Human nature being what it is the privilege was also welcomed both by the serviceman and his family as an additional opportunity to ventilate their side of a dispute even if it had already been exhaustively considered and decided in the normal course. Sometimes indeed it seemed clear that the only object was to cause enquiries that would create trouble for an opposing faction in the village by alleging some fictitious wrongdoing on their part. So a good deal of caution had to be observed in dealing with the petitions, and we were not always – in fact rather rarely – able to return the answer the CO and his soldier really looked for. Nevertheless many genuine grievances were put right and we judged our daily labour to be well worth while.

As the Japanese pushed towards the eastern borders of India and their aircraft carriers entered the Bay of Bengal new areas were threatened and new sources of recruitment had to be tapped for India's entirely volunteer army. Platt as private secretary to the Governor of Madras saw military fads and prejudices about martial and non-martial classes overcome as the Indian Army expanded:

At the outbreak of war it had been drawn almost entirely from North India (very largely from the Punjab) and, except for the Madras Sappers and Miners, the South

Indian Regiments which won fame under Clive and Wellesley (later Duke of Wellington) had been disbanded. Sir Arthur Hope persuaded the Government of India to revive the Madras Regiment. The response was very good and during the war the Madras Presidency provided 250,000 recruits towards the 2 million total. The Punjab, with a more active military tradition, provided 750,000 recruits. Much of the inspiration for recruitment in the Madras Presidency came from the Governor, Sir Arthur Hope. He made regular tours of the Presidency and visited most of the 26 districts at least once a year. He made excellent speeches reviewing the progress of the war which had a good effect both on recruiting and on general morale. He also instituted a Governor's War Fund to provide amenities for troops, British and Indian, stationed or on leave in the Presidency.

Moreover the need was not just for fighting men. The war on the eastern front involved difficult hill country on the Assam and Bengal borders with Burma (lost to the Japanese by May 1942), with very tenuous road and rail links, no aerodromes or supply bases. Pioneers and labour battalions were required – which was where Macdonald, newly appointed Provincial Recruitment Officer in Orissa, came into the picture. Orissa had never been classified as a 'Martial Province' but as Macdonald records:

Traditionally, the people of Orissa had in times past worked in Burma as unskilled labourers, and certain of the aboriginal areas were important as recruiting grounds, as there was considerable rural unemployment in the villages.

The first task, therefore, of the Provincial Recruitment Officer was to obtain men to form two battalions of an Orissa Pioneer Corps, these to work on the Burma frontier in connection with the construction of roads and airfields. The first of the units was formed under the command of a Salvation Army Officer known in that Army as Captain Woods, who had run a mission in Angul for many years, and had a considerable local knowledge of the people. I had, however, to go round different parts of the Province with assistants, endeavouring to enrol men, testing them and arranging for their transport to Angul to the training camp which had been set up there.

By about August 1943 the Pioneer Battalions were deemed to be sufficiently trained to be employed usefully on the north-east frontiers of India, and arrangements were made to despatch them. The departure of the First Battalion was not impressive as most of the men had been issued with boots only a short time before their departure, and had never been accustomed to wearing them. They therefore hung them round their necks and marched barefoot to the station at Angul, which was several miles from the barracks. The result was a rather chaotic departure with the men strung out all along the road – but in fairness it must be reported that when we next heard of the Pioneer Battalion they were doing good work constructing airfields on the Burma front.

Apart from recruiting the Pioneer Battalions, Officers had to be selected and duly gazetted. The young men selected [about twelve per year] were sent off to an Officers Training School at Bangalore in the south of India.

Even in Bengal, another province labelled non-martial, Bell at Barisal found recruiting to the Pioneer Corps and to the Bengal Auxiliary Pioneer Force, the civilian body concerned with construction work in Assam, going well. There was also a strong local force of the Bengal Home Guard whose purpose was to help collect intelligence and enforce the black-out.

The construction of roads, aerodromes, or supply bases involved the district officer in another task, the acquisition of land and other property. As the war flared now on one front, then on another, so did requisitioning work: for Williams in the Punjab, for Paterson at the arsenal base of Jabalpur in the CP, for Maitra in Assam and for Gupta in Calcutta. Williams, in the north-west, led off:

The war situation in early 1942 was critical and there was apprehension of a German break-through in the Caucasus and possible advance through Persia and Afghanistan into India. Defence installations were accordingly being hurriedly improvised along the line of the Indus (the western border of the Attock district), and the local programme involved for me the acquisition of land for two brigade camps and six airfields. This was rather a harrowing task because while the military authorities naturally tried to select their sites so as to avoid taking good agricultural land they had necessarily to find terrain as flat as possible in an area much cut up by small ravines and water courses, and the holdings of the peasant farmers were small. Some had to be expropriated almost entirely, and one sought to make the compensation as generous as possible within the limits allowed.

At Jabalpur, already a military base, land acquisition was pushed through early in 1942 for a complete arsenal, an 'enormous depot built into the hillsides with the magazines projecting about half their length', followed by an expansion of the gun-carriage factory, and still later in 1942 the creation of a shell-filling factory. With these new installations came problems of expanding water supplies, barracks and civilian housing – all work for the district officer and his staff.

Then, as the Japanese pushed a retreating British and Indian Army out of Burma and prepared to advance through Imphal and Kohima towards the Indian plains, it was Maitra's turn, in Assam:

Assam which was thousands of miles from the theatrical frontier along the Khyber and Bolan passes, suddenly became an actual frontier facing the Imperial Japanese Army across its rain-soaked hills covered with spiked bamboos. We civilians saw from a distance General Alexander march out of Burma in defeat. Our jobs were humble – we had to keep up civilian morale. With stories of bombing of Calcutta and Madras going round, the scavengers of Sylhet municipality threatened a general walk out. ARP shelters were made for them and a liberal ration card issued to each family. Our second task was to make available such supplies as were asked for by the military, mainly entirely unsophisticated items like bamboos for hutments and shingles for road making.

By early 1944, though the savage battle at Kohima and Imphal which marked the collapse of the Japanese invasion attempt had still to be fought, the first British counter moves in Burma were under way – largely based upon the new mobility and new ability to supply forward troops which air transport provided. For the district officer on the ground, as Maitra makes clear, it was a period of tension and great effort:

So many things happened at this time and all together that the impression in my mind is like a film that was run too fast and the pictures overlapped. One of the things I had to do for the military was acquire land, and that in a hurry, for air strips. I explained to the villagers that the war left me little choice, but I would see to it that they were generously and promptly paid compensation for their land. I camped and continuously for several days, and half nights by the light of Petromax lamps, paid Rs. 6 lakhs in cash. It was at Hailakandi that I saw the incredible sight of Dakotas towing gliders with nylon ropes for the second Chindit strike into Burma.

From then on, Kohima–Imphal having been safely held in the early summer of 1944, the move back into Burma could begin, the air and land links 'over the mountain Hump' to China could be strengthened and preparations made for an eventual landing in Malaya. It was then Gupta's turn:

War work had now intensified. American troops were pouring in. We had to commandeer extensive grounds, multi-storey buildings, palaces, jute presses, godowns, shops, hotels for them. I was appointed Land Acquisition-Requisition Collector of Calcutta and the 24-Parganas covering all the area from Barrackpore, through the centre of Calcutta and Alipore down to Diamond Harbour. This was a big job of a quasi-judicial nature involving plenty of touring, survey, and assessment after hearing the owners' claims. First we took over the desired premises, prepared inventories of fixtures and fittings, entertained claims of loss of business for professional owners and fixed rent or compensation. Very inflated claims were put in and our main task was to slash them – unpopular work. It was heavy but enjoyable independent work for around three years till the end of 1945.

Three other wartime tasks which often fell to district officers, two of them extensions of familiar peacetime practices and the other absolutely novel, were the raising of War Funds, the dissemination of news or propaganda, and the building up of ARP organizations. Of the first of these Williams in the Punjab writes:

A war fund had been started in each district, and the usual objective was to raise the equivalent of the cost of one or more fighter planes, to be named after the district. In a country of small-holders the degree of stimulus to be applied should clearly be limited, and in Jullundur we depended to a great extent on the receipts of wrestling matches, where some remarkable figures and feats were to be seen.

What was caution in Williams could be positive distaste in others for what easily became an exercise in manipulation and pressure. 'The temptation for Revenue Officers to do something for a rich man, not strictly legal, in return for a big subscription to the fund was great', comments Masterman in Madras, 'and I think corruption of this kind was widespread.' Bowman's reactions were shared in various degree by many others:

The collection of money for the War Fund was a task which I heartily disliked. It was difficult to imagine how Indians could be enthusiastic about contributing to a cause which had very little reality for them. There was a danger that contribution to the War Fund might be regarded by the contributor as entitling him to special consideration; and over-zealous petty officials had to be watched carefully to prevent them from extorting the money by threats. We collected what we could at meetings; but I was disgusted to find that most of the money was being spent on what I regarded as trivialities – amenities for British troops on garrison duty in various centres, band instruments for a battalion in Lucknow and such irrelevancies. At the next war meeting I said that, although we would not refuse money contributions, what we really wanted was the moral support and the prayers of the people to sustain our armed forces in the fight against the Nazi threat to civilisation. One old zemindar stood up and said, 'Let's put up a prayer now'. He intoned the sacred word 'Om' and we all took it up with enthusiasm. There followed a long flow of Hindi intermixed with Sanscrit phrases, and the words 'Hitler' and 'Mussolini' appearing from time to time, pronounced with great venom. The idea caught on. At a High School which I visited, the Head Master announced that his boys were going to hold a 'hawan' ceremony. This was a marathon prayer session, held round a sacred fire for three days and nights without a break, with relays of boys praying for the success of the Allied cause. Just after the completion of the ceremony, news came through that the Allied troops in North Africa had captured Tobruk. The power of prayer was held to be amply demonstrated.

A victory, whether won by arms or prayer, was very welcome. There had been a long run of reverses – Dunkirk, the fall of Singapore, the loss of Burma – and Indian sympathy had been blunted by the refusal of Congress demands for early political advance. The maintenance of morale, the countering of Axis propaganda and of Congress claims, and the task of preparing the country against possible Japanese invasion required a government information and propaganda effort quite new in scale. Orr, in Bihar, like other district officers felt let down by the lack of adequate briefing:

In 1941 when I was in Bhagalpur the Congress Party and the Muslim League were both vociferously staking their claims and exploiting Britain's disadvantage of being at war with Germany and apparently losing it. Knowing nothing of the British Government's attitude I found it difficult at times to know what attitude I should adopt myself towards the nationalist arguments, whether these were quietly and rationally presented by intelligent and cultured patriots, or clamorously by rhythmically chanting crowds responding to a cheer-leader. Towards the end of 1941 a meeting was called by Edwin Prideaux, the District Collector, to stimulate the war effort. The audience to which he spoke had never seen England nor Germany and had no real awareness of why they were fighting each other. They had no concept of the sophistication of modern weapons of destruction nor of the economic and social implications of the modern need for 'total war'. Nor was it easy to counter the Congress Party's assertion that the war had nothing to do with India, and that any India contribution would help only Britain but not India. Needless to say the persons invited to the meeting were thought to be predisposed towards the British cause, and most if not all of them owed their positions of influence and personal wealth to the rule of law imposed and secured by the British. They could at least understand the subtle innuendos of Edwin Prideaux's arguments that in the end they would be more likely to maintain their present privileges if Britain won the war than if she lost it. The immediate need was money, and that they could afford. The next need was recruitment to the forces, and that they could promote without disturbing their own lives. A number of the persons present spoke in support of Britain's cause, with some flattery here, and some reassurance of loyalty there. But the bombshell which really woke up the meeting and shook even Edwin's imperturbability was a speech by a 30-year-old Indian Christian who advocated a massive recruitment not so much to win the war as to obtain the necessary training for the inevitable war of the future between the whites and the non-whites.

It required ready wit and good humour in Prideaux to turn the interruption to his advantage. But there had to be a great deal of inspired improvisation by district officials before a central publicity organization was created and put to work. In Madras Carleston made a special effort to keep schools well informed about the progress of the war, M. S. H. Thompson, the Inspector of European Schools, personally producing a splendid weekly or bi-weekly four-page bulletin for distribution. Hayley similarly initiated a publicity scheme of his own:

We had no system of propaganda in Assam, and I took it upon myself to organize a province-wide news service, combined with propaganda, which I felt was very essential under the circumstances. The Congress Party was in revolt all over India and all the leaders in Assam had to be confined to prison. General Stilwell's army was in North Burma and its supply route consisted of a single railway line up the Bhramaputra Valley and the single trunk road. Both these were vulnerable to Japanese attack, and the fear was that, should the Japanese carry out any bombing raids on Assam, there would be a panic evacuation of the population down this main road.

Army Command in Eastern India, aware of this danger, persuaded the Assam Government to allow Hayley to requisition cars and equip them with loud-speakers and to recruit publicity officers. To them a loose-leaf handbook of publicity points in 'Basic English' was issued, regularly updated. These points, translated into the local languages, were then used, interlarded with news picked up from the radio, in their daily public broadcasts. Only later were regular talking points provided by the Central Government, as Raza then in Sind describes:

In view of the Congress hostility towards the War effort, Lord Linlithgow initiated a movement called the National War Front. The objective of the movement was to explain the war aims to the man in the street and to describe the plight of those free nations in Europe which had been crushed by Hitler. The Chief Minister of the province was nominated as the Provincial Leader with a Committee of prominent citizens of the province to assist him. I was appointed Provincial Organiser of the War Front in addition to my own duties. This assignment necessitated extensive touring and a lot of talking. Sir Percival Griffiths I.C.S. (Retired), a member of the Central Assembly, was the Central Organiser of the National War Front and used to provide us with talking points.

It was something of an uphill struggle, however, for, as Maitra relates, in most Assamese patriotic loyalty did not usually go much beyond 'Better the Devil you know, than the one you don't'. Congress workers were behind bars, the Muslim Leaguers were lukewarm, and as for the members of the National War Front, they, he tartly observes, 'belonged to the tribe known in French Algeria as the *Beni Oui Oui*. They supported Government because of possible gain.' But perhaps the flavour of War Front work by the district officer is best captured by entries in the diary which Dunlop kept as Subcollector at Bezwada in Madras, sometimes discouraged, sometimes stirred:

In the "cold weather" I used to ride to villages and my tents used to be erected in gardens and everything made ready by the time I arrived, having made local inspections en route. Thus I rode on over the river to Erellapad, a large and dirty village, full of sedition – nearly all Congress or Communist. The ryots came in the afternoon and presented a long list of absurd grievances ... a lot of little boys ran about mocking the peons and made a nuisance of themselves, sitting like crows safely out of reach. One boy even shouted the Congress War slogan. ... In the evening I held a meeting and addressed a large crowd most of whom favoured Congress. I urged them to give accurate Census information to the enumerators, told them that their children were the worst mannered I had met ... and then talked about the war ... pointed out how defenceless India would be without Britain ... I was asked and answered a few questions by Congress men e.g. about sending Satyagrahis to jail. The meeting was orderly. I told them that even if they were not allowed by Gandhi to contribute to this War, Gandhi had declared that he had no objections to contributions to the Red Cross. When the meeting dissolved, a small group of leaders at the back shouted "Gandhi-Ki-Jai" then "Down with British Imperialism", a slogan in which the little boys joined but it met with no response among the larger part of the crowd. So home to my camp in the moonlight. This village has contributed nothing to the war effort but satyagrahis and anti-war propaganda in plenty.'

This anti-Government attitude was not usually expressed and I found ryots and village officers, and Zemindars most hospitable and courteous. Thus in Kindapalli 'held a Propaganda meeting this evening. It was very well attended, villagers coming in from as much as 12 miles away. Some very stirring speeches were delivered by members of my Committee who had come from Bezwada – and I felt very stirred and proud myself!'

The press in India in practice remained surprisingly free throughout the war. Midgley notes, for example, that Sir Francis Mudie, Governor of the UP, deliberately advised that the Congress paper at Lucknow, the *National Herald*, should be allowed to go on publishing its critical and sometimes abusive articles throughout the war, with only an occasional clamp-down. But by 1941 a formal structure of press supervision had been established, as Le Bailly, member of the Delhi Press Committee, records:

My colleagues were the editors of the principal papers published in English in Delhi. There was also a representative of the extensive vernacular press but I cannot remember his ever contributing anything of value to our discussion – perhaps he didn't attend very often. The position was that though there was legal provision for prosecution of matter calculated to injure the war effort, it was the policy of the Government not to unless advised to do so by the committee. Actually as the Committee, except for myself, was entirely composed of pressmen the Committee never did recommend prosecution and at most, sometimes in most flagrant cases, the editor was warned and apologised to the Committee. On the whole considering that nearly all the press was of an anti-government persuasion (except the *Statesman*, which was anxious to emphasise its independence of Government and not to offend its fellow journals) the system at least avoided active hostility between Government and the press and generally kept the press from publishing gross misrepresentations of fact.

One case illustrates what might be reported if vigilance was not taken. I happened to be in a street in Delhi when I heard a newsboy announcing (in Urdu) that an allied division had been cut to pieces and scattered (this was during the invasion of Sicily). I immediately took possession of the copies on sale, and found that this startling report was allegedly part of an official communiqué. A reference to the original communiqué showed that it had said that part of a division had been temporarily 'cut off' but had subsequently rejoined the rest of the force. This last bit had, doubtless deliberately, been omitted from the Urdu version, which was being reported fortunately by a newsboy with a very limited circulation.

The overheads of running a printing press in Delhi was apparently small and I was told that it was not uncommon for a young man of literary tastes, unable or unwilling to secure more lucrative employment, to set up as editor of an Urdu journal of which I think, I am right in saying, some 50 were appearing at irregular intervals.

Similar press committees were established in every province consisting of an elected group of newspaper editors and a government official. For him, as Raza at Karachi discovered, the work literally caused many sleepless nights:

We used to meet very frequently and sometimes daily as the news from the War front demanded. There was every effort to appreciate each other's point of view and, on the whole, we got on very well. Since the editors work on their desks at night, I could never sleep undisturbed as they rang me up whenever they were in doubt about the publication of a particular news item.

With ARP the district officer entered upon a task often remote from his own experience and totally so from that of the people of his district. First moves were made in response to Britain's own experience of air warfare, at a time when India's towns and countryside seemed beyond the range of enemy attack, and the digging of slit trenches, amateur camouflage and training in the use of stirrup pumps had an unreal if not comical quality. Midgley at Lucknow catches the flavour – 'I wrote handbooks on air-raid shelters intended to adapt British practice to Indian conditions and, for a short time, had my own radio programme. I was supposed to answer questions sent in by the general public about what to do in air raids. My fan mail was slender, however, and I was soon driven to invent it.'

Belcher in the Punjab records another problem – the language the new ARP instructors should use in their classes:

Urdu speakers were specially highly regarded if they used a high-flown Persianised Urdu even if their hearers could only recognise, not understand it. They felt that using Punjabi in their lectures was beneath their dignity. In consequence I discovered that for explaining such practical matters as the operation of the stirrup pump they were using Urdu to people most of whom appreciated it as a compliment but were hazy about its precise meaning.

In Orr's experience 'the real struggle was not building an effective organization, but winning over the general public first to an awareness of the potential dangers of an air-raid and then to the need to volunteer their services as ARP wardens and fire-watchers'. Masterman, charged with preparing the port of Vizagapatam against possible Japanese attack, would have agreed. Nevertheless, an effective air-raid precaution system was created in Vizagapatam, with the active help of the Municipal Chairman, Pattibhirama Reddy.

He cast aside all his Congress prejudices and was the greatest help in lending us Municipal buildings and in getting the people to co-operate in going to their proper shelters on an alarm, and when the raid *did* come in April 1942, he was to be seen walking about all over the town getting people into their shelters.

The Japanese air-raids had brought war to the shore of India, and for a while invasion was expected. The Madras Government actually moved inland with its more important records, since the city was not really defensible, and Masterman was required to work out a similar evacuation programme for the Europeans at Vizagapatam. In the event there was no invasion, but only a series of carrier-based raids on ports and shipping – Calcutta, Vizagapatam, Ceylon – by the Japanese fleet. Then Japanese attention was drawn eastwards as the great battles of Midway and the Coral Sea developed in the south-west Pacific. But what problems sustained bombing or invasion would have posed for the district officer is well illustrated by Masterman's experience at Vizagapatam, on 6 April 1942:

The first intimation I had was about 8 in the morning, when I saw about 6 planes flying rather low over my bungalow in Waltair. This was rather unusual, but I did not immediately realize that these were enemy planes. Soon afterwards I heard two explosions in the port and I hurried down to the A.R.P. control room in Vizagapatam town. We tried to get into communication with the port by telephone, but failed. (The telephone exchange had been hit by one of the first bombs dropped.) I then went down to the port with the D.S.P. in his car. Six or seven planes were circling round the harbour apparently picking out targets at leisure. There was nothing to hit back with. Some of the ships lying in harbour had some rather antiquated guns, these they fired but the planes were out of range. The planes dropped a few bombs on the harbour and then went off, presumably for lunch on the aircraft carrier, which was visible to the naked eye from the shore.

In the afternoon they came back in greater force. They hit the electricity power house and we were without light that night. They also unluckily made a direct hit on our best shelter and there were 15 casualties. Some ships were hit and damaged – luckily they missed a ship which was carrying high explosives. They did not attempt to bomb the town.

For the most part people went to their allotted shelters quietly. The panic came that night after the raid was over. After nightfall something like two-thirds of the population fled inland in cars, bullock carts, cycles or any other vehicle they could get hold of or by walking. Everyone expected that the planes would come back, either that night or the following day, and everyone was convinced that the town would be the next target and that the bombing of the port was merely a preliminary to a full scale invasion from the sea. They had also observed that the armed forces were quite powerless to resist.

It was not only the poorer classes who fled in panic. Nearly all the vakils [lawyers] and professional men left and most of the shopkeepers, so that on the morning after the raid the bazaars were virtually closed. Generally speaking Government officials and their clerical staffs remained at their posts, but sent their wives and children away.

The most immediate problem was that of food supplies. All the rice merchants had departed, leaving their godowns stored with rice locked up. We had to take matters into our own hands and under my orders the police broke the locks, commandeered the rice and distributed it. But our difficulties were not over. A large majority of the clerks in my office and in other Government offices were Brahmins, who would not eat rice unless cooked by a Brahmin. Normally of course their food is cooked by their wives, who would necessarily be Brahmins in accordance with caste marriage laws. Now, however, all the wives had gone away. With some difficulty the Police found a Brahmin cook on the point of leaving. They arrested him and he cooked for about 100 clerks for 3 or 4 days under police guard to prevent him running away. (This incident is, I think, an illuminating commentary on the sort of way the caste rules affected administration in Madras.)

A branch of Messrs Spencer & Co of Madras normally catered for the needs of the European Community living in Waltair. On the night of the raid, the Manager and the whole of his staff left, leaving the shop unlocked. I put a young I.C.S. British Officer in charge of the shop and with the aid of some Government clerks from my office he sold goods to customers at prices shown in a catalogue which he found in the office. Later we had some difficulty in squaring the accounts with Spencer's Head Office in Madras. They complained that we had used the wrong catalogue, contending that the one we had used was for income tax purposes! Wisely however they did not press the matter.

But our biggest problem was to unload the ships lying in the harbour. Our trouble was that nearly all the coolies working in the Port had run away and could not be induced to return, though we offered very high wages. We did manage to get some back by organising a free midday meal, but not many. A contingent of Gurkhas helped for a time and could be seen happily tossing dangerous shells from hand to hand, although warned that they must be handled with care.

Soon after the raid we were visited by a bomb expert but no-one came near me from the Government of Madras, though as ordered I was sending them a daily report and we were desperately hard up for labour. This, it seemed to me, was carrying the Madras policy of leaving the District Officer alone to run his district without interference from Government to extremes.

Looking back two things strike me: (1) when really subjected to an attack no Congress man was prepared to follow Gandhi's advice and (2) the remarkable loyalty of Government servants, in particular the Police, to the British Government. A great many agreed with Gandhi's views on independence at once, if not with his methods, but I know of no resignations.

Only a handful of district officers were ever in the front line in this way in India, though they were in the thick of it in Burma. But the development of India as a war base involved the movement of large military forces to eastern India – American heavy bombers, SEAC (South-East Asia Command) under Lord Mountbatten with its large command structure, American port and railway battalions to double the capacity of the port at Calcutta and the rail link with Assam, and Indian Army units from the northern provinces. One task for the district officer was that of liaison with these forces, sometimes the informal liaison of open house – 'at odd hours jeeploads of army, sometimes airforce officers would drive up to the DC's bungalow in urgent need of bath, food and drink. My wife was learning her trade' – as Maitra puts it, sometimes formal as when Carleston was made Chief Civil Representative of the Madras Government with the 19th Indian Division, with a staff of twenty civilian liaison officials under him. 'Our duties, as civil representatives', he records, 'were to help with food supplies, assess compensation for any damage to crops or property on exercises, and generally to promote good relations between the military (mostly from other parts of India and speaking different languages) and the local population.' Nor were the military only from other parts of India. When West African troops were flown into Assam, Maitra had to calm agitated villagers asking who were these men 'blacker than crows'. And at Asansol, with its vital coalmines, iron, steel and aluminium works, Woodford had first to soothe the occasional local protest at the 'sexual enthusiasm' of the lads at the new British bases, and then to reconcile American health precautions with the agricultural needs of the peasants:

The US Air force was mightily concerned to keep its men free of malaria. The protection of zones round their bases involved nicking the embankment of irrigation tanks to prevent a great variation of water level. This produced complaints because a maximum head of water was normally required for the watering of the fields. The Air Force Malaria Control Unit (O/C Captain Sherman) was always ready to compromise. The most easterly *thana* had, I believe, a 90% spleen rate. The rate was substantially cut and health visibly improved. These five air bases, little townships, each employing over a thousand civilian workers, almost self-contained and from our point of view unobtrusive, carried the air war into Burmah. In the evening we would hear the sounding of conch shells as their cow-watchers signalled the all clear for take-off. Sometimes we would learn indirectly of disasters at landing or take-off. We would do what we could to back them with our help if the opportunity arose as it did for instance in the matter of steam rollers. At their request we turned over most of our civilian fleet to them for airfield maintenance; our roads had to go without.

There was one other point at which the district officer, in Bengal, was thrown into close contact with the Army – in jointly organizing relief in the harrowing later stages of the Bengal famine of 1943. The famine was a natural calamity, compounded of the disasters caused by the cyclones in 1942 in coastal Orissa and Bengal and shortages in the following year's harvest. But it was made much more desperate and more difficult to relieve by the war – and to an extent by the disruptions caused by the Quit India violence of autumn 1942. The loss of Burma and the occupation of the rice port of Akyab by the Japanese meant that supplies from India's granary in Burma were no longer available. There was dislocation and clogging of road and rail systems caused by troop movements to the Assam and Arakan fronts and much shipping had been diverted to the Mediterranean front. Moreover as Woodford, then at Diamond Harbour at the mouth of the Hoogly, recalls, in spring 1942 the Government had decided on a scorched earth policy: 'Orders came through to collect and immobilise all bicycles. A defence of India Act order was issued: thousands of bicycles, once the pride and joy of their owners were brought in, deprived of their chains and stored, many of them under my house. Then it was the turn of the country boats.' In Bakarganj Bell saw the same order at work:

Cycles were not numerous in this riverain district, but boats there were by thousands, and they were the life-blood of the community. The population and the local administrative and police staff co-operated, and after a short while arrangements were made for the stopping of boat movements South of a defined line, subject only to special exemptions for boats which had received passes for urgent reasons. Boat-owners were required to remove their boats from the 'prohibited area'. A boat-receiving station was set up at Palang, in the Faridpur district, just North of the Bakarganj boundary, and the boat-owners were paid immediate cash compensation on leaving them there. Thousands of boats were received at Palang at the cost of many lakhs of rupees – though perhaps not such vast sums as were being spent elsewhere. It was later asserted by critics of the Government that the 'denial' of boats made a significant contribution to the famine which developed in the following year, for the South of Bakarganj was a rice-exporting area, and this interference with transport must have been some check on trade. My own tour notes referred to complaints that lack of boats hindered the movement of cattle and labourers out to the South, and there was certainly some lack of kerosene and salt in markets in the South.

With a calamitous rise in prices, fuelled by the now dramatic war-induced inflation, all the contributing factors came together to produce famine and mortality in Bengal on a scale which it had been assumed would never be experienced again. 'Those were the days', writes Rahmatullah, then at Howrah, 'when the streets of Calcutta and the railway platforms were all littered with dead bodies, and women reduced to mere skeletons, almost bare bodied, with dead children around and babies on their breasts and the beggar's bowl beside were a common sight in and around Calcutta, including Howrah.' Rahmatullah was soon at work in his own district commandeering hoarded stocks and opening relief kitchens. But the collapse of the Fazlul Huq Ministry in March 1943 and the establishment of Governor's rule under Sir John Herbert, then a sick and dying man, served to prevent a real grip being taken on the problem until October 1943 when Lord Wavell arrived as Viceroy and almost at once visited the famine area, as Bell relates:

Lord Wavell said little but listened much, and very soon after his visit military units were drafted into Bengal to help with the movement of supplies, and also to open emergency hospitals for the very ill. The unit which came to the Midnapore district was a motorised battalion, 17/7th Rajputs. For the next five months they did much good work moving foodstuffs and materials for house-building, but without decrying their good work it would be misleading to say that the army stopped the Bengal famine. They came in November, when the harvest was only a month ahead, and when it was certain that things would get better. It was, however, reassuring to have good supplies established at depots throughout the affected area, as insurance against shortage and panic in the coming year and, indeed, a great deal of relief had to be given until well into 1944. By that time, too, the Government of Bengal had built up a large Civil Supplies organisation, which could procure rice effectively. The 17/7th left quietly and at short notice, early in April, when as later revealed, the Japanese advance into India was threatening Kohima and the Dima-railhead. Relations with our 'famine relief' battalion were happy, and the same can be said of experience with the forces generally.

One factor contributing to the famine condition had been inflation. The growth of India's armed forces – ten-fold by the end of the war – was more than matched by growth in the defence budget. Income tax and a new corporation tax and large loans raised in India paid for part of this, but the rest was met by expanding the money supply. At the same time large quantities of consumer goods were siphoned off to meet military needs, as India became a supply base first for the Near Eastern and then for the South-East Asian war zones. Rapid inflation necessarily followed. By the time of the Bengal famine prices had risen some 250 per cent, and were to go on rising. The demand for food was growing, some sources of supply had been lost, distribution was difficult and for some town dwellers and poorer groups in the countryside foodgrains were being priced beyond their reach. Bengal, in the front line, was the province worst affected. But all the food deficit provinces and then the centre too were gradually driven into state procurement of foodgrains and then into some form of rationing. Belcher demonstrates very clearly the reluctant, step by step way in which provinces shouldered the burden – or rather, asked their district officers to do so:

When the loss of Burma and its rice in 1942 and the increased demands of the Armed Forces for foodgrains forced the Governments in India to intervene in the foodgrains market in order to keep supplies available at a reasonable price to the ordinary Indian consumer, the Punjab Government's first hope was that their own intervention could be kept to a minimum. Deputy Commissioners were simply empowered to fix maximum prices for their Districts when they thought that the situation demanded it. They soon did so, but the consequences were chaotic, since producers or those who held stocks began to hoard and so create shortages and higher prices and enforcement of price maxima proved very difficult. Moreover the situation was complicated by Deputy Commissioners in adjacent Districts fixing different prices so that stocks rapidly disappeared from one to appear in the other. This was soon cured by fixing prices centrally from Lahore, but the system of minimum interference by Government led to all kinds of anomalies and malpractices; consequently more and more Government action had to be taken, until in the end Government procurement and full scale rationing of foodgrains in the towns became unavoidable.

The ad hoc nature of the early stages of grain procurement is well brought out by Paterson's description of his very personal efforts as DC, Jabalpur in the Central Provinces in 1942:

What we tried to do in the first instance was the use of compulsory purchase orders and we used all our local knowledge to find out where stores were being held by moneylenders or by landlords in the hope of rising prices and somehow or other we managed to scrape by. We opened fair-price shops where a limited supply could be bought by anybody and I remember at that time somehow acting with what, looking back, seemed an incredible degree of independence. I hunted all over the place for food supplies, I wrote to Johnny Hancox in Cawnpore, an old Cambridge colleague of mine as I had heard there were better supplies up in the U.P. I heard that Bhopal, a little bit north of Saugor, had supplies and I remember paying a visit to the state authorities in person to see if I could make some purchases there.

Paterson's individual enterprise was naturally soon superseded by more regular procurement procedures. It is interesting to see, however, for how long reliance was placed upon the agency of the district officers rather than upon a new specialist staff. Belcher, in the Punjab, illustrates this use of the DCs:

In those early days we in Rawalpindi were in a particular difficulty since although the country districts could more or less feed themselves the supplies needed to feed the City itself had to come from sources outside which were rapidly drying up. [Lloyd-Jones explains this drying up: 'In normal times the farmers had to sell about a third of their crop to pay their rents and land revenue, and what they sold went to feed the towns. With the steady rise in grain prices caused by wartime inflation it became possible to pay with an ever smaller proportion of their crop. And since there was a shortage of consumer goods to spend money on, the farmer ate more of his own produce and for the first time in his life was reasonably well fed.'] To deal with this increasingly urgent situation the DC was empowered to requisition the necessary supplies from his opposite number in the nearest surplus District, who was to buy what was needed and despatch it by train. This meant discovering from the grain dealers what their unsatisfied needs were, telegraphing to our nearest supplying District, Sargodha, for stocks to be requisitioned and sent, and collecting the price from the dealers against permits enabling them to pick up their grain from the railway station when it arrived. Naturally this was easier said than done. Checking that the requirement stated by the dealers represented genuine non-hoarding needs could only be done in a very rough and ready fashion: the DC Sargodha and his staff did not find it easy to locate and requisition the stocks and organise the rail transport: and the distribution and sale of the grain being in the hands of the trade we had no means of control against abuse other than refusing to arrange supplies.

Problems did not end there: grain supply officers who had no intimate knowledge of the foodgrain trade often bought supplies that turned out to be defective – and those consumers who were offered 'an assortment of rotting grains, of every colour from brown to green' might tell Martin just what he could do with them. But storage was also a major problem:

Stocks which had been requisitioned were generally left where they were in the owner's godown until required. This necessitated guards to check that they were not stolen and inspectors to check the guards, but no one had told us about the rice weevil which in the space of a month can apparently devour a hundred times its own weight in rice. We soon found out when the stocks were due to be distributed. The worst grain of all to store was maize. We did not normally buy maize, as it was looked down on as something the best people did not eat, but the crop of 1945 was particularly good and as we were short of rice we took a gamble and bought several thousand tons as a safeguard against actual famine. When we attempted to distribute it several months later we found we had virtually nothing left except myriads of exceptionally well fed weevils.

Trying to prevent illicit movement of stocks was a problem, as Downing records at Madura in Madras. There the government had made every district a food unit and banned all private movement of food between districts and since Madura was a surplus and its neighbours were deficit districts 'smuggling across the border into these districts was endemic, creating at times local shortages in the Madura district'. But to secure licit movement was just about as difficult. Orr in Orissa tried to help orange growers in his district to market their fruit in Calcutta:

But we never succeeded in reaching Calcutta with any consignments. The reason was not inefficiency, it was corruption. At the mention of perishable cargo every station-master en route between Berhampur and Calcutta metaphorically licked his lips and set in motion a well tried system of blackmail. If the appropriate commission (i.e. bribe) were not paid in advance the cargo would be diverted and delayed until either the shipper paid up or the cargo perished. The system was fool-proof, and even the fact that I as S.D.O. was personally supporting the export scheme frightened nobody. Eight annas per orange remained the true market price in Calcutta because it was not possible to sell for less and still cover all the 'expenses' of transport.

Williams, at Campbellpur, met the same blackmail – though this time it was the government sugar supplies from the UP which were put under levy: 'Suppliers and railway staff were not blind to the advantages of a monopoly position; supplies and wagons there were, but their movement soon came to depend on appropriate private remuneration.' Only some rather high-handed inter-provincial police co-operation got the sugar moving.

Procurement and supply were tackled first, but the establishment of fair price shops in the towns was not by itself adequate, as Gorwala explains:

It meant queues of 500 strong standing outside the grain-shops from early hours in the morning to get their minimum quantities and people returning to buy again and again until it seemed that however great the stocks put into the shops, they would never suffice. It was clear that for any extended period distribution of this kind would not serve. Rationing had to be brought in. It soon became clear that rationing in the cities alone would not do. Provision had to be made too for seeing that the landless labourers and inadequate producers in the rural areas were not starved, which led to the setting up of rural distribution centres and rural rationing.

Though Gorwala mentions rural distribution, rationing for a long time was applied almost exclusively to the towns, often drawing on staff first put together for ARP and Civil Defence purposes. In the UP the five major cities, Cawnpore, Agra, Benares, Allahabad and Lucknow, were the first in which the experiment of rationing was tried – and Banks was one of the first Town Rationing Officers to be appointed, in September 1943, in his case in Agra. The aim was to provide grain at reasonable cost and in reasonable quantity to prevent hardship among the poor and to discourage hoarding for a profit.

Clearly, any such scheme needed to limit the amount any individual could buy. This meant the issue of ration cards, which in turn meant enumerating and listing the population. But we had to take a step even further back – we had to begin by numbering the houses. I had a Deputy Rationing Officer on the distribution side, an elegant gentleman of Persian origin, nicknamed by his friends 'An-dada' or provider of bread. He set up teams of Senior Inspectors and Inspectors, covering the whole city. I think the smallest subdivision was the rationing 'circle', and the largest, covering a quarter of the city was the Area, later to be in charge of an Area Rationing Officer, a member of the Provincial Civil Service. At the start, however, the rationing inspectors were going round their circles with pots of red paint, putting numbers on the mud or brick walls of the houses. Then they set about listing the inhabitants, and probably reached a fair estimate of the number of the population, excluding those who had their reasons for not getting themselves too well documented, and including some fictitious female dependents (invisible in purdah) of those who were far sighted enough to see the possibility of getting extra rations. The population of Agra was about 400,000.

The next step was to issue ration cards, one per family, punched like a bus ticket with the number of units for which it was valid, one for an adult and half for a child. The text was in Urdu, which was the most common language in Agra, but I remember receiving a deputation of Hindus who complained that the cards were printed in a 'foreign' language. Communal strife makes memories long; the foreigners concerned were the Mughals!

I cannot now remember the amount of the rationing unit at the start; it may have been about 8 chhataks (16 ounces) a day. My recollection of Agra is of the ration being for a long time a supplement to the open market and an encouragement to the normal channels of supply to remain open. There was pressure from the Government of India to use rationing as a means of reducing consumption for economic reasons, and I remember a UK rationing expert who was mystified by our permissive attitude. But the UK had close control of imported food, and home producers highly organised and generally loyal and involved in the war effort. To close the town markets by law involved having the confidence that the supply to the rationing scheme was – and would remain – adequate to feed the town without the existence of an open market the extent of which we did not really know.

However, foodgrain supply to the big towns was eventually restricted by law to the official supply through the rationing shops. There had to be exceptions for town dwellers who owned land outside the town and normally looked after their own needs, and no doubt these people 'looked after' a good few others to whom they were not legally allowed to sell. Rationing never became 'total' (though we used the word) in the sense of applying to the whole population. This would have meant attempting to buy up all the supplies and issuing restricted amounts to villagers as well as to townspeople. There would have been no surer way of causing the supply to dry up and famine to ensue.

The pattern outlined by Banks of rationing by household held good, with variation of detail and success in most towns. In Calcutta, however, and possibly elsewhere where there were major concentrations of factory labour, sometimes factory housed, some rations were issued through employers' shops, as Woodford sets out:

Contact with employers in regard to rationing was largely maintained through the efficient secretariat of the Bengal Chamber of Commerce [BCC]. The principle had to be firmly established that employers' shops should be operated without regard to labour relations, and rations issued to all card holders registered in the shops whether workers, ex-workers or strikers. This was accepted universally and, I think, loyally applied. I visited the shops whenever I could. I would issue circulars from time to time not hesitating to mention by name the firms that were going wrong. But in issuing these circulars for me the BCC Secretary would suppress the names leaving blanks in the sentences. In the end I think this was just as effective. It produced interesting rumours and speculation I dare say. I did not insist on names.

The employers' shops were in addition, of course, to the multitude of tiny ration shops for the non-factory population. There the main problem in a vast, swarming, mobile city was numbers:

One huge question mark hung over the whole operation: how to ensure that the number of ration cards corresponded to the population. There was no identity card system. For people to multiply themselves, invent new names and new identities or to take over the card of someone who had left or died was not difficult. Towards the end of my time I devised a scheme for reissuing all cards in a way that could perhaps limit the number of falsifications and duplications. The operation deflated the card issue by 30%.

The distortions of war did not cease with the coming of peace in 1945 and in 1946, as Belcher recalls, in the Punjab the limited Government procurement of wheat for its own purposes and for sale to deficit provinces was enlarged into a complete government monopoly of all trade in grain. Since the Punjab Government also maintained a Provincial Foodgrains Reserve very large operations were entailed, in which the expertise of the Co-operative Department was particularly valuable. There was also the beginning of a major scientific attack upon loss in storage with proper grain silos erected in the railway yards of market towns and fumigation campaigns against weevils.

Moreover though food was the earliest and the most important field in which procurement and rationing schemes were introduced, in the later years of the war other schemes had to be introduced – for cloth, sugar and petrol for example – since government demands became so heavy as to make normal marketing impossible. In the end what would at first have seemed impossible, the rationing of India's villages as well as her towns, had to be attempted. The burden fell upon the district officer – Arthur at Multan had to organize the setting up of a retail depot and the issue of ration books to all heads of families in each of the 2,285 villages of his district!

Other district officers were called to the centre to deal with the new problems. Cook for example was summoned from his dusty UP district of Budaun first to act as custodian of enemy property and later to organize sugar and cloth controls – 'fixing the price of cloth for the Government at a time when the difference of a fraction of an anna in the price per yard meant millions of rupees on the bill. Although a good friend who ran an efficient mill was able to give us his costings, we were never able to force the politically powerful Marwari and Gujarati mill-owners to accept these comparatively low prices.' Lamarque was summoned from Madras to handle mines and minerals – purchasing mica for the electrical industry, sulphur in Baluchistan to replace that lost in Sicily and helping to organize coal output and movement as the demands of war and industry intensified.

War had hastened in India, as in Britain, a major shift in the role of government in the economic life of the country. From the late 1930s the government had been increasingly concerned with economic development, in the countryside particularly. Sir James Grigg, Finance Member of the

Viceroy's Council summed up his achievement on the eve of war by stating 'I have kept two main tasks in view: the financing of the new Constitution [of 1935] and the provision of money for rural development.' By 1944 a first sketch of a national Five Year Plan of economic development had been sketched out at Bombay. In 1945 Kemp found himself transferred from Singhbhum district to be Secretary to the government in post-war planning and author of the Orissa Government's first five year plan. Kemp's experience foreshadowed the rapid growth of planning staffs, the expansion of the provincial and central secretariats so visible in the Delhi or Islamabad or Dacca landscape today. Midgley makes the point:

It was, nevertheless, necessary to concentrate talent in the Secretariats to cope with the new demands of the war. The new breed of Directors and Controllers dealt not only with food, but with steel, cement, petrol etc. and with the development of war industries. Inevitably the priority shifted from the districts to the capitals. District administration suffered but the foundations of postwar industrial development were laid and the beginnings of a fund to finance it accumulated in the form of suspended sterling payments for wartime supplies and services due from HMG to the Government of India.

After VJ day, we began to plan for these developments.

The question was whether at district level the accretion of wartime and development duties would make the old pattern of administration impossible to sustain. Could the district officer carry the old burden of revenue, court, and law and order work and direct or co-ordinate the new control and development staff invading his district? Saumarez Smith at Malda in Bengal set out the problem in a 'Note on the present status and duties of a District Officer' written in mid 1944, in which he reviewed in turn the relations of the district officer with the burgeoning new departments and the adequacy of his instruments:

For the Cotton Cloth and Yarn Control Order, I have been given precisely one untrained Textile Sub-Inspector on Rs. 88/– a month, who is supposed to check the nefarious activities of 1,800 licensees scattered throughout the district. The Hoarding and Profiteering Ordinance has been left entirely to the ordinary district police, who are already overworked with controlling normal crime (when I say 'normal' I refer to the quality, not the quantity of crime). Nearly every Gazette brings some new Order. All I can hope to do is to catch some individual offender, if possible a well-known man, prosecute him, and hope to scare others. The basic evils are corruption among subordinate staff and no public opinion against the profiteer and black-marketeer.

The control of foodgrains stands on a different footing, for since the Famine a substantial staff has been sanctioned. The relations between this staff and the district officer are of particular importance. The Province has been divided into seven regions, each in charge of a Deputy Director of Civil Supplies, an I.C.S. officer of Collector's standing. Under him there is an Assistant Director (a Deputy Magistrate) in each district; the Assistant Directors have a number of Inspectors under them. The Collector has no administrative control over the Civil Supplies staff, but must keep the closest possible contact with the Assistant Director. The Assistant Director is in the difficult position of having to serve two masters.

This leads on to the subject of the Development staff. About five years ago officers were appointed throughout the Province for the regulation of jute. The work entailed licensing individual plots of land, so there was a hierarchy leading up from the modest Primary Licensing Assistant [PLA], through the Assistant Inspector, Range Inspector,

Chief Inspector (in charge of a district), Assistant Controller, up to the Chief Controller. The P.L.A. drew Rs. 30/– a month and was in charge of a Union Board, i.e. a group of about a dozen villages. The Jute Regulation staff later took on Rural Reconstruction and other miscellaneous duties. This year they have been renamed the Development staff, and their duties have become even more varied. They are supposed to cope with the 'Grow More Food' campaign, and are shortly to undertake the most complex and important task of a crop survey of the whole Province. The staff are all young, poorly paid, and inexperienced, but full of enthusiasm for the betterment of the Province. They have nearly all been appointed since the establishment of Provincial Autonomy, and are a symptom of the new system in which patronage is an important weapon.

The relationship between the Collector and the Development staff is extremely vague. I have no administrative control over them whatever. I cannot transfer or punish even a P.L.A., though probably my requests would be granted without demur. The Chief Inspector's office is entirely separate from mine. He, like the Assistant Director of Civil supplies, has to serve two masters.

Saumarez Smith concluded his review by asking whether the collector's role in the district was to be sustained or not, and if so what changes would be required:

There is much talk nowadays of post-war reconstruction, and the economic, agricultural and industrial development of the country on a huge scale. Unless the pattern of administration in the districts is clearly visualized, there will be much waste of money and labour, for lack of co-ordination. The natural tendency of Secretariat Departments, as I have tried to show, is to solve each new problem by creating new cadres of officers under their control, with whom the Collector is expected to maintain some sort of contact. The period after the war will inevitably be most difficult from the political point of view; even moderate people who have realized the obstacles to constitutional progress during the war will be extremely impatient. It will be fatal to weaken the forces of law and order. And if the long-suffering district officer is expected to have a general responsibility for, and interest in, postwar reconstruction as well as for maintaining law and order, there may be a breakdown. I feel sure that in the discussion of postwar constitutional problems it will be as essential to consider the pattern of administration in the districts as the structure of the Governments at the Centre and in the Provinces – if there are still a Centre and Provinces! For the 'dumb millions', beloved of oratorical legislators, still regard the district officer as the symbol of Government.

FURTHER READING

Further reading on the war as it affected India might begin with more traditional military history, such as S. W. Kirby, *India's most dangerous Hour* (London 1958) and *The Reconquest of Burma* (London 1965). S. N. Prasad, *Expansion of the Armed Forces and Defence Organization 1939–45* (New Delhi 1956) and N. C. Sinha and P. N. Khera, *Indian War Economy (Supply, Industry and Finance)* (New Delhi 1962), look at the background to India's military effort. H. Knight, *Food Administration in India, 1939–47* (Stanford 1954) considers the repercussions on civilian life. T. K. Ghosh, *The Bengal Tragedy* (Lahore 1944), gives a brief Indian view of the 1943 famine, while the *Famine Inquiry Report* of 1945 provides an exhaustive and very wide-ranging official view. A recent comprehensive survey is provided by Johannes H. Voigt, *Indien im Zweiten Weltkrieg* (Stuttgart 1978).

CHAPTER 12

END AND BEGINNING

The India the British unified by luck and guile and valour was blown apart of its own volition in terrible circumstances – the doing of an overhasty Government in London submitting to the intransigent demands of politicians in India. Murray

The district administration was the pier of the bridge over which India passed from colonial rule to independence. Venkatachar

Grappling with the new problems thrown up by war – and mastering them – was anxious, tiring and yet exhilarating work. The years between 1942 and 1945 extended young entrants to the service to the full and vastly enlarged horizons for their seniors. Venkatachar admirably sums this up:

Mobilisation for war effort and rationing of food and civil supplies brought in new kinds of jobs unknown to the old district administration. The district administration responded to the new challenges. There was a feeling of security under war-time conditions; officials were full of confidence in discharging their duties. War-time work had added new dimensions to district work and much new skill enriched the experience of officials who assumed responsibilities which could not be thought of in peace-time. The disturbances of 1942 did not weaken the district administration. Paradoxically, it had become stronger. Till the last year of British rule, the district administration showed no sign of visible deterioration.

Moreover once Hitler had invaded Russia and the Japanese had attacked the United States there was a confident feeling that the tide had turned; forces had been unleashed on the allied side which made ultimate victory certain. There were less global boosts to morale too, so Kemp at Jamshedpur recalls: 'One was the news of the great victory at El Alamein and the part played in the western desert by Indian troops, and the other was the arrival locally of a consignment of Scotch Whisky with the label Britain Delivers the Goods.' But as defeat was slowly turned into victory and the end of hostilities approached, political problems set aside since 1942 reappeared with renewed urgency.

In May 1945 the war in Europe ended. The Viceroy, Lord Wavell, was clear-sighted enough to recognize that the strengths of his position – the presence in India of ample military forces and the successful management of the wartime economy – would not last, and so he re-opened the debate about India's constitutional future which the rejection of the Cripps offer in 1942 had violently closed. In March 1945 he had flown home and consulted the Cabinet and early in June returned to order the release from prison of the Congress Working Committee and to invite the main Indian political leaders to Simla. His proposal was that they should join his Executive Council in which all portfolios but Defence would be in their hands. Their tasks would be to conduct the war with Japan – a year of stubborn fighting was expected – to plan post-war reconstruction, and to arrange a constituent assembly. The conference failed, since the leaders were too busy staking out party claims to come together. Of two such leaders Raza writes:

The Buttos and the Khuhros did not hit it off. Although their dislike for each other did not amount to the hatred of the Montagues and Capulets of the Romeo and Juliet fame, yet their quarrels were of public moment.

But the final run-up to independence and partition had nevertheless begun.

To the district officer the distant doings of the India Office or the Simla Conference were items of news only. But when Attlee's Labour Government, elected in July 1945, ordered general elections in India for the winter of that year, politics at once reached down to the district. The re-activation of politics had very different implications in the various provinces. Where Congress had won in 1936 with a large majority – in Madras, say, or Orissa, Bihar and much of the UP – the struggle was first to secure nomination on the Congress ticket as against rival individuals or factions and then to find ways of getting in touch with often illiterate voters in great sprawling rural constituencies. Lloyd-Jones with perhaps a touch of malicious pleasure shows how difficult it was to mobilize the electorate even for Jawaharlal Nehru:

The restrictions on political activity had been withdrawn and preparations for elections to the provincial assemblies were under way. Congress politicians were much in evidence once more and the press was full of speculation about developments towards Indian independence. Jawaharlal Nehru was touring the district as part of the election campaign. But the meetings were poorly attended and at one meeting he turned on the organisers and scolded them in public for not arranging a bigger turn-out. In fact a professional wrestling match held in a village near my camp attracted a bigger gathering than any of his meetings. The truth was that despite claims by the nationalist press that the country was seething with the desire to be free from the hated British yoke, the ordinary inhabitants, provided that they were reasonably prosperous, took little interest in politics and only asked to be left alone. Nehru's speeches at these meetings, as reported to me, made curious reading. He promised his audience that after independence everyone would have a car and electricity in their houses, which was going rather far even for an election promise. At another village he said that after independence administration would be through village panchayats [councils] and not through officials. This perplexed his hearers because the panchayat of their village was hopelessly split by faction and incapable of taking any action at all.

In such provinces, where Congress victory was certain, the task of the district officer was that of maintaining order, preventing fraud or intimidation and controlling very large electorates.

But where there were sizeable Muslim minorities the contest was for their allegiance, a contest between a Congress party which claimed to speak for all Indian nationalists and a Muslim League which Jinnah, at the 1945 Simla Conference, claimed had the sole right to speak for Muslims. In such constituencies, in the UP for example, the district officer had not merely to conduct an election but to prevent hard campaigning leading to disorder, as Lloyd-Jones did in Muzaffarnagar:

As time for the election approached, tension throughout the district increased. The main contests in the Muslim constituencies were between the Muslim League and the Congress Muslims. There were frequent allegations of intimidation and other mal-practices but in fact there was never any real doubt about the outcome. The Muslim League represented the great body of the Muslims while those supporting Congress were regarded as Quislings and renegades. In the event Congress won the province, the League won the Muslim seats.

For Jinnah, however, it was the outcome of the elections in those provinces which he had claimed for Pakistan – the Punjab, NWFP and Sind, Bengal and Assam – that was critical. Since the resignation of the Congress ministries in October 1939, and the imprisonment of the Congress leadership in 1942, the Muslim League had gathered strength. It had been a very considerable Muslim party in the elections of 1936 but by no means the only one. Since then it had added to its strength in by-elections. Nevertheless, in several of these prize provinces it was not only Congress which had to be beaten at the polls, but also well entrenched Muslim leaders who were not ready to sub-ordinate their provincial authority to that of Jinnah and the League.

The two major prizes were the Punjab and Bengal. In both, Muslim leaders had emerged who sought to promote Muslim interests within their own provinces by heading coalitions, drawing strength from a broad appeal to agrarian interests rather than by relying on a narrower communalism. In the 1937 elections no Congress Muslim had won a seat in either province, and comparatively few League Muslims had been elected either. Muslims voted instead for the Unionist Party in the Punjab or the Krishak Proja Samiti (KSP) in Bengal. In 1939 their respective leaders Sir Sikandar Hayat Khan and Fazlul Huq only reluctantly accepted Muslim League interference. But the British search for Indian commitment to the national war effort enhanced Jinnah's standing as the Muslims' spokesman, and the Cripps Mission's tacit acceptance of the possibility of Pakistan even more so. Thus the pressure on provincial leaders to toe the League line intensified. The atmosphere of the period is conveyed by Rahmatullah in north Bengal.

Whilst I held charge of Sirajganj Sub-Division, the historic Muslim League Session was convened. Elaborate preparations were made and a huge pandal (rostrum) erected as Mr. Mohammad Ali Jinnah, President of the All India Muslim League was to inaugurate it. The Dak Bungalow had been specially renovated and redecorated as the Qaid-e-Azam and Miss Fatima Jinnah were to stay there for a few hours. The Session proved to be a grand success, without any official assistance or blessings whatsoever.

Curiously, only a couple of days before the scheduled date of the arrival of Mr. Jinnah I received the intimation of a pucca official visit to Sirajganj of Moulvi A. K. Fazlul Huq, Chief Minister of Bengal, accompanied by Mr. Shamsuddin Ahmad the KSP leader and a Minister in his Cabinet, exactly 24 hours before the time of the arrival there of Mr. Mohammad Ali Jinnah and Miss Fatima Jinnah. As instructed I set up a Reception Committee, received him at the railway station, brought him to the town in my own car and fixed up a public reception for the Chief Minister and the Minister at the Municipal Office. After lunch at my bungalow they went out to meet their workers. Actually the Minister had brought with him dozens of notorious Calcutta 'goondas', obviously to create last minute disturbances, and if possible to set fire to the pandal. Over a thousand devoted, trained and vigilant Muslim League volunteers forced the 'goondas' to run away, and there was no breach of peace. The same Moulvi Fazlul Huq had moved the Pakistan Resolution at Lahore in March, 1940!

When in 1943 Fazlul Huq refused to accept Jinnah's claim to leadership he was overthrown as Chief Minister and a League ministry took over in Bengal. Gupta comments 'Bengal was in the throes of upheaval – communal, famines and corruption. The Ispahanis – leading grain dealers and wholesalers – were alleged to have made piles by hoarding and profiteering.' What is certain is that this was the period when the Ispahanis and other big Muslim firms, sensing the potential for them in Pakistan, began to put their money behind the Muslim League. At the election, though Congress won the general seats, the Muslim League won 113 of the 119 seats reserved for Muslims. It was the League which formed the new ministry in 1946.

In Assam a Muslim ministry held office during the war, and politicians used their power to reward or harass, so Maitra recounts, with some freedom. But the position was unstable since Assam was a Hindu majority province and at the 1945–6 elections Congress emerged the winners. The League did not tamely accept the situation:

Though not more than a third of its population was Muslim, Assam was claimed for Pakistan for strategic and other reasons. The Assamese were determined not to be pushed into Pakistan. The new provincial Government was a Congress Ministry headed by Mr. Gopinath Bordoli, a good man but not suited to be a captain in a storm. Apart from Sylhet which had a Muslim majority, the Muslim League strategy was to unleash a terror campaign in the districts of lower Assam with the help of Muslim immigrants from E. Bengal who had settled there in large numbers to frighten the Hindus into submission. The D.C. was always a political officer – the eyes and ears of Government. He was more so now than ever.

At one stage the Muslim League High Command sent to Darrang two high-grade rabble rousers. One was Sadar-i-ala of the Muslim National Guards [MNG]; the other Maulana Bhasani, the stormy petrel of East Pakistan and Bangala Desh. I issued a prohibitory order forbidding them to enter the district. The leader from Punjab obeyed, but not Maulana Bhasani who as a consequence was arrested and put into Tezpur jail. Here he staged a hunger-strike. I met the Maulana and told him that if he died I would take the trouble to dig his grave with my own hands. He took the hint and broke the fast.

But that was not the end, as Maitra explains, for training camps were established for Muslim National Guards, the para-military wing of the Muslim League, and reputedly arms were being smuggled. Then it was announced that the Bengali immigrants led by the National Guards would attack the district town. Maitra's sources of intelligence confirmed this, and acting through the Chief Minister on tour nearby, Maitra called in the Assam Rifles:

The same night under cover of darkness one platoon of Assam Rifles with two machine-guns under a Jemadar crossed the Bhoreli river by boat – it was the rainy season – and took their position on the Mangaldai highway at sunrise. As the Muslim mob of thousands with their green flags and loud cries approached, they were met by a small band of Gurkhas at the ready. They were told to stop. When they did not, a volley rang out killing two. The mob ran back. The M.N.G. camp was demolished. The Muslim League bid failed and the Congress Ministry did not fall.

In the NWFP the position was reversed. In this Muslim-majority province a Red-Shirt ministry had taken office under Dr Khan Sahib in 1937, in alliance with Congress. He had resigned in response to the Congress call in 1939 and had been succeeded first by Governor's rule and then by a Muslim League ministry. The fate of this was observed by Curtis:

The Muslim League – somewhat mistakenly so far as its own interests were concerned – undertook to form a ministry under Sardar Aurangzeb Khan. Wartime shortages had necessitated the introduction of rationing of sugar, cloth, other commodities and sometimes even of grain. Inevitably there was some suspicion that Ministers were doing well out of this system: and it was not surprising that when, after the conclusion of the war with Germany, parliamentary elections were held again, Dr. Khan Sahib and a Congress Ministry were voted into office.

From the narrow viewpoint of the domestic voter this may have been a satisfactory outcome. The Muslim League ministry had not been impressive. But its impact on the scene of All-India politics was disastrous.

The election to power of a Congress Ministry at Peshawar was greeted with no pleasure by British officers serving in the Province or by the considerable portion of the population which had backed the war effort. It was not easy to forget August 1942.

To Jinnah the 1945–6 result, which seemingly put a province of Pathans, who had the reputation of being fanatically Muslim, within the Congress camp was an affront to the whole concept of Pakistan. On the other hand, when Nehru in October 1946 visited the province he was no less affronted.

He was led to believe that he would be acclaimed as the Liberator of the Nation by both the people of the settled districts and the tribesmen of the independent tribal areas. A successful tour of this kind would show how baseless was the Two Nation theory propounded by Mr. Mohammed Ali Jinnah. Dr. Khan Sahib for his part hoped that the tour would establish him as the leading Muslim in the Congress Party and that he would be able to persuade Pandit Nehru that relations with the tribes should be exercised through him.

What happened then was related by Curtis in a letter to his wife:

On arrival at Peshawar Nehru was greeted with a crowd many thousands strong at the landing ground. They were carrying black flags and yelling slogans. The Deputy Commissioner posted large forces of police at the obvious exit and so drew all the crowd there. He then got Nehru into a car and beetled out of another exit which took him miles out of the way but secured him a free run. A Yank cinema operator took pictures of the arrival of the 'all-popular' leader to the fury of the Hindu press correspondents, and he was then and there dropped from the press party and not taken along. He amused himself taking pictures of a mass meeting at which Nehru was urged to go away.

Next day Pandit Nehru, Dr Khan Sahib and Abdul Ghaffar Khan flew to Miranshah to meet a jirga of the Utmanzai Wazir tribe:

Abdul Ghaffar opened the proceedings by telling the Wazirs that the great Nehru had heard of how they had been oppressed by the Feranghis [foreigners] and had decided to come and investigate their condition. They were poor, ignorant, and jungle folk and the new Indian Government was determined to give them schools, to teach them their religion, to build them hospitals and to civilise them. The Wazir spokesman replied more in grief than in anger that Abdul Ghaffar had got it all wrong. The Utmanzai Wazirs were oppressed by no one nor did they need instruction in the teaching of Islam from a man whose son had married a Parsee and whose niece (Dr Khan Sahib's daughter Miriam) was married to a Christian. This remark infuriated Dr Khan Sahib who called them paid toadies of the Political Agent. This remark was too much for the jirga who leapt to their feet in protest.

Smouldering with indignation the party then departed in Harvards for Razmak. A Mahsud jirga was assembled in the Residency garden. Nehru spoke in Urdu. The Mahsuds probably did not understand much. But when he said that those present were all debauched by British bribery it was too much for old Kaka, Mir Badshah's father, who in the coarse way Mahsuds have, said 'Hindu, if the British pay us money, there's a good reason. Our private parts are of extraordinary size as you will find out to your cost before long'. With that the old boy stumped out.

At this point the Resident urged Nehru to return to Peshawar as his tour was alienating the tribes. But though Dr Khan Sahib agreed with this advice, Abdul Ghaffar Khan pressed Nehru to continue. On the final day, on a road journey from the Malakand pass which came under Curtis's jurisdiction, the car in which Nehru and his party were travelling was stoned, the occupants were cut by flying glass, and dung was thrown into the car. In the end they were transferred to a Frontier Constabulary lorry and returned by side roads to Peshawar. The whole unfortunate visit had revealed, as Curtis argues, that there was no support for the Congress Party among the major tribes of the Frontier. The reality was that the Red Shirt movement was neither Congress nor Muslim League inclined, but was an expression of Pathan particularism. A Mahsud spokesman – 'the tall chap like Mephistopheles but for his red dyed beard' as Curtis described him – made that point, declaring that up till then they had always been free and intended to keep it that way. Nevertheless it was Jinnah's hand which was strengthened by the episode.

In Sind the Assembly after the 1937 elections consisted of thirty-five Muslims, twenty-two Hindus and five Europeans. Raza records of the pre-1945 period:

Most of the Hindu Members belonged to the Congress Party and all the 22 Hindu Members voted in unison. The Muslims were divided into half a dozen groups and the leaders of the groups became Ministers. The Chief Minister was Khan Bahadur Allah-Buksh, O.B.E., a very astute politician who always received the solid support of the 22 Hindu members of the Sind Assembly, along with 8 to 10 members of his own group.

Here too a predominantly Muslim province thus had a ministry strongly Congress in complexion, mainly because the Muslims were as riven by faction and personal rivalry as Congress was disciplined and united. In 1942, however, Allah Buksh followed the Congress leaders in their Quit India campaign and was dismissed by the Governor. The succeeding ministry was within the Muslim League fold, though only nominally so. In 1946, however, League candidates swept the board in Sind.

The most vital area for the Muslim League, however, was the Punjab where for many years Muslim premiers had headed Muslim-dominated ministries, but had done so with only token deference to the League. The situation was closely observed by Belcher, in Rawalpindi from mid 1941 to early 1944:

What touched us closely was the continuing and increasingly determined political quarrel between the Punjab Premier and the leader of the Muslim League, Mohammad Ali Jinnah. Sir Sikander's main concern was with the unity of the Punjab; he therefore believed strongly in the necessity for its Muslim majority to live in harmony with its large Hindu and Sikh minorities. His Unionist Party, which was dedicated to this cause, had won the 1936 elections under the new Government of India Act handsomely, and his Government, containing Ministers representing all three communities was strong and successful. But its non-communal ideal was fundamentally opposed to the new concept of a separate and exclusive Muslim nation, Pakistan, which had been proclaimed by Jinnah in August 1940 and espoused by the Muslim League. Sir Sikander had not felt that he could safely stand aside from the Muslim nationalist cause at the time of the fatal rift between the Congress and the Muslim League following the 1936 elections; and he could not do so now, when the vital struggle with the Congress over the future of the Sub-continent was plainly about to begin, with the evident readiness of the British Government to negotiate over postwar constitutional development. To do so would have been to put at serious risk his position as leader of the Punjab Muslims and consequently his whole political credibility. So he made a tactical obeisance to the slogan of Pakistan – not in any case as yet precisely defined – but thereafter resisted the determined attempts by Jinnah to exert political control over him and his Muslim colleagues – all, since 1937, nominally members of the Muslim League. He argued instead for a definition of Pakistan quite different from that now being advocated by the League leaders. This could naturally not be tolerated by Jinnah, whose Pakistan ideal stood or fell by the adherence to it of the Punjab and Bengal as the two major Muslim majority Provinces.

The public debate between the two was continuous, but Sir Sikander's political standing had enabled him to hold his own, and to prevent Jinnah appealing successfully over his head to the Punjabi Muslims for their support; his unexpected death in December 1942 dramatically changed the situation. The possible threat that this entailed for good relations between the communities in the Punjab was to us as administrators a matter of serious and practical consequence.

Azim Husain, son and biographer of the founder of the Unionist Party Sir Fazl-i Husain, watched the events from Lahore with an even more personal interest. He had seen the base of the Unionist Party eroded somewhat after its 1937 election success – 'Not being in line with the policy of the All India Congress against the war effort, [it] was coming under increasing criticism from urban Hindus, and from urban Muslims in support of the All India Muslim League.' With Sir Sikandar's death late in 1942 however, erosion increased and the party, thereafter led by Sir Khizar Hayat Khan Tiwana, was notably weakened:

The new Premier, who was not so skilled a politician as his predecessor, found his position somewhat uneasy, particularly when he came under strong pressure from the All India Muslim League and the Provincial Muslim League to give support to Mr. Jinnah in pursuance of his policy of partition of the country as the only viable solution of the problem of the Muslim minority in India. As the leader of a party which included not only Muslims but also Hindus and Sikhs who had agreed a programme of development and fair allocation of privileges between the different communities, it was difficult for the new Premier to go along with the policy other than that of seeking a provincial solution to the communal problem. The Premier therefore came into sharp conflict at this stage with the urban Muslims who rejected the concept of a provincial solution of the Muslim minority problem.

Azim Husain was himself appealed to by the leaders of his father's old party to leave the central secretariat, come to their aid and strengthen the hands of the new premier. They secured permission for him to return to the Punjab but he refused the quasi-political career thus offered him.

Williams, who was Deputy Commissioner at Lahore, shows how the British reacted to the threat from the League to a party on whose loyalty and co-operation they had counted for so long. By the time elections had been called in 1945 Khizar Hayat Khan, Williams recalls, was no longer fully master of the situation:

His position had been weakened by the death or retirement of three other of his colleagues from the original Coalition of 1937, and the bonds of that Coalition, which had included all communities, were crumbling. The Muslim League in particular sought to assert itself as the major party in the Province and was resentful of the attention now accorded to Congress at the Centre. Political meetings became more frequent, but fortunately no trouble occurred. As the time for the election approached the Government became more apprehensive about the weakness of the Coalition Unionists as against the Muslim League, and had resort to the usual manoeuvres of shuffling around officers of known sympathies according as they might promote interests or be rendered ineffective. The major tactical stroke in Lahore was to call back into existence the Municipal Corporation, suspended some years before for corruption and incompetence, and arrange for municipal elections only a few short weeks before the general election. The object seemed to be the promotion of distraction and disharmony in the opposition parties; the effect on the district administration and police, already facing growing intensity of political feeling in a potentially turbulent city of huge size, was to impose upon them a tremendous and unnecessary extra burden and make incessant demands on discipline, endurance, and good sense.

The municipal elections passed off well, perhaps because everyone's attention was really focussed on the general election to take place almost immediately afterwards. For the latter I was Returning Officer for all constituencies in the district, and responsible for all election arrangements. A principal and contentious point in these was the selection of the location of the various polling stations, and the choice of the presiding officers; the experience of nearly two years of the district and its officials was invaluable for the decisions. The elections themselves were scenes of much excitement but no real trouble, with perhaps most violence seen at the women's polling stations where figures in burqas could set about each other in the knowledge that only an exceptionally brave man would intervene.

The result was the return of the Muslim League as the largest single party in the Provincial Legislative Assembly, but with a little under half the total seats.* A ramshackle coalition of Hindus, Sikhs, and a few very undistinguished Muslim moderates was patched together under Khizar who again took office as Premier, to the intense anger of the League who denounced him as a traitor to his kind. Feeling in Lahore ran high, and reached a danger pitch when a Muslim youth was killed in a brawl. The League organised a huge funeral procession, to march through much of Lahore, with the possibility of communal explosion. On me lay the responsibility for deciding if it should take place or be banned under local order as likely to cause breach of the peace; much risk lay in a decision either way, but I felt that the chance of averting

* Seven Muslim Unionists won seats in the Punjab Legislative Assembly, and seventy-nine Muslim League candidates.

major disorder would lie best in allowing a carefully shepherded procession to make its way along a selected route, with its members giving vent to their feelings in their chants, rather than in a repressive order entailing the likelihood of having to deal with a variety of widely scattered outbreaks of perhaps increasing violence. So the procession took place under heavy police escort, with the military in Lahore Cantonment alerted to come to the help of the Civil power, if need be. The Superintendent of Police and I accompanied the procession on foot for some eight hours on a hot day, to the accompaniment of almost ceaseless chanting and wailing, intensified at each of the many halts. The virtues of the dead were extolled, but much more vigour was given to the condemnation of Khizar and his new Ministers in every variety of opprobrium. The route agreed was observed, but not without one or two attempts to deviate involving roadside argument with the mob leaders, amongst whom was one I had last seen in 1937 as High Commissioner for India in London. At length the procession came to its cemetery; the dead man was buried; and the processionists dispersed with emotions for the time being exhausted. When at last I got to bed late that night it was to be telephoned by Khizar, who demanded if I had ceased to preserve order in Lahore, since I had allowed a mob to spend the day shouting revilement of the Premier; I suggested that it was just because I had allowed this to happen that he was still Premier at the end of that day.

The elections of 1945–6 demonstrated the almost complete communal polarization which had taken place in India since the elections of 1937. In the Central Legislative Assembly, for example, all thirty Muslim seats had gone to the League, which had taken 86.6 per cent of the Muslim votes. Congress for its part had secured 91.3 per cent of the votes in non-Muslim constituencies. Even at that point the constitutional issue of a federal or divided India had not been decided. But that the decision must be taken swiftly was emphasized by the scenes at the Delhi trial of the Indian National Army leaders who had fought alongside the Japanese, by an Indian naval mutiny at Bombay and by other signs of weakening discipline in various services. In March 1946, therefore, a British Cabinet Mission composed of Lord Pethick-Lawrence, Sir Stafford Cripps and A. V. Alexander arrived in India. Met by Jinnah's flat demand for a six-province Pakistan and a flat rejection of that by Congress, the Mission proposed a three-tiered Indian Union – first the provincial governments, then a grouping of provinces (Western, Central and Eastern), and finally the Union centre, in which Hindus and Muslims would have parity, to handle defence, foreign affairs and communications. The proposal offered Jinnah a full six-province Pakistan within the loosest federal structure – the threat being that should he opt for partition, by his own logic he would lose all those areas of the Punjab, Bengal and Assam where Hindus predominated. Congress were offered a united India, but with only a weak centre. Both were given a chance to participate at once in an interim government, an expanded Viceroy's Executive Council which would be fourteen members strong (six Congress members, five League, one Sikh, Parsi and Indian Christian).

The two contestants now had to decide whether to accept the three-tiered federal structure and enter the interim government. Jinnah said yes to both, seeing that the Cabinet Mission plan offered the largest Muslim homeland he could hope for. Congress accepted the plan with reservations, but refused to enter the interim government. And though later Congress did enter the

government they then declared that they did not accept the grouping proposals as binding, or as Nehru put it on 10 July, that they would be 'completely unfettered by agreements'. The Muslim League thereupon withdrew
its acceptance of the Cabinet Mission plan and Jinnah called on Muslims to
observe 16 August 1946 as 'direct action day'.

For the district officer the period after the ending of the war and the return
to government by elected ministries in all the provinces had been trying
enough, since politicians everywhere were seeking to strengthen their electoral hold by whatever means came to hand. Lloyd-Jones in the UP watched
as the grain procurement system was taken over by the politicians, 'political
friends were favoured and others penalised', and when a force of civic
guards was recruited to assist the police, mainly from among ex-servicemen,
the Congress Government required him to accept men from the Indian
National Army whose leaders had recently been tried in Delhi as traitors.
In Bihar the pattern was much the same, as Ray records:

Nor did I find the Ministers particularly helpful. They toured the districts continually with a large following, not for administrative purposes, but mainly for
political reasons. Seldom was any warning given in advance: a telephone call at any
early hour would inform one that an Hon'able Minister had arrived at the Circuit
House which meant postponing one's work, joining the queue of petitioners and
dancing attendance upon him for the rest of the day. With one or two notable
exceptions they had little idea of the complexities of administration. 'I hear there is a
lot of blackmarketing in the district – look to it at once and let me know next week'
was a fairly typical verbal instruction I once received. Nor were personal courtesies
always very marked. After a tiring day with the Prime Minister I recall being dismissed with a wave of the hand late at night on the railway station with a curt: 'You
can go now'. However objectionable all this did not really matter, but what did
matter was the tendency of Ministers to manipulate affairs with their Congress
henchmen on the spot. Endless intrigue, interference and misunderstanding was the
result. This meant that the District Officer was often isolated and bypassed and had
no idea of important orders passed or decisions taken until long after, often by
rumour. Transfers of subordinate officials without warning or consultation became
commonplace. Nevertheless any failings or shortcomings were attributed to 'sabotage
by British officials', the words of a friendly Congressman to me.

After the breakdown of the Cabinet Mission plan, however, such difficulties would come to seem trivial compared with the disasters of communal violence unleashed by Jinnah's call for direct action on 16 August
1946. Martyn, then in the Home Department of the Bengal Government,
saw the tragedy unfold in Calcutta. The Chief Minister declared a public
holiday, which allowed crowds to assemble and rioting to start. What
followed Martyn recorded at the time in a letter to England:

The result was August 16th – the Great Killing. The worst was over by the 20th but
the hate and tension is still very apparent and the implications of that event are still
being worked out. I was in the Police Control for most of the four days but got out
on one occasion and toured the city with the Governor and party. You will probably
have seen pictures of the bodies lying about. The extent of the inter-communal hate
was amazing, and brought home very forcibly the results of preaching Pakistan
versus Hindustan. When we went on the tour round we saw two people murdered
before our eyes, a hundred yards down the road from where we had stopped – two

oldish men being belaboured with iron rods by three/four youths and, after they had fallen down, two men ran back and finished them off as they rolled on the ground. The Police Inspector and the Armed Guard rushed forward in a truck and fired, but they probably hit nobody.

The exact figures of dead will never be known, but 5,000 plus 15,000 injured would not be an over-estimate. Civil War without doubt. The Europeans/Anglo-Indians etc. were not touched – it was Hindu versus Muslim. There are many authentic stories of this – the European, trying to save a Muslim who was being stabbed to death by Hindus in the main business centre, being told to keep away, and having his bicycle removed out of harm's way 'in case it got blood on it' (by the Hindus before they finished off the Muslim).

The consequences were both immediate – the complete disorganization of the life of a great city noted in a diary by Martyn who was Chief Co-ordinator of the relief operations – and long term, a chain reaction of communal violence across all North India:

The immediate problems thrown up by the disturbances were many – food, hospitals, burial of corpses (all the professional corpse removers and Societies for the Burial of the Poor had been scattered) and an ad hoc Government show with volunteers had to be brought into being and work night and day, prevention of epidemics etc. We had to arrange hasty meetings in the middle of the trouble and do a good deal of improvisation. The Army were most co-operative. The Calcutta Corporation for the first day or two was not in existence. An additional difficulty was the collapse of all transport and the stopping of trains. The stories of the Killing lost nothing in the telling – that was hardly possible – and since then we have been on the edge of a communal upheaval anywhere at any time.

In Dacca the news from Calcutta led to almost immediate violence, and Bell, the DC, at once brought into action the Dacca Defence Scheme prepared in 1941 'a regular printed manual stating where pickets should be posted to check hostile bodies clashing'. The large-scale rioting was quickly checked, as was arson, thanks to the legacy of the wartime ARP organization:

But it was impossible to check all the sudden attacks from the narrow alleys which were and are so common in old Dacca. Shankari Bazar, the settlement of the old established Hindu conch-shell workers, was just west of the Collectorate and the Courts, and there was certainly one incident when a man was killed in the Court precincts by someone who came out of that Bazar, knifed a bystander, and ran back. Even if there was a witness to any outrage, he would certainly not give evidence against a co-religionist. The indirect effects of these attacks were serious. Inhabitants of areas where there were minority groups, tended to move away and to crowd onto other areas of their co-religionists, or into schools, several of which were occupied by refugees. The general sense of fear stopped movement and Government and municipal servants and employees of other public concerns were not carrying out normal duties, or required police protection to do so. All this trouble was caused by the use of weapons which could be found in any home or workshop in the town. Fire-arms were not used. Occasionally 'acid bombs' (acid contained in an electric light bulb) were used, but killing was done by knives and property was attacked by crowbars, or torches made of rag and oil, helped by dry wood and straw.

I was required for constant consultation by the Superintendent of Police, to sign orders and to interview people who complained of lack of police protection, or favouritism. Early in the trouble, and notably when there was damage to property by arson, collective fines were imposed on the supposed guilty community. Curfews were imposed on localities which were the scene of crimes. I believe there were some 160 deaths in four or five months.

Within weeks of the Calcutta killings Hindus in Bihar began retaliatory attacks upon the Muslim minority in that province. A Madras Regiment battalion was deployed in aid of the civil power, but even with this assistance district magistrates were unable to contain the violence and prevent a heavy death toll. Moreover, as Martin in Patna district records, under the intense pressure the discipline of the forces of law and order themselves began to weaken. One incident in which he was directly involved may stand as an example of many more. He reports his actions on hearing of rioters attacking the village of Nagarnausa:

The strength of the party which proceeded to the village was myself, the Commanding Officer [of the Madras Regiment] and his escort of five soldiers, Captain Lathom of the RIAC and five RIAC drivers. We were armed with rifles and sten-guns and two bren-guns, both of these later jammed during the firing and became useless.

On nearing the village we found that there was a large mob gathered. The village is a large one about one mile in its circumference. I would estimate the strength of the mob as approximately 5,000 persons. The military party split up and started to encircle the village from the West and South. Fire was opened independently by the Military as we came within range of the mob. The Military Party was split up into small groups and I was myself detached for some time. I would estimate that during this firing about 20 persons in the mob were killed.

After the mob had dispersed from the village, the Commanding Officer and I went into the interior of the village where we found a large collection of Mohammedans approximately 1,200 in number. They showed great signs of distress and said that they had been attacked continuously for three days. The mosque in the village had been destroyed and I myself saw the bodies of 10 to 15 Mohammedan persons in this area. The Mohammedans stated that a very large number had been killed during the previous fighting and that also a number had been killed as they were attempting to reach Nagarnausa from surrounding villages.

As the evacuees left the village at dusk, about 1,200 of them including women and children, they were again attacked and their escort had to re-open fire. Martin, commenting on the determination of the mob, recalls 'the noise the mob had made when they realised that they would not after all be able to kill the Muslims, old men, women and children and all, when they had thought they had them within their grasp. "Tantum religio potuit suadere malorum".' But he also comments on his feeling that even the disciplined Madras Regiment, who had done valiant work, could not be relied on as Hindus to open fire on fellow Hindus and he observes, by contrast, that the five RIAC drivers in his little force, all Pathans, 'were obviously deeply disturbed by what they had seen going on around them and had no inhibitions about the use of their weapons'.

Meanwhile Wavell had continued his efforts to achieve a constitutional solution. Though the League had announced their rejection of the Cabinet Mission plan, Congress took part in an interim government under Nehru, from 2 September 1946. Jinnah by his call for direct action had demonstrated Muslim disruptive strength and now in October, unwilling to leave the Centre in Congress hands, he nominated five League members to the interim government, though to block rather than co-operate in its working. Wavell, ever more aware of his ebbing power to control events, pressed the British Government for a decision. The British Prime Minister's response was first to try a personal conference in London with Nehru and Jinnah and then when that failed, to announce that Britain would transfer power not later than June 1948, 'whether as a whole to some form of central government, or in some areas to existing provincial governments, or in such other way as may seem reasonable and in the best interests of the Indian people'.

As background in India to Attlee's high-level negotiations in Britain there had been a further chain reaction of communal violence – at Noakhali in eastern Bengal where Hindus were the sufferers, and in the UP and at Delhi where it was the Muslims' turn. It was in Bengal, however, that Gandhi began his great personal campaign for communal reconciliation, which he later continued at Delhi, and which was to end in his assassination by a Hindu communalist on 20 January 1948. McInerny, posted at Noakhali, gives a moving glimpse of Gandhi there:

I attended the prayer meeting which he held at Chaumuhani on the day of his arrival. Here sat a little physically ugly old man talking to a crowd of 5 or 6 thousand people in a language, Hindi, which they did not understand, except to a very slight extent. The speech was translated into Bengali afterwards, but as he spoke I got a feeling that the fact that they did not understand what he was saying didn't matter. This was because of an extraordinary quality in his voice, which expressed perfect detachment but not indifference. It was the voice of the Bhagavad Gita – The Song of God. And they were having 'darshan' – seeing him, and living for some time in his spiritual ambit.

The setting of a date at which power would be handed over, did not reduce tension however, but provoked still further violence, as Williams saw:

The British Cabinet's decision to hand over power in August 1947 was a plain invitation to politicians in power to stay there by whatever means they could, and to those who were not in power to get there by destroying what was in their way. With the Muslim League demanding its own State of Pakistan and the rival communities much intermingled geographically the Punjab, and especially the north-west and centre, soon became a battleground between Muslims and Sikhs, with massacre and looting on a huge scale.

The trial of strength between the rump Unionist ministry in the Punjab and the Muslim League, long waged, was still no more disorderly than usual at the beginning of 1946. Slater at Dera Ghazi Khan, 'a wilderness which had in the past attracted holy men intent on mortifying the flesh, though their successors were mainly scoundrels', handled a January by-election without undue difficulty, aided by a superintendent of police who knew the district inside out, had a superb intelligence system and a well-disciplined force. He could even note with interest the contrast in electioneering styles: 'The Unionist campaigning technique was to nobble influential individuals privately. The League on the other hand relied on mass meetings calculated to stir up religious feelings.'

Once Attlee's February announcement had been made, however, the gloves were off and the League went for a knock-out. And since the League's heaviest punch was the appeal to religious bigotry, what began as a struggle for leadership between Muslims, soon dragged Sikhs and Hindus in too. When Khizar Hayat Khan's ministry resigned in March 1947 communal riots flared. On 5 March Multan boiled over. This was Arthur's district and summoning reinforcements and warning the Civil Surgeon to get ready for riot casualties he moved down into the city:

I issued an order under Section 12 of the Public Safety ordinance prohibiting meetings, processions, the gathering of five or more persons, and the carrying of arms within the municipal limits of Multan. At the same time I issued an order under Section 144 Cr. P. C., imposing a curfew from 6.0 p.m. to 7.0 a.m. Publicity was given to these two orders by the Publicity Officer and his Mobile Publicity Van. I then closed the District Courts and instructed the Additional Deputy Commissioner and all other Magistrates to proceed to Haram Gate Police Station, leaving one Officer in charge of the Treasury to organise its defence should it be attacked. One company of 3rd Dogras arrived at Haram Gate Police Station at about 2 p.m. As soon as the troops arrived, mobile military patrols accompanied by Magistrates were sent out in Military Transport to patrol the Circular road, and one platoon was sent out into the City on patrol on foot accompanied by a Magistrate. I instructed the Magistrates to open fire immediately if the rioters refused to disperse. When a second Company of troops arrived a strong force was located at the Flour Mills to protect the City grain supply. By this time, fires had broken out in several parts of the City on the Circular road and the Municipal Fire Brigade and the Military Fire Brigade were sent to deal with these fires as best they could. The riot broke out about twelve noon and the situation was under control by 3.0 p.m. Unfortunately, by that time parts of the City had been set on fire and it was impossible to bring these fires under control.

In a letter home on 28 January Arthur had written, 'So far all has gone well here but who can say what will happen. The slightest thing may give a communal tinge to the whole business and then we shall have a communal riot of no mean proportions on our hands.' Just two months later he was counting the cost of the communal riot that had occurred – 194 dead, 183 injured, Rs 14 lakhs damage from arson and looting, and collective fines to the same amount imposed.

Belcher, also in Multan, never forgot his first communal killing when he saw 'a group of Muslims armed with staves launch a sudden murderous attack upon a single Sikh on the roadside, obviously simply because he was a Sikh, recognisable as such by his beard and turban'. But by May single murders were commonplace in the cities and as Williams at Lahore relates:

In the countryside the entire religious community of one village would take part in the wholesale slaughter of those of an opposite religion, and cases were known of Indian army officers on leave organising mass attacks of this kind.

In Amritsar, in June, murder and arson and destruction of property reached such a pitch that a 48 hour curfew was imposed. Apart from the great number of deaths a problem was created of the salvaging and custody of property buried in the ruins of houses, and the tracing of owners who had probably, if still alive, fled the city. Normal legislation did not suffice, and I went to Amritsar to try to appreciate the physical difficulties. It was one of the most eerie experiences I have known to walk about in a huge Indian city of over half-a-million inhabitants, through street after street of smouldering ashes and demolished houses, with every door and shutter closed, and to see no human being save my police guides and hear no noise save the drip of water from a broken pipe or the collapse of another charred roof timber. An emergency Act was prepared and promulgated, but it could be little more than a paper exercise to try and deal with an immense human and financial problem in the dying days of the Province.

When Attlee in February 1947 announced his final date for the transfer of power in India he also announced that Lord Louis Mountbatten was to take over as Viceroy from Lord Wavell. Mountbatten arrived in India on 22 March and found that the Congress Working Committee had already recognized that partition was inevitable. The new Viceroy too, soon accepted that even the loose federation proposed by the Cabinet Mission was now impossible. He first considered a devolution of power to the individual provinces, which appalled Nehru as an incitement to fragmentation, and then proposed the two-Dominion solution worked out by the Reforms Commissioner, V. P. Menon, which was ultimately accepted. On 3 June, the Cabinet in London having expressed their approval, the leaders in India broadcast their acceptance of partition. Next day Mountbatten announced that the date for Independence had been brought forward from February 1948 to 15 August 1947.

At the same time the Indian leaders were presented with a statement of the consequences of their actions – a contingent plan, suggested by V. P. Menon, and drafted by Christie, now on the Viceroy's staff:

My partners in this exercise were two senior I.C.S. colleagues, Hindu and Muslim respectively, H. M. Patel and Chaudhuri Mohammed Ali (who was later to be a Prime Minister of Pakistan). This document was called 'The Administrative Consequences of Partition', and it set out what would be involved in dividing the assets and liabilities of India, in the event of partition, from rolling stock to currency reserves, from the national debt to the armed forces; and it made proposals for carrying out the division.

It was drafted, mainly by Patel and Mohammed Ali, but edited and stitched together by me, at a series of private lunchtime meetings of the three of us in my house, not without heat and hard bargaining, and the occasional risk of a 'walk-out' by one or other of the protagonists.

Patel and Mohammed became a steering committee of the Partition Council under the Viceroy. I waited in my office every night for the fruit of their day's labour, twenty or thirty files, each a separate judgement of Solomon, and sent them on to Mountbatten, sometimes not before midnight, with any precis or recommendation which might be necessary in the rare cases on which they had not been able to agree. He would study them in bed – and once or twice I was summoned to an early morning levée, to elucidate some point while the Viceroy was dressing – and was ready to present to the Partition Council at 9 a.m. the agreed proposals which, at that stage, they were ready enough to accept.

Delhi was preoccupied with hammering out the final constitutional drafts, with preparations for the plebiscites which would vote Assam out of Pakistan and the North West Frontier Province into it, and with the drawing of the surgeon's knife through the living flesh of the Punjab and Bengal which were now to be divided. But for the district officer there were other pre-occupations – how to sustain as much of the normal administration as he could, and what to do about his own future. Normal administration had of course become a relative term, for India, about to be partitioned, had never more clearly displayed its variousness. In the experience of the district officer it had always been false to talk about India or the Raj as a unity. He and his fellows in the ICS were members of one all-India service, but their working lives were spent in provinces which were semi-autonomous kingdoms, governed by different traditions and modes of administration. So while in some districts preparations for partition were hurriedly pushed forward in a crisis atmosphere in others routine revenue work continued in a quiet countryside.

The immediacy of partition is described by Faruqui, then Collector of Karachi, 'a sprawling town with colonial style buildings – small and ill-equipped', who heard on 3 June that Pakistan would be born on 15 August and that Karachi would be its capital. With one engineer colleague he had to prepare the city for its new role:

And the first special train bringing the staff of the Constituent Assembly of Pakistan secretariat from Delhi arrived on July 27, 1947. There were make-shift arrangements for office and residential accommodation. There were to be special trains every 2 or 3 days or sooner. We made make-shift arrangements for office and residential accommodation by working day and nights in temporary electric light. Contractors cheated and defaulted. The non-Muslim artisans and labour left *en masse* without notice. We had to bring replacements by air in those days when there was no regular air service. We even put up tents for the men, women and children who were not used to living in tents. Even such unsatisfactory arrangements would have broken down had the special trains arrived regularly. But the Hindus and Sikhs way-laid them, robbing and killing indiscriminately. These ghastly tragedies however gave us more time to prepare such arrangements as we could. To add to our misfortunes, heavy rain poured upon us in Karachi where it hardly ever rained or even drizzled in August. After one such downpour I visited a tented camp and found men, women and children sitting with their pitiable belongings on the cots in their tents with water rushing underneath. I commiserated with them. 'It is nothing', they said, 'we will put up with anything for the sake of Pakistan'. It is a small example of heroism and spirit of martyrdom which inspired our people in those days, which must not go unrecorded.

Martyn in Bengal saw the same process from the other end, for he arrived in his office one day to find that 'all the chairs in the room (except my favourite chair that I had used for ten years) had been removed. They had been carted off to the Docks on the way to Dacca. The sight of furniture from the rooms of one of the Muslim Ministers being carried down the verandah – each item daubed with green paint, the colour of Islam – was another sign. Those going eastward were going either into the Wilderness or the Promised Land.'

In South India, however, all was calmly normal. Downing at Chicacole in Vizagapatam district of Madras was busy in solving the problem posed by a petition by tobacco cultivators for a remission of land revenue and in unmasking their attempted fraud. As he noted:

So far as the work of the division was concerned, it was surprisingly unchanged by the evolving political situation. Madras was blessedly untouched by the communal strife that was tearing North India apart. There was a Congress Ministry in office, the local Congress Member of the Legislative Assembly was a frequent and friendly caller at my office, but none of this made any obvious difference to the functioning of the administrative system in the districts.

Even in North India there were some quiet centres in the storm. Lloyd-Jones in the UP reports that his district, Muzaffarnagar, remained quiet though tense throughout. Waiting for his release from the service he went out into camp for the last time:

Out in camp things did not seem to have changed. India might be on the verge of momentous changes but the ordinary villager went about his business unconcerned. I received the usual friendly and respectful greetings with the same requests and complaints. As far as the people were concerned I was what represented government and they could not imagine any different system. The landowners, the retired government servants and the men of some education who knew what was happening in the world outside used to come and talk to me. They also found it hard to believe that the British were going. As one said to me, 'After all you fought the Germans to decide who should rule India.' A narrow view of our war aims perhaps, but understandable. Who heard of a victor throwing away the prize of victory? As for Congress and the political agitations, no one took them seriously; it was a sort of game and everyone knew that the British could clamp down on Congress whenever they wished, as was shown during the war.

I continued my normal routine in camp with careful inspections and detailed reports, feeling rather like the captain writing up his log as the ship goes down. Even if things were to continue without trouble, I doubted if there would be many inspections by my successors, but at that time I felt sure there would be civil war and chaos after independence.

It is not proposed here to review the events which followed partition and independence on which Lloyd-Jones thus reflected, either the great successes or the disasters. Of the former too little has perhaps been written, of the latter too much. But Williams's last glimpse of the Punjab and his thoughts upon it ought perhaps to be included:

My last day as a serving officer was the 14th August 1947. A few British Officers were still left; to obtain any pay at home for the last leave we would now take we needed last pay certificates from the Accountant General, but his office, like many others, had been deserted, with many of its clerks refugees from Lahore. We traced one official who could still be found, and brought him to his desk where he made out certificate after certificate to save us from immediate penury in England. On the 15th after seeing the Governor off from the airfield where his last view of Lahore was of billowing clouds of smoke from a burning city I went to the Cantonment to see if the Army could help with transport to Delhi, since trains were not running after a pitched communal battle the night before in Lahore railway station. A small convoy was in fact to leave next day, and on the early morning of the 16th a few British civil officers joined it to dash through a sort of no-man's-land, now the battleground of warring communities.

In the wider scale of the independence of a sub-continent this appalling disaster practically escaped notice, or was dismissed as an inevitable price to pay when the political rights of some 300 millions were involved. But it was by any standards a major catastrophe in history, and should not have happened.

There can have been few North Indian district officers who did not share that view and did not ask the question could the bloodshed at partition have been prevented, was not the pace unduly, disastrously hurried. Lloyd-Jones for example wrote home in June, 'Attempting to set up two new states in two months would be impossible in any part of the world, but knowing the speed with which things move in India, it is sheer irresponsibility'. He adds, 'In order to safeguard life and property, it had always been our custom to spend weeks in taking precautions and preventive measures before a festival when the danger of Hindu-Muslim conflict was expected. Yet here was the likelihood of the most stupendous explosion of all, and less than two months allowed for the organization and planning of counter-measures.' Belcher, however, makes one point particularly germane to the study of the key role of the district officer. In discussing the reasons which led to unprecedented mass migrations across the Punjab borders he gives most weight to two factors. One, evidently, was the already present fear created by the communal rioting of the past months which was now to break out again. The other was the gap at the heart of the district administration,

A consequence of the requirement that senior Indian officials on each side of the border should be of the 'right' community on Independence Day; it followed from this that at the very moment when minorities were feeling most vulnerable and in need of reassurance they found that senior District officials of their own community who might have given them that reassurance had themselves disappeared over the border. Almost all the British ICS officers had left at Independence, as had – under the orders I have already described – all the non-Muslim senior Indian officers, so that a number of Districts were in the hands of relatively inexperienced men, some only recently appointed to them. And the Muslim officers from India who had opted for service in Pakistan were mostly still *en route*, many held up for long periods by the very violence and disruption they were so desperately needed to cope with – some actually in personal anger, as happened when Sikh mobs took over the airport at Delhi, killing such Muslims as they could find there, until the Air Control managed to warn planes with any Muslims on board not to land. So for the critical days and weeks the administration was simply overwhelmed.

This picture of district officers leaving India altogether or transferring from one new Dominion to the other is a reminder that, for most members of the ICS, 1947 was a year of personal decision. The ICS was a covenanted service, its terms of service embodied in a contract, and in 1947 two white papers, Cmd 7116 in April and Cmd 7189 in August, set out the options before its members. They had now a choice to make, as Belcher describes:

With all these uncertainties, rising communal passions, rumours and alarms, it was hard to carry on with one's normal tasks with proper application; indeed it was doubtful how far one's orders and decisions would carry into the future. And I had now my own future to think about. Following the June announcement of the partition scheme all the members of the ICS were given the choice of serving in either of the two new Dominions, assuming they were acceptable to its Government, with guarantees that all the terms of their existing contracts of service would be honoured; the non-Indian members were also given the alternative of leaving the Service, either immediately on Independence or after a period in one of the new Dominions, with the proportunate pension they had earned and compensation on a fixed scale for loss of career. Later came an offer to British officers who decided to leave the Service of staying on in the Sub-continent to join the staff of one or other of the two new High Commissioners for the United Kingdom who were now being appointed; it was planned to send one of the Civil Service Commissioners from London to make a preliminary selection, those taking up High Commission posts having to go through the full normal selection process when they returned to the United Kingdom at the end of their first tour of duty.

Belcher's own choice was to offer his services to Pakistan, though in case he proved unacceptable, since the Muslim League 'suspected the British ICS officers in the Punjab – or at least the more senior among them – of having consistently worked against them in favour of the Unionists', he hedged his bet by having an interview with the British Civil Service too.

Mudie, too, stayed on:

I had long been in favour of the Pakistan solution to India's future Government and as I had seen a good deal of Nawabzada Liaqat Ali Khan, who was destined to be the first Prime Minister of Pakistan, I wrote to him, asking what I should do. He replied asking whether I would go as Governor to the West Punjab. I agreed.

Lamarque in Madras was briefly tempted to stay, but in the end felt it wiser to say no:

As for myself I had little hesitation before deciding that, at my age of 34, I too must quit India and seek another career, and so I went to London in April 1947 to be interviewed for a job in the British service. I had first a long talk with my minister C. Rajagopalachari, wisest and kindliest of Indian statesmen. He strongly advised me to stay, on the grounds that India needed all the administrative talent she could get, and that there would still be a career for me in India. I replied, with complete honesty, that if it was just a question of continuing to work for him I would readily stay, but that one day there would arise a new king, which knew not Joseph, and then my future would be uncertain.

Often Indian political pressures and expectations did make it difficult for Ministers, however anxious to retain experienced men, to invite foreign administrators to stay after India had secured its independence. This seems to have been the case in Orissa, and in the UP Midgley declares 'Any doubts I might have had were quickly settled by the Chief Secretary, now of course an Indian colleague, who wrote from Lucknow to say "Some European officers have expressed their willingness to continue in service. They need not trouble." ' Many British ICS, however, had no intention of staying on, certainly not Lloyd-Jones:

The Congress Government made an offer to all British members of the service to stay on on a three year contract. Even the 'liberators' wanted some continuity. But for my part I could never consider remaining. One would continually be faced with the prospect of having to carry out unpalatable orders, perhaps to the detriment of those who had been one's friends and supporters. I had a feeling that Congress were rather hurt when the British members of the ICS opted in a body, with very few exceptions, to quit. But what could they expect?

The last few weeks were busy preparing to hand over the district, attending farewell parties and listening to speeches. Even my old enemies, the Congress, gave me a farewell party and I was again approached personally with a request to stay on. [But] my mind was made up. It was nonetheless sad; the saddest part was looking into the hurt eyes of men who felt themselves betrayed, men who had stood stalwart by the British, and who, especially the Muslims, feared for the future.

Hayley, on the other hand, who had been accepted for a Civil Service post in England, was delighted to be asked by the Congress Chief Minister of

Assam to stay on as Secretary for Rural Development in charge of a major plan with a four and a half million pound budget. He had a very good three years and evidently was particularly pleased to have been personally chosen by the Assam cabinet to make the contract with the Bombay mills for Assam's supply of cloth when cloth rationing had to be re-introduced in India. 'No-one in that meeting batted an eyelid, but I was very conscious of the fact that I was the only white face there.'

The choices before Indian district officers in 1947 in one sense were not so wide. As Maitra rather tartly relates: 'Sardar Patel brow-beat Under-Secretary Henderson at the time of the transfer of power to deny Indian officers what was offered to their British colleagues – retirement with pension and a generous lump sum for loss of career.' He adds, however, that in his opinion few would have cared to retire. That had been the position taken by the April white paper: 'In the case of Indian officers [HMG] feel that senti-ments of patriotism will impel them to continue to serve their country and that they can look for a positive improvement in their prospects.' Compen-sation was therefore restricted to those not invited to serve their new govern-ment, whose actions while in British service had damaged their prospects, or for whom no transfer could be arranged from a province within which their safety was uncertain. The arrangements for Burma were similar, but the Government of India declined to guarantee pay and conditions 'as favour-able as those enjoyed at present'.

For some non-British district officers, independence brought no immediate change in their service duties: Narasimham had an eight-month spell as Collector of Salem in Madras; Bonarjee who was Commissioner at Benares in 1946 moved to be Commissioner of Rohilkhand in 1947; and Faruqui, who was born in the West Punjab in what became Pakistan, served that Dominion. Rahmatullah, however, though born in Bihar and serving at independence in Midnapore, chose Pakistan – 'nobody in the District ever thought I would be opting for Pakistan and leaving them on August 10, 1947. The representatives of all political parties and elements opposed to British Raj came to bid me good-bye and with tears in their eyes wished me well in Pakistan.' Raza, too, made Pakistan his choice though his home was in the UP, and he was Collector of Karachi when it became the capital of the new Dominion. Gupta whose boyhood had been spent in the UP but who was serving in Bengal in 1947 moved back to his home province: 'My cadre was changed at my request from Bengal, which had a surplus of officers to the UP.' His pleasure at this homecoming was soon marred, however, by the outbreak of communal violence spreading from the Punjab borders and the murder of Gandhi. Maitra, also, changed his province. He had been too independent to get on well with some of the Assam politicians, and had always felt rather isolated, and never very sure how far even British adminis-trators would support him in his stance:

A Muslim officer, even from distant Punjab, could count upon the support of Muslim Ministers. Assamese officers (mostly in the Provincial and very few in the Imperial services) could look for patronage to the Assamese ministers. But a Bengali Hindu like myself, who had no patron either in the high official echelon or in the ministry was nobody's baby.

In 1947, therefore, he says, 'I took transfer to Bengal soon after Independence, exercising the only option offered to an Indian ICS officer.'

Whether the district officer was staying put, changing province or dominion or leaving India altogether, 15 August 1947 was a memorable day, a point from which to look back and forward. Raza entitles his contribution 'My Apprenticeship to Service in Pakistan', and on 15 August many Muslim members of the ICS must have seen, as Venkatachar understandingly puts it, 'new vistas and horizons in a Muslim state. Here was a challenge to work for an ideal without begging for favours from the Hindus.' For those like Rahmatullah who had left a homeland to follow that Muslim dream, the day also meant a parting too – Such a morning had arrived, as the Urdu couplet has it, as turned one's own folk into strangers – 'Aik savera aiysa aaya, apne huey paraye'. Murray records that moment too:

On Independence Day in 1947 I was up at Razmak, the army camp on the march between North and South Waziristan and the Indian Army units there, Hindu and Muslim, were breaking up in preparation for their reorganisation into two armies, giving tea parties to each other, recalling past shared hardships and triumphs and saying goodbye for ever as the Indian companies and squadrons would be going back on Partition to India. It was an emotional occasion with the happy prospect of national independence stretching out securely ahead and the recent series of massacres and counter massacres, which had convulsed north India forgotten for the moment. Alas the progress of army units moving east and west was not to be unimpeded.

Shukla reached a new post at Budaun just in time to celebrate Independence Day:

It was a moment of pride and joy; the country, an ancient country which had been the cradle of civilisation and which has gifted many things to the world and contributed to civilisation, had, after centuries of political subjection and humiliation, become independent, once again free to order its life according to its own values and to contribute to world civilisation. A historical moment indeed! To men in the Civil Services, as well as in Defence forces, new opportunities opened out to serve their country. So far, for the Englishmen the I.C.S. had been a mission, to Indians a career; now for Indians too it became a mission.

But the 15th was certainly not just a day for philosophizing. 'It was a good attendance at the Parade yesterday', writes Dunlop, 'I've never seen a bigger crowd in Madras. A good-natured holiday feeling crowd ... In the evening had to abandon the car in a terrific traffic jam – no policemen in sight. Crowd in very gay mood. No doubt about the pleasure they feel in their Independence.' Hayley in Assam, at the crowd's request, fired a 31-gun salute with his shot-gun at the midnight ceremony. Next morning he discussed with the strongly Congress Speaker of the Assam Legislative Assembly the procedure for the formal parade.

I asked him if he wished me to be on the maidan to greet him when he arrived, or if he would like me to accompany him from his bungalow to the parade ground. 'Oh please Hayley', he said, 'come and escort me from the bungalow, before this, every time I have been escorted from my bungalow, it has been to be put in jail'.

In Calcutta a cheerful Martyn records his paradox:

It was ironic, but nevertheless highly symbolic, that after being for ten years in close touch with the forces of Law and Order, the last event I witnessed (as a spectator without responsibility) was one of chaos. It was the sight of hundreds and hundreds of shouting, cheering, laughing Bengalis (Hindus and Muslims alike) surging into the imposing grounds of Government House and storming up the state staircase into the public and private rooms and, for some, finding a seat on the Throne itself. I could almost hear Curzon turning in his grave and I rejoiced at the scene.

But as with all holidays on the morrow it is back to work, the old routine. Maitra catches both the special quality of 15 August and the way in which next day the district officer on tour through his villages, in court, or at his desk settled back to his duties:

I well remember the mid-night fireworks and the chanting of Vedic hymns to usher in the new dawn. It was a moving experience. Next day in scorching sun the armed police paraded. Our first child, then just over one year old, was taken to see the *tamasha* wrapped in a new tricolour flag. The Union Jack had been lowered from the flag post in D.C.'s bungalow the evening before. There was a great deal of sober rejoicing, but no trace of anti-British feeling. There was a request from local Congress leaders for jail delivery and let out the criminals, which I did not agree to. Next morning as I went to my office the same old files were there. I wrote D.O. letters in the same old note-papers bearing on the righthand corner the familiar lion and unicorn emblem. It was difficult to realise that over-night an Empire had vanished.

FURTHER READING

Beside the works already mentioned in chapter ten may be set V. P. Menon, *The Transfer of Power in India* (Calcutta 1957), L. Mosley, *The Last Days of the British Raj* (London 1961) and Penderel Moon, *Divide and Quit* (London 1961), three varied viewpoints, and the monumental N. Mansergh and E. W. R. Lumby (eds), *The Transfer of Power, 1942–47* (London 1970 – in progress), seven volumes to date.

On the leading figures there are individual studies such as B. R. Nanda, *Mahatma Gandhi* (London 1957 and 1965), M. Brecher, *Nehru: a political biography* (London 1959) and, more recent, S. Gopal, *Jawaharlal Nehru: a biography*, vol. I, 1889–1947 (London 1975) and B. N. Pandey, *Nehru*, (London 1976). Khalid Bin Sayeed, *Pakistan: the Formative Phase*, 2nd edn. (London 1968) is a wider study, but perceptive on the personality of Jinnah. Two biographical studies are H. Bolitho, *Jinnah, Creator of Pakistan* (London 1954) and M. H. Saiyid, *Muhammad Ali Jinnah, A Political Study* (Lahore 1962). For the British side there are J. Glendevon, *The Viceroy at Bay: Lord Linlithgow in India, 1936–43* (London 1971) and P. Moon (ed.), *Wavell: the Viceroy's Journal* (London 1973). A considered study of Lord Mountbatten in India is still to be written, meanwhile there is a committed study from A. Campbell-Johnson, *Mission with Mountbatten* (London 1951).

On the partition period Lieutenant-General Sir Francis Tuker, *While Memory Serves* (London 1950) gives a soldier's view and Khushwant Singh, *Train to Pakistan*, (reprinted Connecticut 1976), that of a sikh, cast in a semi-fictional form.

GLOSSARY

Agrahara village/land given to Brahmins free of tax or subject to a nominal rent.
Ahlmad superintendent.
Amin surveyor.
Anicut dam.
Ashram place of retreat.
Babu a title for Hindus in some parts of India corresponding to Mr; an Indian clerk.
Bania, Banya merchant; shop-keeper; money-lender.
Bearer personal servant.
Bhadralokh high caste, educated (Bengali) Hindu.
Busti a settlement or collection of huts.
Chaprassi orderly; messenger.
Chaukidar watchman; guard; village policeman.
Chela disciple; follower.
Dacoit armed robber.
Dacoity gang-robbery.
Dak bungalow publicly maintained rest-house for travellers.
Dehat sudhar rural uplift.
Dewan finance minister or prime minister of an Indian State.
Dhoti loin cloth worn tucked between legs and fastened at waist.
Diara land rich fertile land which is left when floods recede.
Fakir poor person, usually religious mendicant living on charity.
Godown warehouse.
Hartal stoppage of work; strike.
Id Muslim festival, especiailly Id al-Fitr at the breaking of the fast of Ramazan and Id al-Azha, the sacrificial festival.
Jagir rent or revenue – free grant; freehold estate.
Jhuming slash and burn cultivation in India. For Burma see *taungya*.
Jirga tribal council.
Kacheri, cutcherry office/court room of district revenue official.
Karnam South Indian term for village accountant.
Kisan sabhas peasant associations.
Lakh a hundred thousand units.
Lambardar village headman, see *patel* .
Lathi thick, iron-tipped stick or bludgeon.
Lugale see *bearer*.
Mahar village servant.
Mahasabha assembly; party; grouping.
Majlis parliament or council.
Malik tribal elder.
Mamlatdar see *tahsildar*.
Marumakkathayam matriarchal system of law practised in Malabar district of Madras (now part of Kerala).
Moffussil country as distinct from town; rest of district/province as distinct from its headquarters/capital.
Muharram period of fasting and public mourning observed during the first month of the Muslim lunar year to commemorate the deaths of Hassan and his brother Husein (AD 669 and 680).
Mulaqati visitors.

Nawabs Muslim aristocrats.

Nazir office superintendent or manager.

Nazul land owned by government in urban areas.

Panchayat village council.

Paniwallah waterboy.

Partal verification of *patwari*'s entries in village accounts and registers.

Patel headman, see *lambardar*.

Patwari North Indian term for village accountant, see *karnam*.

Peon see *chaprassi*.

Peshkar judicial officer's reader; court clerk.

Punka, punkha ceiling fan

Purna swaraj complete independence.

Qanungo revenue inspector, responsible for revenue administration in a circle of villages, usually twenty to fifty, in a *tahsil*.

Raiyat, ryot farmer; cultivator; tenant.

Ryotwari word used to denote a land system under which each cultivator holds his land in severalty and is responsible for payment of the revenue.

Sarkar district; government.

Satyagraha Sanskrit word meaning 'reliance on truth', a name for Gandhi's passive resistance to British rule in India.

Suttee practice of widows immolating themselves on the funeral pyres of their husbands. The practice was abolished in 1828.

Swaraj self-rule.

Syce groom.

Taccavi agricultural loan, often payment in advance for seed purchase.

Tahsil the revenue division of a district containing up to several hundred villages.

Tahsildar, mamlatdar, township officer officer in charge of *tahsil*.

Taluk term used in Bombay and Madras for *tahsil*; a tract of proprietary land owned by a *talukdar* (*taluqdar*).

Tank lake; reservoir; pond.

Taungok headman/chief of hilly district in Burma.

Taungya Burmese equivalent of *jhuming*.

Tazia emblem in shape of tower carried by Muslims at time of *Muharram*.

Thana police station.

Township see *tahsil*.

Ulema body of professional theologians, expounders of the law in a Muslim country.

Vakil lawyer.

Zaildar headman of a group of villagers.

Zamindar, zemindar landholder.

Zamindari word which denotes a land system under which the village is owned by a landlord or group of landlords who are responsible for the payment of land revenue to the government.

INDEX

Agency Tracts, 136–8, 140, 143
Agra district (UP), 132–3, 221–2
agrahara (*see* glossary), 7
Agricultural department, 56, 100
ahlmad (*see* glossary), 77
Air Raid Precautions (ARP), 163, 211, 214–17
amin (*see* glossary), 50, 146
Amritsar, xxvii, 30–1, 239
Andaman Islands, 147
Anderson, Sir John, Governor of Bengal, 117
anicut (*see* glossary), 52
Arthur, A. J. V., 30, 31, 71, 79, 81, 84, 92, 96, 101, 102, 104, 239
ashram (*see* glossary), xxix
attachments during training, 39, 100
Attlee, Rt Hon. Mr C. R. (later Earl Attlee) British Prime Minister (1945–51), 188, 227, 238, 240

babu (*see* glossary), 83
Baksi, N., 5
Ballia district (UP), 201, 202
Baluchistan, 33–4, 150–1, 152
bania, banya (*see* glossary), 102
Banks, J. D., 221–2
Bareilly district (UP), 34
Barty, D. C., 110, 130–1, 185–6, 206–7
Bastar State, 143–4
bearer (*see* glossary), 125
Belcher, R. H., 6, 14–15, 54, 62, 66–7, 97–8, 111, 129, 208, 215, 219, 220, 223, 239–40, 243–4
Bell, F. O., 6, 31–3, 44–5, 50–1, 102–3, 105–6, 113, 133, 180, 206, 209, 218–19, 236–7
Benares district (UP), 201–2
Berhampur district (Orissa), 117
bhadralokh (*see* glossary), 32, 33
Bijnor district (UP), 48
Bonarjee, N., 3, 47, 86–7, 88, 89–90, 95, 182, 245
Bowman, A. I., 18, 42, 55, 71, 111, 112, 128–9, 132–3, 142, 207, 211–12
Brayne, F. L., 54–5
Brown, Mrs J. B., 123–4
Buddhism, Buddhists, 156, 162

Burma: Civil Service, 82; elections, 158, 175; evacuation of, 164–6, 167–71; Indians in, 161, 162, 167, 168; military administration of, 172–4; oil fields in, 103, 160, 163, 166–7; reoccupation of, 174–7, 211; separation from India, 10, 156, 158, 159
Burmese National Army, 174
busti (*see* glossary), 17

Cabinet Mission to India, 234–5
Carleston, H. H., 15, 41–2, 109, 111, 146, 180–1, 212
chaprassi, chuprassee (*see* glossary), 63, 98, 158
Chauk (Burma), 103
chaukidar (*see* glossary), 73 (*see also* village servants)
chela (*see* glossary), 31
Chingleput district (Madras), 51
Chittagong (Bengal), 190
Chittagong Hill Tracts, 117, 136, 139, 140, 142
Christie, W. H. J., 45, 95, 112, 117, 136, 139–42, 240
Civil Service Commission, 8, 9, 10
clubs, 28, 29, 33, 126, 127, 128
Cockburn, G. W., 37–8, 72, 135, 142–3, 161, 167, 172–4, 175–7
commissioners, 115, 116
communal disorders, 92, 181–5, 235–7, 239–40, 242
Congress party (Indian National Congress), xxxiii, 189, 191–4, 195, 197, 198, 226–7, 231, 235, 237; attitude to Government of India Act (1919), xxvi, xxvii, 187; attitude to war effort, 199, 200; boycott of Simon Commission, xxx; civil disobedience campaign (1930–1931), 101, 158, 187, 188, 191; constitution, xxvii; position after 1945–6 elections, 229–31, 234; rebellion of August 1942, 202–4
Conjeeveram (Madras), 182
Cook, B. C. A., 30, 223
Co-operative Department, 101
court clerk, reader, 62, 69, 77, 81 (*see also* peshkar)

Map showing the administrative boundaries of India in the early and mid 1930s. Based on the small-scale standard Survey of India map showing provinces and districts. In the reduction of the source map it was not possible to show every individual boundary.